The University and the People

The University
and the People

*Envisioning American
Higher Education in an
Era of Populist Protest*

Scott M. Gelber

THE UNIVERSITY OF WISCONSIN PRESS

Publication of this volume has been made possible, in part, through support from
the **Anonymous Fund**
of the College of Letters and Science at the University of Wisconsin–Madison.

The University of Wisconsin Press
1930 Monroe Street, 3rd Floor
Madison, Wisconsin 53711-2059
uwpress.wisc.edu

3 Henrietta Street
London WC2E 8LU, England
eurospanbookstore.com

Printed in the United States of America

Library of Congress Cataloging-in-Publication Data
Gelber, Scott M.
The university and the people: envisioning American higher education
in an era of populist protest / Scott M. Gelber.
p.   cm. — (Studies in American thought and culture)
Includes bibliographical references and index.
ISBN 978-0-299-28464-0 (pbk.: alk. paper)
ISBN 978-0-299-28463-3 (e-book)
1. Public universities and colleges — United States — History — 19th century.
2. State universities and colleges — United States — History — 19th century.
3. Populism — United States — History — 19th century.
I. Title.   II. Series: Studies in American thought and culture.
LB2328.62.U6G45   2011
378′.050973 — dc22
2011011569

Portions of chapter 3 were published as "'City Blood Is No Better Than Country Blood': The Populist
Movement and Admissions Policies at Public Colleges and Universities," *History of Education Quarterly*
51 (3) (August 2011).

Contents

Illustrations

Acknowledgments

This book would not have been possible without the guidance of Julie Reuben, who has provided encouragement and constructive comments throughout this process. I have been blessed by her advising. I am also grateful to Nancy Cott and James Kloppenberg for their questions, advice, and kind support. Harold Wechsler, Chuck Dorn, Chris Loss, and Robert Cherny read portions of the manuscript and provided helpful feedback. I would like to thank my colleagues who discussed pieces of this work in the Boston history of education reading group, the Harvard nineteenth-century American history workshop, and the Harvard History of American Civilization colloquium. Mary Lee Griffin and Vicki Bartolini, my colleagues at Wheaton College (Massachusetts), have provided an exceptionally warm environment in which to finish this book. Gwen Walker and Paul Boyer at the University of Wisconsin Press have been welcoming and professional from the start of the publication process. Along the way, I have been fortunate to receive financial assistance from Wheaton College, Harvard University, the Spencer Foundation, the Woodrow Wilson Foundation, and the Charles Warren Center for Studies in American History. I am indebted to the commitment of the interlibrary loan staff at Harvard University and Wheaton College, as well as the archivists of Kansas State University, the University of Kansas, the Kansas State Historical Society, North Carolina State University, the University of North Carolina at Chapel Hill, the University of Nebraska–Lincoln, and the Nebraska State Historical Society. I am most profoundly thankful for the support provided by family and friends. In particular, I have been lucky to share this experience (and my life) with Emily Farbman. To Sam and Sid, whose births highlighted the past three years, I look forward to more stories with you.

The University and the People

Introduction

Academic Populism

In the fall of 1895, the University of Chicago sacked Edward Bemis, a controversial sociology professor who supported labor unions and public ownership of utilities. While editorializing about Bemis's fate, *Harpers Weekly* pondered
whether socialism or populism could ever provide a sound philosophical basis
for an institution of higher education. "A Populist university would be an
interesting experiment," mused the columnist, "but neither Chicago University
nor any other American university is at present ready, we are happy to say it, to
be made the corpus vile for such an experiment."[1] Populism seemed like an
awkward fit for universities because the movement championed farmers and
laborers, while doubting the virtue of professionals and scholars. Culminating
in the most successful third party campaign since the Civil War, the Populist
movement vaulted self-styled representatives of "The People" into state legislatures and governors' offices during the 1880s and 1890s.[2] Less than two years
after *Harpers Weekly* raised the possibility of an experiment in radical higher
education, Populist politicians dismayed respectable opinion-makers throughout
the nation by reorganizing the Kansas State Agricultural College (now Kansas
State University). In one of its first official actions, the college's new board of
regents hired Edward Bemis.[3]

This episode, along with similar takeovers in other states, dramatized the
relationship between the so-called people's revolt and American institutions
of higher education. Fueled by rural dissatisfaction, the Populist movement
promised to defend small producers by supporting cooperative ventures and
increasing government regulation of banks, railroads, and wholesalers.[4] A
subset of the movement also believed that state colleges and universities

(terms used interchangeably in this book) could advance the cause of Populist egalitarianism. While Populist advocacy for informal education and common schools has been well documented, this counterintuitive enthusiasm for *higher* education remains underappreciated.[5] As indicated by the *Harpers* columnist, skeptics viewed the movement's forays into college politics as hostile raids and suggested that Populism was inconsistent with true higher learning. However, some Populists became surprisingly passionate about the core ideals of the state university at a time when only 2 percent of 18- to 24-year-olds attended college nationwide.[6] Electoral victories in the movement's southern and western heartlands briefly enabled these Populists to influence public institutions of higher education.

Populists and their allies focused primarily on colleges supported by the Morrill Act of 1862, which provided federal land grants to institutions that provided practical education to the "industrial classes." The Populist vision of these agricultural and mechanical colleges was neither unprecedented nor unique; the movement amplified a triad of common expectations for state-supported higher education: accessibility, utilitarianism, and public service.[7] Populist priorities, especially the movement's demand for applied subjects and outreach programs, also coincided with the emergence of similar interests among the mainstream leaders of America's fledging universities. Yet the Populists' unparalleled fervor for accessibility and practicality highlighted the special challenge of defining public higher education in a democratic nation.

In the language of historian Laurence Veysey, Populists epitomized a "grassroots" vision of state universities that rivaled a "higher" emphasis on the benefits derived from scientific research and advanced study.[8] Populists promoted minimal admissions requirements and widespread remediation, whereas more elite supporters of public higher education sought to require four years of high school. Populists demanded free tuition or generous scholarships, whereas some commentators complained that these policies were inappropriate uses of public funds. Populists lobbied for increasing the study of agricultural science and the mechanical arts, whereas many university presidents prioritized pure science and training for prestigious professions. Finally, Populists defended the right of professors to endorse controversial causes, whereas academic leaders typically embraced the ideal of nonpartisan expertise. In all of these domains, Populist pressures on state universities exposed enduring tensions between egalitarianism and elitism.

Scholars have carefully examined these tensions and explored the manner in which American intellectuals sought to reconcile their expertise with the spirit of a democratic society.[9] But fewer historians have looked closely at the sentiments of those unruly citizens who questioned academic authority. The Populist movement provides a vivid (albeit imperfect) proxy for the kinds of popular attitudes that prompted intellectuals to tread lightly—attitudes that fueled important debates about the nature of higher learning. Of course, Populism did not distill the views of the entire population; contrary to the movement's propaganda, Populist ideology was more prevalent in some communities than in others. Yet Populist organizations represented a broad swath of farmers and workers whose ideas about higher education rarely appear in the historical record. Populist leaders, many of whom possessed college degrees, courted the relatively unschooled men and women who attended their lectures, read their articles, and perhaps saw their leadership as proof of the power of higher learning.[10]

These Populists seemed to instantiate academia's worst fears about outside intervention. While late-nineteenth-century college presidents contended with a variety of external pressures, Populist campaigns generated special anxiety because they appeared so alien to traditional allies of higher education. College presidents and professors tended to demonize Populism because of the movement's controversial economic policies, demagogic rhetorical style, and eagerness to intervene in college affairs. The Populist movement, in general, emphasized economic grievances instead of the ethnocultural issues (such as prohibition) typically discussed by Republican and Democratic leaders.[11] Fervent believers in the power of democratic governance and the state's obligation to serve ordinary citizens, Populists also insisted that laypersons should gain greater control over public institutions, including public colleges. Most academic leaders, therefore, regarded Populists as fearsome intruders.

Drawing on sources penned by these unsympathetic witnesses (and fed by their own anxieties about fascism and McCarthyism), historians writing during the mid-twentieth century reinforced this portrayal of Populist hostility toward higher education. In particular, Veysey referred to agrarian advocacy as unfortunate "tampering" and concluded that "academic and popular aspirations seemed rarely to meet."[12] These interpretations were consistent with Richard Hofstadter's influential *Age of Reform*, which characterized the Populist movement as irrational, bigoted, and anti-intellectual.[13] Whereas Hofstadter's criticism of Populism has been thoroughly revised by historians over the decades, his analysis has lingered within the history of higher education, where it has only just begun to be reconsidered.[14]

Hofstadter's interpretation of Populism cast a long shadow on the history of higher education because it resonated with scholarly predispositions against public interference and because it can be substantiated with colorful evidence of Populist hostility. Populists exemplified typical nineteenth-century criticisms of college training. Populist commentators routinely mocked college graduates for lacking practical experience, extraordinary ability, or special insight. "An educated fool is the most hopeless of all fools," announced the *Progressive Farmer* while recounting the story of a Boston professor who could not fit through his front door with an open umbrella until a laborer across the street solved the "terrible dilemma into which the philosopher had fallen." "What stupendous folly," the Populist newspaper exclaimed, "to place such blubber-heads at the head, or even at the other end of our public enterprises."[15] The organ of the Farmers' Alliance of Randolph County, North Carolina, complained that the vogue of higher education was "nauseating nonsense" because the state already had too many "thin-faced gentry with high-sounding honorary titles, which appear as a bubble beautiful and dazzling for a moment, then burst and disappear into empty nothing."[16] Adopting a harsher tone, another radical newspaper complained of "learned jack asses who add a string of big letters to their insignificant names" and pride themselves on speaking foreign languages rather than disseminating useful information to the common people.[17] The *Manhattan Republic*, published by Kansas Populists, boasted that the absence of formal higher education allowed Populist politicians to think in practical terms and remain "in close touch with the common people."[18] When acknowledging that some Populist leaders possessed college degrees, supporters often hastened to add that they had worked their way through school. For example, the Kansas People's Party Handbook mentioned that State Superintendent of Public Instruction William Stryker attended college, but "he had to work for and earn it."[19]

This disparaging rhetoric reflected Populist fears that a small clique of privileged college graduates could dominate state politics. Georgia Populists, for example, worried that a diploma might become a prerequisite for holding public office because so many politicians were alumni of the state university.[20] These concerns energized a longstanding debate over whether American universities constituted democratic oases or bastions of aristocracy—divergent perspectives on higher education that stemmed from rival interpretations of the nature of democracy itself. Most nineteenth-century college presidents, professors, and students embraced Jeffersonian ideas of representative government. They lauded universities for promoting a meritocratic society. Inspired by Jacksonian political movements, others maintained a majoritarian view of democracy. They worried that universities could monopolize knowledge and limit access to political power.[21] Palpable in the wake of the American Revolution, this suspicion intensified during the Gilded Age, when college credentials gradually became more valuable to young people who aspired to professional or business careers.[22]

Some Populists wondered if colleges eroded popular sovereignty while merely earning distinction for a small number of faculty and students. Educators, after all, routinely boasted about the political aptitude of college graduates. United States Commissioner of Education William T. Harris hoped that highly educated leaders would counteract the attraction of the masses to "all mere *isms* and one-sided tendencies like socialism and anarchy and anything that has the form of a universal panacea."[23] Offensive to Populist sensibilities, this justification of public higher education appeared regularly in student newspapers. Students claimed that their familiarity with Greek and Roman history and experience debating in literary societies immunized them from the lure of demagogues. A student at the University of Kansas was confident that college-educated voters and candidates could accomplish the "elevation and purification of politics." A student at the Colorado State Agricultural College agreed that his classmates could beat back the impulses of "the untutored mass of humanity."[24]

Populists resented the manner in which some students and professors implied that the masses were unfit for self-government.[25] A correspondent of Populist editor Luna Kellie responded to these sentiments by announcing that "kingship, priestcraft, and titles, and all official positions that assume that . . . the parties are better than what are called common folks, is [*sic*] all bosh."[26] William Jennings Bryan proclaimed that the great problems of the era must be remedied by the masses, not "those who measure men by diplomas and college degrees."[27] In Kansas, a radical newspaper accused institutions of higher education of cultivating "a surface mysterious sort of pretense to fool the uneducated into believing that a college education is too deep to fathom." These concerns fueled Populist criticism of the "priestly" aspects of higher education, such as the caps and gowns worn during commencement ceremonies.[28]

Of course, Populists overstated these concerns. Many college presidents hoped that mass education could improve the effectiveness of democratic institutions.[29] Still, Populists felt compelled to argue that the average self-educated farmer was at least as competent as a college-educated politician. The movement acted on this premise by endorsing mechanisms of direct democracy, such as the ballot initiative and referendum.[30] To inform adherents about public policy proposals, Populist organizations published newspapers, sponsored discussions of economic issues, distributed reform literature, and hosted lectures.[31] Convinced that their movement constituted a true people's college, some Populists questioned whether universities should receive any state funding whatsoever, especially because provision for primary- and secondary-level education was inadequate in many rural locales.

When the movement won control of legislatures or university governing boards, therefore, professors and administrators braced for salary cuts or worse. The aforementioned takeover of the Kansas State Agricultural College (KSAC), during which Populist regents dismissed several faculty members, appeared to confirm these grim expectations. Even though Populist demands for accessibility and practicality resembled the wishes of generations of reformers (including the presidents of many leading universities), faculty at land grant institutions had ample reason to expect hostile intrusions whenever Populists assumed power.

However, the archival record reveals that Populist interventions did not fully conform to a predictable pattern of anti-intellectualism and demagoguery. Although they did not renew the contracts of a few professors, KSAC's fusionist administration tolerated some ideological dissent and increased the number of faculty with PhD's. Motivated by a measure of anti-intellectual suspicion, Populist advocacy for low entrance standards also stemmed from serious concerns about the inadequacy of rural secondary schooling. While the movement promoted vocational education, many Populists valued courses in classics, rhetoric, and social sciences. Even after scrutinizing university budgets, Populist-controlled legislatures passed appropriation bills that exceeded previous levels of funding. Reexamination of the Populist orientation toward state universities uncovers a complex track record that partially confirms and partially belies conventional expectations.

As historian Charles Postel has demonstrated, Populists were neither ignorant rubes nor nostalgic socialists. The Populist stance toward state universities reinforces this interpretation.[32] Despite the movement's bitter attacks on ivory tower elitism, many Populists still evinced a precocious enthusiasm for mass higher education. These Populists shared the improbable belief that higher education could still be egalitarian. In particular, they hoped that public colleges and universities could disperse intellectual capital and soften distinctions of professional status. At the turn of the century, as the nation's leading institutions of higher education embarked on a long and fruitful romance with academic expertise, Populists advocated for this alternative set of priorities. There are good reasons to be skeptical about whether these ideals represented the will of "The People," and there are even more reasons to be grateful that these priorities never won full sway over public higher education in the United States. Populist policies probably would not have produced the scholarly excellence, advanced research, and academic freedom that have ranked many state universities alongside the finest in the world. Nevertheless, the Populist vision of higher education included thoughtful and idealistic components.

The Populist perspective emphasizes the extent to which the classic characteristics of public higher education were forged by principle and deliberate policy, as well as by necessity. While universities maintained low entrance standards in part because of a dearth of public secondary schooling, Populist observers endorsed those college presidents who embraced accessibility with the most enthusiasm. While universities initially kept costs down in part because they had little choice, Populists encouraged administrators who continued to resist fee increases even after enough students were willing and able to pay. While universities added new courses in part to attract students interested in applied studies, Populists also stressed the connections between vocationalism and egalitarianism. Compelling or troubling, Populist ideas about each of these facets of public higher education warrant careful consideration. By reintegrating the Populist movement into the history of American higher education, the following chapters suggest that the widely applauded missions of state universities evolved out of a tense, yet productive, relationship between public pressure and academic authority.

Populism resists a straightforward definition. Its murkiness stems from its roots in the Latin word *populus*, which ambiguously refers to a whole population as well as to poor people in particular. In late-nineteenth-century North Carolina, for example, a newspaper editor complained that Populist leaders defined "the people" as "those who are dissatisfied," rather than as the majority of all American citizens. This rhetoric camouflaged socioeconomic rifts and enabled Populism to inspire a mass movement within a heterogeneous nation.[33] This movement emerged out of deep and widespread cultural traditions. During the late nineteenth century, many farmers and laborers who never formally identified themselves as Populists still shared the movement's skepticism toward elite professionals and the bureaucratization of modern life. In the southern and western Populist epicenters, many unaffiliated citizens railed against the influence of eastern city dwellers. Perhaps most significantly, Populism resonated with the egalitarianism and millennialism of evangelical Protestants.[34]

Populist activism thrived within a diverse assortment of local, regional, and national organizations. Although the term originated with national and state People's Parties that formed during the 1890s, historians have retroactively attached the Populist label to earlier agrarian reform associations. While these organizations proposed different strategies, each responded to burdensome debt, crippling deflation, low and unstable crop prices, monopolistic railroads, exploitive wholesalers, political disempowerment, and cultural disrespect. Whereas the Grange served as the preeminent agency of agrarian protest during the 1870s, the Farmers' Alliance emerged as the most influential Populist organization of the 1880s and early 1890s, when a large network of local and state alliances evolved into the National Farmers' Alliance and Industrial Union (NFAIU). In many southern states, roughly half of all those eligible to join (rural whites over the age of twenty-one) became NFAIU members.[35] Farmers' Alliances organized local agricultural cooperatives and urged Democrats and Republicans to endorse a variety of redistributive policies: the monetization of silver; government regulation of railroads, banks, and telegraphs; and a public system of cooperative crop marketing known as the subtreasury plan.

Frustrated by the response of the two mainstream parties, state alliances began to sponsor independent political campaigns, which coalesced around a national People's (or Populist) Party in 1892. The Party's platform called for public ownership of utilities, civil service regulations, silver coinage, a graduated income tax, public savings banks, redistribution of land owned by speculators, and the subtreasury plan. In addition to its rural base in the NFAIU, the party included prohibitionists, Christian socialists, single-taxers, greenbackers, and workers affiliated with organizations such as the Knights of Labor.[36] In several states, the People's Party supported compromise platforms after resorting to "fusion" with Republicans or Democrats. The Party achieved its greatest electoral success in the Great Plains, and won short-lived victories in far-western states such as Colorado and Washington. Although Farmers' Alliances and Granges saturated the Midwest, Populist politicians fared poorly in this region, where they were hampered by relatively healthy agricultural economies and co-optation by the two major parties. Despite the power of the Southern Farmers' Alliance, widespread fraud and racial divisions prevented the Party from gaining a firm foothold in the South, even in states with vigorous Populist movements. The lone southern exception occurred in North Carolina, where Populists allied themselves with Republicans and won control of all branches of state government.[37]

Allegiance to Populism evolved out of a vibrant democratic culture fostered by local newspapers, church and schoolhouse meetings, and massive rallies.[38] The movement attracted support from relatively uneducated constituents, and its leadership tended to be less privileged than their Republican and Democratic counterparts. Yet under the ideological umbrella of *producerism*, Populism drew adherents from a wide array of class backgrounds. Producerism distinguished between hardworking, wealth-generating "producers" and corrupt "parasites" who exploited the labor of others.[39] While this philosophy promoted solidarity with the downtrodden, Populism was not a working-class movement in the modern sense.

To the extent that they used the term "class," most Populists referred to the wholesomeness of a broadly defined "middle class" consisting of farmers and workers, as well as small-town merchants and manufacturers who exhibited sympathetic attitudes. While Populists criticized drastic economic inequality, most did not object to significant differences in wealth resulting from the pursuit of income through "honest means." Populism, therefore, mobilized wealthy planters committed to elevating the status of agriculture as well as poor farmers dedicated to combating economic inequality. This diversity prompted a North Carolina farmer to wonder if Populism could ever fully unite "the 'cracker' element" with "the more refined type of the office holding gentry." Indeed, as the movement grew, it struggled to absorb this combination of "genteel" and "mudsill" cultures.[40]

Asserting that elites exploited male and female laborers alike, Populists also attempted to unify the men and women of the producing classes. Populists tended to conform with Victorian ideology by referring to rural women as "farmers' wives" who were special protectors of domestic virtue. Unlike conventional nineteenth-century gender norms, however, Populist rhetoric often stressed that all rural husbands and wives labored to sustain the economic viability of the farm. For example, the *Lincoln Independent* reasoned that farm-women should ally themselves with the movement because they were hard-working "home builders."[41] Indeed, women and men both assumed leadership positions within the Farmers' Alliance, which counted women as upward of one-quarter of its membership. In the West, Populist women won election to political offices, such as school superintendent and register of deeds. Populist women were also active as editors, organizers, and lecturers, although the movement's gravitation toward electoral politics over the course of the 1890s limited the avenues for women's leadership. Pressure from the southern wing of the movement also dissuaded national Populist organizations from endorsing full legal or political rights for women.[42] Yet Populists tended to support the expansion of college access for women by promoting coeducation in the West and single-sex colleges in the South, approaches that were consistent with regional tendencies.

While efforts to forge a movement that encompassed men and women were moderately successful, Populism's potential to promote interracial solidarity fell tragically short. Especially during election years, some white Populists hoped to build biracial coalitions. Tom Watson, a white Populist leader from Georgia, initially worked to unite struggling farmers across racial boundaries. Benjamin

F. Foster, a black Populist from Kansas, encouraged African Americans to join the "party of the poor man."[43] Yet many white Populists remained reluctant to share political power or patronage. Although the movement claimed to be democratic and egalitarian, white Populists often endorsed racial discrimination. The Southern Farmers' Alliance excluded African Americans altogether. In North Carolina, the majority of white Populists continued to espouse white supremacy, even as they benefited from a political alliance with black Populists and Republicans. In the Great Plains, most white Populists also rejected the concept of social equality with their black allies. Meanwhile, a segregated Colored Farmers' Alliance (CFA) emerged out of Houston, Texas, in the late 1880s and included perhaps one million members across the South by the end of the decade.

The issues confronted by black Populists were never high on the agenda of most white Populists. In particular, white Populists tended to ignore lynching, unequal educational facilities, violations of voting rights, and exploitation of black tenant farmers. This schism proved fatal in 1891, when fifteen African Americans were murdered during a CFA-sponsored cotton-picker strike. White alliances stood idle, partly because many of their members relied on black workers to harvest their crops. As other politicians effectively capitalized on racial fears, white Populists became even more reluctant to align themselves with the movement's black wing.[44] Ultimately, neither the western nor southern branches of the white movement focused on racial injustices in higher education.

The ideological, organizational, and racial diversity of Populism has generated substantial scholarly debate over which regions, leaders, policies, and political strategies represented the purest form of the movement. Historian Lawrence Goodwyn, in particular, differentiated between genuine Populists committed to cooperative economic organization and various "shadow movements" that focused on silver coinage and fusion with the Democratic Party.[45] Since many Populist organizations drifted away from the movement's original radical platform, Goodwyn's conclusion is understandable. Identifying a prototypical case of Populism, however, can become a subjective and anachronistic enterprise.[46] Regardless, these debates are tangential to Populist views of higher education because they focus on political strategy (fusion vs. independence) and economic policies (currency, cooperatives, and public regulation).

While these issues are important in and of themselves, no consistent relationship seems to have existed between a Populist's economic and political stances and his or her posture toward state universities. Instead, two fundamental aspects of Populist ideology contributed to the movement's vision of higher education. First, Populists celebrated the capabilities and virtues of ordinary citizens. Second, Populists agreed that a small number of elites tended to monopolize resources at the expense of farmers and laborers. Influenced by these sentiments, Populists expressed concern about whether public universities were beholden to voters and welcoming for the children of the masses. It seems appropriate, therefore, for a study of higher education to construe Populism *broadly* as a commitment to the movement's core principles of egalitarianism and producerism.[47] This study also recognizes that the majority of Populists envisioned the ideal student as the white son, or sometimes the white daughter, of a rural family.

This book concentrates on a loosely defined collection of "academic Populists" who were the most vocal proponents of the movement's vision of higher education. These men and women tended to occupy three sorts of positions: university presidents or trustees who were appointed, elected, or endorsed by Populists; faculty members or students who had direct ties to the movement; and Populist leaders or editors who expressed special interest in higher education. Most academic Populists were relatively privileged individuals. As Veysey noted, few academic leaders ever had "genuine grassroots connections" or ongoing engagement with farm labor.[48] Nevertheless, academic Populists identified with the movement's ideology and believed that state universities could demonstrate solidarity with the struggles of ordinary farmers and laborers. This book also draws on partisan newspapers and letters to the editor to provide a sense of Populist attitudes at the grassroots. Low prices and aggressive door-to-door sales around the turn of the century expanded the market for Populist newspapers into unprecedented numbers of rural homes, including a wide range of landowners, renters, and tenant farmers.[49] Unfortunately, neither newspapers nor personal papers have survived to provide thorough accounts of African American Populists; and the voices of white female Populists, though more plentiful, are also underrepresented in the historical record. Limited by these constraints, this book examines these perspectives wherever possible. By necessity, this book primarily documents the ideas of white male advocates for Populist higher education.

The following chapters concentrate on contextualizing and analyzing the ideology of these academic Populists, rather than endorsing or condemning particular university policies. Indeed, most claims about the movement's impact must remain tentative because the few instances of administrative control were too short-lived and too incomplete to provide sufficient data. Furthermore, the pervasiveness of populistic egalitarianism within American culture prevents clear quantitative comparison of university policies in "Populist" regions such as the Great Plains as opposed to "non-Populist" regions such as New England—influential university presidents were (un)sympathetic to Populism regardless of geography, while agrarian organizations made similar demands on state universities across the nation.[50]

This book concentrates on the South and the West, where the intensity of academic Populism was greatest. Not only did Populism thrive in these states, but the movement's engagement with public universities also resonated with proud stereotypical distinctions between local democracy and northeastern aristocracy. These perceptions were fueled in part by variations in regional enrollment patterns. Whereas eastern state universities enrolled roughly 10 percent of the region's college students during the 1890s, state universities accounted for up to 25 percent of enrollment in the South and 60 percent of enrollment in the West, where a relatively homogenous population promoted an especially expansive vision of public higher education.[51]

Political victories empowered academic Populists in Kansas, Nebraska, and North Carolina, in particular. Simultaneous to the aforementioned takeover of KSAC, Kansas Populists governed the purse strings of the University of Kansas intermittently during the 1890s. Populists also controlled appropriations for the University of Nebraska for most of the decade and elected a majority of its board of regents between 1900 and 1904. In North Carolina, the state agricultural college (now North Carolina State University) was founded in 1887 when Farmers' Alliance leaders wrested control of federal land grant funding away from the University of North Carolina (UNC). During the 1890s, North Carolina Populists also supported the founding of separate state colleges for women and African Americans and engaged in vigorous debate over UNC's funding. Brief episodes of academic Populism also transpired after elections in other states, such as Missouri, Colorado, the Dakotas, and Washington State.

These states do not constitute a representative sample of American public higher education. Rather, their stories provide dramatic examples of Populist pressures that faced virtually all state universities, especially institutions that received proceeds from federal land grants. In states such as Wisconsin, this pressure peaked in the 1870s when the Grange was in its prime, rather than during the peak of the Farmers' Alliance in the 1880s or the Populist Parties of the 1890s. Other states, such as Texas and Georgia, had strong Populist movements but appear infrequently in this book because their state Populist parties never gained formal control of a public university. Some politicians, most notably Governor "Pitchfork" Ben Tillman of South Carolina, capitalized on resentment toward state universities, yet are not a main focus of this book because of their equivocal commitment to Populist egalitarianism.[52]

The first two chapters of the book survey the origins and political history of academic Populism. Populistic critics questioned whether institutions of higher education were appropriate for a democratic nation as early as the 1790s. As described in chapter 1, attacks on public and private higher education swelled during the Jacksonian era, when anti-elitist politicians and labor leaders accused colleges of reinforcing aristocratic privilege. A number of mechanics institutes and agricultural colleges attempted to resolve these concerns by emphasizing accessibility and utilitarianism. By the dawn of the Populist movement, agrarian leaders had become optimistic that land grant institutions could provide superior training without the exclusivity or refinement typically associated with institutions of higher learning. Introducing case studies in North Carolina, Kansas, and Nebraska, chapter 2 reveals the extent and the limitations of this Populist interest in public higher education. Contrary to conventional wisdom, the movement was not uniformly hostile to state colleges and universities. Many Populist leaders had attended college and believed that public institutions of higher education could empower ordinary farmers. Whereas this aspiration occasionally encouraged the movement to promote equal access for young women, most white Populists endorsed or ignored racial barriers to higher education.

The next two chapters analyze Populist campaigns for academic and financial access to public colleges. Chapter 3 focuses on Populist advocacy for low entrance requirements, ample remediation, and semiformal extension programs. Populists and likeminded administrators argued that public colleges discriminated against rural students if they aligned admission standards with stronger urban school systems. Whereas most colleges longed to dispense with remedial courses, Populists argued that preparatory departments remained vital bridges to higher education. Populists also encouraged greater investment in agricultural short courses and farmers' institutes designed for the general public. Chapter 4 documents how Populists allied themselves with state university leaders in favor of free tuition and in opposition to critics of "socialistic" state subsidies. Academic Populists believed that universities could only combat elitism if they were free or heavily subsidized. Populist ideology also encouraged support for now-common elements of financial assistance, such as campus employment and student cooperatives.

The next two chapters discuss Populist views of curricula, research, and academic freedom. Chapter 5 complicates common assumptions about Populist curricular preferences. As expected, Populist support for state universities depended on the extent to which these institutions embraced agricultural education and domestic science. Populists (mistakenly) assumed that these subjects would be most attractive for rural students. Less commonly noted, Populists hoped that teaching agriculture and home economics at the college level would reduce invidious distinctions between mental and manual labor. Populists also insisted that land grant colleges provide courses in the humanities and social sciences in order to cultivate informed citizens within all classes. Predictably, neither the Populists' romantic view of manual labor nor their ambivalence toward social mobility took root within state colleges. Chapter 6 details how academic Populists struggled to resolve tensions between their respect for scholarly insight and their enthusiasm for popular rule. Occasionally, Populist-controlled governing boards displayed unexpected tolerance for the emerging ideal of academic freedom. Other Populists suspected that the mantle of academic objectivity would never protect critics of laissez-faire economics and self-servingly declared that *the people* should be able to dictate the politics of college professors. Although academic Populists failed to reconcile these conflicting impulses, they raised precocious questions about whether the privilege of academic freedom should only extend to scholars deemed to be nonpartisan or uncontroversial.

The last chapter demonstrates Populist support for funding public higher education. Populists prioritized spending on rural common schools and sought to lower faculty salaries, which were attractive targets for an egalitarian movement during hard times. Yet despite the movement's rhetoric, Populists still tended to pass typical appropriations for state universities whenever they formed legislative majorities. While Populists often demanded reductions in state budgets, they encouraged the expansion of the public sector insofar as it benefitted the movement's supporters. When Populist legislators could make the case that universities served ordinary farmers, they sometimes even increased funding for these institutions. In particular, Populists supported appropriations designed to expand the physical capacity of state universities.

This book concludes by tracing the ebb and flow of populistic ideas on higher education throughout the twentieth century and into the twenty-first century. After the Populist movement faded, state universities and land grant colleges faced less vigorous resistance when they raised standards or increased fees. For better or worse, state systems of higher education began to rely on new and less prestigious schools in response to the kinds of expectations that Populists had once directed toward flagship institutions. Yet just as Progressive reformers championed key aspects of the Populist political and economic platforms, academic Populism reverberated beyond the movement's short-lived period of formal political power. Demands for access and practicality have remained common, though they have rarely been backed with equivalent political strength or egalitarian fervor. The rhetoric of Populism has also been invoked to support causes that are distant from the spirit of the original movement. Nevertheless, the history of academic Populism can still inform new proponents of mass higher education.

While illuminating the ambitions of academic Populists, each of the following chapters also recounts the limits, contradictions, and failures of their activism. Along with the movement writ large, the Populist vision of public higher education was marred by bigotry and narrow-mindedness. Yet, like the broader movement, academic Populism nevertheless raised essential questions about the development of modern America. Populists who engaged with state universities exposed deep tensions between equality and opportunity, popular sovereignty and expertise, and democracy and meritocracy. While exemplifying certain misguided tendencies of popular pressure, Populist demands also invigorated some of the core egalitarian principles of public higher education. Despite his ultimate condemnation of Populist anti-intellectualism, even Richard Hofstadter still admired the "humane and democratic sentiments" that energized the movement. Hofstadter encouraged scholars to recognize the complexity of a movement that embodied these ideals alongside less savory elements of American culture.[53] Taking Hofstadter's sage advice to heart, I have attempted to honor the aspirations of academic Populists without overlooking the pitfalls of their campaign.

1

Preludes to Populism

Anti-Elitism and Higher Education, 1820–1885

In 1877, the regents of the University of the State of New York warned that
meddlesome politicians might pervert institutions of higher education.
"Happy is the community," concluded the regents, whose colleges cannot
be "trammeled by popular clamor or subjected to partisan interference."[1]
Throughout the nineteenth century, leaders of American colleges worried
about this sort of pressure from laypeople outside of the academic realm.
Small and financially precarious, colleges could not ignore public opinion if
they hoped to survive. Every student demand, every request from a wealthy
donor, and every legislative investigation brought varying degrees of pressure
to bear on college presidents. However, populistic movements produced some
of the most dramatic forms of public pressure in the history of American higher
education. The anti-elitism of farmers, artisans, and their champions appeared
to clash diametrically with conventional college mores. Although the Populists of
the 1880s and 1890s generated an unprecedented intensity of this sort of
pressure, their movement reiterated longstanding concerns about higher education. This chapter situates the Populist vision within this larger tradition by
reviewing how earlier egalitarian campaigns shaped public colleges.

Criticism of the inaccessibility and impracticality of colleges proliferated
after the American Revolution and intensified within workingmen's organizations during the 1820s and 1830s. Farmers and artisans rarely distinguished
between public and private colleges in this era. When these institutions grew
more distinct after the Civil War, citizens increasingly expected public colleges
to offer practical courses to a broad spectrum of young people. As training for
secular vocations replaced ministerial training as the primary purpose of

higher education, legislators and agrarian leaders compelled state colleges to develop curricula for farmers, artisans, and engineers. Most prominently, the Patrons of Husbandry (also known as the Grange) sought control over state colleges that were supported with federal land grants authorized by the Morrill Act of 1862. To a certain degree, the Grange's efforts to reform these public colleges aligned with concurrent shifts in mainstream academic priorities. Many professors hoped to replace the antebellum emphasis on mental discipline and piety with utilitarianism and scientific research. Motivated by their admiration for European models, their desire to attract additional students, and their interactions with donors and legislators, American university leaders encouraged institutions to develop new courses of study. Adding their intemperate voices to the debates over these reforms, educators associated with the Grange began to advocate for a model of public higher education that they hoped would provide the greatest benefit to ordinary rural youth. Prefiguring the aspirations of academic Populists of the 1880s and 1890s, these activists started to believe that accessible and practical state colleges could be both "higher" and egalitarian. The pursuit of this unlikely combination helped to enshrine accessibility and utilitarianism as core ideals of American public higher education.

The Jacksonian Critique: 1820 to 1862

The dichotomy between public and private institutions did not apply to the original American colleges, which were established by colonial or royal authorities. Instead, colonial colleges were quasi-public entities chartered, partially funded, and occasionally governed by elected officials. Although public universities were established during the early republican era in North Carolina, Georgia, South Carolina, Tennessee, and Vermont, and in the old northwest states (such as Michigan and Wisconsin) during the antebellum period, these schools shared many curricular, socioeconomic, and administrative characteristics with private institutions.[2] Debates over state appropriations revealed widespread suspicions about whether any college could serve the broad public interest or whether they each catered to particular regions, social classes, religious denominations, or political parties. In 1798, for example, a New England farmer accused colleges of reproducing America's ruling class. With republican fervor, the farmer argued that the primary purpose of colleges was to establish "places for men to live without work."[3] Similarly, a commission studying higher education in New York concluded that colleges were "devoted almost exclusively to the rich."[4]

This critique intensified during the so-called Jacksonian era of the 1820s and 1830s, when the core ideology of late-nineteenth-century Populism began to crystallize in conjunction with the political victories of a loose alliance of small farmers and artisans.[5] Symbolized by the election of President Andrew Jackson, this coalition presented their lack of traditional schooling as a political asset. Supporters of Jackson's presidential campaign praised their candidate for being untainted by excessive formal education.[6] In 1835, an Illinois legislator boasted that he had been "born in a briar thicket, rocked in a hog trough, and . . . never had . . . [his] genius cramped by the pestilential air of a college."[7] Jacksonian-era labor leaders, such as the newspaper editor George Henry Evans, emphasized that advanced learning was not a prerequisite for intelligent citizenship. Evans urged his readers to listen carefully to the political ideas of their co-workers "even though they should not be so well read." Instead of the high-brow forms of oratory taught in college courses, Jacksonian Democrats preferred plain speech.[8]

While skeptical of college, the Jacksonian wing of the Democratic Party advocated for universal elementary-level education. Spokespeople for working-men's organizations questioned the merits of public expenditures on high schools and colleges at a time when access to common schools remained limited for poor farmers. In 1829, Davy Crockett spearheaded opposition to university land grants in Tennessee by arguing that universities benefited elites at the expense of his humble constituents. Crockett claimed that ordinary Tennesseans considered themselves lucky if they had access to a school "convenient enough to send our big boys in winter and our little ones all the year." "We think ourselves fortunate," Crockett continued, "especially if we can raise enough Coon-Skins and one little thing or other to pay up the teacher at the end of every quarter." As a representative in the U.S. Congress, Crockett explained that he opposed public funding for colleges because "this college system went into practice to draw a line of demarcation between the two classes of society—it separated the children of the rich from the children of the poor." The president of the University of Nashville lamented this sort of "levelling" [*sic*] spirit, which encouraged the perception that colleges exuded "odious pre-eminence."[9] These sentiments encouraged antebellum colleges to seek more egalitarian reputations. Most colleges ceased the traditional practice of ranking students according to their fathers' social status. Harvard, Princeton, and Yale reduced their tuition and increased their scholarship funds.[10] Several campuses experimented with schemes to lower their costs (and honor the dignity of labor) by requiring students to build and maintain college facilities. The founders of Oberlin College, for example, expected all students to work on the college's farm, split firewood, or tend buildings and grounds.[11] In New York City, workingmen's organizations and Jacksonian Democrats campaigned for an accessible "Free Academy," which evolved into the City College of New York.[12] Although most never rivaled the democratic achievements of City College, very few antebellum colleges came close to resembling the elitist enclaves depicted by critics. The majority of colleges faced constant financial peril and enrolled large proportions of students who depended on charity and seasonal employment. Nathanial Hawthorne, for instance, characterized the Williams College class of 1838 as "rough, brown-featured, schoolmaster-looking, half-bumpkin, half-scholarly figures"—a far cry from the white-gloved student aristocrats pilloried by Jacksonian politicians. These detractors also overlooked the manner in which the classical curriculum offered by antebellum colleges prepared many students for the ministry, instead of only serving the predatory professions condemned by agrarian and labor leaders.[13]

Nevertheless, colleges failed to persuade skeptics that they were democratic institutions. Tuition, living expenses, and familial obligations still constituted severe obstacles for all but the wealthiest students. Even typical admission requirements pertaining to "moral character" posed a special challenge to poor applicants, who were less likely to have relationships with local leaders who could provide the requisite letters of recommendation. The frequency with which college students became urban or small-town professionals also contributed to the sense that colleges were institutions of privilege. By the 1850s, for example, 72 percent of University of North Carolina graduates became lawyers, doctors, businessmen, bankers, or manufacturers. Some Jacksonian leaders even believed that the monopolization of higher learning by elite professionals had contributed to the economic panic of 1837.[14] These attitudes imperiled public funding for higher education across the nation. State appropriations to private colleges became rare because of the financial cost of supporting growing numbers of institutions and the political cost of favoring particular denominations.[15] Meanwhile, Jacksonian Democrats directed populistic attacks against funding for public institutions. Protestors ridiculed a request for an appropriation to build a house (or "mansion") for the president of the University of Georgia; one critic of the university objected to "giving the people's money to support a set of lazy professors."[16]

Similar attitudes prevailed among urban mechanics and artisans. In 1830, an organization of New York workingmen objected to public funding for colleges designed "almost solely for the benefit of the rich." The Philadelphia Working Men's Committee agreed that public funding for higher education "may serve to engender an aristocracy of talent, and place knowledge, the chief element of power, in the hands of the privileged few." The committee warned that colleges might generate a "monopoly" of knowledge that would condemn the masses to a state of "comparative ignorance." In contrast with Jeffersonian enthusiasm for an "aristocracy of talent," these workers argued that democracy could only flourish if "equal knowledge" became the "common property of all classes."[17] These critiques posed a troublesome question to proponents of public higher education: Did colleges and universities invariably create undemocratic status distinctions?

A number of antebellum educational societies addressed these concerns by eschewing the exclusive collegiate culture of Latin, entrance examinations, and diplomas. These mechanics institutes, lyceums, library associations, and mutual improvement organizations multiplied during the middle decades of the nineteenth century. Whereas the pursuit of higher learning tended to be a gentlemanly activity prior to 1800, these clubs dedicated themselves to the dissemination of every form of "useful knowledge." Inspired by the example of Benjamin Franklin, nineteenth-century proponents of self-improvement defined their subject matter in broad terms because they believed that all scientific and philosophical truths had vocational or civic applications. This orientation to learning attracted educational reformers because it stripped higher education of its association with aristocratic idleness.

Indeed, mechanics institutes appealed to radical educators, even though most of their classes emphasized scientific or technical subjects rather than political economy. Most notably, William Maclure, a Scottish-born educator who accused colleges of avoiding truths that could elevate the producing classes, supported a Working Men's Institute at his utopian settlement in New Harmony, Indiana. More commonly, organizations such as the influential Franklin Institute for the Promotion of the Mechanic Arts in Philadelphia intended to cultivate politically moderate workers. Over time, these ventures attracted increasingly large audiences while migrating away from vocational subjects and toward scientific subjects with popular appeal. For example, the New York Society for Mechanics offered a lecture in 1850 on "Natural Relations Between Animals."[18] The evolution of these institutes revealed core tensions that would challenge subsequent efforts to create egalitarian forms of higher education. On one hand, mechanics institutes promoted the democratic ideals of self-instruction while intentionally avoiding the institutionalized curriculum, trained faculty, and formal pageantry of collegiate higher education. Yet organizations of moderate "mechanics" (as well as their more assertive "workingmen" cousins) also contained small manufacturers and skilled workers who sought to differentiate themselves from the growing ranks of unskilled industrial labor. When mechanics institutes sponsored formal schools, they highlighted the sort of dilemma that would complicate the quest for Populist higher education decades later. These schools could either emphasize a distinct vocational (and ideological) curriculum, or they could focus on becoming stepping-stones to more prestigious high schools and colleges. The Franklin Institute, for example, faced this difficult choice when some mechanics objected to the exclusion of Latin from the institute's proposed secondary school.[19]

Presaging the proposals of late-nineteenth-century Populists, some antebellum reformers attempted to resolve this dilemma by combining the curricular structure (and physical infrastructure) of colleges with the egalitarianism of mutual improvement societies. They shared Franklin's belief that incorporating vocational applications into college curricula could create a classless form of advanced education. These initiatives gained steam along with the spread of applied scientific pursuits within the mainstream of American higher learning. Originating with the U.S. Military Academy (1802), technical higher education was also pioneered at the Rensselaer Institute and the Gardiner Lyceum during the 1820s. Wealthier colleges, such as Harvard and Yale, founded separate scientific schools, albeit with emphases on academic rather than practical dimensions. More commonly, local political and economic pressures encouraged antebellum colleges to expand their popular appeal by adding utilitarian courses.[20]

Some populistic educators sought to channel these energies into new "colleges" that emphasized vocational instruction in order to blur the distinctions between manual and mental labor. In 1847, the Farmers' College outside of Cincinnati began to offer short courses on practical subjects to students who lacked the time or money for a conventional college course. Founded in 1857 by a mechanics mutual-benefit association and led by a self-educated carriage maker, a People's College in Havana, New York, briefly provided vocational courses.[21] Illinois farmers also attempted to organize a college with a flexible schedule, practical curriculum, and opportunities to work on college facilities in lieu of room and board charges. Jonathan Baldwin Turner, a Yale graduate who turned to agriculture after religious disputes compelled his resignation from Illinois College, led lobbying efforts at the state legislature in the 1850s. Turner argued that private classical colleges created "clans and castes" and "undue deference to mere learned authority," instead of promoting equal status for farmers and artisans. He repeated common Jacksonian warnings about the danger of concentrating power "in the educated head of the body politic—cold, crafty, selfish, and treacherous." Turner wrote that an agricultural college that emphasized observation of natural processes would inoculate ordinary Americans against tyranny by imparting a spirit of lifelong learning and

encouraging faith in divinity rather than in leaders.[22] Turner's radically democratic vision encouraged the establishment of the Illinois Industrial University
in 1867, forerunner to the University of Illinois and one of the first institutions
supported by the Morrill Act. During the following decades, these land grant
agricultural and mechanical colleges attracted the passions of those, like Turner,
who dreamed of anti-elitist higher education.

The Morrill Act and the Grange: 1862 to 1885

Enthusiasm for applied public higher education increased modestly after the
passage of the Morrill Land Grant Act of 1862. A U.S. representative and later
senator from Vermont, Justin Morrill was a self-educated son of a blacksmith
who hoped to encourage the growth of colleges that were dedicated to practical
subjects. The act that bears his name granted each state a portion of federal
land, which they could sell in order to generate funding for colleges teaching
agriculture, the mechanic arts, and military training. Along with most advocates
of applied higher education, Morrill assumed that children of an ill-defined
"laboring" class would find these subjects more attractive than the traditional
college curriculum. Morrill also shared the widespread conviction that college
instruction in farming would raise the prestige of the occupation. Although
many states mismanaged their grants and the initial public response was tepid,
proceeds from sale of the federal land bolstered some struggling public colleges
and facilitated the creation of others.[23]

The ambiguous language of the Morrill Act generated rancorous disputes
over what curriculum was most appropriate for these institutions. The legislation stated that the "primary object" of land grant colleges "shall be, without
excluding other scientific and classical studies, and including military tactics, to
teach such branches of learning as are related to agriculture and the mechanic
arts . . . to promote the liberal and practical education of the industrial classes
in the several pursuits and professions in life." Most supporters, including
Morrill himself, interpreted this language as a broad mandate encompassing a
variety of liberal arts courses. In particular, administrators of impoverished
state universities hoped that land grant proceeds would strengthen the traditional offerings of their institutions along with some additional investment in
the sciences. In contrast, many agrarian leaders fastened onto the phrase
"primary object," expected dramatic new agriculture programs, and rejected
the claim that investment in conventional sciences fulfilled the terms of the
federal land grants.[24]

For the first few decades after the passage of the Morrill Act, a scarcity of qualified agricultural educators settled this debate in practice but not in spirit. Applied research in this field dated back to the 1840s, when Justus Liebeg published his influential *Organic Chemistry in its Applications to Agriculture and Physiology*. Yet even land grant college presidents who were committed to applied agricultural education struggled to find experienced instructors. The Florida State College of Agriculture responded to the dearth of agricultural expertise by hiring a scholar of the classics to fill a chair of "Agriculture, Horticulture, and Greek." In 1885, a professor of agriculture confessed that many who claimed to be experts in the field were not even knowledgeable enough to feed pigs.[25]

These circumstances, along with their own inclinations, encouraged most land grant college presidents to emphasize courses in the arts and sciences instead of focusing narrowly on vocational curricula. In 1867, for example, the first report of the trustees of Illinois Industrial University explained that their mission was to train scientists rather than farmers or mechanics. The early trustees of the Ohio Agricultural and Mechanical College erased the A&M component of its name in 1878 (Illinois followed suit in 1885 by deleting its "Industrial" moniker). Land grant college presidents, such as George W. Atherton of Pennsylvania and Andrew Dickson White of Cornell, argued that the power of higher education resided in its ability to achieve breakthroughs in basic scientific research. They insisted that land grant colleges should not be judged according to the size of their enrollments in vocational courses.[26] Any observer who evaluated land grant colleges according to their A&M enrollments quickly realized that the schools were failing. While students at some institutions gravitated toward new engineering courses, few wanted to enroll in agricultural programs. At Illinois, where there was not even a professor of agriculture from 1870 to 1875, an average of only ten students opted for this course of study each year until the turn of the century. No student graduated from the agriculture course at the University of Wisconsin until 1880 or at the University of Minnesota until 1899.[27] Advocates for applied higher education grew frustrated with these enrollments as well as with the inability of land grant faculty to protect farmers from economic or ecological disasters. One agricultural newspaper referred to professors as "classical idiots" and looked forward to an "impending day of reckoning."[28] Responding to a North Carolina farmer who vented similar outrage, the editor of the *Southern Cultivator* agreed that "the industrial classes have been shamefully cheated out of their just rights."[29]

The slow development of agricultural education at land grant colleges attracted the attention of the Grange, the nation's most powerful agrarian organization. Formed in 1867 by federal bureaucrats concerned about the deterioration of the economy and culture of rural America, the Grange spread rapidly through state and local chapters. Although it was led by large land-holders and distrusted by some poor farmers, the Grange won wide support by vocalizing rural dissatisfaction and providing an attractive ritualistic community. Nonpartisan on the national level, local Granges petitioned legislatures and occasionally allied themselves with third-party campaigns against railroad monopolies, high interest rates, and unscrupulous financial middlemen. The Grange soon exceeded the influence of relatively conservative agricultural societies that had been the main vehicles of agrarian political empowerment during the antebellum era. Membership in the Grange peaked in 1873 and 1874, when multiple local chapters formed every day. The movement began a steady decline beginning in 1875 after its plan for creating cash-based marketing cooperatives failed and many of its legislative attempts to regulate railroads ended in frustration.[30]

During the 1870s and early 1880s, Grange leaders became prominent spokespeople for popular demands on public higher education. State Granges formed education committees to monitor the progress of the fledgling land grant colleges, which the organization believed could increase the prestige and profitability of farming. The education committee of the North Carolina State Grange, for example, hoped that agricultural higher education could help farmers' children avoid becoming mere "hewers of wood and drawers of water."[31] Heralding later aspirations of the Populists, Grangers also believed that agricultural college graduates could advocate more effectively for farmers' political interests.[32] Low investment in these agricultural programs angered Grangers across the nation, sparking protests in states as far flung as Vermont, North Carolina, Minnesota, and California. After conducting an investigation in 1876, the national Grange resolved that land grant colleges should operate under the exclusive control of working farmers.[33] James Patterson of Kentucky A&M was not the only land grant college president who complained about the "unreasoning obstinate hostility" of the Grange.[34]

The Grange's demands for vocational curricula fit squarely within the tradition of public pressures on higher education. Grangers agreed that rural youth would profit from utilitarian agricultural instruction more than from basic science or a classical curricula.[35] Equally important, Grangers continued to assume that vocational colleges would be more wholesome and more egali-tarian. In California, where the Grange lobbied for farming courses at the state university since its founding convention, the organization inveighed against control of public higher education by "the blighting hand of a selfish and moneyed aristocracy." Ezra Carr, a Granger who also taught agriculture at the

University of California, proclaimed that the state required at least one institution "free from the temptations to college extravagance, where plain living and high thinking can be illustrated in all appointments." The Grange's campaign came to a head during a state constitutional convention in 1879, when delegates narrowly rejected a proposal to ban intangible subjects, require manual labor, and elect regents by popular vote. Instead, the convention established a college of agriculture within the university and limited the grounds for subsequent political intervention.[36] Grangers were more successful in their efforts to increase agricultural studies at Illinois Industrial University. In 1873, agrarian activists and their allies in the state legislature pressured the school to abolish the chair of classics, require all students to take A&M courses, and install Jonathan Periam as the university's superintendent of practical agriculture. A Granger and editor of the *Western Rural*, Periam accused land grant colleges of ignoring agriculture and serving instead as "easy-chairs for college dons, retired clergymen, decayed politicians, or theoretical farmers."[37]

Motivated by similar impulses, Grangers were aggressive advocates for agricultural education in Kansas, where they helped transform the state's land grant institution from a denominational school into an A&M institution. Kansas's land grant college had evolved out of Bluemont Central College, a Methodist Episcopal school in Manhattan that was chartered in 1858, only three years after the arrival of white settlers from the northeast. Bluemont's founders regarded themselves as missionaries of New England culture and hoped that the institution could transplant eastern civilization to the sod houses of the Great Plains. After barely keeping its doors open amid an impoverished frontier community, Bluemont won the state's land grant designation in 1863 and changed its name to the Kansas State Agricultural College (KSAC). The college, however, retained the entire Bluemont faculty, a traditional curriculum, and a governing board appointed by the Methodist Church. Between 1867 and 1874, no KSAC graduate worked in agriculture or a related field. In the spring of 1872, the Kansas State Board of Agriculture concluded that the college was preoccupied with studying "the musty classics."

Many Kansas Grangers hoped that KSAC could be transformed, in effect, into an extension of their organization.[38] By the early 1870s, amid the devastation of a grasshopper plague, drought, and economic depression, Kansas agricultural advocacy groups had established a statewide reform movement. In 1872, a splinter group of reform Republican candidates fused with Democrats and challenged conventional stances on currency, banking, tariffs, taxation, and transportation. Two years later, a full slate of candidates ran as members of a new Independent-Reform Party, a movement that attracted the Grange's considerable support.[39] Starting with a meeting of forty-six farmers in Brown County during the spring of 1872, the Kansas State Grange would represent three-quarters of the state's farming population within two years.[40] In 1873, Grangers convened in Topeka with members of other Kansas farmers' clubs and county agricultural societies in order to form the Farmers' Cooperative Association (FCA) of the State of Kansas.[41]

Like their counterparts in other states, Kansas's agricultural leaders demanded that farmers control the state's land grant institution. An FCA leader referred to the presumption that farmers and mechanics were incapable of managing a college as a remnant of "the dark ages when Kings and Popes were born with spurs on their heels and the people with saddles on their backs."[42] Governor Thomas Osborne and the state legislature responded to the Grange by dismissing the entire KSAC board of regents. The new regents promptly eliminated Greek from the college.[43] After the resignation of KSAC's original president, the board hired James A. Anderson, a Presbyterian minister with a degree from Miami University and an unflagging enthusiasm for technical education. Perhaps equally important, Anderson took pride in his reputation as an unrefined man of the people. A friend recalled that "any old bum" felt comfortable approaching Anderson, who could often be seen chatting on street corners "without the slightest clerical air in dress or manner, oftentimes with a cigar in his mouth." After preaching in Stockton, California, and serving as an army chaplain during the Civil War, Anderson took charge of a congregation in Junction City, Kansas. Although endorsed by Kansas's powerful agricultural interest groups, he faced a hostile reception at KSAC. Anderson was greeted by hisses from students as he approached the chapel platform for his first presidential address. Local newspaper editors were abusive, and sympathetic students were subjected to doggerel rhymes and ridicule from the college literary societies. Kansas Populists would later note how opponents created the impression that he was "an escaped lion or tiger that was eating up the children and old women raw."[44]

Anderson promised that KSAC would emphasize practical subjects rather than "Latin or Greek rubbish" or "fancy 'ologies' or 'osophies.'"[45] He abolished instruction in the classics, German, and French, while requiring fifty minutes a day of labor on the farm or in the workshop. Along with many contemporary college presidents, Anderson doubted the traditional claim that studying the classics provided essential "mental discipline" or "culture."[46] He argued that too many professors of science prioritized "inductive discovery" and pursued practical applications only as afterthoughts. Instead, Anderson wanted to hire professors who viewed "the same science from the wholly different standpoint of 'Will it pay the farmer?'" And like most Grangers, he wanted KSAC graduates to become farmers rather than agricultural "missionaries."[47] In order to create the impression that college students somehow remained within the ranks of the laboring masses, Anderson believed that the KSAC campus should resemble a prosperous farm or "a little hamlet of thriving artisans." He argued that the campus should consist of "cheap, stone buildings, one or two stories, scattered among the trees . . . not requiring costly foundations and tall, heavy walls, not finished as are parlors, nor wasting space in broad corridors."[48] KSAC's new regents were thrilled with the manner in which Anderson rid the college of "superfluous bosh."[49] Professor J. D. Walters agreed that KSAC's curriculum had sorely needed adaptation to "the wants of the poorer class."[50]

General Stephen Dill Lee's administration of the Mississippi State Agricultural and Mechanical College also embraced the Grangers' curricular priorities. In 1871, the University of Mississippi and Alcorn University were designated as the state's land grant institutions for white and black students respectively (the Grange restricted membership to whites only and paid little attention to Alcorn). Although the University of Mississippi hired a soil chemist, it had attracted only a handful of students to its agriculture course by 1876, when it discontinued the department. The Mississippi Grange responded by lobbying for a bill that transferred the federal land grant proceeds to a new state A&M college. Signed in 1878, the bill required that a majority of the trustees of the new college be farmers or mechanics. When the college opened its doors in 1880, a board of trustees dominated by Grangers hired General Stephen Dill Lee to be the college's first president. After the fighting for the Confederacy, Lee struggled to make profit as a farmer and became active in the Mississippi Grange, where he protested the manner in which "the rich have grown richer, the poor poorer, and the lines have been drawn between these two classes very strongly."[51] Under Lee's leadership, the Grange and the college remained closely affiliated through the 1880s, as the school hosted a variety of extension programs and drew its student body disproportionately from counties with high levels of Grange membership.[52] Like John Anderson in Kansas, General Lee shared the Grange's concern that partisans of traditional higher education regarded A&M subjects as "poor kin at the rich folks house." At Mississippi A&M, therefore, afternoon hours were reserved for farm labor and maintenance of the college campus, including lessons in ditching, fencing, and clearing stumps. Grange leader Putnam Darden celebrated that agriculture had become the school's "overshadowing theme."[53]

The Grange's enthusiasm for vocational education dovetailed with demands for college access. At Cornell, agitated Grangers encouraged the university to stop charging tuition for students in the agriculture department, a policy change that led to a dramatic increase in attendance. In Maryland, the Grange spearheaded a campaign against the expense of attending the state land grant college, which required Latin and catered to the sons of gentlemen farmers. Ultimately, Maryland Grangers were satisfied by a reduction of entrance requirements and elimination of tuition.[54] Jonathan Periam, the Grange leader who taught at Illinois Industrial University, insisted that the school should be accessible to all students with a common school education. Periam worried that agricultural colleges might restrict admissions in order to train future professors rather than enroll "the industrial masses."[55]

At KSAC, John Anderson also worked to decrease admissions requirements to the level of the average rural common school graduate: 14 years of age and basic skills in reading, writing, and arithmetic. He was more than willing to sacrifice institutional status even if it meant that KSAC would never become "a university for 'the higher education' whatever that phrase may happen to mean." The new standards resulted in significant increases in enrollment at KSAC. Anderson also reduced the length of the KSAC program from six to four years in order to lighten the financial burden on "boys and girls who have to work their own way through college and life." He sought to hire student workers and to reduce expenses for students whose parents struggled to earn "every cent by hard labor."[56] Bill Sikes, who attended KSAC from 1875 to 1879, recalled that most of his classmates worked, lived simply, and struggled to pay their bills. Sikes tended fires on campus and wore clothes sent as charitable donations from New England churches.[57]

Mississippi Grangers also expected that the state A&M college would be accessible to the sons of ordinary farmers. When appointing the committee that first explored the creation of a separate agricultural college, the state Grange stipulated that tuition should be inexpensive or nonexistent.[58] The college opened free of charge, although students were required to pay $55 up front for three months of room and board, books, fees, and a uniform. However, all students were paid to work fifteen hours a week on the school farm, and many met most of their expenses by working overtime. While the school also enrolled some of the wealthiest youth in the state, college officials claimed that uniforms and military discipline blurred class distinctions between students. While proud of the socioeconomic diversity of the school, trustees hoped that Mississippi A&M would be "emphatically a school for the poor." By the end of the 1880s, college officials could boast that two-thirds of students were sons of small farmers.[59]

Grangers also encouraged the college to welcome students who possessed little academic preparation. General Lee did not object to large enrollments in remedial courses because he recognized that higher admission standards would put the college out of reach of many rural youth with "poor school advantages." Lee was proud that his college enrolled students even if they were older and "very backward in their studies," instead of limiting itself to the education of "those (so considered) brighter boys, destined by their parents for the so-called learned professions." In order to better accommodate these students, Lee also tried to keep class sizes low so that teachers could provide individual attention. "We ought to put the diploma within reach of every country boy," Lee told an assembly of land grant college presidents, not just those whose fathers were rich enough to afford the tuition of city high schools or private academies.[60]

The Grange was also at the forefront of several campaigns for college access for young women. The Grange dedicated itself to the uplift of the farm family and granted full membership to women, including voting rights and access to officer positions. While Grangers by and large did not believe in full gender equality, the organization proclaimed that women were the special repositories of eternal rural values. Especially in midwestern chapters, women Grangers led local meetings and frequently rose to upper levels of state hierarchies. Grange leaders believed that education and involvement in their organization could expand the horizons and enrich the social and intellectual lives of rural women.[61] To this end, Grangers were early advocates for domestic science courses and included a plank in their 1874 Declaration of Purposes urging state agricultural colleges to teach "all the arts which adorn the home."

Just as they attacked "useless" classical curricula at male colleges, Grangers ridiculed ornamental education at female academies. In Michigan, Granger Mary Mayo argued that domestic science would liberate farmwomen from drudgery while agricultural science would do the same for their husbands. Mayo and other Grangers protested that the Michigan Agricultural College failed to teach domestic science despite a requirement in its charter. The Michigan Grange lobbied the legislature to build a women's dormitory in the 1870s, since the lack of accommodations prevented many women from enrolling. Grangers also lobbied for coeducation and investments in departments of domestic science at the universities of Minnesota and Connecticut.[62] At KSAC, where enrollments were split evenly between men and women, President Anderson stated that women had an "inalienable right" to liberal and practical education. He maintained that women were vital to the farm economy and were entitled to industrial education. During Anderson's administration,

KSAC became one of the first colleges in the nation to include domestic science courses in a curriculum leading to a BA. KSAC also provided equal access for women to all liberal arts classes.[63] After the establishment of the state agricultural college for men, Mississippi Grangers lobbied for a public industrial college for women. In 1884, the state Grange celebrated the establishment of the Industrial Institute and College for Women in Columbus.[64]

When Grangers were dissatisfied with the lack of access or lack of vocational courses at state universities that contained land grant divisions, they campaigned for increased control or for institutional secession of A&M departments. Although the creation of separate colleges required redundant investment in physical plant, many Grangers came to believe that land grant institutions needed to be independent in order to avoid the misappropriation of resources toward classical education and the stigmatization of vocational programs. This stance foreshadowed unintended consequences stemming from Populist demands for distinct colleges for the masses. Ultimately, isolating practical education from liberal education might have exacerbated this stigma more than if they had remained side by side. Nevertheless, Louisiana Grangers vigorously opposed the merger of the new Louisiana Agricultural and Mechanical College with the classical Louisiana State University (LSU) in 1876. Even after he appointed two Grange leaders to the school's governing board and offered the organization meeting space on campus, LSU president David F. Boyd reported that the Grangers were still "howling" about a lack of agricultural coursework and lobbying for a reversal of the merger until the mid 1880s.[65]

After weathering a Granger effort to establish a separate agricultural college, University of Minnesota president William Watts Folwell confided that he suspected that other institutions would not survive unscathed. It was rumored, for example, that Grange complaints had brought the entire University of Nebraska faculty to the brink of resignation.[66] Folwell's prediction was accurate. In West Virginia, where Grangers constituted one-sixth of the state's voting-age population, the organization successfully lobbied the state legislature for a bill transferring (temporarily, as it turned out) land grant proceeds from the state university to an independent agricultural college.[67] Concerns raised by the New Hampshire Grange prompted a series of investigations of Dartmouth's use of the federal land grant, culminating in the establishment of a new state agricultural college in Durham in 1891.[68] Ultimately, agrarian protesters succeeded in wresting land grants away from private schools or comprehensive state universities in several other states, including Connecticut, Rhode Island, and as will be described in the following chapter, North Carolina.[69]

Accounts of Grange interventions in higher education typically characterize these campaigns for independent colleges as attacks on state universities
rather than as maneuvers to protect agricultural education. However, when
satisfied with the development of state agricultural colleges, Grangers did not
hesitate to lobby legislatures for funding. In 1875, a Wisconsin legislature
dominated by Grangers passed an appropriation for a new science building at
the state university. The Michigan Grange opposed expenditures on a gymna-
sium "where the delicate sons of wealth may become athletes," but supported
increasing funding for faculty salaries at the state agricultural college after a
beloved professor was lured to Purdue. At the Colorado State Agricultural
College, where seven out of eight of the original trustees were Grangers, members
of the organization waved banners at the school's opening ceremony and urged
legislators to pass generous appropriations bills. Grangers supported Texas
A&M, even though they had drafted plans for their own college. The invitation
of the Grange's Grand Master to be the featured commencement speaker in
1884 and the establishment of an agricultural experiment station in 1887
further rallied Grange support for the college as it competed with the University
of Texas for state funding. After an initial period of suspicion, the New York
State Grange ultimately supported Cornell University during state budget
deliberations in the 1870s and 1880s.[70] In Kansas, the Grange opposed the
diversion of funds from the agricultural college to other institutions and lobbied
for additional support for agricultural extension.[71] In Mississippi, Grangers
asked their legislators to guarantee annual appropriations for the state agricultural and mechanical college.[72]

Conclusion

During the middle half of the nineteenth century, anti-elitist organizations
qualified their disdain for higher education and began to demand that public
colleges and universities embrace a distinct mission. While these pressures often
struck academic leaders, such as University of Michigan President James Angell,
as "unintelligent and mischievous criticism," agrarian groups helped to establish
accessibility and practicality as core ideals of American state universities.[73] By the
late nineteenth century, when the Populist movement emerged as a powerful
political force, the principle of equal higher educational opportunity rivaled earlier
elitist views of colleges and universities.[74] In 1878, before the heyday of Populism,
the chancellor of the University of Kansas confidently predicted that the next
generation of farmers would no longer regard educated people as members of "a
kind of superior caste" limited to children from wealthy families.[75]

As Americans developed these ambitious expectations, Grangers lobbied for a particularly anti-elitist form of public higher education. Decades of curricular reform and industrial development, punctuated by the Morrill Act, encouraged Grangers to contemplate a striking vision of the state college. Unlike the Jacksonian Democrats who challenged the very concept of public higher education, Grange leaders hoped that an accessible and vocational course of study could enrich the lives of workers without necessarily promoting class divisions. This aspiration persisted into the 1880s and 1890s, after a new set of Populist organizations supplanted the Grange as the vanguard of rural activism.

A number of academically oriented Populists continued to apply egalitarian ideals to the realm of public higher education. Allies of a more radical and broader-based movement, these Populists attempted to enact a bold democratic agenda at state universities. Compared to their earlier counterparts in the Grange, Populists tended to preserve more comprehensive records of their stances toward academic standards, affordability, curricula, scholarly freedom, and public funding. The Populist insurgency also coincided with a watershed era of the American university. The movement's agenda either reinforced or countered new trends regarding academic standards, financial aid, research practices, and state appropriations. As documented in the following chapter, Populist political victories energized three especially vivid attempts to promote egalitarian higher education.

2

Scaling the Gilded Halls of the University

Populism and Campus Politics

The Populist movement celebrated the virtue of citizens who hailed from outside of privileged circles. The *Nebraska Independent*, for instance, paid tribute to members of the hardscrabble "lower classes," who not only produced the nation's wealth and defended its borders, but also taught themselves poetry, science, and philosophy.[1] Disturbed by this combination of "popular contempt for higher education and . . . popular pride in the self-made man," University of North Carolina (UNC) President Edwin Alderman worried that Populist legislators might starve his institution of public funds.[2] Indeed, some Populists argued that the movement's informal educational network should supplant established colleges. Yet anti-elitist skepticism did not blind all supporters of Farmers' Alliances or People's Parties to the possibility that universities could promote egalitarian social reform. A segment of the movement augmented the Grange's early advocacy for accessible and practical state colleges. Compared with their predecessors in the Grange, academic Populists were empowered by an even more ambitious political coalition.

This chapter begins by surveying Populist interventions at universities in North Carolina, Kansas, and Nebraska—the three states where the movement won its greatest political victories. While Populist politicians often relied on alliances with one of the two major parties, the movement still gained a substantial degree of influence within institutional governing boards and legislatures in these states.

The second half of this chapter argues that these takeovers were not merely guided by ignorance or bitterness. Populist editors, trustees, faculty, and politicians believed that state universities could empower the producing classes. Many of these Populists were wealthy, politically connected, and college educated. Nevertheless, they helped lead a mass movement comprised of supporters who possessed less formal education, on average, than members of the Democratic or Republican Parties. Academic Populists sought to persuade the movement's rank and file that college did not necessarily alienate young people from the wholesomeness of the farm or the workshop. Despite indulging in some demagogic criticism of college snobbery, a number of Populists declared that higher education could prepare the children of farmers and laborers to advance community interests. While the movement sponsored informal education through lectures, newspapers, and local meetings, academic Populists also sought to boost college enrollments. These Populists occasionally advocated for increasing the higher education of rural women, in particular. Yet white Populists typically ignored or endorsed racial barriers to college. Severely limited by this bigotry, Populism promoted a radical, yet incomplete, vision of public higher education.

Populism on Campus in North Carolina, Kansas, and Nebraska

Populists attempted to bring state colleges and universities into greater conformity with the movement's ideals. These intentions emerged most clearly in North Carolina, Kansas, and Nebraska, where academic Populists seized control of public institutions of higher education.

In North Carolina, Populist pressure was instrumental to the founding of the state's agricultural and mechanical college. Impoverished and embroiled in partisan struggle following the Civil War, UNC closed in 1871 and reopened in 1876 under the leadership of President Kemp Plummer Battle, scion of a prominent piedmont family. Although Battle directed additional resources toward courses in botany, mineralogy, and chemistry, disenchanted farmers noted the lack of applied agricultural training and questioned whether UNC merely provided "rich men's sons" with the opportunity to perfect their aristocratic airs. One farmer accused Battle of being a pompous "humbug" and acting like an "uncrowned king."[3] UNC faced mounting criticism, especially from citizens dissatisfied with Battle's allocation of the proceeds of the Morrill Act land grant.[4]

This discontent coalesced around a campaign for a separate state college of agriculture and mechanic arts. Most accounts of the founding of this school focus on a group of young professionals who called themselves the Watauga Club. Including figures such as Charles Dabney, Josephus Daniels, Charles McIver, and Walter Hines Page, the club epitomized the "New South" vision of economic development. Frustrated with the leadership of the Confederate generation, whom they denigrated as "fossils" and "mummies," the Wataugans lobbied the state legislature of 1885 to charter an industrial school dedicated to training engineers and manufacturers (the bill's sponsor, Thomas Dixon, Jr., would later write *The Clansman*, a white supremacist novel that inspired the film *Birth of a Nation*). Although the Wataugans modeled their school on the Massachusetts Institute of Technology, they included agricultural coursework in order to win approval from a legislature dominated by farmers.[5]

Indeed, agrarian advocacy would prove crucial to the establishment of the school. Although North Carolina legislators granted a charter for an industrial school in 1885, they did not allocate funds. After two years without further progress, the Watauga Club sponsored a "mass meeting." However, instead of the Wataugans who were scheduled to speak on behalf of the school, a group of farmers led by Leonidas Lafayette Polk hijacked the meeting and passed their own set of resolutions calling for the diversion of UNC's land grant funding toward a new state agricultural college. Polk, a former Granger who would emerge as a leader of the Farmers' Alliance and Populist Party, promoted this agenda by organizing a "Farmers' Mass Convention" two weeks after the Wataugan's meeting. According to Polk, farmers who were "unschooled and unaccustomed to public speaking" controlled the convention. One farmer even proposed that no one should be allowed to vote on resolutions unless they tilled the land. Polk proudly noted that farmers remained in charge even though "the polititions [*sic*] put forth their earnest efforts to capture the convention." The North Carolina Knights of Labor, who were at the peak of their political influence, also supported the creation of a new public college.[6] One state senator reported that the popularity of this idea was so widespread that he had won his election by pledging support for the institution "upon every stump in my county."[7]

In the wake of the farmers' convention, the legislature reallocated the state's federal land grant funds from UNC to a new North Carolina College of Agriculture and Mechanic Arts (NCCAMA), which later evolved into North Carolina State University.[8] Although initially dismayed by the loss of UNC's land grant income, President Battle ultimately appreciated that the university had been freed from "the constant demand to build stables and work shops."

Battle, who led UNC until 1891, became content to relinquish the land grant designation and to "let the farmers have it and use it as they wish."[9] However, politically connected WatXXX prevented agrarian leaders from gaining complete authority over NCCAMA. When the college opened in the fall of 1889, only three of its fifteen trustees belonged to the Farmers' Alliance.[10] Yet farmers and Populist advocates still shaped the original contours of the land grant college. NCCAMA enrolled an inaugural class of seventy-two young white men, who divided their time equally between traditional academic recitations and hands-on "practice" in agriculture, horticulture, shop work, and mechanical drawing.[11] A decade later, NCCAMA remained a no-frills institution whose students, according to one new enrollee, were a "tough looking set of boys."[12]

After forming an independent political movement, North Carolina Populists continued to influence the development of public higher education in the state. Initially, the North Carolina Farmers' Alliance (NCFA) had been content to pressure the Democratic Party into supporting various reform proposals, such as railroad regulation. Dismayed by Democratic opposition to their proposals for government-subsidized crop marketing, the more radical elements of the NCFA established the North Carolina Populist Party during the early 1890s. In 1894, the Populists formed a strategic alliance with the state's Republican Party, which was popular among African Americans in coastal counties and whites in mountainous western counties. Together, Populists and Republicans won 78 percent of the legislature in 1896 and elected Governor Daniel L. Russell.[13] Between 1897 and 1899, this "fusion" administration assumed control of the NCCAMA board of trustees, headed by J. C. L. Harris, a pro-reform Republican attorney and newspaper editor with an affinity to Populism.[14] At UNC, the movement managed to win places for three Populists on the governing board during the 1890s. Governor Russell exclaimed, with some hyperbole, that "the people" of North Carolina had won control of the university.[15] UNC loyalists, such as President George T. Winston (1891–1896), were acutely aware of the university's dependence on Populist goodwill. Although UNC's Populist trustees were loyal alumni of the university, the Populist bloc in the state legislature seemed less reliable. Winston warned his colleagues at the National Education Association that "political control" of public universities represented the greatest challenge facing American higher education. Like many other opponents of Populism, Winston likened the movement to the unprincipled "spoilsmen" of Reconstruction and asserted that its vision of "so-called colleges for the people" was pure "folly." Winston worried that Populist influence could undermine the university's ability to serve as a bulwark against mob rule in North Carolina.[16]

During the 1890s, Populists also unsettled the faculty and administration of the University of Kansas (KU) and took full control of the Kansas State Agricultural College (KSAC). When the state Republican Party failed to respond forcefully to an agricultural crisis during the late 1880s, many Kansas farmers gravitated toward the platform of the Southern Farmers' Alliance. The alliance grew rapidly in Kansas, especially in regions where newcomers were heavily mortgaged and vulnerable to economic downturns. By 1890, alliance membership totaled 100,000 in the state, with as many as fifty new suballiances formed each week. In June of that year, a collection of former third-party activists and erstwhile Republicans coalesced around the power of the Farmers' Alliance and formed the People's Party of Kansas. The People's Party also attracted support from the Knights of Labor, urban Citizen Alliances, the Grange, single-tax clubs, and remnants of a Union Labor Party. In a state where both major parties had been dominated by urban professionals and businessmen, the People's Party provided a refreshing option for rural voters. In 1890, the People's Party won four out of every five races for the Kansas House of Representatives. After fusing with the state Democratic Party in 1892, Kansas Populists suffered from internal dissension but nevertheless maintained partial control of the legislature and elected Governor Lorenzo Lewelling.[17]

KU Chancellor Francis Huntington Snow prided himself on being "a good Republican" and could not have been pleased about the prospect of a fusionist (Democrat-Populist) governor appointing members to the university's board of regents.[18] The chancellor had already faced Populist criticism for spending university funds on his personal transportation from the Lawrence railroad depot, as well as to heat, light, clean, and maintain his residence. Populist William Henry Sears had also objected to the membership of Snow, the university's regents, and most of its faculty in fraternities or secret societies. Sears, who grew up on a farm outside of Lawrence and graduated from KU, concluded that "the university people" are a "gang of lick-spittles" who "set themselves up on a pedestal too high and lofty to be criticized by the common people and taxpayers." Sears claimed that the university escaped accountability because local elites coveted institutional business contracts and invitations to KU social events.[19] A Populist newspaper agreed with Sears's assessment of the "aristocracy and seclusiveness of the clique in power." "Don't be a toady," the paper urged its readers, "set down on those snobs."[20]

Although rumors circulated that fusionist politicians were scheming to create a majority on the board, Governor Lewelling could only fill three open seats on the seven-member body.[21] Ultimately, Chancellor Snow managed to maintain cordial relations with the fusionist regents who served during his tenure. In fact, Snow reported that Lewelling's appointees defended the university against a stream of critical editorials published by the Populist *Jeffersonian* in 1894. According to Snow, one fusionist appointee even resigned from the board in order to protest these columns.[22] After assuming office in 1897, fusionist Governor John Leedy privately renewed interest in taking control of the board. According to an ally, Leedy wanted to ensure that the university would be "non-partisan" by giving Populists, Democrats, and Republicans representation throughout the campus. Leedy reportedly considered pressuring a Republican regent to resign by digging up reports that he had thrown a bomb while in college.[23] After other plots failed, Chancellor Snow continued to pray that Populists would never win control of the university or the state normal school in Emporia.[24] To his relief, both of these institutions remained in Republican hands.[25]

In contrast to KU, KSAC experienced far more dramatic Populist intervention. According to Professor Julius Willard, the election of Governor Lewelling in 1892 spread "considerable anxiety" among KSAC faculty and President George T. Fairchild. Lewelling was able to appoint Populists and allied Democrats to fill four vacant seats on KSAC's seven-member board of regents.[26] Fairchild, who had run the college since 1879, had good reason to be concerned. A former Congregational minister, English professor, and loyal Republican, Fairchild anticipated that his policies would be challenged by fusionist regents. In particular, Fairchild had raised KSAC's admissions standards and defended the school's liberal arts offerings.[27] Populist Regent Harrison Kelley, a farmer, former congressman, and director of the state penitentiary, was a particularly unnerving appointment for Fairchild because Kelley had previously criticized the lack of social science at the college. Regent Edward Secrest, also a farmer and former legislator, had been endorsed by the Riley County Farmers' Alliance. Having sent four children to KSAC, Secrest was enthusiastic about having "a chance to change the order of things."[28] A transformation of sorts was already evident by the fall of 1893, when the regents invited Populist leader "Sockless" Jerry Simpson to give a chapel address. Secrest also invited Governor Lewelling to speak on campus, promising that the college audience would warmly welcome "a live *heretical* governor."[29]

During the Lewelling administration, academic Populists focused on increasing the number of social science courses at KSAC. Appointed to the board of regents in 1894, Christian Balzac Hoffman emerged as a driving force behind these curricular reforms. Hoffman had attended Central Wesleyan College in Missouri and earned a small fortune in the flour, woolens, and timber industries. In 1881, Hoffman attended a meeting of antimonopolists in Dickinson County, became concerned about "the rapid disappearance of 'chances' for the poor man," and joined the reform wing of the Kansas Republican Party. During the following decade, he served as mayor of Enterprise, Kansas, and won election to the state legislature, where he sponsored Kansas's first railroad regulation bill. Ultimately, Hoffman allied himself with the Kansas People's Party and became increasingly radical, even as he continued pursuing lucrative business ventures.[30]

Shortly after his appointment to the KSAC governing board, Hoffman led the search to fill a new chair of political economy. On the strength of a recommendation from B. O. Flower, editor of the *Arena* reform journal, the board hired Thomas E. Will, who would eventually play a crucial role in the Populist-led reorganization of KSAC.[31] Born in Adams County, Illinois, in 1861, Will spent his teenage years working on his family's farm during the day and studying at night. At the age of nineteen, he was working as a country schoolteacher, attending the Illinois State Normal School, reading Henry George's *Progress and Poverty*, and losing his faith in the nation's political economy. He went on to study economics first at the University of Michigan and then at Harvard, where he was disappointed by a curriculum consisting of what he considered to be "dust and ashes, a boundless jungle of sophistries, contradictions and non-sequitors." While he was in Cambridge, Will's sister died on a struggling Nebraska farm. He vowed to wage "eternal warfare" against the capitalist culture "that could thus crush and blight and wither the fairest flower." Will chaffed during his time at Harvard, which he referred to as "the citadel of a murderous economic system."[32] After earning a master's degree in economics, Will spent two years teaching at Lawrence College in Appleton, Wisconsin.

When he was offered the KSAC position, Thomas E. Will was lecturing, writing for reform periodicals, and serving as secretary of a Christian Socialist organization called the Boston Union for Practical Progress. Will never formally joined the People's Party, but his political orientation was clear. He supported perennial Populist causes, such as bimetallism and public ownership of utilities, and identified as a reformer committed to "democratizing government, religion, education, social privilege and rank." The Populist *Manhattan Republic* eventually urged Will to run for governor.[33] Even Julius T. Willard, a conservative KSAC professor and no friend to Will, acknowledged that his colleague was "really sympathetic with the oppressed."[34]

For four years, the fusionist regents of KSAC increased the school's offerings in political economy but otherwise provided little cause for excitement.[35] But in 1896, after electing fusionist Governor John Leedy, Populists took renewed interest in the college.[36] On December 23, Leedy convened a two-hour meeting with Will, Hoffman, and J. N. Limbocker, one of his new appointees to the

Christian Balzac Hoffman (Kansas State Historical Society)

Thomas Elmer Will (University Archives, Kansas State University)

KSAC board.[37] According to Professor Willard, Governor Leedy asked the three men to "revolutionize things at the Agricultural College."[38] Hoffman agreed that a reorganized college could counteract the forces that were increasingly dividing "the masses from the classes."[39] In particular, Hoffman pledged that the agricultural college would rededicate itself to the provision of vocational education alongside courses in progressive economics and civics. "One becomes enthusiastic in contemplating what an institution like the K.S.A.C. could accomplish," he wrote to Regent Harrison Kelley, "if it put itself into the van of progress instead of bringing up the tail-end."[40] President Fairchild claimed that Kelley looked forward to manipulating his involvement with the college in order to counter Republican charges that the Populists were "the party of the ignorant."[41]

When the fusionist-controlled legislature convened in Topeka in the spring for their 1897 session, Populist leaders agreed that they should replace Fairchild with a new leader willing to increase instruction in economics and applied agricultural studies. The legislature voted to end the college president's role as *ex officio* regent and extended each regent's term of service. Afterward, the fusionist board replaced President Fairchild with Thomas E. Will.[42] Following this reorganization, Regent Limbocker exulted that the people had "scaled the gilded halls of the universities."[43]

Populists also sought control of the University of Nebraska (NU), whose industrial college received the proceeds of Nebraska's federal land grant. Nebraska farmers had organized a statewide alliance during the 1880s to lobby for lower railroad shipping rates. Frustrated with Republican leaders, the Nebraska Farmers' Alliance created the Nebraska People's Independent Party in 1890, along with the Knights of Labor and other reform groups. Based in local clubs, the Party swelled as the result of Republican inaction in the face of devastating crop failures. Populists and Democrats fused into a coalition and won majorities in the legislatures of 1891 and 1893.[44] Despite this success, Populists did not control NU. While Populists dominated the fusionist legislatures, NU's governing board was elected by popular vote and remained under the control of a Republican majority.[45] Faced with the task of courting a fusionist legislature, this board asked James Hulme Canfield to become university president during the spring of 1891.

With conventional academic credentials as well as Populist sympathies, Canfield appeased all factions of NU's political universe. Born in Ohio to a transplanted Vermont Episcopalian minister, Canfield graduated from Williams

James Hulme Canfield (from *Semi-Centennial Anniversary Book: The University of Nebraska, 1869–1919*)

College and eventually taught at the University of Kansas. Canfield wooed rural audiences with self-deprecating tales of how frequently he missed the pail while milking cows as a child.[46] As chancellor, he also earned goodwill for describing his relationship with the public as "a man who breaks bread with them under their roofs—without regard to social distinction or condition; who listens to their suggestions and studies their needs . . . who feels himself to be their 'hired man' in a peculiar sense of the words."[47] Canfield also defined himself against East Coast tradition by favoring vocational training as much as the pursuit of highbrow culture. After graduating college, he had turned down his father's invitation to tour Europe and instead traveled west to work at a lumberyard and on the Iowa branch of the Chicago, Milwaukee, and St. Paul Railroad.[48] Canfield was sympathetic to the agrarian revolt and criticized northeastern disdain for the Farmers' Alliance. At KU, Canfield assigned radical tracts on political economy and cutting-edge texts by Richard T. Ely. Popular among students, Canfield earned the respect of editors of the Republican *Nebraska State Journal* as well as Populist papers such as the *Alliance-Independent* and the *Farmers' Alliance*.[49]

When Canfield stepped down in 1895, the NU board of regents replaced him with George MacLean, an English professor from the University of Minnesota. A native of Connecticut and graduate of Williams, Yale, and Leipsig, MacLean articulated a more elitist vision of higher education. Not only did MacLean lack Canfield's aura of folksy accessibility, but he also emphasized scholarly research and advanced coursework.[50] During MacLean's administration (1895–99), control of state politics and the NU board continued to be divided among Republicans and their rivals in the fusionist camp.[51] Unlike Canfield, MacLean did not satisfy both constituencies. *Nebraska Independent* editor Frank Eager believed that MacLean was an aristocrat who should be closely monitored by the two Populist regents who were elected in 1897 (George F. Kenower and E. Von Forell). The *Independent* reported that the university had been "getting further away from the people" during MacLean's tenure and editorialized that the chancellor had "sniffed contemptuously at the farmer boys" on campus. The paper concluded that MacLean was lacking in "democratic spirit," disrespected manual labor, and encouraged the growth of "society circles" on campus.[52] In 1899, excited by the prospect of winning control of NU, Populist newspapers urged voters to elect John L. Teeters and Edson Rich to the board of regents. Campaigning on anti-MacLean, anti-corporate platforms, Teeters and Rich won their races, creating a board with two Republicans and a ruling alliance of two Populists, a reform Democrat, and a pro-silver Republican. This fusionist board would govern the university from 1900 to 1904.[53]

University of Nebraska Board of Regents, 1899. E. V. Forell (*top right*) and G. F. Kenower (*middle right*) were elected on a fusionist ticket. (Archives and Special Collections, University of Nebraska–Lincoln Libraries)

When the University of Iowa offered its presidency to MacLean, he jumped at the opportunity to escape out from under an antagonistic board. According to the *Nebraska State Journal*, the specter of Populist control of NU unnerved all right-thinking Nebraskans. Disturbed by news of the Populist takeover of Kansas's agricultural college, the *Journal's* editor predicted that the university would be subject to bald-faced cronyism.[54] Despite these predictions, the fusionist board convened in 1900 with little fanfare or drama. The board reviewed bids for campus construction projects, hired a philosophy professor to replace a deceased faculty member, and discussed upcoming maintenance needs. In contrast to events at KSAC, NU's period of fusion rule generated relatively little partisan rancor. Even after the end of the fusionist majority, Teeters was elected by his Republican peers to be president of the NU board.[55]

Populist Higher Education

While most faculty and administrators in North Carolina, Kansas, and Nebraska still felt threatened by these takeovers, Populists often belied stereotypical assumptions about the movement's attitude toward public higher education.

Consider the movement's stance toward intercollegiate athletics. Critics of North Carolina Populists were quick to describe any interest in athletics as proof of the movement's anti-intellectualism.[56] However, Kansas Populists seemed more likely to question whether it was appropriate for institutions of higher learning to host sporting events. In November 1895, readers of the Populist *Jeffersonian* complained to the newspaper's editor about the overemphasis on football at KU. One reader grumbled that studious students received less respect than "the athlete whose sole endowment is a bushy head and No. 9 boots." Another reader wondered if football served to distract taxpayers from paying close attention to KU's curriculum.[57] In 1897, the *Jeffersonian* called for the university to fire its football coach, arguing that his salary could not be justified when farmers struggled to make ends meet. Later that year, the newspaper worried that the university only focused on academics in the winter, when the weather was too cold for football. The *Kansas Commoner*, another Populist organ, also editorialized against football at KU.[58] This sort of criticism hints at the distinctiveness of academic Populism, an egalitarian campaign that nevertheless believed in the value of higher learning for farmers and their advocates.

After all, a large portion of the movement's leadership had attended college themselves, including prominent figures such as Tom Watson of Georgia (Mercer College) and William Jennings Bryan of Nebraska (valedictorian of Illinois College class of 1881).[59] In Kansas, college-educated Populists included

John G. Otis, head of the state's delegation to the U.S. Congress in 1890, and Stephan McLallin, editor of the *Topeka Advocate*.[60] Luna Kellie, Secretary of the Nebraska Farmers' Alliance and editor of the *Prairie Home*, attended Rockford Seminary (alma mater of Jane Addams), while Marion Todd of Illinois attended Hastings Law School.[61] Several of the most prominent African American Populists were also college graduates, such as Walter Patillo (Shaw University), John B. Rayner (Shaw University), and Benjamin F. Foster (Fisk University and the Chicago Theological Seminary).[62]

As many as one-quarter of the officers of state Farmers' Alliances had some form of higher education—a proportion far in excess of the education level of the population as a whole.[63] In Georgia, most candidates at the top of the 1892 Populist Party state ticket had attended college, though the party leadership still had less education and fewer ties to the University of Georgia than leaders of the state Democratic Party.[64] Among the seventeen Populist state senators serving in North Carolina during the 1897 session whose educational backgrounds could be determined, seven had attended college.[65] In Kansas, 45 percent of Populist leaders had attended college, and at least 35 percent had graduated. As in Georgia, this college-attendance rate was much higher than the state average but still lower than the rate of the leaders of the mainstream parties.[66] The evidence from Nebraska reveals a similar dynamic: 26 percent of Populist leaders attended college, compared with 36 percent of Republicans and 34 percent of Democrats. Typically, mainstream politicians had attended a state university, whereas more of the college-educated Populists had attended small denominational colleges or normal schools.[67]

Populists and fellow travelers even inhabited the ranks of the professoriate. Reportedly, at least one professor at every major North Carolina denominational college (Wake Forest, Davidson, Trinity, and Guilford) belonged to the Farmers' Alliance or wrote for an Alliance newspaper.[68] At Trinity College, for example, Professor N. C. English led the Randolph County Farmers' Alliance and contemplated running for political office.[69] In Missouri, Farmers' Alliance leader Urial S. Hall served as president of a small college.[70]

Many of the Populists who were elected or appointed to be regents or trustees of state colleges or universities also had attended institutions of higher education. Whereas increasing numbers of professionals and business leaders replaced ministers on governing boards after the Civil War, Populists were more likely to fill these positions with farmers, small-town editors, and career reformers.[71] Although their backgrounds were often unconventional, many Populist trustees and regents had nevertheless attended college. All three Populist trustees at UNC were alumni of the university.[72] Out of the fifteen regents of KU and KSAC who were appointed by fusionist governors, at least six had attended college.[73] In Nebraska, every fusionist regent had attended college.[74] In Washington State, all of Populist Governor John R. Rogers's appointments to the governing board of the state university were reported to have been "well educated."[75]

Populist newspapers routinely cited trustees' education as evidence of their qualifications for those positions. In Kansas, the Lawrence *Jeffersonian* endorsed Governor Lewelling's appointment of a regent who was "an educator and a literary man," while the Topeka *Advocate and News* expressed satisfaction with another regent's Harvard diploma.[76] In Nebraska, the *Alliance Independent* praised a Populist candidate for NU's board of regents for being "a fine scholar." The *People's Poniard* supported Elia Peattie's candidacy for the same position because she was a woman of "culture, education, and accomplishments in a literary sense." A self-taught journalist and fiction writer who published primarily in the *Omaha World-Herald*, as well as the *Chicago Tribune* and *Harper's Weekly*, Peattie campaigned for William Jennings Bryan and coauthored an allegorical story promoting free silver. Bryan thanked her with a volume of poetry by William Cullen Bryant, wryly inscribed "To my friend Elia Peattie, the first Bryan man." In 1899, the *Nebraska Independent* even criticized two Republican candidates for the board of regents because neither had graduated from college.[77] Despite the movement's skepticism of academic credentials, some Populists nevertheless preferred to elect or appoint college-educated trustees.

The prevalence of educated leaders helps to explain the extent to which Populist newspapers interspersed favorable coverage of campus events alongside their criticism of certain institutional policies. The reform press enthusiastically reported opening ceremonies, inaugurations, and commencements at public and private colleges alike. Many movement papers devoted regular columns to campus news. The *Jeffersonian*, for example, celebrated "the magnificent halls of learning" of KU and other institutions of higher education that had begun to produce practical, vigorous graduates. The Topeka *Advocate and News* devoted a lengthy article to the appointment of a new professor of engineering and mechanic arts at KSAC. The *Hickory Mercury* boasted about the quality of North Carolina's institutions of higher education.[78] In turn, colleges and universities purchased advertising space in Populist papers, a practice indicating that the schools believed that Populist parents were not opposed to enrolling their children.[79]

And they were not. University of Colorado President James Baker reported that "radical" farmers and laborers asked "profanely" for access to higher education.[80] Indeed, Populist students outnumbered Republicans and Democrats at the Colorado State Agricultural College (CSAC) during the early 1890s. The CSAC student newspaper endorsed Davis "Bloody Bridles" Waite's Populist campaign for governor. Students celebrated James Weaver's success in Colorado during the presidential race of 1892 by firing cannon until confronted by a pistol-wielding night watchman who happened to favor the Republican Party.[81] At NCCAMA, a student loyal to the movement delivered a strident commencement speech in 1898 lamenting the unequal distribution of wealth and urging the organization of the working class.[82]

At the KSAC, roughly 15 percent of the class of 1891 identified themselves as Populists.[83] Encouraged by her Populist father, Mamie Alexander sold her heifer "Lovely" in 1898 to cover the expense of entering KSAC.[84] KSAC students formed a Free Silver Club in 1896, which held debates with representatives of the college's McKinley Club. At a joint meeting with the Bryan Club of Manhattan, KSAC's Free Silver Glee Club sang rousing versions of "Rally 'Round the Flag" and "Good-bye, McKinley, Good-bye."[85] Students at KU, NU, and the University of Minnesota also formed Populist or pro-silver clubs.[86] The *Lawrence Journal* claimed that the KU was almost evenly divided between Republicans and Populists. On the campus of NU, speeches by William Jennings Bryan regularly drew enthusiastic crowds of students.[87] Frank O'Connell, a young Nebraskan who identified with the "Pops" at a young age, is one example of a Populist youth who gravitated toward higher education. Despite the distance between their Nebraska farmstead and the nearest secondary school, as well as the great sacrifice of sparing the children's labor, Frank's mother was determined to send her children to college.[88]

This Populist attraction to higher education further complicates formulaic distinctions between working class and elite culture. As documented by historian Jonathan Rose, British workers consumed a diverse mix of popular and classic literature.[89] Alvin Johnson, who grew up in a Populist family and later served as president of the New School of Social Research in New York City, illustrates the point within an American context. Johnson's mother, who had received an informal but thorough education, wrote poetry and asked Alvin to read aloud to her from Dickens, Thackeray, George Eliot, and Victor Hugo. Inspired by Edward Bellamy's utopian novel *Looking Backward*, Alvin joined the Farmers' Alliance at the age of sixteen, read reform newspapers, committed himself to "liberating the masses," and became the official lecturer of his local sub-alliance. Johnson's parents encouraged his educational aspirations. Having attended a small rural common school, Johnson entered the University of Nebraska's remedial department, where he encountered other Populists. At NU, Johnson noticed a gulf between rich and poor students and continued to identify with Populist principles by socializing "with the masses and regard[ing] with contempt the aristocratic pretensions of the sons of usurers and crooked paving contractors."[90] Early encounters with literature, science, and art did not determine Johnson's class identity, nor did formal higher education cause him to disassociate with farmers. Instead, higher education encouraged him to imagine new worlds beyond the boundaries of his childhood.

Perhaps influenced by these sorts of experiences, many academic Populists argued that public higher education could equalize the opportunities afforded to privileged and ordinary youth. In Nebraska, a Populist journalist became a particularly vocal champion of this aspect of the state university's mission. Born on a homestead in Lancaster County, Frank Dewitt Eager entered the preparatory department of the state university and ultimately earned a bachelors' degree. After serving as state secretary of the Nebraska Populist Party, selling real estate, and operating a theater business, Eager purchased and consolidated various Populist newspapers into a single organ, *The Nebraska Independent*.[91] While the *Independent* acknowledged that many people succeeded without attending college, the paper editorialized that NU provided "a great advantage" for farmers' children. The *Independent* praised NU for being a school for earnest youth instead of an "institution for literary dudes and rich men's sons." Apparently self-conscious of the movement's reputation for anti-intellectualism, Eager claimed that Nebraska Populists loved the state university "as much as anybody can love it." The *Independent* also claimed that the state university was "the one purely Populistic institution in the whole state" and was the pride of "the wild and wooly pop."[92] A letter to the editor from an Ashland farmer reinforced Eager's statements by boasting that Nebraska had "more college-bred men behind the plow than any other state."[93]

Eager and other academic Populists believed that higher education could promote a more egalitarian society by providing farmers with the social and political status previously associated with educated cosmopolitans. A Kansas Populist urged the state's public colleges and universities to provide rural young people with access to the same sort of knowledge "as can be learned in the schools and universities of the foremost army-ridden countries of Europe."[94] In South Carolina, populistic Governor "Pitchfork" Ben Tillman endorsed liberal arts requirements at the state's land grant institution (Clemson Agricultural College) so that its graduates could meet graduates of traditional colleges on equal footing.[95] Marion Butler, a powerful North Carolina Populist, promoted a similar view of the state agricultural college. The son of a moderately wealthy farmer, Butler attended UNC, where he excelled in rhetoric and law. Compelled to abandon a legal career and return home after the death of this father, Butler edited the *Caucasian*, an influential Populist paper, and rapidly ascended within the movement. As a journalist and politician, Butler supported public higher education and eventually served on UNC's board of trustees. Butler also endorsed NCCAMA, stating that the agricultural college could promote social justice by achieving a status equal to any other institution in the state.[96]

Academic Populists hoped that farm youth who attended public colleges and universities would continue to identify with the producing classes and return home to advance the interests of their communities. A North Carolina Populist newspaper, for example, editorialized that farmers' lack of higher education handicapped them in a political sphere dominated by lawyers and doctors. "Any class that is not educated," stated the paper, was "at the mercy of all educated classes."[97] Motivated by these sentiments, the Kansas Farmers' Alliance sent a farmer to attend courses at the University of Michigan Law School after his election to a local judgeship. Although the man had already won the confidence of his neighbors by briefly studying law and mediating many of their disputes, the alliance hoped to legitimize his election and update his knowledge.[98]

Some members of the Farmers' Alliance proposed establishing their own "Alliance University" dedicated to transforming farmers into lawyers, bankers, doctors, and other professionals who could serve rural communities.[99] This proposal was reminiscent of Ruskin College and the Workers Educational Association, which trained working class intelligentsia in Britain. Despite concerns that formal education would de-radicalize young people, many memoirs reveal that students' intensified their commitment to social reform while developing new arguments and a heightened sense of educational inequality. Finding revolutionary lessons in subjects such as Dante's punishment of corrupt leaders, Ruskin College students believed that their liberal education was not necessarily inconsistent with radical politics or working class allegiance.[100] In the United States, labor leaders and socialists would eventually develop similar schools, such as the Brookwood Labor College, which provided one- to two-year programs that trained activists and adult educators.[101]

While Populists pursued similar goals, they more often targeted established institutions of higher education rather than seeking to create their own schools (though movement supporters founded a few short-lived colleges, including Ruskin College in Missouri). Academic Populists believed that their vision meshed closely enough with the official mission of state colleges and universities. These Populists also maintained that formal higher education—including courses in classics, rhetoric, and political economy—would empower farm youth by preparing them to participate in public life.

Like most nineteenth-century leaders, Populist orators learned to employ historical, philosophical, and literary metaphors in their speeches.[102] Although a speaker at a North Carolina farmers' club complained that colleges merely "teach a great many 'ologies'" and "show boys how to stuff a canary bird," he ultimately asserted that college-educated farmers would be better able to lobby the state legislature.[103] The author Hamlin Garland, who lectured on behalf of the Farmers' Alliance and People's Party, illustrated this purpose of higher education in his novel, *A Spoil of Office*. Garland told the story of Bradley Talcott, a farm laborer who became a Populist politician. After realizing that "a feller ought o' know how to speak at a school meetin' when he's called on," Bradley saved up in order to attend a small-town seminary. Ultimately, Bradley flourished in the seminary's rhetoric class and debating club, attended law school, and ran successfully for public office. Garland's fictional account of Bradley mirrored the experience of actual Populist leaders such as William Jennings Bryan, who honed his oratorical skills during college extracurricular activities.[104]

Leonidas Lafayette Polk, a prime mover behind the creation of NCCAMA, became one of the most vocal advocates for this Populist vision of public higher education. Descended from state legislators and military leaders, Polk referred to himself as the son of a "plain old farmer," even though his father had owned 32 enslaved people and nearly 2,000 acres. In 1855, Polk enrolled as an "irregular student" at Davidson College because he lacked sufficient preparation in Greek and Latin. Polk studied at Davidson for a year, taking agricultural chemistry, logic and rhetoric, mathematics, declamation, and composition while participating in the debating competitions of the college's Eumenean Society. Following his time at Davidson, Polk immersed himself in the culture of the gentleman farmer, reading the *North Carolina Planter*, experimenting with new agricultural techniques, joining the North Carolina Agricultural Society, and building a substantial personal library of history, biography, poetry, philosophy, and theology. After the Civil War, Polk returned to his farm, petitioned for a post office, and founded "Polkton," which grew into a town of 200 by 1880. Polk also experimented with several ill-fated financial investments, including an attempt to sell a patent medicine called "Polk's Diphtheria Cure."

Aided by his folksy charisma, Polk became a leader of the North Carolina State Grange and the state's first commissioner of agriculture. According to one witness, Polk "delighted in crowds and they delighted in him." In February 1886, Polk solidified his position as one of the most prominent agrarian leaders in the state by starting the *Progressive Farmer*, which quickly became the largest newspaper in North Carolina. The North Carolina Farmers' Alliance ultimately elected Polk as its secretary and named the *Progressive Farmer* as its official organ.

Leonidas Lafayette Polk (North Carolina Collection, University of North Carolina Library at Chapel Hill)

In December 1889, Polk was elected president of the National Farmers' Alliance and Industrial Union and was favored to win the People's Party nomination for U.S. president before his death in 1892.[105]

Polk attacked UNC and argued that a new state agricultural and mechanical college would enable farmers to protect themselves from exploitation by lawyers and bankers. He believed that the state should provide farmers with "a liberal education of a high grade" to facilitate their comprehension of agricultural science and to confer political status equal to urban professionals.[106] Polk hoped to convince white rural youth that technology had ended the "age of muscle" and inaugurated the "age of brains." "Let me tell you if you have not already learned it," he told an audience in Winfield, Kansas, on the Fourth of July, 1890, "that the God of mercies has endowed you with brains. . . . That nation which neglects to educate its masses of people to higher ability and to a higher plane of thought and action is on a sure road to inevitable decay and death." Before a North Carolina crowd, Polk was explicit that this education included pursuit of formal credentials. "It will be a glorious day for North Carolina and for the South," Polk said, "when our young men shall not be ashamed to hang their diplomas in their work shops, their machine shops, their art galleries, their laboratories, their school rooms, their counting rooms, and their farm houses."[107] Combining criticism of traditional universities with optimism about the democratic potential of a public higher education, Polk epitomized academic Populism.

Polk also personified the racism of many white Populists. An opponent of proposals to found a state industrial college for African Americans, Polk speculated that black people were incapable of learning scientific agricultural methods.[108] After the Second Morrill Act of 1890 required North Carolina to offer some form of A&M education to African Americans, white Populists supported the establishment of the North Carolina Colored Agricultural and Mechanical College (now North Carolina Agricultural and Technical State University) rather than the integration of NCCAMA. Before the threat of losing federal support for the all white agricultural college, state legislatures with substantial Farmers' Alliance representation had defeated proposals for a similar institution.[109] Even after the state Populist Party forged an alliance with African American Republicans, black North Carolinians remained concerned over the fate of their A&M college.[110] Unsurprisingly, white Populists did not press for the desegregation of UNC, where "blacking" was a form of freshman hazing.[111] In one region of North Carolina, white Populists did not even support state funding for black common schools. In Alabama, white Populists sought to transfer public funds from black to white schools. Only in Texas did the Southern Farmers' Alliance concern itself with the education of African Americans, albeit without challenging segregation.[112]

In Kansas, where some older Populists had participated in abolitionist campaigns, the movement's advocacy for college access did not target racial inequalities.[113] KU and KSAC were both officially colorblind; KU enrolled a small number of black students between 1870 and 1910, while KSAC did not graduate a black student until 1899.[114] White Populists do not seem to have campaigned explicitly to expand black enrollment at either institution. While KSAC's Thomas E. Will responded sympathetically to a letter from a penniless African American father who wanted to send his sons to college, Will characterized the inquiry wholly as an example of the disadvantages of poverty.[115]

Uninterested in race-based advocacy, white Kansas Populists apparently ignored Western University, the one institution in the state that was expressly dedicated to the higher education of African Americans. In 1898, President William Tecumseh Vernon, known as the "Booker T. Washington of the West," pledged to recruit black voters in exchange for a promise of public funding from Republican gubernatorial candidate William E. Stanley. After winning the election, Governor Stanley fulfilled his end of the bargain in the face of opposition from Populist legislators.[116] Kansas Populists also paid little attention to the Haskell Institute, the state's most advanced Native American school.[117] This response to racial discrimination indicates the manner in which Populist majoritarianism could promote apathy or hostility toward minorities. Despite occasional rousing calls for unity, movement leaders responded most consistently to the grievances of a particular interest group of white "producers." The movement's focus on this group, whose children could almost achieve respectability after a mere four years of college, perhaps helps to explain the Populists' enthusiasm for higher education.

Regardless, this indifference toward racial disparities in higher education is consistent with the broader history of the Populist movement. Less predictably, there is little evidence that African American Populists campaigned against discrimination in public higher education. Risking their lives by advocating for fundamental human rights and equal funding for common schools, black Populists may have viewed access to higher education as a less pressing issue.[118] African American Populists may have also believed that the public black colleges supported by the Second Morrill Act of 1890 were already fully committed to accessibility.[119] Alternatively, it is plausible that black Populists' may have had low expectations for state colleges that were governed by white legislators and trustees. The president of Mississippi's Alcorn State College, for example, reported that nearly half of the school's trustees actually questioned the higher education of African Americans. Black colleges with a land grant designation faced an external mandate to focus on vocational education and often answered to administrators who hailed from outside of local communities. In contrast, private black colleges, especially those founded by black churches, such as the African Methodist Episcopal denomination, could be expected to be more responsive to the wishes of their students and their families.[120]

Whereas most white Populists promoted or ignored racial barriers to higher education, Populist class consciousness occasionally prompted the movement to encourage the higher education of women producers. While most states provided opportunities for women to attend public institutions of higher educa-tion (typically coeducational universities in the West and single-sex colleges in the South), roughly half as many women attended college as men during the heyday of Populism.[121] Women also faced discrimination on campus, including exclusion from extracurricular activities and discouragement from taking science and engineering courses.[122] Some academic Populists demanded the equal higher education of women in either coeducational or single-sex settings. Elia Peattie, the Nebraska Populist who had run for university regent, granted that private denominational colleges had the right to remain single-sex institutions, but asserted that all public universities should be open to men and women alike.[123] Populists argued for coeducation in Colorado and Kansas, where Thomas E. Will supported the education of women on "equal terms" as men.[124]

Populists believed that college training could reduce the drudgery of field-work and prepare women to work as teachers, telegraph operators, or clerks in case of economic depression or widowhood. Jennie Dixon, who edited the Populist *Southern Mercury's* "Home Circle" section, promoted a form of higher education that might prepare farmers' daughters "for some kind of business."[125] For similar reasons, populistic Governor "Pitchfork" Ben Tillman lobbied for coeducation at South Carolina College and the Citadel, as well as for the estab-lishment of a state industrial college for women.[126] The North Carolina Farmers' Alliance resolved in favor of college access for women at its annual meeting in 1890, explaining that higher education "alike for males and females" would benefit all of "the industrial classes." The following year, a state legislature dominated by members loyal to the Alliance established the North Carolina Normal and Industrial School (NCNIS) for white women.[127] According to a Populist mother, NCNIS would attract "farmers' daughters who crave the advantages of town girls."[128] Yet Populists did not lobby for coeducation at UNC, where proposals to admit undergraduate women were rejected in 1897,

1898, and 1899.[129] And at the NCCAMA, the fusionist board of trustees only allowed women in the textile department and as non-degree students.[130]

Elsewhere, Populists sometimes advocated for women's access to the most privileged positions on campus—faculty appointments and governing board seats. At the time of the Populist movement, land grant colleges employed women as assistants, technicians, and instructors, but rarely as full faculty members. In Nebraska, Populist editor Frank Eager attacked the state university for replacing two female teachers with men who were no better qualified and for only hiring women to fill low-level administrative positions. Protesting that NU no longer had any female professors, Eager's *Nebraska Independent* accused Chancellor George MacLean of snobbishly favoring East Coast elites while alienating the "earnest young women" who attended the university.[131] Similarly, the Lawrence *Jeffersonian* complained when KU's regents did not promote a female assistant to the rank of full professor. Noting that many years had passed since the KU faculty had included a woman, the paper argued that KU's female assistants were exploited as "the drawers of water and the hewers of wood for the professor who dons his knee breeches." When Populist regents of KSAC had the chance to act on these concerns, they filled the chair of mathematics with Mary Winston, the first woman with a PhD to ever teach at the college.[132] Fusionist Governor John Leedy also appointed Susan St. John (a prohibition activist and wife of a former governor) to the KSAC board.[133] In Nebraska, the Populist Party nominated Elia Peattie to run for a seat on the NU board of regents. Peattie, who lost the race, was the only woman in any political party running for a statewide office in Nebraska during the election of 1895.[134]

Conclusion

Richard Hofstadter, perhaps the keenest observer of American anti-intellectualism, recognized that egalitarian movements still tended to respect the awesome power of higher learning.[135] The Populist movement was no exception. Concerned that entrenched privilege had trumped fair play and honest labor, Populists looked to public institutions of higher education for remedies. Motivated by visions of reform rather than destruction, academic Populists embraced opportunities to influence state colleges and universities. L. L. Polk, Frank Eager, Thomas E. Will, and others encouraged these institutions to embrace the movement's anti-elitist ethic. Despite their overwrought rhetoric and skepticism toward traditional academic leadership, many academic Populists still believed that mass enrollment in state colleges and universities could promote a democratic civil society.

While this campaign sometimes encouraged women's access to higher education, most white Populists embraced racial discrimination and segregation. This bigotry highlights a pitfall of the majoritarianism that both energized and degraded the movement; white Populists tended to advocate for *the masses* (an imaginary and often racially homogenous category), rather than emphasizing universal, individual, or minority rights.

Despite these tragic limitations, academic Populism sought to assure the masses that their children could benefit from college without absorbing elitist attitudes. The remainder of this book explores this tension between Populist enthusiasm and Populist anxiety. Academic Populists hoped to resolve these mixed feelings about higher education by lobbying state colleges and universities to emphasize a particular constellation of policies. These interventions often exhibited unexpected thoughtfulness as well as stereotypical demagoguery. Indeed, the passion of the movement's critique of higher education arose from the conviction that these institutions had not yet committed themselves to the promotion of full-fledged democracy.

3

The Greatest Good
for the Greatest Number

Populism and Academic Access

In November 1897, Kansas State Agricultural College (KSAC) president Thomas E. Will received a letter from William Coleman, a thirty-three-year-old manufacturer of hosiery. Although Coleman had not attended school for seventeen years and doubted if he could pass KSAC's entrance examinations, he hoped to attend chemistry and mechanics classes during the winter. Recently appointed by a fusionist board of regents, President Will scribbled "can we make a special arrangement for him?" in the margins of the letter.[1] Will's desire to maximize attendance was not unique. During the nineteenth century, most state colleges and universities maintained low admission requirements, conducted extension programs, and admitted nondegree "special students" who attended part time or could not pass entrance examinations. While some faculty preferred to focus on smaller numbers of gifted students, many Americans believed that mass enrollment was the core mission of public universities.[2] Passionate advocates for this point of view, academic Populists entered into a longstanding debate about whether public institutions of higher education should target disadvantaged, average, or exceptional students.

As early as the era of Andrew Jackson, Americans had questioned whether public schools could cater to students with extraordinary preparation or intellect without violating the nation's egalitarian ideals.[3] But whereas Jacksonian Democrats tended to rail unreservedly against the hierarchical nature of colleges, Gilded Age Populists exhibited more conflicted attitudes. Many Populists retained Jacksonian skepticism toward the most common rationale for public higher education—that small cadres of talented graduates would serve the entire population. Populists continued to argue that college graduates could monopolize intellectual capital and exploit the masses in the same fashion as monopolies of utilities, railroads, or manufacturing. However, as secondary schooling became more widely available, Populists infused these anti-elitist rants with increasing optimism about state universities. Academic Populists believed that accessible public higher education could supply "the greatest good to the greatest number" by reducing status distinctions between children of producers and children of the privileged.[4]

The movement expected land grant colleges and universities to serve large numbers of white rural youth by maintaining remedial courses, low entrance requirements, and numerous extension programs. On first inspection, college admission standards may have seemed virtually nonexistent during the nineteenth century, when frail secondary school systems and parochial applicant pools constrained the requirements of even the oldest and most storied institutions. According to Populists observers, however, colleges with even slight entrance standards still discriminated against worthy but unprepared farm youth. Populists urged land grant institutions to reject the recommendations of out-of-state universities and national educational associations until rural youth had access to quality high schools. Retelling the history of entrance requirements from the Populist perspective emphasizes this early politicization of admission standards. In particular, this history demonstrates how advocates for disadvantaged *white* students challenged the justification for selective admissions at public universities.

"Selective" Admissions in the Late Nineteenth Century

Historians of higher education have demonstrated that inadequate secondary schooling and parochial recruitment spheres limited admission standards during the nineteenth century, when virtually all colleges sought to bolster their status by enrolling larger numbers of students.[5] Before 1870, most colleges only examined prospective students in classics and mathematics, and professors often administered these tests with considerable discretion. A professor of Greek at the University of North Carolina (UNC), for example, allegedly passed an otherwise weak student because he demonstrated a wealth of knowledge about a local mountain. As high school enrollment rose steadily, colleges sought to increase the quality and quantity of requirements, gradually adding examinations in subjects such as geography, history, and the natural sciences. Yet secondary school principals successfully lobbied colleges to add flexibility by allowing applicants to replace Greek or Latin requirements with examinations in scientific subjects or modern languages. By the 1880s, many colleges and universities also offered alternative degrees, such as the Bachelor of Letters or Bachelor of Science, which required applicants to demonstrate more familiarity with modern subjects instead of the classics.[6] Western and southern public universities often maintained even fewer and less exacting requirements than eastern private institutions. In particular, several of these universities did not require applicants to show proficiency in a foreign language.[7]

In order to remain viable, most colleges also admitted applicants who failed entrance examinations and granted these students a period of time in which to become proficient. Even elite private institutions, such as Columbia University, admitted nearly half of their students with these "conditions" at the turn of the century.[8] In 1899, the president of UNC reassured applicants that entrance examinations rarely prevented students from enrolling as long as they were willing to catch up on missing subject matter. Indeed, between 1899 and 1903, 30 to 50 percent of UNC freshman had conditions in Latin, 50 to 72 percent in English, and 31 to 41 percent in mathematics.[9] In order to serve these borderline applicants, most colleges and universities operated preparatory departments. At many institutions, enrollment in these departments matched or exceeded enrollment in college-level courses. For example, the University of Colorado enrolled 71 preparatory students and 25 students in its liberal arts college during the 1887–88 school year. Nationwide, preparatory students constituted over 40 percent of college enrollment in mid-1880s.[10]

Starting with the University of Michigan (UM), public institutions of higher education pioneered another strategy for easing students' transition from local school systems. Impressed by the close relationship between German universities and *gymnasia*, UM President Henry S. Frieze directed professors to inspect and certify Michigan high schools. In 1870, UM pledged to admit all students who had been endorsed by their principals and completed the college-preparatory track of any certified high school. By the early twentieth century, this "admission by certificate" system became the most common method of gaining entrance to state universities.[11]

In 1892, the National Education Association appointed a prestigious "Committee of Ten" in order to coordinate this varied and idiosyncratic set of entrance requirements. Chaired by Harvard University President Charles Eliot, the committee promoted four options for college preparatory curricula: classical, scientific, English, and modern languages. Each curriculum contained similar core subjects (in varying intensities), along with different foreign language requirements. The committee also agreed that each course of study should require a full four years of high school.[12] Compared to more familiar twentieth-century admissions standards, the committee's recommendations may appear quite modest. Indeed, the liberal reformers who comprised the committee did not seek to increase exclusivity. To the contrary, they hoped that uniform academic requirements would provide clearer routes to college.

Yet when viewed from a Populist perspective, even minimal requirements proposed by UM or the NEA could still be "selective" if they ignored the extent of rural disadvantage. While public high schools operated in most large cities and towns by the late nineteenth century, many rural counties provided no free opportunities for college preparation. Charles Eliot estimated that as many as three out of four Americans, including "the masses of the rural population," lacked access to adequate secondary schooling. Throughout Nebraska, for instance, only one-third of counties offered secondary-level classes during the 1890s.[13] Educational opportunities also varied widely from one district to another. High property valuations or railroad revenues enabled some Kansas districts to hold school for nine months, while adjacent districts only operated for four months. In North Carolina, most rural students attended common schools for two to three months a year, while students in densely populated districts attended for up to eight months.[14] Rural school attendance also declined during planting and harvesting seasons.[15]

Unless they could afford private education, rural students confronted an arduous road to higher education. Relatively few rural students graduated from accredited high schools and gained automatic admission by certificate. Although proponents of this method of admission and the Committee of Ten intended to expand the pipeline to higher education, few rural schools offered the requisite number and level of courses. Even within accredited schools, most students pursued an insufficient number of college-preparatory courses. In 1900, only one-third of American high school graduates had taken a college preparatory course sequence.[16] Less than 50 percent of high school students studied Latin, and only 5 percent studied Greek. The proportions taking courses in modern languages were no higher, with roughly 10 percent and 15 percent studying French and German respectively. Mathematics requirements were within reach of more students, but still challenged the 50 percent of students who did not take algebra and the 75 percent who did not study geometry.[17] Even in Michigan, many rural students could not pursue admission by certificate until after 1909, when the state forced all counties to build high schools or reimburse students who attended schools in other counties.[18]

Predictably, many students also struggled to enter college via the traditional series of entrance examinations. Although often characterized as having essentially open admissions, even state institutions such as the University of Nebraska (NU), the University of Texas, and North Carolina College of Agriculture and Mechanic Arts (NCCAMA) rejected roughly 25 percent of applicants during the 1890s.[19] While these applicants could gain conditional admission and take remedial courses, they still faced daunting challenges on the path toward regular enrollment. The novels of Willa Cather, who attended NU between 1891 and 1895, dramatize the labors of those rural youth who managed to thrive at state universities. In *The Professor's House*, Cather told the story of Tom Outland, a young man without formal secondary education who impressed NU faculty members after teaching himself Latin (including the entire *Aeneid*) and high school mathematics. Jim Burden, protagonist of *My Ántonia*, compensated for the shortcomings of his rural high school by learning trigonometry before entering NU and studying Greek during the summer after his freshman year. Cather honored Jim and other students who "completed the course by really heroic self-sacrifice." Cather, herself, had spent a year in remedial classes after graduating from a high school that had not offered a full preparatory curriculum.[20] Yet examples of rural students who failed to overcome these challenges were also common. For instance, UNC President George T. Winston regretted that half of the freshmen in his Latin class were doomed to fail. Regarding these unprepared students, Winston remarked that it was "a dangerous experiment to pitch a boy into a deep stream to sink or swim. The majority will go down."[21]

In this context, it is not surprising that most colleges responded cautiously to the entrance requirements proposed by the Committee of Ten. The majority of public as well as private college presidents struggled simply to keep their institutions afloat and dreamed of large enrollments more than uniform standards. Concerned that the committee's proposed language requirements would be beyond the capacity of public high schools, the University of Wisconsin rejected a direct request from Charles Eliot to align its admissions standards to the report.[22] Some state university leaders preferred to embrace the ideal of broad access rather than seek to codify firm entrance requirements. University of Illinois President Andrew S. Draper, for example, proclaimed that public institutions "must not try to keep people out; they must help all who are worthy to get in."[23]

Yet other faculty and administrators were torn between the pursuit of higher standards and the necessity of remaining accessible. Believing that their primary mission was to train the most talented and accomplished youth of their regions, some state university presidents insisted that their entrance requirements were appropriate as long as they did not discriminate explicitly against rural students. In 1882, University of Kentucky President James Patterson explained to the state legislature that the school should educate students who managed to prepare themselves for college rather than focusing on "their weaker companions."[24] Faculty members often looked forward to the day when they might purge their institutions of what one observer called the "ungraded, un-lettered, and unwashed."[25] Subscribing to a similar philosophy, President James H. Baker hoped to transform the University of Colorado into the academic equal of Harvard and Yale. Inaugurated in 1893, President Baker believed that true universities provided a form of "special education" that was too advanced for the majority of young people.[26]

Conventional advocates of public higher education hoped to justify this degree of selectivity by portraying colleges as meritocratic institutions that evaluated ability rather than social pedigree.[27] President Baker explained to Colorado residents that the university created a beneficent "aristocracy of intellectual power."[28] In order to illustrate the democratic nature of these institu-tions, allies cited examples of poor students who excelled. For instance, University of Wisconsin Professor Frederick Jackson Turner celebrated public universities for sinking "deep shafts through the social strata to find the gold of real ability in the underlying rock of the masses."[29] Administrators of public universities also routinely declared that the education of relatively small number of students trickled down to benefit all state residents. President Patterson assured Kentucky's taxpayers that "the few who push their way to eminence by the cultivation of the talents which are their birthright mould the character and shape the des-tinies of the State." University of Kansas (KU) Chancellor Joshua Lippincott argued that although few students attended KU during the 1880s, the univer-sity existed "through these few for the masses." To justify why the state should pay for expensive repairs after a devastating campus fire, University of Missouri President Richard Henry Jesse stated, "One single great man developed in the university was cheap at a million dollars and twenty years of time." These proponents frequently referred to the selfless leadership of college graduates in scientific, economic, and political domains.[30]

Unimpressed by these arguments, laypeople expected state universities to provide ready access for the underrepresented masses. State university presi-dents risked inciting protests if they attempted to make their schools more selective by increasing minimum standards for admission. Well before the peak of Populist political power, public outrage prompted the trustees of Ohio State University to veto an increase in the rigor of its entrance examinations. After the head of Illinois Industrial University proposed requiring a Latin entrance examination in 1886, opponents of the measure demanded his resignation. During the same year, Cornell University President Charles Kendall Adams appeased New York farmers by allowing students over the age of eighteen to enter the state's agricultural college without examination. Southern state universities felt particular pressure to shed the perception that they were training grounds for heirs of the antebellum plantation elite. Charles Dabney of the University of Tennessee acknowledged that raising entrance requirements during the 1890s might jeopardize the school's funding. A professor at the University of California claimed that "popular clamor" also compelled western land grant colleges to maintain low standards. Even in New England, not typically regarded as fertile ground for populistic agitation, New Hampshire legislators attempted to compel the state agricultural college to admit all common school graduates.[31]

In states where they came to power, Populists advanced to the vanguard of this campaign for mass higher education. Focusing especially on the ideal of equal educational opportunity, Populists emphasized that public institutions of higher education could either align their standards with established urban high schools or remain accessible to ordinary rural students. Consistent with the priorities of the majority of the movement's supporters, academic Populists lobbied for geographical equity and tended to ignore or endorse racial discrimination. Instead, the movement emphasized the educational disadvantages facing the sons (and sometimes the daughters) of white farmers. One Populist, for example, argued that monopolies placed rural youth in a position as handicapped as a man wrestling a bear.[32] "In what respect are the children of the poor equal to the children of the rich," asked the *Alliance Independent*, "have they an equal opportunity to secure an education?"[33]

Populists suggested that uniform college admission standards could never be legitimate in the midst of unequal preparation. They believed that for every exceptional rural child who managed to enter a state university, many others failed to compensate for their lack of quality secondary schooling. Alvin Johnson, a Populist youth who was able to overcome these odds at the University of Nebraska, observed that most of his rural classmates had been unable to do so. Johnson noted that rural students whose language had been "limited to the daily speech of the farm or the small town" were "terribly handicapped." Johnson recalled that many of his friends "who had perfectly good brains nevertheless were dismal failures as students."[34] In an attempt to reconcile these concerns with their overall optimism about public universities, academic

Populists hoped to broaden access to higher education and decouple its relationship with socioeconomic status.

In order to reduce the disadvantages faced by Alvin Johnson's classmates, Populists attempted to improve rural elementary and secondary schools.[35] In Colorado, where Populists elected Governor Davis "Bloody Bridles" Waite and a plurality of the state legislature during the election of 1892, the movement protested dramatic inequalities between rural and urban educational facilities. Waite's superintendent of public instruction advocated for a statewide tax earmarked toward the equalization of local school funding.[36] Harry Gaines and William Stryker, Kansas's Populist state school superintendents, were also concerned about the gulf between rural common schools and the state university. Kansas youth from counties without public high schools were forced to pay tuition fees if they traveled to attend urban schools. Although the Kansas legislature of 1886 had attempted to facilitate the construction of regional high schools in rural areas, only three had been established as of 1894. Gaines and Stryker criticized the unequal resources of school districts and proposed remedies such as a state education tax, district consolidation, and public transportation. A reader of the Populist *Topeka Advocate* was enthusiastic about these proposals and asked, "By what process of reasoning can anyone conclude that town children are entitled to better school facilities than their country cousins?" "If human laws fail to make men more nearly equal," the reader concluded, "they are radically wrong."[37]

Nebraska Populists waged a similar campaign against unequal educational opportunities. In 1895, Nebraska's Populist legislature outlawed tuition charges for nonresidents who did not have access to free high schools in their own districts. Much to the dismay of the Populist press, a state court overturned the law two years later. Like his counterparts in Kansas, Nebraska's Populist school superintendent also called for a new state tax to benefit impoverished rural districts.[38]

Remediation

In the meantime, Populists argued that college policies should not discriminate against rural students. Thomas E. Will believed that the KSAC should cultivate the "latent possibilities" of all citizens, instead of only enrolling "favored individuals and classes."[39] To this end, Populists promoted preparatory departments designed to bridge the distance between rural school systems and institutions of higher education.

In contrast, most professors reluctantly tolerated these programs. While recognizing that preparatory departments facilitated the enrollment of additional students, professors regretted the manner in which these programs impeded the growth of local high schools and distracted universities from their primary missions.[40] College presidents and professors often argued that preparatory departments tainted the nature of higher education at their institutions. President Edward Orton of the Ohio State University complained that remedial courses designed "to bring up the work of backwoods districts" created a mongrel school that violated the "sacred" purpose of higher education. Similarly, University of Minnesota President William W. Folwell stated that combining preparatory "blackboard drudgery" and college-level "humanizing, literary, reflective subjects" in the same school was akin to breaking a "natural law."[41] As public high schools multiplied and strengthened their curricula, most university leaders were eager to eliminate preparatory departments. As early as the 1860s and 1870s, when systems of secondary education were in their infancy, professors were already advocating for the end of remediation. Encouraged by the growth of public secondary schools and the hope that the admission by certificate system would increase college access, more professors supported termination of remedial programs during the 1880s and 1890s.

Indeed, the state universities of Iowa, Minnesota, and Wisconsin abolished their preparatory departments a few years after implementing systems of high school accreditation.[42] In 1888, University of Tennessee President Charles Dabney judged that preparatory departments had "no place in a university." Declaring that most preparatory students were "hopelessly backward" and that the university was not the "proper place for them to make up their lost opportunities," Dabney began a gradual and incomplete campaign against remediation.[43] In 1895, when the Southern Association of Colleges and Schools established itself as the accreditor of the top tier of higher education in the region, the organization denied membership to colleges that maintained preparatory departments.[44] At the 1897 meeting of the Association of American Agricultural Colleges and Experiment Stations, University of Missouri President Richard H. Jesse questioned whether it was even legal for land grant institutions to maintain these programs according to the terms of the Morrill Act.[45]

The history of UNC illustrates the conventional opposition to preparatory departments. Like most nineteenth-century universities, UNC enrolled many students who lacked extensive secondary-level education. President Kemp Battle regretted the manner in which these students slowed the pace of instruction, but worried about the economic and political consequences of the significant reduction in enrollment that would result from increased standards. In his report to UNC's governing board, Battle described the dilemma posed by the large numbers of these students and asked, "what is to be done with them?" He understood that because many students lacked classical training near their homes and could not afford to board at private academies, enforcing higher entrance standards would "close our doors practically to many communities of our state." Nevertheless, Battle was more determined to preserve UNC's "growing reputation for scholarship."[46]

When UNC lost its land grant status to NCCAMA and was no longer legally mandated to maintain lower entrance requirements for students studying agriculture or the mechanic arts, the university notified secondary schools across the state that it would henceforth reject students who lacked three years of high school Latin, algebra, and English.[47] President Battle opposed continuing remedial courses because he believed that they "infallibly lower the character of the institution." "If a student cannot keep up with the rest," he reported, "let him submit to his fate." Battle recommended that students who required additional tutoring should "pay for it out of their own pockets" or attend another college that was "less exacting as to admission."[48] Although UNC continued to allow students to enter with conditions in two subjects, the university rejected one-fifth of its applicants and filled most of its spots with graduates of private academies (as late as 1903, only 16 percent of freshman had attended public secondary schools).[49] In 1899, when Democrats regained control of the NCCAMA board of trustees after two years of fusionist administration, the college also abolished its preparatory department. Afterward, NCCAMA's president (former UNC Latin Professor George Winston) responded to inquiries from poorly prepared applicants by stating that the A&M college was "not a preparatory school."[50]

It is widely understood that colleges and universities endeavored to close preparatory departments, but it is less commonly noted that it was not self-evident when institutions should take this step.[51] Drawing attention to the contentiousness of these decisions, academic Populists expressed greater concern about how the elimination of preparatory departments would disrupt the educational opportunities of rural youth. As late as 1895, 17 percent of full-fledged college students had finished their preparation in these programs rather than proceeding directly from high schools.[52] Populists had more tolerance for remediation because they were less interested in the sanctity of higher education. For example, Nebraska's *Alliance Independent* stated that university professors were "simply teachers in other rooms from those occupied by the teachers in the graded schools."[53] So when faced with proposals to abolish remedial courses, many Populists preferred to err on the side of caution.[54]

While other schools cut remedial programs, KSAC's fusionist administrators enrolled increasing numbers of students in its preparatory courses. During the tenure of President Thomas E. Will (1897–99), attendance in these courses rose by 65 percent. In the fall of 1898, KSAC's regents hired the college's first full-time instructor for preparatory courses. Noting that remedial classes had previously been taught "somewhat indifferently" by undergraduate and graduate students, the regents hoped that the new hire would conduct these courses in a more thorough fashion.[55] Responding to the Populists' comfort with these courses and their relative disinterest in advanced instruction, the dean of the KU graduate school complained that the movement's ideal form of higher education was merely a "high school for the education of farmers boys."[56]

The Populists who monitored developments at NU also believed that widespread remediation was consistent with the institution's land grant designation. NU accepted students from country schools into a two-year preparatory department, which was called the Latin School because this subject was typically the tallest hurdle for rural youth. High school graduates who had studied Latin and algebra but lacked full preparation enrolled in the Latin School's second year.[57] Although the NU faculty had voted to close the Latin School in 1890, the board of regents overruled this decision after protests from the Nebraska Farmers' Alliance and other residents of rural counties.[58] Chancellor James Hulme Canfield, a popular figure among Nebraska Populists, was more supportive of the Latin School than most of his faculty. Canfield argued that because 80 percent of Nebraskans lacked access to adequate high schools, remedial courses served as NU's primary connection to ordinary residents of the state. The chancellor noted that only public colleges with preparatory departments were able to enroll large numbers of rural students.[59] Canfield also understood that Populist support for NU would deteriorate if he eliminated the Latin School. Some legislators had threatened to cut the university's funding if it canceled remedial courses.[60] Canfield's successor, George MacLean, rejected the Populist perspective on remediation and announced plans to close the Latin School. Proclaiming that his administration would focus on the quality rather than the quantity of students, MacLean told students, "In the republic of letters there is always an aristocracy."[61]

Unconvinced, the *Nebraska Independent* exclaimed that this decision "deprived thousands of sons of farmers of the opportunity to secure a higher education." The paper argued that NU's preparatory courses provided a free high school

This yearbook cartoon from 1897 prematurely memorialized the University of Nebraska's Preparatory "Latin" School. The board of regents preserved the school after the state supreme court overturned a law that had banned high schools from charging tuition to nonresident students. (Archives and Special Collections, University of Nebraska–Lincoln Libraries)

for country youth who had no other public pipeline to the university. The *Independent* accused MacLean of being "stylish" and favoring city youth over country youth. The paper charged that ending the preparatory courses was "a scheme to shut the 'hayseeds' out of the university and reserve its privileges for the benefit of Nebraska's aristocracy." Populists were not satisfied with MacLean's attempt to compromise by continuing remedial classes in a few subjects, advertising private tutors, and sponsoring a private secondary school in Lincoln.[62] In 1897, the Nebraska Supreme Court temporarily resolved this dispute by overturning a law that had forbidden public high schools from charging tuition to nonresident students. In the absence of free secondary schooling for most rural students, NU's regents refused to dismantle the Latin School.[63] During a decade in which public high school enrollment rose dramatically, Populists epitomized this argument for preserving the preparatory function of state colleges and universities.

Entrance Requirements

In addition to generating support for preparatory departments, Populist concern for underserved white rural youth motivated the movement to advocate for low prerequisites for the college-level courses of land grant institutions. After struggling to attract students during their early years, land grant institutions eventually developed into reputable state colleges or strong A&M entities within state universities.[64] Yet land grant institutions often continued to maintain more modest admission standards than traditional colleges or universities. Often only requiring an eighth- or ninth-grade level of preparation, many agricultural programs maintained an intermediate status between secondary and higher education.[65] When UNC had received land grant funds, for example, state law required the university to exempt A&M students from its standard entrance requirements.[66]

Therefore, when Leonidas L. Polk campaigned for a separate state agricultural college, he followed local precedent by arguing that the school must recognize "the disadvantages under which the farmer's boy labors in the struggle for education." Polk envisioned that North Carolina's land grant college would be within the reach of "any farmer's boy who has obtained the rudiments of a common school education."[67] Led by Polk, farmers lobbied for the establishment of NCCAMA, which originally admitted any white male over fourteen years of age who could demonstrate moral character as well as comprehension of "ordinary English," "simple arithmetic," and "a fair knowledge of geography and state history."[68] These requirements situated NCCAMA within the lowest tier of land grant colleges in terms of admission standards. During this period, 83 percent of NCCAMA's peer institutions required applicants to their college-level divisions to know algebra, 43 percent required geometry, and 39 percent required English proficiency at a high school level.[69] Along with most colleges in the nation, NCCAMA issued conditional acceptances to applicants who failed one or two entrance examinations and required professors to provide remedial tutoring. In the event of "some unusual circumstance or promise in the applicant," NCCAMA trustees also authorized the enrollment of students who had failed three or more exams.[70] Although NCCAMA's professor of English regretted that many of his pupils were "sadly deficient," the college only sent home six of its seventy-nine students during the 1890–91 school year.[71] In 1893, NCCAMA established a formal preparatory department to serve these students, who totaled more than one-quarter of the college's enrollment.[72]

North Carolina Populists never obtained full control over NCCAMA, and it began to adopt more conventional academic norms. Alexander Holladay, NCCAMA's first president, withstood pressure from those who wanted to peg the college's standards to the level of "the whole mass of the people."[73] After a brief period of Populist/Republican control between 1897 and 1899, the Democratic Party regained a majority of seats on the NCCAMA board and promptly raised the college's entrance requirements. The college added an algebra requirement and closed its preparatory department in 1899, even though large portions of North Carolina remained without access to free high schools. Afterward, NCCAMA denied admission to significant numbers of applicants.[74]

During their administration of KSAC, Populists' permissive attitude toward admission standards also clashed with the outlook of traditional academic leaders. Similar to their counterparts in North Carolina, Kansas Populists tolerated high requirements at the flagship state university, yet defended relatively low standards at the state land grant institution. On the eve of the fusionist takeover in 1893, KSAC had raised its entrance examination to a level only just beyond the common schools of the state. The college also accepted any applicant who presented a diploma from a recognized grammar school.[75] As in the case of NCCAMA, these requirements were low compared to other state agricultural colleges.[76] KSAC's fusionist regents refused to substantially increase these standards during the next six years.[77] In 1894, KSAC's board rejected the Committee of Ten's guidelines for college entrance standards, despite a personal request from Harvard President Charles Eliot. Earning commendations from the Populist press, the regents responded that they were obligated to keep KSAC within reach of graduates of the state's public school system.[78] In contrast, the Republican *Manhattan Nationalist* protested that any student who completed the seventh grade could enter KSAC. "Elevate the standard regardless of the numbers attending," the paper urged. The *Nationalist* also argued that the college's modest requirements had been enforced more strictly before the start of the fusionist era. The paper claimed that forty to sixty applicants had failed each examination during the several years preceding 1897, whereas virtually all students passed the test in 1897.[79]

After Republicans swept the statewide elections of 1898 and ended the fusionist majority on KSAC's governing board, they looked forward to raising the college's entrance requirements. Frustrated with the number of unprepared students attending his chemistry courses, Professor Julius T. Willard hoped that Republican regents would reinstitute previous admission policies. Despite the drop in enrollment that might accompany an increase in entrance standards, Willard believed that "the confidence of the people can be retained and *regained* so that the better class will come in to make up for what must be shaken off for low grade work."[80] KSAC students petitioned the board of regents in June to maintain its standards. The petition, endorsed by a vote of 396 to 24, echoed Populist concern for rural students.[81] The Populist *Manhattan Republic* sought to remind the new board members that KSAC was "not a professional men's college, but a farmers' and mechanics' college" that should remain "in close touch with the country people of the state."[82] Nevertheless, the Republican board immediately raised admission requirements by adding exams in English composition, bookkeeping, physiology, and algebra.[83] The *Student Herald* objected that graduates of rural common schools would require a term of remedial work. The *Herald* editorialized that these new standards were challenging for "even the strongest students" from rural areas. The student editors argued that country schools should be improved before college standards were raised. "We believe in reform," they stated, "but we do not think it should be applied at the wrong end."[84]

In Nebraska, Populists were pleased with Chancellor James Canfield's support for lax admission standards. Unlike North Carolina and Kansas, Nebraska designated its land grant program as an "Industrial College" within the flagship state university. Although NU had initially maintained lower standards at the land grant program, the university raised the industrial college's entrance requirements to the equivalent of its liberal arts division in 1885.[85] These entrance requirements were similar to NU's peer institutions—applicants either presented diplomas from accredited high schools or passed examinations in common school branches, plus algebra, geometry, history, and foreign languages.[86] Nebraska Populists did not demand that NU reverse this decision, but they did expect the university to administer its admissions policy with a measure of sympathy for rural youth. Canfield agreed that the gates to the university should not be guarded "with locks that respond only to golden keys." In his letter accepting the NU chancellorship, Canfield announced his intention to have the university "minister to the needs of the greatest number," instead of attempting to reach an academic "ideal" far removed from the level of the typical country school system. Canfield promised that the university would open its doors to all graduates of "a good country school."[87]

According to Alvin Johnson, Canfield lived up to these promises. When Johnson initially inquired about attending NU, Canfield advised him to prepare his powers of memorization by reading a page of history and a page of fiction every morning. "Read a page of each very carefully," the chancellor suggested, and "in the evening, after your farm work, reproduce these two pages from memory." Johnson dutifully complied, using *Uncle Tom's Cabin* as his work of fiction. When Johnson arrived late to NU after harvesting his family's crop, Canfield warned that he would struggle to catch up, but concluded, "If you want to try it, the chancellor has no right to forbid you."[88] Nearly sixty years later, Johnson recalled that Canfield had "focused his great human intelligence upon me when I was an ill equipped boy from the farm, and jammed me past all the reasonable restrictions imposed to exclude such a boy as I was."[89]

Canfield instructed the evaluators of university entrance examinations to err on the side of rural students. He even permitted examiners to conduct oral interviews of applicants who had not completed their tests during the allotted time. Canfield asked examiners to be conscious of the "rust" that students accumulated over the course of the summer or during the years between leaving school and applying to university. "The standard of the university is to be maintained rather by the quality of the work which we do here," Canfield told the examiners, "than by our criticism of the work which has been done elsewhere." While the chancellor agreed that NU should have a rigorous course of study, he urged examiners to "let our entrance gates turn rather easily."[90] Faced with a tight budget and an office crowded with prospective students, however, Canfield was compelled to reject the least qualified applicants. In 1893, he turned away as many as one-fourth of all applicants.[91] Still, Canfield's permissive philosophy unnerved many professors. While the chancellor advocated for accessibility, the majority of the faculty requested an increase in the amount of Latin required of applicants to the classical course.[92] Canfield also clashed with President Nicholas Murray Butler of Columbia University at the 1894 annual meeting of the National Education Association. Canfield challenged Butler's recommendation that all professional schools should require applicants to possess a bachelor's degree. Canfield argued that the NU Law School accepted students directly from high school in order to "keep American education in touch with American people." Canfield concluded that the nation had not yet "reached the time when there is a very numerous class in this country with sufficient time and means at command to do the work proposed by Dr. Butler."[93]

On hearing that Canfield had accepted the presidency of the Ohio State University, the *Nebraska Independent* worried about his successor's attitude toward entrance requirements. The newspaper was concerned that Chancellor George MacLean, a former professor of English at the University of Minnesota, might raise admission standards beyond the level of the average rural school system. "City blood is no better than country blood," the *Independent* argued, warning that high requirements would be viewed as tantamount to "discrimination" against rural students. Asserting that any student who was capable of doing college work should be enrolled even if other students were far more advanced, the *Independent* also opposed any movement toward selective admissions.[94] In 1900, when an alliance of two Populists, a reform Democrat and a pro-silver Republican took control of the NU board of regents, MacLean departed for the presidency of the University of Iowa. After hiring Chancellor E. Benjamin Andrews, whose critique of social inequality endeared him to the new regents, the board indicated that Populists would consent to increasing standards under certain circumstances.[95] Comforted by the growth of Nebraska's public school system and the recent passage of a statute prohibiting tuition payments at high schools, the fusionist board approved a faculty request to raise the high school credit requirements to fourteen yearlong units—the emerging entrance standard for American universities.[96] Still, the regents cautioned professors against raising entrance requirements without formal authorization from the board.[97]

Extension Programs

The proliferation of extension programs and the establishment of affiliated agricultural high schools may have alleviated some of the Populist pressure on the entrance requirements of NU and other land grant institutions. To placate the state Grange, the University of Minnesota had opened the nation's first agricultural high school in 1886.[98] Chancellor Canfield attempted to start a similar School of Agriculture and Mechanic Arts in Nebraska (not to be confused with NU's more advanced Industrial College). Canfield asserted that the school would serve some of the 80 percent of the state's young people who would otherwise have only common school opportunities.[99] As a professor at

Minnesota prior to becoming NU's chancellor, George MacLean had witnessed how an agricultural secondary school could appease rural concerns without compromising university entrance standards. MacLean, therefore, coupled his proposal to abolish NU's preparatory department with an endorsement of Canfield's high school plan. Opened in the fall of 1895, NU's School of Agriculture offered a three-month winter course and a more academic three-year program, neither of which required formal entrance examinations. Most of the school's students enrolled in the winter course, which focused entirely on vocational subjects, such as soil analysis, livestock, dairy, horticulture, pest control, and farm accounting. The average age of students during the school's first years of operation was twenty-one, suggesting that most of its students returned to formal education after working for several years. MacLean argued that the school provided the "missing link" in the Nebraska school system and fulfilled NU's obligation to be a "people's university."[100] Although the school opened with only fifteen students, its enrollment increased to over fifty during the 1897–98 school year, and more than one hundred students in 1899–1900.[101]

When fusionist candidates were elected to the NU board of regents, they unanimously endorsed the agricultural high school. At their first board meeting in February 1898, George Kenower and Ernest Von Forell formed a committee to explore methods of increasing enrollment. The committee concluded that the school should add a fourth year and lengthen its semesters. Although the committee agreed that the program should remain "a technical high school," they recommended making the fourth year of the curriculum equal the rigor of the first year of a college course.[102] The Populist press approved of the school's low entrance requirements and accessibility to farmers' children.[103] The school's enrollment continued to grow, reaching 353 in 1906, roughly 16 percent of the university's total attendance.[104] Inspired by Nebraska and Minnesota, twenty-nine agricultural colleges would eventually establish similar secondary school programs.[105]

Their support for Nebraska's agricultural high school indicates that Populists understood that many students would not pursue full years of college regardless of the ease of admission. The movement, therefore, also lobbied for the development of extension programs that could benefit a broader swath of the citizenry.

Inspired by British universities and the Chautauqua lecture program, these efforts to extend college instruction to the general public multiplied during the Gilded Age. As early as the 1870s, professors at Johns Hopkins University began offering public lectures.[106] Edward Bemis, later hired by KSAC's fusionist administration, conducted one the nation's first formal extension programs in 1887 under the auspices of the Buffalo Public Library. By the 1890s, extension courses were offered at a number of institutions, most prominently at the University of Wisconsin and the University of Chicago.[107] Some university leaders began to worry that extension programs and special students would erode the prestige and residential spirit of college life. Yale University President Timothy Dwight, for instance, predicted that the presence of informal students would "demoralize" regular students.[108] Yet agrarian advocates enthusiastically encouraged extension programs and seemed oblivious to the possibility that farmers might feel stigmatized on campus.

In particular, Populists expected land grant institutions to offer agricultural short courses during lulls in the farming cycle. First offered at the University of Michigan in 1867, these short courses could span a few days or weeks.[109] In Wisconsin, officials established a short course during the 1880s after the state Grange protested against the scarcity of farmers' children on the Madison campus.[110] The Populist movement continued to support the development of short courses in the 1890s. The *Weekly Commoner* of Colfax County, Washington praised the state agricultural college for offering a short course to the "grim-visaged sons of honest toil."[111] The Nebraska Farmers' Alliance supported the introduction of a short course at the state university in 1892, while the fusionist general assembly of 1897 earmarked public funding for these courses for the first time.[112] That same year, the fusionist regents of KSAC resumed a lapsed wintertime extension program. President Will listed these courses among his proudest accomplishments.[113] During its fusionist era, KSAC also offered a dairy course open to any resident over the age of eighteen who possessed a common school education.[114] KU established a formal extension program in 1891, after the success of an economics course offered to the Farmers' Alliance of Vineland.[115]

Populists were also enthusiastic about university-sponsored farmers' institutes. Dating back to itinerant lecturers dispatched by antebellum agricultural societies, agricultural colleges institutionalized these traveling conferences during the late nineteenth century in order to woo public support for scientific farming. In Wisconsin, for example, university-sponsored institutes instructed farmers to diversify their crops and invest in dairying.[116] During the 1870s and 1880s, Granges and Farmers' Alliances often demanded that land grant colleges sponsor mobile institutes. In Michigan, farmers' institutes helped win over Grange leader Cyrus G. Luce, who had been one of the state agricultural college's most influential critics. The Grange and Farmers' Alliance helped organize institutes in many other states, including Mississippi, Georgia, and California.[117]

In Nebraska, the development of farmers' institutes was intimately linked with agrarian protest. NU's regents first launched an institute program in 1873, as a response to rural dissatisfaction with the university. The governing board directed the professor of agriculture to spend at least one-third of his time at farmers' institutes or otherwise engaged in the promotion of the university around the state.[118] By 1890, with the program suffering from a lack of funding and administrative support, the dean of the agricultural college tried to explain to the state Farmers' Alliance why so few institutes were offered.[119] Chancellor James Canfield shared the Populists' interest and reinvigorated the institutes during his reign. Canfield argued that the institutes helped to fulfill NU's mission of reaching "the greatest number with what the greatest number demands and needs."[120] Under Canfield, NU increased the number of farmers' institutes from ten in 1891–92 to forty-nine in 1895–96, with average attendance of roughly one hundred farmers at each event. In 1897, the fusionist majority in the Nebraska state legislature provided a dedicated funding stream of $1,500 to support the program.[121] In 1899, a fusionist regent spearheaded the authorization of extension courses offered by the school of domestic science.[122]

Academic Populists in Kansas also embraced farmers' institutes. Thomas E. Will's commitment to university extension programs preceded his tenure at KSAC. In 1894, Will had coordinated a "People's University" associated with the Boston Union for Practical Progress, a Christian socialist organization. Modeled on the Chautauqua lecture series, the People's University was intended to provide higher education to the masses. The program's first event was a four-day institute offering instruction in music, theology, and social science to the residents of Cornville, Maine. Will had hoped that these programs would encourage participants to read reform periodicals and start their own informal study groups.[123] After departing KSAC in 1899, Will attempted to form a similar program in Boston. Professor Frank Parsons, hired by KSAC's Populist board, would later found Boston's Breadwinners' Institute, a part-time school for workers interested in learning "the elements of broad culture."[124] KSAC Regent Christian Hoffman, along with Eugene V. Debs, eventually organized a "People's College" in Missouri that was dedicated to moving higher education outside the confines of the traditional university.[125]

These individuals united to increase the number of farmers' institutes offered by KSAC. During the 1896–97 school year, at the end of President George Fairchild's administration, the college had conducted nineteen institutes. From 1897 to 1899, the years of the Will presidency, KSAC sponsored ninety institutes. In 1898, the board of regents earmarked $500 for the farmers' institute program,

KSAC's largest allocation up to that point. According to Will, the number of institutes offered between 1897 and 1899 constituted nearly half of the total number of institutes conducted during all of the 1890s.[126] Enthusiastic about this trend, the Populist *Advocate and News* called for funding the institutes until they could be offered yearly in each county.[127]

These programs promised to resolve stubborn tensions by expanding rural access to higher education without compromising admissions standards. In theory, public universities could concentrate on molding exceptional students into state leaders, while auxiliary programs served those who would otherwise have been excluded.

Conclusion

While Populists contributed to the growth of extension programs, conclusions about the movement's impact on actual college enrollment must remain tentative because of the brevity of their formal control, the extent of exogenous forces, and the difficulty of determining which students might have been rejected in the absence of Populist activism. Furthermore, academic Populists did not always revise official policies; occasionally they urged land grant colleges and universities to administer existing admissions and remediation procedures with a sympathetic attitude toward rural white students. Although there may never be a conclusive explanation, the rate of enrollment growth did increase during the fusionist administrations of KSAC and NU.[128]

While one might assume that the Populists' permissive stance toward entrance requirements would have also increased attrition rates, the results seem to be mixed. Graduation rates at all institutions of higher education were relatively low during the nineteenth century—at some land grant colleges as few as 10 percent of entering freshman classes graduated in four years. Besides academic failure, there were many other reasons for a student to leave, such as an appealing job opportunity, familial obligations, and lack of funds.[129] During its first years of operation, NCCAMA saw half of its students leave between the freshman and sophomore years, a rate that was not unusual compared to similar institutions.[130] Freshman attrition also remained unremarkable during the fusionist era of KSAC. Nor did the agricultural college retain substantially more students after 1899, when the new Republican board of regents increased admission standards.[131] Similarly, attrition at NU did not spike during the era of fusionist permissiveness. However, retention rates did increase after NU raised its entrance standards in 1900.[132] These numbers suggest that the movement may have retarded efforts to screen out unprepared applicants. Regardless, academic

Populists did not seem troubled by this tradeoff, or at least they were loath to suggest that underprepared rural students were incapable of succeeding in college.

Although motivated by a degree of demagogic anti-intellectualism, this resistance to admissions requirements also reflected the movement's more principled concern with the inequalities between rural and urban schools. For brief periods in several states, Populists became the loudest participants in an ongoing debate over the extent to which colleges should accommodate disadvantaged students. Populists sided with those academic leaders who believed that it was unjust to calibrate admissions standards to the level of city high schools and private academies. The movement supported policies that compensated for the uneven capacity of school districts and blurred the distinctions between secondary schools and colleges.

Yet academic Populists never fully rejected the standards of higher education by boycotting universities or attacking their graduation requirements. While they hoped that increased enrollment would dilute the prestige of college, academic Populists did not abandon the emerging physical and human infrastructure of public higher education, nor did they seek to eliminate diplomas. Apparently, these Populists believed that colleges and universities could provide advanced political and vocational training that was worthy of special recognition. Perhaps because of their own personal attachments to college, academic Populists seemed to accept that even major increases in enrollment would merely reduce, rather than eliminate, the exclusivity of higher education. Undaunted, Populists challenged the notion of academic meritocracy and argued that public institutions of higher education should serve the masses despite unequal levels of preparation.

4

Looking Forward

Populism and Economic Access

During the late nineteenth century, the idea of mass higher education could seem like a distant fantasy. In his utopian novel *Looking Backward* (1887), Edward Bellamy imagined that it would take over a century to realize this dream. While telling the story of a Bostonian who was transported to the year 2000, Bellamy imagined that higher education would become available to all citizens "without condition" until age thirty-five.[1] In *Equality*, the less renowned sequel to *Looking Backward*, Bellamy predicted that every resident of twenty-first century Boston would attend school until at least age twenty-one. Dr. Leete, Bellamy's guide to the future, explained that all young people received the equivalent of a nineteenth-century college education, which Leete described as "the required minimum of culture" necessary for citizenship. Bellamy recognized that a drastic change in attitudes toward financial aid would be necessary to achieve this revolution. Twenty-first century Americans would understand that universal college enrollment required "maintenance of the pupil without economic return during the educational period."[2]

While Bellamy hoped that this scenario would materialize by the twenty-first century, some Populists lobbied for mass higher education in the late *nineteenth* century.[3] Kansas State Agricultural College (KSAC) President Thomas E. Will told an audience that access to affordable advanced training was a "natural right" as early as 1898. Asking rhetorically who should attend college, Will answered "without hesitation or qualification, all!" Will denounced tuition as a de facto "property qualification to higher education, barring with gold the gates that should be thrown wide open to all."[4] According to the *Lincoln Independent*, Nebraska Populists aimed to fund institutions of higher learning "until every young man and young woman in the state who desire it can have a university education."[5] Academic Populists believed that if state colleges became accessible to all citizens, then public higher education could promote majoritarianism rather than inequality or elitism. During a series of important yet underappreciated episodes, Populist advocacy drew attention to the early politics of financial aid.[6]

Populist demands for affordable higher education may appear at first blush as the product of demagogues determined to find fault with existing institutions. Indeed, contrary to Populist propaganda, virtually all college presidents embraced the ideal of equal educational opportunity. Most institutions struggled to reduce financial barriers in order to enroll enough students. As the number of high school graduates doubled during the 1890s, these leaders hoped that higher education could be affordable for this larger pool of potential applicants.[7] Academic Populists stood apart from the mainstream only because their expectations regarding the enrollment of poor (white) youth seemed particularly ambitious.

When viewed from the Populist perspective, the rhetorical commitments of state university presidents did not always align with the accessibility of their institutions. Some academic Populists gravitated toward cooperative ventures and hoped that public campuses could demonstrate how to form model communities that would be immune from the heartlessness of the cash economy. Yet despite their strident, even propagandistic, tone of voice, most Populist proposals defended or expanded preexisting policies—policies that would ultimately become the centerpieces of a national campaign for college access during the twentieth century. More than five decades before the era that is typically regarded as the beginning of the drive for mass higher education, academic Populists advocated for free tuition, scholarships, campus work programs, and low-cost room and board.

Poor Students at State Universities in the Gilded Age

Most nineteenth-century colleges struggled to remain financially solvent by keeping costs low and enrolling sufficient numbers of paying students. Fledging public institutions, in particular, attempted to be affordable because of principle as well as necessity. On principle, President Richard Henry Jesse of the University of Missouri declared that free tuition was part of the very definition of a public university. Some state constitutions, such as Indiana's, mandated free tuition, while other states passed legislation to this effect. When Justin Morrill conceived of the federal land grant program, he also assumed that A&M colleges would be free.[8] Out of necessity, many public colleges and universities felt compelled to be free of charge in order to attract enough students to justify their existence. Arkansas Industrial University, for example, ended tuition in order to stem the flow of young men who left the state to attend other colleges.[9]

These state universities struggled to remain tuition free, especially when officials mismanaged federal land grants. Faced with growing enrollments and increasing costs, most state universities began to charge tuition by the 1880s.[10] Still, these institutions subsidized the enrollment of between one-third and one-half of their campuses, typically by offering scholarships to a number of students per county. For example, when the Tennessee legislature accepted the terms of the Morrill Act, it compelled the state university to provide full scholarships to three students from each county.[11]

At some public universities, these policies facilitated the attendance of large numbers of poor students. By 1879, there were so many indigent scholars at the Arkansas Industrial University that its trustees established a fund to pay for student burials. A professor at the University of Oklahoma reported that the school's first students had struggled "to keep the wolf from the door."[12] According to journalist Ray Stannard Baker, the majority of students at Michigan agricultural college worked their way through school during the 1880s. Baker recalled that some of his classmates were "genuine backwoods characters," including one who walked barefoot through the campus.[13] Many of the students who enrolled at the University of Nebraska (NU) during this period had little money remaining after paying for books, room and board, and a five-dollar matriculation fee. A student from the class of 1886 recalled that poverty was a "perfectly normal condition" at the university and noted that the janitor could afford more fashionable clothing than most of the student body. Another NU student from this era described a campus culture in which there seemed to be "something disreputable about being rich."[14]

Nevertheless, familial obligations and even modest costs of living prevented the children of many poor farmers and laborers from completing college. KSAC President George Fairchild reported in 1886 that attendance fluctuated according to the number of students who were compelled to leave school to work on their families' farms.[15] Professors at the North Carolina College of Agriculture and Mechanic Arts (NCCAMA) frequently informed students that they would have to leave if they did not pay their debts. Applicants for admission who arrived in Raleigh without sufficient money were preemptively rejected during the late 1880s and early 1890s.[16] At the University of North Carolina (UNC), one hundred students left during the 1887–88 school year because of inability to meet their expenses. After receiving many letters from needy applicants, UNC President Kemp Plummer Battle estimated that thousands of additional students would attend if not for financial obstacles.[17] Of course, there were other factors contributing to low attendance and high attrition in this period. During the late nineteenth century, a college degree was far from essential for ambitious youth; it was not uncommon for students to forgo or leave college in favor of more attractive opportunities.[18]

While money was not the only variable influencing college enrollment, student bodies tended to be disproportionately wealthy, even at public campuses. Two of the most thorough studies of this subject concluded that few poor students attended state universities in the Gilded Age.[19] Students at public institutions became increasingly affluent by the turn of the century. For instance, the members of the University of Illinois' Delta Tau Delta fraternity marked special occasions with oysters and crab by the 1890s, whereas students had subsisted on mush and milk during the 1860s and 1870s.[20] Theodore Dreiser keenly felt his relative poverty while attending the University of Indiana from 1889 to 1890. Dreiser, who could enroll only after receiving a gift from his schoolteacher, characterized the majority of his classmates as "pampered pets, in short, of pampered parents—the usual college lah-de-da or social loafer." Never invited to join a fraternity and rarely noticed by female students, Dreiser dropped out of Indiana, forever resentful of the "social segregations" within the "so-called democratic" university.[21] When Alvin Johnson returned to NU in 1906, he was struck that students no longer walked to campus in order to save the cost of train fare, as most had done during the early 1890s. "All the students had money and bicycles," he observed.[22] Mass magazines began to warn middle-class readers that their children would be spoiled by four years of comfortable college life.[23]

However, contrary to Populist insinuations, even elite university presidents did not celebrate luxury or seek to exclude poor students such as Dreiser. During his inaugural address in 1869, Charles W. Eliot hoped that Harvard University would attract students "from all conditions of life." Eliot stated that scores of Harvard students entered with no money whatsoever and survived on a combination of work and scholarships. "If they prove themselves men of capacity and character," Eliot claimed, "they never go away for lack of money." Indeed, Eliot dispensed large sums of financial aid and hoped to avoid raising tuition. Similarly, David Starr Jordan of Stanford University talked about clearing a "path from the farmhouse to the university." Princeton University attempted to combat the perception that it was a "rich man's school" by offering scholarships to ministers' sons and ministers in training. In general, the leaders of private colleges and universities loudly denounced campus opulence and paid tribute to earnest hardworking students.[24]

Naturally, allies of public institutions also celebrated the education of poor students. At the University of Kentucky, President James Patterson hoped to make the institution "accessible to the poorest youth in the land." During the 1880s, Patterson invited members of the state legislature to visit the campus and count the number of homespun-clad boys "with bronzed features and hard hands."[25] When arguing against proposals to charge tuition at the University of Michigan, President James B. Angell proudly labeled the school "the university of the poor" and asserted that any institution "within reach of the rich alone" was repugnant to American instincts. Angell asserted that accessible public universities would prevent the West from becoming divided into factions marked by class and education.[26] In his celebrated vision of the University of Wisconsin, President Charles Van Hise emphasized that higher education should be available to "poor and rich alike."[27] In contrast with Dreiser's perception, a trustee of the University of Indiana boasted that it was "especially a school for persons of limited means," located in an earnest town with a minimum of "lavish" display.[28]

According to historian John Thelin, the self-supporting student became a prized "folk hero" on college campuses.[29] Advocates of higher education appreciated these students for a number of reasons. Not only did successful students from hardscrabble backgrounds corroborate the meritocratic rhetoric of college presidents, but they also helped promote an antimaterialist aura. For example, Charles W. Eliot liked to say that higher education represented the virtue of "plain living against luxury."[30] Like many Americans, college presidents believed that the struggle to overcome poverty developed moral character. The *Biblical Recorder* of Raleigh, North Carolina, explained that "whether rich or poor, it is best for all boys at school to *feel* poor." Exclaiming "ho for the poor boys," the *Recorder* editorialized that "anybody who is ashamed to dress plainly and save money at school had better stay at home and live and die in the obscurity that he deserves."[31] In 1899, a poll of college presidents revealed their unanimous support for the notion that wealth impeded academic effort and achievement.[32]

Willa Cather's fictional depictions of NU illustrate this romantic view of college poverty. In her novel *My Ántonia*, Cather celebrated the "serious young men" who arrived at NU "straight from the cornfields with only a summer's wages in their pockets, [and] hung on through the four years, shabby and underfed." A few years later, Cather wrote *The Professor's House*, in which the title character rued the influx of affluent students. Cather's professor was reinvigorated by the arrival of Tom Outland, a hardworking and self-supporting protégé.[33]

Academic Populists shared much of this enthusiasm for poor students, though they were more prone to criticize their underrepresentation on college campuses. William Jennings Bryan told one university audience that 99 percent of its student body belonged to the ranks of "the idle rich."[34] Similarly, Populist Frank Burkitt accused Mississippi A&M College of catering to "the favored circle" of the state. According to Burkitt, most poor farmers could not pay for their children's train fare, room, and board at the Starkville campus.[35] Populists accused students at the University of Georgia of being "dandies and dudes," who spent their time "dancing and rioting and drinking liquor."[36] Nebraska Populists asserted that Cornell University exemplified the manner in which land grant institutions sometimes betrayed their original mission by charging tuition and building expensive laboratories. "What good old uncle Ezra founded for the benefit of the poor," stated the *Nebraska Independent*, "has been stolen by the rich."[37]

Populists also amplified widespread concerns about the aristocratic nature of college fraternities during the 1880s and 1890s. Fraternities, which had disconcerted college leaders since the antebellum period, became increasingly troublesome sources of mischief and exclusivity toward the end of the nineteenth century.[38] Faculty and administrators worried about the undemocratic nature of Greek societies and the forms of social discrimination experienced by poor students, such as Theodore Dreiser. In 1890, three-fourths of college presidents surveyed by the National Educational Association opposed the spread of sororities and fraternities because of their tendency to promote extravagance and institutionalize class distinctions within the student body.[39] UNC President Edwin Alderman complained that Greek societies were "incompatible" with the purpose of the university because they promoted "a contest apparently between the rich and the poor." At the North Carolina Normal and Industrial School (NCNIS) for white women, President Charles McIver not only banned sororities, but also supervised the assignment of students to campus organizations in order to prevent segregation by social class.[40] At Purdue University, President Emerson White attempted to ban fraternities by requiring all students to sign an anti-fraternity pledge (this policy was overturned by an Indiana court).[41]

Populists were particularly vigilant critics of Greek societies. In 1897, a Nebraska Populist legislator attempted to outlaw fraternities and sororities at NU in order to keep all students "on a level footing."[42] Populists were troubled by the discomfort poor students felt when surrounded by classmates who spent freely on clothes, fraternity fees, and parties. As fraternities and sororities proliferated at the University of Kansas (KU), the Populist *Jeffersonian* complained that "a boy without dude clothes and gold rimmed eye glasses is snubbed and belittled by the faculties."[43] Similarly, the *Nebraska Independent* imagined that poor students would feel out of place if they could not afford to participate in "the cotillions, the junior ball, [and] the masque." The paper worried that students from modest rural backgrounds were "already ill at ease" on college campuses and easily discouraged by social exclusion.[44] Alvin Johnson, a NU student from a rural Populist family, also sensed that some students seemed to disdain poor rural classmates. Johnson recalled that his peers "adored" Chancellor James Hulme Canfield because he was "a true democrat, who used all his influence to abate the snobbishness of the students from families that composed the rising middle class." Johnson added that whereas there were many Populist students in his preparatory courses, few entered the college proper, where he felt "alien" and "rarely discussed politics at all."[45] For Populist leaders, increased attendance of poor rural students was insufficient; they argued that colleges must enroll a large percentage of these students in order to form a supportive campus culture.[46]

In response to these Populist pressures, leaders of state colleges and universities in North Carolina, Kansas, and Nebraska worked hard to counter accusations that they catered to the rich. In 1890, the same year as the formation of the Kansas People's Party, the governing board of KU disputed the perception that only "the sons and daughters of wealthy men, of bankers, of successful professional men, [and] of capitalists" could afford to attend. The regents began reporting the background of KU students, 40 percent of whom were children of farmers or artisans. KU's regents argued that the university was "manifestly an institution offering the poor young man an equal chance with the rich one." By 1896, the regents claimed that the KU was "the embodiment of the democratic spirit."[47] The editor of the Republican *Lawrence Journal* came to the defense of the university by offering to name a hundred KU graduates who had arrived in Lawrence penniless and paid their way through college by delivering papers, sawing wood, and caring for horses. The newspaper reported that less than 10 percent of KU students came from wealthy families. KU's student newspaper also defended the school by arguing that the student body belonged to the mass of "poor people."[48]

In 1894, the first year in which Populists controlled the KSAC board, President Fairchild also added a new section to the college's annual report. He developed a new chart entitled "Industrial Classes Represented," which illustrated how the children of farmers constituted the majority of the college's student body.[49] Likewise, NU first reported on the occupations of its students' parents in 1890, the year that state's People's Independent Party was established. NU publications would continue to boast that the university enrolled substantial numbers of farm youth and exhibited a "genuinely democratic spirit" by welcoming the children of hardworking producers and helping these students to support themselves.[50]

North Carolina provides the most intense example of these dynamics. After the founding of the North Carolina Farmers' Alliance in 1887, UNC President Kemp Plummer Battle added a section to his annual report entitled "Benefits to Poor Young Men." The new section listed the number of scholarships and claimed that roughly half of UNC's students arrived on campus "with hands brown with toil." Battle romanticized those UNC students who suffered "in the coldest weather without great-coats, hovering over scanty fires, but with the flames of noble resolutions burning in the breasts." The report profiled a few individuals, such as W. G. Randall, who walked three and a half miles to school "through rain and snow," and traveled on foot for days to reach Chapel Hill with just 30 cents in his pocket.[51]

George Winston, Battle's successor at UNC, continued to refute the notion that the university belonged "only to the rich." Winston claimed that one-third of UNC students supported themselves by working as typesetters, lab assistants, teachers, clerks, and boarding house janitors. He insisted that wealthy UNC students were not regarded "with a particle more favor than he who waited on table to work his way through college."[52] In 1894, amid mounting Populist representation within the North Carolina legislature, Winston printed a broadside that included testimonials from twenty "talented poor boys" who received loans, scholarships, and campus jobs. He concluded that UNC was built on the attendance of "the people themselves, the great mass of plain, toiling people."[53]

In addition to Battle and Winston, a cohort of liberal advocates vigorously campaigned to convince Populist skeptics that public higher education in North Carolina was accessible to poor white youth. Committed to a creating a "New South" based on individual merit and industrial development, these education reformers celebrated the ideal of the self-made individual. Foremost among them, Edwin Alderman and Charles McIver had attended UNC during the 1870s when, according to Alderman, most students were "poor boys" from "simple homes of self-denial and self-sacrifice."[54] In 1896, during his inauguration as UNC President, Alderman claimed that many UNC students left behind parents who struggled mightily so that a "child of their flesh may know the life denied to them." Alderman reminded skeptics that more than half of UNC students were sons of farmers and proudly concluded that the state university prevented the development of "aristocracy in education."[55] A wealthy father even worried that UNC had become so "democratic" that professors discriminated against his son. After a professor refused to reconsider a low examination grade that prevented the son from earning honors, the father complained to Alderman that he felt "very much hurt and thoroughly humiliated."[56] As president of NCNIS, Charles McIver also declared that the school was "a great blessing for poor girls." McIver claimed that (white) women attended NCNIS because the school did not charge tuition to students who pledged to teach in North Carolina public schools. He also boasted that farmer's daughters constituted 40 percent of the NCNIS student body between 1892 and 1894.[57]

Tuition and Campus Employment

Unimpressed, academic Populists attempted to push the issue of affordability to the forefront of state education policy. Populists defended the principle of free or inexpensive higher education against critics who raised concerns about the potential moral hazards associated with tuition subsidies. During the nineteenth century, the very notion of scholarships could provoke controversy; even some state university leaders questioned the wisdom of enrolling students free of charge. Chancellor Henry Tucker of the University of Georgia worried that free higher education might attract "indolent" or "undeserving" students. While chancellor of the University of Nebraska, E. Benjamin Andrews wondered if free tuition might make students ungrateful for their opportunities.[58]

Predictably, leaders of private institutions directed particularly spirited criticism toward the idea of free public higher education. Harvard President Charles W. Eliot argued that state-subsidized tuition would erode students' commitment to the ideals of free enterprise. Eliot criticized public colleges for "insidiously teach[ing] communism in the guise of free tuition."[59] Similarly, the principal of an Alabama secondary school warned that proposals for free tuition cultivated "a sort of communism" and were merely "the bid of the demagogue for the patronage of the populace."[60] John C. Kilgo, president of Trinity College (later Duke University), agreed that free tuition was "socialistic" and morally corrupting. Arguing that free tuition imparted "lessons of helplessness," Kilgo urged UNC to stop asking the state to subsidize students' education. "A pauperized manhood is a poor substitute for a college diploma," Kilgo concluded.[61]

In states where public universities charged tuition, some citizens questioned the legal basis for providing scholarships to limited numbers of students. In

Missouri, Indiana, and New York, citizens sued public universities for using tax revenues to pay the tuition of select individuals. The plaintiffs argued that a scholarship was an unconstitutional use of public funds dedicated to the entire state.[62] Skeptics also questioned whether these scholarships were easily manipulated to benefit politically connected students. John Kilgo claimed that many recipients of UNC scholarships figured "largely in society," wore expensive clothing, and rode trains "as though they owned the road." Testifying before the education committee of the state legislature, a Trinity College professor reiterated the charge that UNC awarded scholarships to the "sons of the most well-to-do citizens of the state."[63] Perhaps because of these concerns (as well as a lack of funds), it was common for state colleges to provide loans rather than grants.[64]

During these debates, Populists tended to urge public universities to eliminate tuition or provide plentiful scholarships.[65] In 1887, Arkansas politicians aligned with the Farmers' Alliance forbid the state university from charging tuition to students taking vocational courses.[66] In North Carolina, Leonidas L. Polk argued that NCCAMA should be free or inexpensive. Although the state legislature of 1887 rejected two proposals for free tuition at NCCAMA, it limited tuition to twenty dollars, required the college to grant 120 scholarships, and authorized the college president to accept promissory notes in lieu of tuition. Including living expenses, annual costs ranged from $100 to $130, half the amount spent by students at UNC. The same legislature reduced UNC tuition by fifteen dollars, ordered the university to enroll all young men "of good moral character" regardless of ability to pay, and required the free education of ministers' sons, candidates for ministry, disabled men, and teacher trainees.[67] During Missouri's brief era of Populist-Democrat governance, the state university first started a scholarship program and then eliminated tuition altogether.[68] In Nebraska, the organ of the state Farmers' Alliance applauded the public university, which had always been legally barred from charging tuition. "The son of a rich man can go to Harvard, Yale, Columbia, or Princeton, and pay the $150 to $200 per year demanded by these institutions for tuition," the *Farmers' Alliance* stated, "but the boy from the poor man's home cannot do this . . . the free state university is his only hope."[69]

In 1888, Mississippi Populists supported a need-based scholarship policy at the state A&M college for white men and the state industrial college for white women. The Populists preferred need-based awards because they predicted that merit-based scholarships would be "gobbled up" by the well-educated children of urban merchants and professionals. To end the overrepresentation of wealthy students at these schools, the Mississippi legislature allocated a number of scholarships to each county on the basis of their white population. A Populist newspaper editorialized that the movement endorsed scholarships for "the wool hat boys and sun bonnet lassies" who could only attend school for a few months a year in log cabins.[70]

President Thomas E. Will of KSAC personified Populist advocacy for free access to public higher education. According to Will, public universities that charged tuition were a "mockery and a mirage to the boy or girl without money." Will celebrated the tuition-free status of KSAC and stated that he would not be satisfied until every state enabled "the most wretched guttersnipe in the metropolis" or "the most forlorn herdsboy in the frontier dugout" to obtain as much education as they could absorb.[71] During a commencement address in 1898, Will criticized those who argued that "the school of self-help" was the only way to develop character. Will demanded the creation of "scholarship ladders with their feet in free kindergartens and their tops in free professional and technical schools, and free postgraduate courses in universities." Elsewhere, Will proclaimed that "democracy should tolerate no tollgates on the educational highway." "Fie upon the people's higher schools," he declared, "if they are to be but rich men's schools!" Will asserted that college tuition should be subsidized by the state because Americans should never depend on "the kindly offices of a bishop, the initiative of the profit-monger nor the paternalism of the plutocrat that their children may receive the benefits of a higher education."[72]

Populists also targeted the miscellaneous fees that students paid in addition to tuition. Even in states that had constitutionally or legislatively mandated free public higher education, state colleges usually charged laboratory fees, library fees, diploma fees, and "incidental" fees. In 1890, incidental fees were twenty dollars at the University of Michigan and twenty-five dollars at the University of Minnesota, nearly half the amount of tuition at many private colleges.[73] Unsympathetic to the institutions' desire to supplement their modest amount of public funding, Populists tended to oppose these user fees.

In 1894, Kansas Populists objected to a proposed five-dollar library fee at KU, which had a longstanding tradition of tuition-free education. KU's *Student's Journal* editorialized that fees would exclude poor students and transform the campus into "a small body of fashionable, society-loving men and women." When eighty students refused to pay the fee, the Populist *Jeffersonian* supported their contention that the fee violated a state law forbidding tuition charges at the university. The paper also proudly noted that the only regent who had voted against the fee was the Populist H. S. Clarke (the *Jeffersonian* neglected to note that three other Populist appointees had originally voted for the fee in 1892). The *Jeffersonian* celebrated when the attorney general ultimately ruled that the fee was illegal.[74] In 1895, a proposal to legalize fees inspired Populist predictions that KU would eventually exclude "every poor boy or girl in the state." Under the headline "Education Must Be Free," *The Jeffersonian* called another proposed ten-dollar fee "an exhibition of asinine stupidity" that would create a "property caste" in Kansas and betray the principle of "equal privileges before the law." In contrast, Lawrence's Republican newspaper editorialized that charging fees would ultimately benefit the state by countering the dangerous presumption that the state was responsible for ensuring individual welfare.[75]

Like their counterparts in Kansas, Nebraska Populists also protested against fees. Dating to 1869, the establishing legislation of NU had included a five-dollar matriculation fee but stipulated that no tuition could be charged to residents who were full-time students in the arts and sciences, engineering, normal, or graduate divisions. Although NU remained free from tuition charges, the cost of room, board, and assorted fees ran as high as $175 per semester during the 1890s.[76] In 1901, after the Republican Governor Charles Henry Dietrich vetoed a $90,000 appropriation bill, NU regents raised funds by instituting an additional fee of three dollars per semester. The *Nebraska Independent* labeled the new fee the "Dietrich Tax" and complained that the governor's veto made "poor students have to foot the bill" for their education.[77] An editorial cartoon illustrated the tenor of Populist opposition. The cartoon portrayed the governor as a bandit pointing two pistols toward an alarmed student outside the university gates. While the governor wore an expensive suit and dress shoes, the barefoot student resembled an innocent Huck Finn, sporting overalls and a straw hat. Standing just behind the confrontation, a member of the governor's administration held a bulging moneybag and awaited the conclusion of the robbery.[78]

Two years later, NU faculty and administration still wrestled with whether fees were permitted by Nebraska law. Professor Roscoe Pound believed that the fees were legal because they paid for equipment, whereas state law only forbade charging students for "tuition" (i.e., instruction). An associate of an NU regent, however, argued that fees were illegal and threatened the public character of the university. Ultimately NU's faculty voted to continue collecting the fees.[79]

Populists recognized that even without tuition or fees, living expenses could present insurmountable obstacles for poor students. In his final report as president of KSAC, Thomas E. Will explained that modest costs for room, board, and books could "prove as effective a barrier to many students as would an expense account of $1,000 per annum."[80] Between 1897 and 1899, therefore, KSAC's fusionist administration attempted to employ student laborers and create cooperative institutions in order to reduce the cost of living on campus.

Cartoon from the *Nebraska Independent*, October 24, 1901.

Attractive to many Populists and other reformers, the concept of economic cooperatives dated back to the Rochdale Society of Equitable Pioneers, a cooperative society founded during the 1840s in Rochdale, England. Inspired by the ideals of Robert Owens, proponents of the "Rochdale Plan" attempted to form communities in which residents relied on their own labor with minimal dependence on the market economy. Populists and the residents of these utopian settlements shared a similar ambition—establishing cooperative alternatives to competitive industrial capitalism. Indeed, the membership of these movements overlapped.[81]

Several Populists active in KSAC affairs during the 1890s also participated in cooperative ventures. In particular, Regent Christian Balzac Hoffman had spent several years trying to start a utopian settlement in Topolobampo, Mexico.[82] As president of KSAC, Thomas E. Will believed that the same principles that informed Populist support for the cooperative subtreasury plan of crop marketing could also make the college more affordable. Will asked Hoffman whether he had "ever considered what a field this college offers for genuine cooperation." Will had pondered the question and was "greatly impressed with what seem to me the possibilities." He hoped that cooperatives could insulate the college from the volatility of the cash economy (with the exception, naturally, of professors' salaries). In theory, students who constructed and maintained the campus would be paid with "certificates for labor performed," redeemable at college dormitories, a bookstore, and a dining hall. This dining hall would be student-run and supplied with food produced on the college's farm. Confident that this cooperative system could substantially lower student costs and boost enrollment, Will asked Hoffman to apply the lessons he learned at Topolobampo to the development of KSAC.[83]

Will and Hoffman were not the only KSAC radicals who believed in cooperatives. After leaving KSAC, Will, Regent Carl Vrooman, and professors Frank Parsons and Henry Cottrell would all accept jobs at Ruskin College, the educational wing of a cooperative settlement in Missouri that was inspired by Ruskin Hall in Oxford, England. Founded by Charles Beard and Walter Vrooman (Carl's older brother), Ruskin Hall trained labor leaders at minimal expense by rotating cooking and housekeeping responsibilities among students. At Ruskin College in Missouri, students were also supposed to work at an affiliated laundry, store, farm, or factory.[84] Between 1911 and 1913, Will and Hoffman would also explore the possibility of establishing a cooperative agricultural community in Florida. After suggesting that the co-op could grow guavas and sell jam, Will gushed that community members could become financially independent and "snap our fingers at the World, the Flesh, and the Devil."[85]

While less ambitious than the Rochdale Plan, Topolobampo colony, or Ruskin College, KSAC's fusionist administration hoped to reduce student expenses by opening a bookstore and dining hall.[86] Prompted by Hoffman, the college sold books and supplies at cost, resulting in discounts of between 5 percent and 50 percent for students. The college's new dining hall was never able to rely solely on produce from the college farm, but it did provide affordable meals to 150 students a day. According to President Will, the KSAC dining hall was a modern-day version of "the public tables of Sparta," where "students, professors, employees and regents, regardless of rank or sex, sit side by side, eat from the same bill of fare, and pay the same price."[87] In addition, the fusionist administration planned to build a dormitory using student labor, decades before most public universities began to invest heavily in campus housing.[88]

Although college bookstores and dining halls would become commonplace at institutions of higher education, they could spark controversy at the end of the nineteenth century. The Republican-dominated establishment of Manhattan, Kansas, accused KSAC's governing board of introducing socialist institutions into the town. These opponents called the cooperative dining hall a "soup kitchen," characterizing it as a threat to free enterprise and student morality.[89] In 1899, after Republicans won state elections and regained control of KSAC, students met for two hours and voted by a large margin to petition for retaining the bookstore and dining hall. Nevertheless, the new board closed both operations during its first meeting.[90] Upset at having to eat at expensive and inferior restaurants or boarding houses, students eventually persuaded the new administration to reopen the dining hall, albeit as a private entity open only for lunch.[91] Like most other aspects of their prescription for higher education, the Populists were enthusiastic promoters of cooperatives, but they were not the originators or sole supporters of these initiatives. The first recorded instance of a college cooperative store occurred at Harvard in 1882. When University of Nebraska students founded a cooperative bookstore in 1897, they were inspired by the Harvard co-op, not by radical sentiments.[92]

Still, in addition to the developments at KSAC, Populists or their fellow travelers were involved in the start of several other cooperative or college-subsidized student facilities. During the 1890s, Populist sympathizer John Commons encouraged his students at Syracuse University and the University of Indiana to create cooperative stores. As in Kansas, the students encountered vigorous protest from local merchants. The Syracuse governing board closed the store and by the time Commons joined the faculty of the University of Wisconsin he believed that private-sector opposition would always cripple student cooperatives.[93] In 1887, a Populist-controlled legislature funded construction of a dorm at the University of Arkansas in order to reduce the cost of housing. During the administration of Governor "Pitchfork" Ben Tillman, Clemson Agricultural College was required to board students at cost. At the University of Georgia, President Walter B. Hill was an early Populist supporter who spearheaded the construction of low-cost dorms for poor rural students. And at NU, the fusionist board of regents endorsed a student club dedicated to providing low-cost meals for students in the college of agriculture.[94]

Populists were also enthusiastic advocates of other forms of campus employment. Hiring poor students to perform maintenance had long been a common practice at American colleges. These jobs represented one of the few ways that financially precarious colleges could provide support for students. Some schools, such as the Iowa State Agricultural College, even mandated that students work on campus in order to reduce the cost of running the institution.[95] By the turn of the twentieth century, land grant colleges reported that 73 percent of their students worked on or off campus during the school year.[96] While semiformal work programs were ubiquitous among institutions of higher education, Populists dedicated particular attention to these efforts.

When lobbying for a separate agricultural college, Leonidas L. Polk noted the advantages of paying students to work on the school farm. And when NCCAMA opened, many of its students were employed at campus jobs paying as much as twenty dollars to thirty dollars a term.[97] In 1887, Arkansas Populists required students at the state university to work in the college fields or shops for three hours a day and allocated $5,000 to pay their wages.[98] During the first years of Clemson Agricultural College, students were paid to work on the school farm at rates of up to nine cents an hour.[99] In Lawrence, the Populist *Jeffersonian* criticized KU's chancellor for hiring tradesmen instead of students to repair his sidewalk.[100]

At KSAC, once again, Populist support for campus job opportunities emerged most clearly. In 1897, KSAC's fusionist administration promised that students with "moderate or inadequate means" could secure jobs on campus.[101] During the 1897–98 academic year, the regents spent an impressive $14,000 out of the college's $60,000 income on student wages. This sum represented nearly 40 percent of KSAC's budget for salaries. Professor Edward Bemis estimated that these campus jobs allowed between 50 and 100 students to attend KSAC who would otherwise be unable to afford higher education. Bemis also asserted that that KSAC spent a greater proportion of its income on student labor than other agricultural colleges. Echoing this claim, President Will told a prospective student that more jobs were available at KSAC than at any other institution. Eventually, the governing board asked if the college was spending too much on inefficient student workers.[102]

Toward the end of his tenure, Will urged the state legislature to earmark funds to support student jobs. Unless every needy student could find a job, Will argued, public higher education could not actually be considered "free."[103] Even after the Populists' efforts to reduce the expense of attending KSAC, two-thirds of the freshman class of 1899 still had to rely on support from family or friends.[104] Nevertheless, because they were concerned that working students were distracted from their courses, the Republican appointees who retook control of the KSAC governing board in 1899 were unenthusiastic about providing more campus jobs. These regents recommended that all students arrive in Manhattan with substantial savings.[105] Of course, there was nothing inherently Populist about providing campus jobs—the practice evolved out of institutional necessity to find the cheapest means of providing financial support to students. Populist enthusiasm for work-study policies merely indicates how this longstanding approach to college access could resonate with radical as well as liberal and conservative values.

Conclusion

In general, historians have not been able to determine the extent to which free higher education or plentiful scholarships actually increased student access.[106] Because formal Populist influence over public universities was short-lived and because Populist agitation overlapped with campaigns by mainstream supporters of financial aid, it is especially difficult to measure the movement's impact. However, it seems clear that administrators in states with strong Populist movements felt special pressure to prove that their schools were accessible to poor white students.

University records cited by these administrators lend some credence to their assertions. Between 1886 and 1899, one-half to two-thirds of UNC students paid no tuition (because of private or state scholarships) or paid with promissory notes. The majority of students received some help from their families, but most also covered expenses by teaching during the summer or working on campus.[107] Meanwhile, roughly 60 percent of NCCAMA students received county scholarships and paid no tuition during the early 1890s. Nearly half worked for the college as carpenters, gardeners, janitors, or waiters.[108] In Kansas, the state university reported that 34 percent of its students were wholly self-supporting, and another 11 percent worked to pay for a portion of expenses during the 1889–90 academic year. During the next several years, as Populists exercised intermittent control of the state, KU regents continued to advertise the number of students who worked their way through school.[109]

While officials emphasized the extent to which public universities served the masses, many Populists remained dissatisfied with these statistics. Indeed, poverty remained a common cause of attrition. Even at NCCAMA, whose publications declared the college's dedication to poor youth, many students struggled to pay their expenses. During the late 1890s, President Winston assured students that the college would accept promissory notes if they could not afford to pay tuition up front, but also warned of stiff competition for scholarships and discouraged students from coming to Raleigh without funds.[110] Nevertheless, the vigor of the institutional responses at these campuses suggests that grassroots Populist pressure reinforced state universities' commitment to financial accessibility. Indeed, while the Populists spouted passionate and perhaps overheated rhetoric about the economic barriers to college education, most of their requests either supported longstanding traditions or prefigured policies that would become standard in the twentieth century.

Populist demands also compounded some of the challenges facing administrators tasked with developing tuition and scholarship policies. In particular, Populists never seemed to consider that low tuition rates subsidized the education of wealthy students and reduced the level of resources that could be targeted to low-income students.[111] Perhaps academic Populists were keen to avoid the stigma that might be associated with this approach, or perhaps they concentrated on the symbolism of People's Colleges accessible to all students on equal terms.

Regardless, the history of Populist advocacy emphasizes how financial aid policies could develop out of principle, as well as out of necessity. Academic Populists expected public higher education to remain affordable even after the emergence of greater numbers of students who were willing and able to pay tuition. In pursuit of a more cooperative commonwealth, Populists also highlighted the belief that colleges and universities should be special institutions, insulated from competitive commercial values and receptive to public subsidies and collective enterprises. Above all, the movement's campaign for financial aid underscored the hopefulness of academic Populists, who believed that public universities might someday become institutions of mass higher education.

5

Producers and Parasites

The Populist Vision of College Curriculum

In 1899, during the final throes of the Populist movement, Thorstein Veblen argued that wealthy Americans favored the traditional college curriculum because it epitomized the luxury of "wasted time." According to Veblen's *Theory of the Leisure Class*, elite youth attended college primarily in order to reinforce their social status by engaging in conspicuous inactivity. While Veblen understood that American institutions of higher education had diversified their curricula during the second half of the nineteenth century, he noted that academic subjects still enjoyed higher status if they were considered "decorative" and therefore aristocratic. Raised by Populist parents on a Minnesota farm, Veblen's critique of higher education emerged from a culture of rural egalitarianism. Passages from the *Theory of the Leisure Class* reflected widespread populistic concerns about the impact of university education on the children of farmers and mechanics. Did higher education inevitably exacerbate social distinctions? Could the children of farmers attend college and still identify with the struggles of the producing classes? Would college alienate talented rural youth from their communities and seduce them into parasitical professions?[1]

Fueled by these anxieties, academic Populists urged state universities, especially land grant institutions, to emphasize practical subjects such as agriculture and home economics. Populists joined an ongoing campaign for applied higher education that included supporters inside and outside of the academy. Some professors of the liberal arts and sciences resisted, complaining that these priorities revealed the anti-intellectualism of the masses and the narrow self-interest of business leaders. At a National Educational Association panel in 1888, a professor explained that demands for vocational education illustrated laypeople's failure to understand "higher spiritual wants."[2] Sometimes betraying similarly condescending attitudes, scholars have struggled to engage in fruitful dialog with skeptics of the liberal arts and sciences.

By analyzing the arguments of Populists, who were among the most outspoken of these skeptics, this chapter uncovers a thoughtful, though still flawed, rationale for vocational education. Academic Populists articulated a vision of college curricula that shared a great deal of common ground with the philosophies of Jane Addams and John Dewey. In contrast with corporate supporters of applied higher education, Populists hoped that vocational courses could minimize the gulf separating workers and professionals in American society. Academic Populists also believed that utilitarian higher education, if conducted in this spirit, could emphasize communal interests rather than individual upward mobility.

These aspirations were only partially realized. Although academic Populism encouraged additional vocational offerings at state colleges, these courses did not necessarily foster egalitarianism. No matter how often Populists celebrated the righteousness of the masses or promoted nostalgia for idealized rural communities, they could not dissuade college students, including the children of Populist farmers and laborers, from pursuing exclusive professional credentials. The movement's campaign for vocational education exposed some of the most fraught elements of academic Populism—tensions between loyalty and ambition, mental and manual labor, radicalism and accommodation. Academic Populists struggled to synthesize the practical with the intellectual and failed to reconcile the ideals of individual advancement and social equality. Nevertheless, Populist pressure on college curriculum animated Veblen's important and perhaps disconcerting questions about the nature of higher education.

Populist Advocacy
for Vocational Higher Education

Drawing on Platonic and Aristotelian ideals, nineteenth-century advocates for classical education proudly rejected vocational purposes. These philosophers associated labor with slavish worldly affairs, and associated purely intellectual pursuits with truth and freedom (hence "liberal" education).[3] While praising the spiritual benefits of higher education in the 1850s, British Cardinal John Henry Newman famously argued that the virtue of the classical curriculum resided precisely in its irrelevance to earthly applications. The American writer Walter Hines Page recalled how his teacher more bluntly defended this tradition in terms of social class by asserting that "a Boy must know Latin or he cannot be a gentleman."[4]

Yet Americans also embraced utilitarian education. Vocational training at the college level gained momentum during the Jacksonian era and spread rapidly in the second half of the nineteenth century. Small denominational colleges began to offer commercial instruction and other applied courses in order to encourage much-needed enrollment and local aid.[5] More prominently, the Morrill Act of 1862 provided federal assistance for agricultural and mechanical colleges, whose leaders united to lobby for the Hatch Act of 1887 (providing funds for experiment stations) and the Second Morrill Act of 1890.[6] Outside of land grant institutions, influential university presidents such as Daniel Coit Gilman at Johns Hopkins and William Barton Rogers at MIT encouraged the practical application of scientific research. American universities also accommodated increasing numbers of applied subjects by permitting elective courses and establishing graduate schools. These reforms reflected revolutionary changes within the community of scientists, who had begun to emphasize how academic inquiry could yield new insights with the potential for useful application.[7]

This increased attention to utilitarianism also resonated with other developments within modern America, especially industrialization and professionalization. Business leaders, in particular, expressed disenchantment with the implicit antimaterialism of the classical curriculum.[8] These institutional, intellectual, and economic currents promoted practical courses within state universities well before the heyday of the Populist movement. These trends were particularly well established in the South and the West. Advocates for a New South viewed practical higher education as a means to increase agricultural productivity and industrial development.[9] In the West, utilitarianism had been part of the original mission of most public universities. An Illinois farmer, for example, lobbied for a state agricultural college while dismissing the value of studying "all the metaphysical fools from Aristotle down."[10]

While they sometimes reiterated traditional agrarian skepticism, Populist leaders ultimately joined this movement for applied higher education. Accustomed to managing their fields according to intuition and experience, farmers had often expressed ambivalence toward the science of agriculture, which threatened farmers' prized sense of self-sufficiency. Advocates of scientific agriculture also tended to promote capital-intensive techniques that could be implemented only by the wealthiest landholders. Associated with ominous consolidation of farm ownership and increasing tenancy rates, state A&M colleges did not earn universal support from farmers. Farmers also may have recognized that agricultural science initially provided unreliable guidance about practical matters such as fertilization, virus prevention, and plant growth. A professor at Iowa State Agricultural College later quipped that he "might as well have looked for cranberries on the Rocky Mountains as for material for teaching agriculture."[11] Agricultural experiment stations directed by A&M colleges also struggled to win farmers' appreciation. Station scientists disappointed farmers whenever they focused on basic research rather than the dissemination of best practices, evaluation of soil samples, and inspection of commercial fertilizers.[12] Populists occasionally contributed to cynical coverage of agricultural colleges in the rural press. In North Carolina, the Populist *Progressive Farmer* accused educated people "who don't get their living by the sweat of their face" of having masqueraded as experts in order to swindle farmers out of their rightful due. The newspaper suggested that agricultural education might be a conspiracy to distract farmers from more important political and economic topics.[13]

Despite this tension between scholars and farmers, Populists did not reject the promise of agricultural education. They expected professors to spend most of their time demonstrating profitable methods and responding to personal queries from farmers—demands that frustrated most agricultural scientists. Despite this shortsighted opposition to basic scientific research, the movement did not object to agricultural science altogether. Indeed, academic Populists complained that land grant colleges were not committed enough to the endeavor. They remained hopeful that these fledging institutions would improve crop yields and spearhead economic development in rural America.[14]

North Carolina Populists typified this response. Even though the University of North Carolina (UNC) had received land grant status in 1875 and established an experiment station, UNC's agricultural courses remained theoretical and small because the university did not own farmland. While President Kemp Plummer Battle stated that finances, not ideology, prevented the university from offering agricultural instruction, Populists had good reason to be skeptical. A UNC professor, for example, had responded to the prospect of a department of agriculture by stating, "We do not want that piggery at Chapel Hill."[15] These sentiments prompted the North Carolina Farmers' Alliance to campaign for the revocation of UNC's land grant status and the establishment of a separate state college of agriculture. "Shoot in the direction of Chapel Hill," exhorted Daniel McKay, a farmer from Harnett County. McKay told Leonidas L. Polk that "our people have had enough of junk in that stereotyped lecture defining the *relations* the university has to the farming interests of N.C. . . . we want something more tangible."[16]

Sensing that this would be a popular issue among a large segment of rural North Carolina, Polk put UNC in the crosshairs of the *Progressive Farmer*. Starting with the inaugural issue of the newspaper, Polk attacked President Battle for using "hair-splitting technicalities" to defend UNC's use of land grant funding for courses in zoology and geology. Noting that the university did not open a department of agriculture until 1885 (a decade after UNC obtained the federal land grant), Polk quipped that this was a "very long hatching period for such a small chicken." Polk also editorialized on behalf of state support for the higher education of farmers' daughters in applied fields such as hygiene, dairy, botany, and cooking.[17]

During the establishment of the North Carolina College of Agricultural and Mechanic Arts (NCCAMA), Polk and his supporters lobbied for a strong vocational focus. A reader told the *Progressive Farmer* that "practical" farmers should be included among the NCCAMA faculty. "I care not how many D's they may have strung on to the tail end of their names," the reader concluded.[18] These attitudes explain why NCCAMA initially compelled all students to study agriculture, horticulture, shop work, and mechanical drawing. The college's daily schedule consisted of three hours of classroom recitation followed by three hours of manual training. Out of its eight original faculty members, three were professors of agriculture, one was a professor of "pure and agricultural chemistry," one was a professor of mechanics, and another was a professor of mathematics and mechanics. Even NCCAMA's professor of English was listed as a "professor of English and bookkeeping." Only the professor of history held a position with no explicit responsibilities for vocational training.[19]

Although the movement never assumed full control of the college, Populists used the opportunity provided by NCCAMA's brief period of fusionist rule (1897–99) to support Professor Wilbur Fisk Massey and experiment station head W. A. Withers, who both prioritized utilitarian advice rather than basic research.[20] This orientation outraged Gerald McCarthy, a botanist and entomologist with a doctorate from the University of Chicago. McCarthy, a former faculty member who hoped to be rehired by the college, complained that agricultural scientists should be "religiously devoted to original investigation" instead of "elementary teaching and popular lecturing." McCarthy called Massey "a superficial quack" whose only purpose was to "astonish the ignorant multitude."[21] Populist Trustee William J. Peele worried whether NCCAMA would be able to withstand these calls to redirect the college toward "theoretical, literary, and ultra-scientific education."[22]

Western Populists advocated for vocational higher education with equal fervor. At the Kansas State Agricultural College (KSAC), Populists complained that President George T. Fairchild increased offerings in the humanities and core sciences rather than adding agricultural courses.[23] A graduate assistant in the experiment station claimed the majority of students had come to regard the agricultural component of the college with "utter contempt." Populist sources such as the Lawrence *Jeffersonian* accused "a class of pig headed professors" of disrespecting farmers and laborers.[24] Frustration with the college's lack of commitment to agricultural education motivated the fusionist reorganization of KSAC during the 1890s. While still endorsing the liberal arts, President Thomas E. Will believed that the college must fulfill the mandate of the Morrill Act by providing practical courses to "those who perform the nation's work in overalls and roundabouts, who callous their hands and begrime their faces."[25]

Under Will's direction, KSAC established more specialized curricular tracks in agriculture, engineering, and domestic science. The fusionist administration instituted a threefold increase in the number of credit hours available in agriculture and directed the experiment station to focus on the "cash value" of experiments on kafir corn, sugar beets, and grasshopper extermination. The Populist majority in the state legislature of 1897 supported Will's administration by allocating more funds to the KSAC farm than during the previous seven years combined. KSAC students responded to the spirit of the new regime in the fall of 1897 by forming a farmers' club.[26]

Kansas Populists also endorsed the field of domestic science and supported construction of a building for this program. KSAC had been one of the first colleges in the nation to begin instruction in this field (also known as home economics), offering a course as early as 1873. To bolster their program, KSAC's Populist regents hired Helen Campbell, a former student of Richard T. Ely at the University of Wisconsin. Like advocates for agricultural higher education, proponents of domestic science believed that studying the subject would increase efficiency and social status while reducing drudgery. Although a fluid division of labor existed on most farms, women tended to take responsibility for housework, kitchen gardens, and poultry, while men tended to take responsibility for fieldwork (gender spheres overlapped in the barnyard and dairy). Thus, gender-specific home economics courses seemed appropriate to many rural advocates for vocational education. While celebrating the opening of KSAC's new domestic science building, Populist activist and editor Annie L. Diggs described herself as "one of those old fashioned women who believe that the home is woman's especial sphere." Domestic science resonated with Populist values because it fed contrasts between wholesome farmwomen and ornamental "doll-women."[27]

Populists also pressured administrators to increase investment in utilitarian education at the University of Nebraska (NU). Like most land grant institutions, NU's agricultural college struggled during its early years. Founded in 1872, the college had no students until 1874 and averaged only twelve students a year until 1881. The school failed to boost attendance or satisfy skeptics by renaming itself as the "Industrial College" and counting all enrollees in NU's science classes as its students. In 1891, a farm newspaper accused NU of being "a one-horse classical college where young gentlemen wear brass buttons and study Latin during college and practice law and seek political office afterward."[28] James Hulme Canfield, NU's chancellor between 1891 and 1895, grew concerned that the university was not using its land grant proceeds to maximize vocational offerings and woo skeptical residents. Under Canfield, NU added a forge room, carpentry shop, and electrical program.[29] Nevertheless, some Populist legislators still claimed that the school provided insufficient attention to agricultural students. Populist criticism intensified during the administration of Chancellor George MacLean (1895–99). The *Nebraska Independent* wondered whether MacLean intentionally misled audiences at farmers' institutes. "We can't help thinking that he is 'working' us," stated the paper, which also wryly predicted that land grant proceeds might someday be redirected to the College of Fine Arts.[30]

Between 1900 and 1904, when an alliance of Nebraska Populists, Democrats, and Silver Republicans controlled the NU board of regents, agricultural education moved toward the forefront of the university's agenda. Elected on a fusionist ticket in 1897, Regents George Kenower and E. Von Forell expanded NU's commitment to vocational subjects. While in the minority, Regent Kenower had introduced a successful motion to start school of domestic science.[31] Once in the majority, fusionists doubled the NU teaching force in agricultural subjects between 1901 and 1902 (while eliminating instruction in Sanskrit).[32]

The fusionist regents also hired Chancellor E. Benjamin Andrews (1900–1909). Andrews ran Chicago's school system and had resigned the presidency of Brown University after clashing with trustees over his advocacy for the monetization of silver. Born into a family of prominent New England ministers, Andrews had flirted with socialism and maintained that education was crucial to ending the exploitation of workers. In 1897, the *Nebraska Independent* had commented that Andrews' conflict at an eastern university suggested that he "would make good western timber and should be transplanted."[33] A supporter of industrial and agricultural education at the college level, Andrews pledged to allocate all of NU's land grant funds to vocational departments. Andrews also hoped to require two semesters of manual training for all students and proposed that male graduates should be able to "create a ruler, a hammer, a pair of tongs, a door, a tool chest, a jackscrew, a wagon wheel, or . . . responsibly survey a section of land or keep a double entry set of books."[34]

Populists outside of North Carolina, Kansas, and Nebraska also exhibited this commitment to agricultural higher education. The national umbrella organizations of the Grange and the Farmers' Alliance supported the Hatch

Act of 1887 and the Second Morrill Act of 1890.[35] In Connecticut, hardly a hotbed of Populism, Grangers protested against Yale's Sheffield Scientific School's use of land grant funds to support basic agricultural research rather than training for practicing farmers. In Arkansas, after Populists won control of the legislature in 1887 and replaced the state university's trustees, the new board added vocational course requirements (including three hours of manual labor per day) and invested in the campus farm.[36] "Pitchfork" Ben Tillman, populistic governor of South Carolina, rose to political prominence in 1886 while launching a similar campaign. Tillman compared the land grant status of South Carolina College (precursor to the University of South Carolina) to "a child [put] to nurse in the house of its enemies." According to Tillman, the state college trained "future masters," not honorable farmers. Two years later, with the help of the estate of Thomas G. Clemson, Tillman transferred the land grant designation to a new state agricultural and industrial college.[37]

It is possible that a critical mass of black Populists also supported vocational higher education, though few official or personal papers document the activities of the Colored Farmers' Alliance (CFA) or African American members of the Populist Party. In the face of violent opposition from white supremacists, CFA leaders and other black Populists operated in a quasi-clandestine fashion. White Populists, such as Tom Watson of Georgia, claimed that Booker T. Washington's vision of industrial education epitomized Populist curricular preferences among whites and blacks alike. Indeed, Washington's Tuskegee Institute catered to the children of farmers and celebrated the virtue of manual labor.[38] Sparse evidence also reveals that some black Populists endorsed the Tuskegee model of higher education. Although they defended their political rights more assertively, CFA leaders often articulated a Washingtonian strategy of self-help and economic development. George Washington Murray, a former South Carolina CFA leader, attempted to secure federal funds for schools modeled after Tuskegee. John B. Rayner, an African American organizer for Texas Populist Party during the 1890s, also campaigned later for industrial education. Starting in 1904, Rayner attempted to transform the Conroe-Porter Industrial College into Texas's version of Tuskegee. Black Populists also lobbied for agricultural education at Prairie View A&M University, Texas's black land grant institution.[39]

Despite these clues, Tuskegee may provide an inaccurate proxy for black Populists' views of college curriculum. There is no evidence in Washington's papers that he found common cause with the CFA or the Populist Party of Alabama, which enjoyed success in some of the most violent white supremacist regions of the state, including the countryside just north of Tuskegee. It was not surprising that Washington aligned himself with local Democrats (though he would have preferred to remain nonpartisan).[40] Aside from the matter of political affiliation, Washington's cooperation with paternalistic elites and pragmatic embrace of industrial education clashed with Populist values. During an era in which white supremacists propagandized about the intellectual limitations of African Americans, traditional academic training subverted the planter regime in a manner consistent with Populist faith in the masses. Whereas white Populists complained about the graduation of parasitical young professionals from state colleges, black Populists might have appreciated that college-trained African American doctors, lawyers, and ministers challenged the myth of racial inferiority.[41] It seems unlikely, for example, that many black Populists would have disapproved of the career path of Lutie Lytle, a Populist who attended Central Tennessee College and became one of the nation's first female African American attorneys.[42] Furthermore, during the peak of black Populism in the late 1880s and 1890s, most African American colleges focused on providing secondary-level instruction to students preparing to teach school— few offered substantial upper-level liberal arts coursework.[43] In this context, black Populists would have had little reason to object to the provision of liberal arts education to a new generation of schoolteachers.

Although white Populists may have been more inclined to attack liberal arts curricula, Populist opposition toward these subjects can be easily overstated. While vocational training was central to most white Populists' vision of higher education, the movement did not entirely reject the liberal arts. After all, many of the movement's leaders had themselves benefited from traditional forms of higher education. Some of these Populists embraced classic tributes to the anti-materialism and democratic idealism of liberal education (particularly the study of ancient Greece). Academic Populists, along with many scholars of the humanities, believed that the modern university could civilize industrial America by integrating classical and practical education. A letter to the editor of the *Wealth Makers of the World* asserted that colleges could provide students with "higher conceptions of success" instead of ambition for mere wealth and self-promotion. Written by a "Populist educator," the letter argued that NU could help inoculate students against enslavement to material temptation and counteract the influence of "these sordid, mammon-worship times."[44]

Similarly, KSAC President Thomas E. Will stated that courses in natural science, history, ethics, aesthetics, and theology prevented higher education from becoming a crass exercise in "money grabbing."[45] Disappointed by his own experience as a Harvard student, Populist Regent Carl Vrooman also believed that KSAC's liberal arts courses could dissuade students from becoming "materialistic and cynical."[46] Indeed, after the fusionist reorganization of the college, KSAC students could still opt for a general course featuring English, history, science, and mathematics. Populists were not opposed to the humanities or the pure sciences as long as these subjects could be harnessed to shrink the cultural distance dividing humble country dwellers from influential elites.

Populists also increased offerings in the social sciences at each institution under their control because they believed that these courses would protect farmers from exploitation. While academic Populists were enthusiastic about college courses for farmers and mechanics, many recognized that narrow vocational education could become a double-edged sword. Trade training promised to elevate the status of America's producers, but did not necessarily empower students to negotiate for better financial terms or to participate confidently in a democratic society. Indeed, a committee of mainstream state legislators hoped that the new Georgia Institute of Technology would "stop drift the drift towards communism, and insure subordination to law and order in all classes."[47] Wary of these motives, John Dewey declared that vocational education would train workers to be "mere appendages to the machines which they operate" unless the curriculum included social science courses.[48]

Years before Dewey and Jane Addams translated these ideas into more refined language, leaders of state Farmers' Alliances and Populist Parties advocated for political economy courses at public A&M colleges. Whereas conventional wisdom held that increasing agricultural productivity would improve the condition of farmers, Populists believed that cutting-edge social science would prove that lawyers and bankers diverted profits away from the rural masses. The *Nebraska Independent* exalted that training the children of farmers and mechanics "in the higher powers of analysis, science and organization" would doom any efforts to monopolize higher learning for the benefit of the "privileged classes."[49] The *Weekly Commoner* of Washington State argued that limiting the education of farmers to vocational subjects would doom rural youth to remain "mere hewers of wood and drawers of water."[50] At KSAC, Thomas E. Will declared that those who opposed teaching political economy to farmers were akin to masters opposing the education of slaves. Will accused capitalists of supporting narrow vocational training in order to educate "blind Samsons, left to grind through life in the prison house of the modern Philistines of wealth." KSAC's fusionist board of regents and the Populist press of Kansas agreed.[51]

Vocational Education
and Populist Egalitarianism

Although they believed that liberal arts courses would empower the children of farmers and laborers, many academic Populists worried that colleges would exacerbate class divisions if they focused entirely on these subjects. To begin with, Populists (at least within the movement's white majority) argued that traditional colleges would never enroll large numbers of rural students who had imperfect academic preparation and little free time. They presumed that the children of farmers and mechanics preferred to attend institutions that offered courses related their parents' occupations.

Populists were not the first to associate vocational curricula with college access. Yet because of their belief in the superiority of rural life and their pessimism about the odds of social mobility, Populists were especially convinced that public colleges would never attract the children of the masses unless they offered agricultural and mechanical courses. Populists also worried that students of agriculture would be ridiculed and discouraged if they attended schools in which they formed small minorities of the college population.[52]

Assuming that children wanted to (or inevitably would) follow in the footsteps of their parents, Populist commentators on the purpose of the Morrill Act often conflated A&M students with "the sons of farmers and mechanics." Convinced that farmers' sons would not or could not pursue higher education in order to master "the dead languages, mathematics, polite literature and all the ologies," Leonidas L. Polk argued that the absence of agriculture from school curricula led to high dropout rates among the "children of the masses." For Polk, an agricultural college *was* a "people's college."[53] William Stryker, Populist superintendent of Kansas public schools, also asserted that "popularizing" education required making it more "practical." "If less than four percent of the school population enters our high school, much less the college," Stryker reasoned, "there is a reason for it, and the school must be partly to blame." Stryker concluded that schools taught "too much lawyer, teacher and doctor and too little merchant, mechanic, and farmer; too much preparation to live in the parlor and too little for the kitchen and the workshop."[54] Similarly, California farmers complained that the state university spent too much time "teaching rich lawyers' boys Greek with the farmers' money."[55]

In addition to assuming that courses in agriculture, mechanics, and home economics would attract poor rural students to state colleges and universities,

Populists feared that other forms of higher education estranged these young people from wholesome manual labor and converted them into members of parasitical professions. These concerns echoed a time-honored tradition— many advocates for vocational education had claimed that classical colleges directed students away from the ranks of noble producers.[56] Senator Justin Morrill, for example, believed that colleges were graduating too many lawyers and bankers rather than farmers who "do not produce, vend, or consume luxuries." Eugene V. Debs accused traditional colleges of encouraging students to become "arrogantly hostile to labor."[57]

Populists joined this chorus. The Populist *Manhattan Republic* was disturbed by reports that forty-eight law students graduated from the University of Kansas (KU) in 1897. A Populist editor in Mississippi was dismayed that the state's A&M college "educated our boys out of the ranks of the producers into those of consumers." At NCCAMA's opening, therefore, President Alexander Holladay assured farmers that the school would teach students to pursue an "honest living" instead of careers "secured by doubtful methods and modern tricks of the trade."[58] Populists also worried that traditional higher education could accelerate the migration of young farmers into cities, where their moral compasses would be impaired.[59] Although some parents encouraged their children to pursue opportunities elsewhere, relocation clashed with conventional agrarian expectations that children would dedicate themselves to wholesome labor and family welfare. One Populist farmer protested that NU functioned as "a great exportation depot" for Nebraska youth.[60]

During his campaign for a state agricultural college in North Carolina, Polk accused conventional colleges of teaching youth to pursue "genteel" occupations. According to Polk, excluding agriculture and the mechanic arts from college curricula would be "absolutely suicidal, both morally and materially."[61] Marion Butler published similar sentiments in the form of a speech by a Thomas Dixon, a Baptist preacher and ally of the Farmers' Alliance. Dixon recommended vocational higher education while denouncing the manner in which traditional schooling taught the blacksmith "to despise his anvil and the clodhopper to look with contempt upon the plow." Dixon complained that college graduates "rise to 'higher' things" by becoming "lawyers, and doctors, and preachers, and bankers, railroad men and politicians."[62]

Like Dixon, "Pitchfork" Ben Tillman of South Carolina implied that traditional forms of higher education could corrupt young men. Tillman courted voters during his campaign for governor by attacking South Carolina College for graduating "drones and vagabonds" who did not "sweat none the four years."[63] He also associated liberal education with femininity. Tillman labeled the Citadel, South Carolina's military college, as a "military dude factory," which transformed the state's youth into haughty loafers. The president of Clemson Agricultural College, an institution born out of Tillman's dissatisfaction with South Carolina College, also promoted the moral value of manual labor and criticized "namby-pamby" students.[64] The nineteenth-century classical college was prone to these charges of femininity because of its emphasis on piety and culture, arenas often associated with womanhood.[65]

While they tended to focus on the education of male college students, many Populists also recommended that young women take vocational courses in order to increase their productivity, preserve their moral fiber, and prepare themselves for the possibility of widowhood. As mentioned before, Kansas Populists supported college courses in domestic science. Populists in North and South Carolina endorsed the establishment of public industrial and normal colleges for women. A North Carolina Farmers' Alliance paper, for instance, advised parents to steer their daughters away from any "fashionable college" where young women merely learned "how to smile, and sing, and recline, and languish." North Carolina Populist Marion Butler relayed a cautionary tale about a woman unable to support her ill husband despite having been schooled in "all those 'accomplishments' which are supposed to fit women for the 'best circles of society.'"[66]

According to Populist orthodoxy, traditional college curricula divorced young rural women and men from *the people.* Part of this concern may have derived from widespread popular ambivalence toward notions of high culture, which implied that a hierarchy of taste distinguished noble individuals from the masses.[67] Indeed, the Ladies Faculty Club at NU dedicated itself to combating "uncouthness and roughness" among rural students so that they would no longer be perceived as "a set of clod-hoppers, fresh from the verdant country."[68] A North Carolina woman wrote to the *Progressive Farmer* to express her resentment over this sort of condescension and to mock the perception that college education would hasten the approach of a "millennium for farmers' daughters." The letter writer resented the implication that "none of us need stay in the poor, miserable country to raise ducks, chickens, etc."[69]

Novelist Willa Cather, a political centrist who attended NU from 1891 to 1895, witnessed these populistic anxieties.[70] In *One of Ours* (1922), a farmer opposed his son's desire to transfer from a small denominational college to NU because he was concerned that his son would become effete, uppity, and aloof. The farmer preferred the local church-sponsored college because its shabby-looking students "were less likely to become too knowing, and to be offensively intelligent at home."[71] Set during the 1890s, Cather's *O Pioneers!* (1913) associated this suspicion of college curricula more directly with the Populist movement. Cather identified Lou and Oscar Bergson as ignorant Populists who rejoiced over the manner in which William Jennings Bryan "gave Wall Street a scare in ninety-six." Cather illustrated the Populist critique of higher education by describing Lou's and Oscar's resentment after their bright younger brother Emil enrolled at NU. The older brothers, who were "sore" with Emil from the moment he left for university, objected to his change in manners and disinterest in agriculture. Lou and Oscar even hoped that Emil would fail out of school. After Emil engaged in a particularly tragic extramarital affair, Lou and Oscar claimed that it was his attendance at NU that had "ruined him."[72]

The novel *Voice of the People* (1900) by Virginian Ellen Glasgow also dramatized this Populist anxiety about college.[73] Glasgow told the story of Nicholas, the son of Amos Burr, an uneducated and inefficient farmer. Like Cather, Glasgow set the drama of the *Voice of the People* against the backdrop of an antielitist uprising—in this case the Virginia Readjuster Movement of the 1880s. Amos Burr muttered vague populistic complaints about the government and said that he had "never saw nothin' come of larnin' yet, 'cep'n worthlessness."[74] Nicholas, however, cultivated a relationship with a local judge by appearing in his house and resisting all attempts to shoo him back to the farm. After the judge helped him through secondary school as well as the University of Virginia, Nick was elected governor. In the process of becoming educated, Nicholas Burr became "baffled by the massive ignorance he confronted" among the farmers who populated his childhood community. After a conversation with a neighbor who argued that the legal profession was inherently corrupt, Nick wondered, "If he could be really of one flesh and blood with these people." Like *O Pioneers!*, *Voice of the People* depicted the manner in which rural Populists could perceive college education as an experience that estranged students from their wholesome roots.[75]

Alongside the suspicions of these ordinary Populists, movement intellectuals were also apprehensive about the alienating effects of higher education.[76] For example, Veblen's acidic criticism of leisured higher education may have evolved out of his own personal estrangement from agricultural labor. Veblen grew up in a tight-knit rural community prior to attending Carleton College, where he pursued a classical curriculum. Veblen's college studies left him with little enthusiasm for farm work, prompting one of his relatives to accuse him of behaving like a "conceited jackass" during his school vacations. According to John Dos Passos, Veblen's brothers did not cease "grumbling about this sardonic loafer who wouldn't earn his keep."[77]

Hamlin Garland, a Populist sympathizer who had also left his family's farm to pursue higher education, recorded a similar encounter in an autobiographical tale, titled "Up the Coulee: A Story of Wisconsin" (1891). In this short story, an urban playwright and producer revisited his rural childhood home and recoiled from the hardships of farm life. The author encountered bitter resentment from his younger brother, who complained, "We fellers on the farm have to earn a livin' for ourselves and you fellers that don't work." Garland illustrated the discomfort of the playwright as he greeted an old woman and felt her calloused hand on his soft flesh. Garland's guilt-ridden protagonist attempted to make amends with his brother by agreeing, "Circumstances made me and crushed you. That's all there is about that. Luck made me and cheated you. It ain't right."[78]

Decades later, John Williams wrestled with these feelings in the pages of his autobiographical novel *Stoner*. A creative writing professor who hailed from Northwest Texas, Williams noted how his protagonist, William Stoner, entered a state university and felt that he had abandoned his family and their farm. After dropping agricultural science and becoming a professor of English litera-ture, Stoner sold his deceased parents' farmland in order to pay down the mortgage of his house near campus. Yet Williams suggested that Stoner still retained "blood knowledge" of rural life, which rendered him profoundly sympathetic for the plight of dustbowl farmers during the Great Depression. Williams then drew an awkward parallel between the stamina of starving farmers and the stoicism of a professor assigned to undesirable courses by a vindictive department chair.[79]

This sort of guilt encouraged students and professors to prove that they were workers as well as scholars. Mainstream magazines often highlighted stories about graduates who worked their way up from blue-collar positions within a corporation, suggesting that college students could thereby shed any snobbish orientation toward manual labor.[80] These sentiments were common on campuses touched by the Populist revolt. During the brief Populist reign in Colorado, students at the state agricultural college boasted that they worked harder than Yale or Harvard students who grew "pale and weary when confronted with the necessity for honest toil."[81] In Nebraska, a university newspaper editorialized that students were "truly laboring men" because they routinely worked to pay for room and board after attending classes and studying. The *Nebraska Indepen-dent* reported that some students harvested wheat during their summer vacation in order to disprove the perception that they were "educated loafers" or "use-less athletes." Populist student Alvin Johnson worked on a sugar beet farm during a summer break so that he could remain in touch with ordinary

Nebraskans.[82] In this spirit, the *Independent* noted that a journalist who the Populists nominated for the NU board of regents was still essentially a laborer. The paper reported that the nominee, Mrs. Elia Peattie, was a diligent worker "earning her daily bread" while also "sewing, darning, and mending."[83]

As an antidote to these strains, many white Populists argued that vocational courses would blur distinctions between farmers and professionals and thereby encourage college students to return to agriculture.[84] As signaled by the proliferation of derogatory terms, such as "hick," "rube," and "yokel," the status of farmers decreased relative to urban professionals during the second half of the nineteenth century.[85] In response, rural leaders hoped that land grant colleges could train farmers in such a way as to revive the prestige of agriculture. NCCAMA President Holladay revealed the populistic overtone of this ambition by predicting that the spread of agricultural higher education would decrease the gap between rich and poor until "the oppression of the many by the few shall cease."[86]

Agrarian advocates, Populist and non-Populist alike, hoped that A&M colleges would demonstrate that farming required as much expertise as any other vocation. A speaker at a North Carolina farmers club, for instance, declared that the perception that farmers required less education than doctors or lawyers was "monstrous nonsense."[87] In 1886, Leonidas L. Polk voiced the common expectation that college-educated farmers and mechanics would be "dignified by the very systems under which they are prepared and trained." Over a decade later, the *Progressive Farmer* continued to anticipate that when a critical mass of farmers obtained college degrees, "clod-hopper, hayseed, and such appellations . . . will become obsolete."[88]

Populists and other nineteenth-century proponents of egalitarian social reform also believed that privileged college students would be less likely to feel superior to laborers if they were required to take vocational courses. In his utopian novel *Looking Backward* (1888), Edward Bellamy predicted that all citizens would have to perform manual labor for three years in order to promote universal respect for the dignity of all vocations. Henry Demarest Lloyd, influential author of *Progress and Poverty*, favored manual training courses because they "put the son of the millionaire by the son of the stoker at the forge and the lathe."[89]

Leonidas L. Polk explained that vocational courses would help students at state colleges "keep sympathy with the interests they are being educated to benefit." In this spirit, NCCAMA pledged to increase labor's "respectability."[90] At NU, Chancellor James Hulme Canfield supported vocational training because he agreed that agricultural students would be stigmatized if no other college students worked with their hands. Canfield objected to dividing the university between students seeking "the education of a gentleman" and those preparing to be an "all-round chump." Unless all students worked in the university's shops or fields, Canfield feared that agricultural students would feel that they were told to "go over there in the corner and stay there."[91] The *Nebraska Independent* went so far as to forecast that NU's vocational courses could destroy "the old division of mankind into wealth producers and wealth consumers."[92] During its fusionist period, KSAC broadcast similar messages. A graduate of the college boasted that KSAC taught students to be "imbued with a deeper and more wholesome respect for the average walks of life." After the end of the fusionist era, the KSAC catalog continued to state that physical work "awakens and deepens sympathy with industry and toil" and "impresses the student with the essential dignity of labor."[93]

Perhaps because of its demagogic element or its lack of rhetorical sophistication, this Populist vision of vocational education has remained unappreciated compared to the views of Jane Addams and John Dewey. However, these Progressive philosophers echoed Populist hopes. An advocate for settlement houses in which college graduates and workers commingled, Addams hoped to reduce philosophical and sociological divisions separating intellectual and manual labor. Addams promoted a broad version of vocational education designed to engage workers in the history, political economy, and social function of their respective industries. At Hull House in Chicago, Addams hoped that cross-cultural exchange and the study of applied subjects would not alienate working-class children from their communities. Similar to Populist commentators, Addams regretted the propensity for rural families to send a daughter to normal school or college in hopes of increasing her social status.[94]

Influenced by Addams, John Dewey's theory of vocational education became one of the most respected academic treatments of the subject. Dewey also sought to promote workers' participation in government and industrial management.[95] Prompted by his discomfort over the enmity of intellectuals toward railroad employees during the Pullman strike of 1894, Dewey hoped that a synthesis of vocational and liberal education could obliterate the "barriers of distance" separating workers and professionals. He repeated previous calls to "intellectualize" industrial and agricultural labor by revealing their scientific complexity and economic contributions. Dewey seconded the Populist belief that instruction in physical sciences could enable workers to improve the technical aspect of their vocations, while instruction in social sciences could empower workers "to become masters of their industrial fate." Dewey also argued that students who did not intend to work in fields or factories after graduation should still take courses in manual training in order to "increase sympathy for labor."[96] Ultimately academic Populists, along with Addams and Dewey, believed that an interdisciplinary, broadly conceived form of vocational education could diminish status hierarchies between various occupations.

"High Fallutin' Now": The Failure of the People's College

While Dewey hoped to eliminate class differences altogether, distinctions between righteous masses and corrupt elites remained integral to the Populist worldview. The Populist (and socialist) vision of agricultural and mechanical higher education, therefore, embodied an awkward tension. Like other proponents of workers' education, academic Populists believed that land grant colleges and universities could enhance the status of young farmers and mechanics without destroying their identification with the producing classes. For example, Walter Vrooman, brother of KSAC Populist Regent Carl Vrooman and cofounder of Ruskin College in Oxford, England, asserted that the purpose of workers' education was "to bring up the laborer to the professional class, and still be in the working class."

This balancing act was challenging enough at semiformal schools such as Ruskin College or Brookwood Labor College in New York (where students often prepared to work within unions or schools), let alone at credential-granting state colleges.[97] Land grant college leaders often sought to create transformative institutions that would create new opportunities and promote leadership among students from modest backgrounds."[98] More important, the idea of a Populist college conflicted with the aspirations of most students and with the credentialing function of the college degree itself. Regardless of their ideological loyalties, few students attended college in order to perform manual labor or maintain a sympathetic connection with agricultural or industrial workers. Academic Populists were unable to prevent rural students from leveraging their college degrees in order to leave the ranks of the producers—higher education proved to be slippery terrain for the preservation of working-class identity. In Upton Sinclair's cynical terms, poor college students were quickly absorbed into "the psychology of the dominant classes."[99]

The majority of college students hoped to achieve or reinforce middle-class status by entering commercial and professional fields. When the Illinois Industrial University (ancestor of the University of Illinois) opened in 1868, it did not offer diplomas to its graduates because the school's administration wished to distance their institution from all trappings of classical elitism. However, student demand for the status conferred by formal degrees compelled a rapid change of university policy.[100] College degrees signaled that graduates had gained advanced literacy skills and perhaps a modicum of expertise based in scientific empiricism. The college credential also signaled to employers that graduates could abide by the social and cultural standards of a modern bureaucratic environment.[101] The power of this credentialing effect counteracted the egalitarianism of Populist curricular reform. Regardless of the extent to which college curriculum might honor manual labor, the diploma elevated graduates into privileged occupations.[102] Like most boosters of A&M education, Populists were slow to realize that white-collar occupations had become the fastest growing sector of the labor market.[103] Populists also failed to realize that many students pursued liberal arts education in order to increase their career options by delaying vocational specialization. A KSAC student, for example, stated that he preferred broad "potential education" instead of education for a particular job.[104]

Regardless of whether they were in regions with strong Populist movements, A&M colleges struggled to attract students to courses in agriculture — the subject dearest to the movement. While farming provided deep satisfactions, rural life also entailed long hours, hard labor, and financial volatility.[105] Many students attended college precisely in order to escape the strain and insecurity of farming. A member of the first class of NCCAMA, for example, recalled that he decided to enter school because he saw little prospects in farming and was tired of hollering at an uncooperative mule. The president of the Colorado State Agricultural College argued that Populist rhetoric about the superiority of farming rang hollow because all people wanted to work less, earn more, and abandon the "slave life of labor." Acknowledging that few students studied agriculture at the University of Tennessee, a Farmers' Alliance leader worried that nine-tenths of ambitious rural young people were "sick and disgusted with farming."[106] Enrollment numbers confirm these observations. Only three students enrolled in agricultural courses at Arkansas Industrial University in 1893. During the fusionist administration of KSAC, 10 percent to 15 percent of students opted for the agricultural track. In each of NCCAMA's graduating classes from 1898 through 1901, only two students took a full agricultural course of study.[107]

Never high on the agenda of agrarian Populists, engineering may have come closest to realizing the movement's vision of a hybrid intellectual / physical occupation. Spurred on by industrial development, this field became the most popular offering at many land grant colleges during the 1890s.[108] Although graduates explicitly contrasted themselves with laborers, these programs still blurred the lines between a profession and a vocation by moving engineering away from its elite roots and closer to a middle-class occupation.[109] Arguably, teacher education, the largest vocational field within many universities, could also be considered a successful example of egalitarian higher education because of the ambiguous class status of teachers.[110]

While land grant institutions produced growing numbers of engineers and teachers, less than 2 percent of their graduates pursued farming or other agricultural profession by 1900. Between 1889 and 1922, the most common occupation for graduates of A&M colleges consisted of some form of commercial activity, followed by teaching, and then engineering. Even within the pool of students who decided to take agriculture courses, roughly half ultimately worked in other fields.[111] A poem about a Purdue University student provided a light-hearted commentary on this trend. Assuming the perspective of a rural student who returned home and objected to his chores, the poet wrote:

> And I says: "Mam, I'm a student now,
> You can't treat me like a cow;
> If you keep on, I'll get chagrined
> And scoot back to old Purdue." Mam grinned,
> And she said she 'lowed I's right and said
> "You go up stairs and crawl in bed,
> Dot and me will feed the cow,
> I know you're high fallutin' now."[112]

Even land grant colleges under the influence of Populist administrations produced few farmers. Between 1894 and 1897, during the height of Populist power in North Carolina, only a handful of NCCAMA students farmed after graduation.[113] A student at NU reported that the agricultural college was viewed with "contempt" and that "nobody went back to the farm." The student exaggerated only slightly. During the 1890s, the number of all NU graduates who became farmers hovered between 2 percent and 4 percent of their respective classes.[114] KSAC produced a higher percentage of farmers, both before and during its Populist period. Even so, roughly the same numbers of male KSAC graduates entered commerce or the professions as entered agriculture. Most female graduates taught school or performed unsalaried domestic labor.[115]

Among the small number of students who studied agriculture, the ambiguity of farmers' status frustrated Populist hopes that A&M colleges could muddy the distinction between laborers and professionals. Despite Populists' monolithic use of the term, the manner in which "farmer" encompassed field hands as well as managers obscured the extent to which graduates of agricultural colleges constituted a privileged class.[116]

Regardless of Populist rhetoric about the wholesomeness of the rural work ethic, most students pursuing agricultural courses in college were preparing to supervise the labor of others. Land grant courses tailored to women students also tended to assume that graduates would hire others to perform many menial tasks.[117] In general, agricultural colleges promoted large-scale commercial production managed by experts rather than the small-scale, owner-operated farms romanticized by Populists.[118] The NCCAMA catalog, for example, announced that the college's agricultural courses taught students to supervise "the great army of uneducated muscle which constitutes our farm hands." President George Winston elaborated that the college would transform "a 50-cent fellow into a $5 man; and a $5 man into a $20, $30, or $50 a day skilled worker, thinker, designer, supervisor."[119] The North Carolina A&M College for the Colored Race also advertised that its graduates could manage farms and "handle" unskilled laborers.[120] The KSAC *Industrialist* reprinted an article arguing that native-born white farm youth should train to become effective employers of immigrant laborers from Italy and China.[121] The graduation speech of a NCCAMA student revealed the extent to which he saw himself and his classmates as supervisors rather than workers. The student eagerly anticipated the invention of a cotton-picking machine, even though he recognized that it would spell disaster for "many toil-worn, poor hand-to-mouth creatures," who could not be expected to understand to the long-term benefits of the technology.[122] Perhaps because of their inability to afford fertile land, 60 percent of students taking agriculture courses in land grant colleges between 1889 and 1922 proceeded to postgraduate study—more than double the percentage of arts and science students who continued their formal education.[123]

Attracted to the image of the professional farmer, some Populists endorsed the goal of training experts and supervisors who could increase the status of the entire farm sector. Although the Populist *Watchman* encouraged the preservation of "a true yeomanry," the paper celebrated the numbers of agricultural college graduates who managed large commercial operations. The editor of the *Nebraska Independent* enthused over the letters he received seeking to hire graduates of the NU agriculture school to manage commercial estates.[124] At least as many graduates of land grant agricultural programs in North Carolina and Kansas became salaried managers or experts as became working farmers.[125]

Anecdotal evidence suggests that Populist students contributed to the exodus of educated country youth from the ranks of agricultural labor. Even though children of Populist parents often attended rallies, marched in parades, sang campaign songs, delivered speeches, and sold newspaper subscriptions, they did not pledge their lives to farming, especially after attending college.[126] A

Populist sympathizer and son of a Wisconsin Granger, Hamlin Garland recalled that the local institution of higher education "gave farmers' boys like
myself the opportunity of meeting those who were older, finer, more learned
than they, and every day was to me like turning a fresh and delightful page in a
story book, not merely because it brought new friends, new experiences, but
because it symbolized freedom from the hayfork and the hoe." Garland and his
brother spent only a year attending the seminary, but it was enough to place
"the rigorous, filthy drudgery of the farm-yard in sharp contrast with the care-
free companionable existence led by my friends in the village."[127]

While lecturing on behalf of his local Nebraska Farmers' Alliance chapter,
Alvin Johnson contemplated becoming a doctor before pursuing NU's classical
course and a career in academia.[128] Frank O'Connell, who grew up in family of
Nebraska Populist farmers, wanted to attend college in order to become an
engineering expert. Frank told his brother of his intention to pursue a college
degree in order to "be a perfessor. Teach the lunks around here how." Full of
ambition, Frank eventually moved to New York City, took an inspirational
course from Dale Carnegie, and pledged "to become a leader or to hold any
worth-while position." Meanwhile, Frank's younger brother aimed to become a
lawyer, while his sister Ona wanted to enter the University of Nebraska in
order to move to a city, marry rich, and become "a genteel lady."[129] Mamie
Boyd, a KSAC student with a Populist background, eventually became a
journalist, as did C. J. Lamb, a Populist graduate of the University of Kansas
Law School. During the heyday of Populism at KSAC, even a self-proclaimed
"radical" student went to work for a bank after graduation.[130]

Many rural parents, Populists and conservatives alike, encouraged their
children to pursue courses that could train them for nonfarm careers. According
to the president of Arkansas Industrial University, most parents wanted their
sons to "take the course of study that will best open the way for distinction.
Hence preference is given to the classics, to literature, oratory, etc."[131] UNC
president Kemp Plummer Battle claimed that nine out of ten North Carolina
farmers wanted their sons to study the classical college curriculum. Indeed,
even Daniel McKay, a proud farmer engaged in North Carolina agrarian politics,
told Leonidas L. Polk that he hoped his children would learn "*anything* else but
farming." McKay told Polk that if he had sons, he would "*break their legs* if they
had any inclination that way."[132]

Hamlin Garland's mother supported his desire to raise himself "above the
commonplace level of neighborhood life."[133] Similarly, Alvin Johnson remem-
bered that whenever he expressed enthusiasm for farm life his mother would
"douse my ardor with cold water."[134] Frank O'Connell's mother was also

determined that her children attend college so that they might "amount to something." She did not let her anger at "nasty bankers" prevent her from hoping that a college education could transform her son into "a doctor—or an engineer, lawyer, or the like" or even take him "right to the top in some big corporation or the like of that."[135]

Because the goal of celebrating the dignity of hard work seemed irrelevant to many A&M students, most agricultural colleges encountered resistance to their manual labor requirements. At the Michigan State Agricultural College, the labor program evolved into an unpopular routine of brute farm work and campus maintenance. Resentment toward Professor Samuel Johnson's supervision of this three-hour-a-day requirement boiled over in 1885. After a student was expelled for repeatedly calling Johnson "Sammy," the ex-student led his classmates to Johnson's house, where he threw the professor to the ground before Mrs. Johnson dispersed the crowd with a horsewhip.[136] The Tuskegee Institute also failed to convince many students, professors, and other skeptics of the value of merging intellectual and physical labor. Booker T. Washington struggled to persuade his academic faculty to "dovetail" their courses with lessons from the school's fields and workshops.[137] At land grant colleges across the nation, many professors of agriculture opposed manual labor sessions because they drained students' intellectual energies and reduced resources available for scientific experimentation. By 1898, the Association of American Agricultural Colleges and Experiment Stations resolved that land grant schools should no longer require physical work.[138]

Even schools under Populist control eventually abolished these requirements. At NCCAMA, a policy mandating that all freshman work on the college farm was discontinued in 1895. Attempts to inspire enthusiasm by awarding a medal to the hardest working student could not prevent students from shirking their responsibilities or flinging produce and clods of dirt at each other. Within ten years of its founding, NCCAMA evolved into a traditional academic and professional school.[139] According to Chancellor Canfield of NU, manual training was a "bugaboo" among the faculty, who believed that it would lower the "tone" of the institution and displace other courses. A faculty committee also expressed concern that requiring manual training might discourage prospective students and decrease support for the university among "some of the best people of the state." Ultimately, manual labor became optional for liberal arts students after the end of Canfield's tenure in office.[140] Despite its fusionist administration, KSAC also converted manual labor in its agriculture course into an elective after freshman year. In 1897, KSAC ended labor requirements in the "mechanics" course while also changing its name to the more professional-sounding course in "engineering." According to school news-papers, many KSAC students exhibited the "traditional prejudice" against having to work on college buildings or fields.[141]

The demise of manual training requirements was merely the most visible symptom of the failure of Populist advocacy for a synthesis of labor and intellec-tualism. Despite Populist hopes that vocational education could meld elite and mass forms of higher learning, schools continued to reinforce these distinc-tions. Although state colleges and universities established a new class of profes-sional agriculturalists and engineers, the increased status of these occupations did not fundamentally alter the elitism inherent in higher education. Indeed, the Carnegie Foundation for the Advancement of Teaching would instruct land grant colleges to differentiate between "agriculture as a profession and farming as a trade."[142] This story is the inverse of the more familiar failure of democratic visions of vocational education at the secondary school level, where the prescriptions of Addams and Dewey were overwhelmed by narrowly tailored occupational training.[143]

Conclusion

In August 1897, a colleague eulogized Harrison Kelley, one of the first of the Populist appointees to KSAC's board of regents, as an individual who envisioned that the college could fight against the division of "the masses from the classes."[144] The promotion of vocational courses at KSAC and other colleges influenced by Populists became one of the movement's main strategies for achieving this ambitious and counterintuitive goal. There was nothing inherently Populist about the concept of vocational education, which preceded and out-lasted the movement, while often taking forms that did not promote producerist values. Indeed, the campaign for vocational education included Populists and corporate leaders who agreed on almost nothing else—though they were at-tracted to these courses for different reasons.

Academic Populists hoped that vocational courses would dramatically increase college access among disadvantaged rural students, thereby blunting the extent to which higher education reinforced class boundaries. More signifi-cantly, Populists believed that trade training on the college level could erode the very basis for status inequalities between professional and physical occupations. This aspect of the movement's agenda ended in disappointment, though Popu-list pressure contributed to the enshrinement of vocational subjects within universities. Academic Populism failed to prevent state colleges and universities from perpetuating the distance between manual and intellectual forms of labor. Land grant colleges and state universities have expanded the number of professional occupations, but rarely have they encouraged students to reject upward mobility or question the line separating professionals from workers.

By 1918, Thorstein Veblen understood all too well what was happening in American universities. Veblen's distaste for the prevailing emphasis on vocational success rendered him almost nostalgic for the classical form of higher education that he had attacked two decades earlier in *Theory of the Leisure Class.* In a new book, *The Higher Learning in America*, Veblen yearned for the return of academic exploration unencumbered by practical application. Blaming businessmen as well as the masses, Veblen rued the evolution of college education toward the single-minded pursuit of private gain. He mourned the abandonment of disinterested higher learning and repeated the conventional scholarly assertion that practical higher education was "a contradiction in terms." Veblen had become discouraged because vocational and professional training appeared to increase the advantages of a select group of privileged youth rather than benefiting the "common run" of citizens.[145]

Populism did not temper the elitism of advanced vocational training, nor did the movement establish a lasting network of alternative schools. The Populists' utopian vision of vocational higher education would never flourish at degree-granting colleges; either rural students would attend prestigious universities where they might drift from their roots, or they would attend agricultural colleges that distinguished their graduates from the masses. While increases in college access could assuage Populist anxieties, persistent concerns over this inherent exclusivity fueled the movement's questions about the legitimacy of any form of social or political status predicated on college training.

6

The Tastes of the Multitude

Populism, Expertise, and Academic Freedom

In April 1897, when the fusionist governing board of Kansas State Agricultural College (KSAC) replaced several veteran professors, student editors at the University of Kansas (KU) "shudder[ed] at the spectacle prefigured" and predicted that the new faculty would browbeat students into espousing "ultra-radical" theories.[1] The dismissals, which outraged professors and college presidents across the nation, became emblematic of the vulnerability of faculty at public institutions of higher education. Although governors had always appointed the KSAC board of regents, the startling victories of the Populist Party attracted special attention to college politics. Populist control of state universities was not more political, or more democratic, than governance by either of the two major parties. Yet Populist takeovers highlighted the politics of higher education because the movement was more blatant about its desire to influence campus affairs.

During the administration of President Thomas E. Will, KSAC embraced Populist causes and appeared to violate conventional expectations that scholars should remain, in the words of Harvard University President Charles W. Eliot, immune from "the passing wishes or tastes of the multitude."[2] Indeed, most scholars believed that the obscurity of academic policies and the intellectual authority of professors would prevent universities from being governed by majority rule. Faculty and administrators, therefore, ritualistically saluted popular wisdom without fearing that voters would make many specific demands.[3] In contrast, Populist and fusionist regimes seemed to present a unique challenge.

To a certain extent, President Will acknowledged that the impact of political pressure on universities was "highly ambiguous" because elected officials might

126

not represent the best interests of the masses. Nevertheless, Will was certain that this risk did not justify transforming KSAC into a "state within a state." He predicted that autonomous state universities would revert to forms of "priestly education" that would betray the public interest and generate "warfare between the gown and the town." Asserting that Oxford University had "been on the wrong side of every great question before the English people," Will had little faith in the judgment of scholars who were insulated from the influence of elected officials.[4] Will and other academic Populists often romanticized the prospect of majority rule over state universities and ignored the host of problems that might stem from this most radical definition of "democratic" higher education.

While there are many sources of scholarly anxiety about academic Populism, this tolerance of public pressure ranks among the most powerful. Indeed, a section of Walter Metzger's *Academic Freedom in the Age of the University* (published in 1955 along with Richard Hofstadter's *Academic Freedom in the Age of the College*) has remained one of the most extensive treatments of Populism and higher education for more than fifty years. Basing his analysis primarily on the KSAC takeover, Metzger confirmed typical scholarly concerns about Populists and other "militantly democratic communities." *Academic Freedom in the Age of the University*, however, relied on the statements of two opponents of Kansas Populism.[5] Drawing on hostile as well as sympathetic sources, the following chapter explores the movement's transgressions while also demonstrating its conflicted respect for scholarly expertise.

As suggested by Metzger, Populists questioned whether citizens should defer to professors. Instead of honoring traditional institutions of higher education, Populists often emphasized the virtues of common sense, autodidacticism, and community-based learning. Local Granges, Farmers' Alliances, and People's Party chapters established informal educational networks by sponsoring lectures, libraries, and newspapers.[6] Encouraged by these organizations, Populists had no patience for professors who criticized their agenda. Yet the movement still believed that Populist ends could be promoted by scholarship, especially research within recently professionalized social science disciplines. The study of economics, politics, and sociology spread through American universities during the 1880s and 1890s, when strife between capital and labor saturated this research with ideological passion. Accustomed to being a persecuted faction within institutions of higher education, academic Populists craved the protection offered by emerging ideals of scholarly autonomy and celebrated the concept of a scholarly community immune from plutocratic influence.

However, Populists also noticed the inconsistent protection afforded to controversial speech and doubted if the ideal of academic freedom would ever safeguard radical scholars. While university administrators argued that only temperate or *neutral* professors deserved academic freedom, Populists observed that these definitions appeared to be established by power more than principle. Some academic Populists questioned whether they ever could (or should) stand beyond the fray of partisan conflict. During an era in which social scientists wrestled with inchoate professional standards, academic Populists struggled to resolve the contradictions between their interest in scholarly freedom and their allegiance to a popular movement. As suggested by Thomas E. Will, some Populists wondered if grassroots activism could counteract corporate influence over universities more effectively than the principle of academic neutrality.

While the persecution of socialist professors has understandably attracted the preponderance of research on academic freedom during this era, reviewing academic freedom from the Populist perspective reveals how radicals understood this issue during their brief moments of institutional empowerment.[7] Allied with a movement that celebrated participatory democracy, academic Populists faced a particularly intense dilemma with respect to the politics of academic freedom. Ultimately, the Populist track record includes a substantial degree of hypocrisy, as Will and others criticized intolerant conservatives while enforcing their own ideological litmus tests. Yet Populists occasionally belied common predictions about the close relationship between anti-elitism and intolerance. In the process, academic Populists illuminated enduring questions about whether academic freedom should depend on professorial nonpartisanship.

Social Scientific Authority in the Gilded Age

While academic Populists hoped that professional social scientists could advance their reform agenda, other supporters of the movement wondered if academia could ever serve the interests of the masses. Regardless of the type of knowledge produced within universities, Populists remained concerned that college professors and graduates could undermine the political authority of farmers and laborers. Others suspected that established educational institutions would never endorse radical economic theories. But rather than reject social science altogether, academic Populists hoped to introduce ordinary farmers to political economy while also increasing the number of farmers' children who studied this subject in colleges under Populist control. This two-pronged strategy attempted to moderate the prerogatives of scholars and college-educated politicians, while still encouraging a measure of academic respectability for the movement's ideals.

Populist leaders often encouraged laypeople to master social science topics through informal venues. *The Alliance Weekly* recommended that readers learn economics and civics from local suballiances rather than from schools that tended to silence any "bright boy or girl who thinks outside of the old books."[8] The Nebraska *Alliance* promised that it would explain the principles of economic reform in a manner "so plain that it will not require an expert to analyze the prescription."[9] In particular, Charles Macune's *National Economist* published a twenty-part series on "Political Economy" and a thirty-part series on the "History of Land." Starting in 1892, the paper also devoted a section to "Economist Educational Exercises." Referring to these efforts, an alliance leader claimed that the organization had "done more to educate the great mass of people in the principles of government than all the schools and colleges have in the past century."[10] This attitude exasperated Kansas journalist William Allen White, who complained that Populists embraced leaders who boasted that they were "just ordinary clodhoppers, but they know more in a minute about finance than [former Treasury Secretary] John Sherman."[11]

Populists often argued that ordinary voters equipped with informal education were the most capable of solving social problems. "When reform comes in this country," William Jennings Bryan proclaimed, "it starts with the masses. Reforms do not come from the brains of scholars." KSAC's Populist Regent Carl Vrooman, though he possessed a Harvard diploma, agreed that commoners would be at the vanguard of progress.[12] Disturbed by academia's chilly reception to William "Coin" Harvey's popular pro-silver publications, the *Nebraska Independent* boasted that thousands of "old Hayseeds in Nebraska" could outdebate "anyone of these gold bug professors in three rounds and come out of the fight without a scratch."[13] If, as these Populists asserted, citizens could understand the intricacies of political economy, then there would be less justification for insulating professors from public criticism.

Indeed, Populists questioned whether college professors merited special protection. Whereas institutions of higher education celebrated the genius of their faculty, Populists sometimes doubted if scholars possessed unique gifts. The Lawrence *Jeffersonian* asserted that "any sensible young man" could quickly become as effective as most professors.[14] Alvin Johnson, a Populist student at NU, shared this workaday attitude toward scholarship. Johnson believed that "the ordinary man, if patient enough and bold enough, could achieve original scholarship."[15] Rejoicing that "the wide diffusion of popular education has practically destroyed the scholar's monopoly," KSAC's Thomas E. Will also

enthused about the capabilities of laypeople.[16] Often unimpressed by the
research pursued within university settings, many Populists saw professors
primarily as disseminators of information rather than as experts whose authority
should not be regulated by popular opinion.[17]

Not only did Populists doubt whether professors possessed special insight,
but some also questioned whether universities were capable of promoting
objective scholarly norms. Populists who paid close attention to heated economic
debates wondered if social scientific research consisted of partisan clashes
rather than professional exploration. During an era when distinctions between
the rigor of professional and layperson scholarship were only just developing,
this question was not entirely unfounded. The traditional professoriate of the
Gilded Age engaged in relatively unspecialized academic pursuits and tended
to associate closely with the views expressed by local elites and denominational
leaders. In this context, the differences between amateur and professional
scholars could seem more ideological than methodological in nature. Vernon
Parrington, for example, drew this sort of contrast between conservative
Gilded Age "academic economists" and radical self-educated economists such
as Henry George, Sarah Emery, and William "Coin" Harvey.[18] Academic Populists sympathized with these amateurs while accusing established social scientists
of catering to the interests of wealth and power. Harvey illustrated this suspicion
in his novel *A Tale of Two Nations*, in which a shady operative paid professors to
write books defending the gold standard.[19] Henry George unnerved an audience
at the University of California by suggesting that academic economists spouted
"pretentious quackery" in the service of elites.[20] Prompted by this skepticism,
Nebraska's Populist legislature considered forbidding colleges from awarding
degrees in social science unless they gave course credit to students who studied
with unaffiliated scholars.[21]

Yet academic Populists also celebrated the emergence of a new generation
of university professors who advocated for economic reform. A cohort of
young scholars, including Richard T. Ely, John Bates Clark, and Henry Carter
Adams, chose to promote social uplift through academic study. Many were
children of Protestant ministers and infused their research with social gospel.
Inspired by German economists who believed that the principles of government intervention in the economy could be determined by empirical study,
these scholars challenged the British laissez-faire theories that dominated most
college courses. These professors reinforced the convictions of an array of Populists, Christian socialists, and other reformers who hoped that the modern state
could establish a "cooperative commonwealth." According to this theory,
government intervention (stopping short of widespread state ownership) could

reconcile liberal individualism and social-democratic collectivism by promoting cooperation and preventing gross inequalities of wealth.[22] These new social scientists found positions at universities that were beginning to embrace modern academic ideals of research and public service. Pioneering university presidents such as Daniel Coit Gilman at Johns Hopkins and Andrew D. White at Cornell saw this social science research as a modern expression of the ethical core of higher education.[23]

Although employed at major universities, these scholars promoted economic and civic reform with an evangelical fervor that resonated with the passionate crusade of the Populist movement. For example, Alvin Johnson was inspired to become an economist after witnessing a disease-stricken army camp while training for the Spanish-American War. After studying classics in college to the detriment of his "equalitarian zeal," Johnson awakened to "thoughts of militant democracy" and saw economics as a means of doing his part "in the struggle for justice, for the restoration of the democratic ideal, badly battered by a generation of monopolistic greed and political chicanery." Johnson pledged to challenge the teachings of conservative departments of economics, which "stood with all four feet solidly planted against the popular movements seething in the industrial cities and among the farming population." After stints at Columbia, Cornell, the University of Texas, and the University of Chicago, Johnson would attempt to reconcile his egalitarianism with his commitment to higher learning as a professor at the New School in New York City.[24]

Populists readily incorporated new scholarship produced by the likes of Johnson into the movement's propaganda. Embraced by leaders such as Kansas Senator William Peffer and National Farmers' Alliance President H. L. Loucks, Richard T. Ely's work on public ownership and railroad economics became especially influential.[25] The *Nebraska Independent* even boasted that the fundamental tenants of Populism were "sustained by the writings of the great scholars and thinkers in all parts of the world."[26] Enthusiasm for these scholar-advocates encouraged some academic Populists to believe that state university professors could be political allies.

Although they sought professional status within universities and did not personally identify with Populism, many of these new social scientists also shared the movement's desire to erode distinctions between academia, popular discourse, and civic reform. Barred from many faculty positions, women social scientists especially gravitated toward the role of applied researchers and reformers in the public health and social welfare sectors.[27] In a more conventional academic capacity, Professor John Commons was determined to become the sort of scholar who could serve as "a guide the army of discontented may trust and follow."[28] Richard T. Ely considered his lectures at the Chautauqua summer school between 1884 and 1891 to be the most significant of his career because they reached the "common people."[29] However, even Populist sympathizers such as Ely, Edward Bemis, and Thorstein Veblen still bristled against the expectation that they focus on their own undergraduate students.[30]

Nevertheless, many scholars oriented toward social reform attempted to present scholarship as a form of common sense that was accessible to all concerned citizens. While a professor at the KU, James Hulme Canfield chose to subtitle his book on taxation as "A Plain Talk for Plain People."[31] Populists encouraged this approach, while objecting to professors who, in the words of Nebraska's William "Crookneck" Taylor, spoke "a different language than us hayseeds do."[32] This sentiment became a staple of populistic commentary on academia. Henry George, for example, proclaimed that there was no need for abstruse language because economics was really a "simple and attractive science."[33] If scholarship could be readily accessible to laypeople, then Populists could confidently judge the contributions of professors employed at public institutions of higher education.

An episode from Nebraska illustrates this expectation. In the fall of 1895, G. R. Roach, a self-identified "ordinary working man" sent the following query to twelve professors at the University of Nebraska (NU): "Dear Sir: After reading several economic articles in the reviews and magazines I find myself in a perfect fog. Will you be kind enough to inform me what "value" is?" Roach was outraged when five of the professors did not respond even though he had included stamped self-addressed envelopes. Five other professors dismayed Roach by instructing him to consult a dictionary or some other colleague. But the response of W. G. Langworthy Taylor, NU's conservative professor of political economy, was especially distressing. Taylor mentioned an article that he had published, but cautioned that the concept of "value" could only be understood after a prolonged period of study. The editor of the *Lincoln Independent* expressed indignation over the implication that laypeople of "ordinary understanding and education" might not understand basic concepts of political economy. After defining value as "what a thing will fetch," the editor challenged Nebraskans to read professor Taylor's article on the subject. "If anyone, aside from God and himself knows what the said professor W. G. Langworthy Taylor was trying to tell," the editor fumed, "he certainly does not reside in the United States of America." The *Independent* published an example of Taylor's prose and accused the professor of "trying to befog a very simple subject for the purpose of making it appear mysterious and not to be understood by the average

English scholar." As a remedy, the editor suggested that professor Taylor work on a farm for five years.[34]

Academic Populists urged state universities to increase their offerings in social science and to staff these courses with professors sympathetic to social reform and the democratization of scholarship. In North Carolina, the fusionist administration of the North Carolina College of Agriculture and Mechanic Arts (NCCAMA) introduced a class in agricultural economics.[35] In Nebraska, Populist leaders promised to support NU's appropriation if the university established a school of social science. William Jennings Bryan personally sought to encourage these pursuits by funding a $250 prize for the best student essay in political science. By 1898, the Nebraska Populist platform included a plank demanding an increase in the study of social and economic issues at the state university. For the first few years of the twentieth century, NU became a haven for left-leaning political economists. After Edward A. Ross was expelled from Stanford, for example, he became the head of NU's sociology department. The state universities of Missouri, Montana, Wisconsin, North Dakota, and Washington also served as temporary refuges for radical social science professors.[36] In states such as Minnesota and Alabama, where Populists never controlled state universities, they lobbied to include economics in the program of university-sponsored farmers' institutes.[37]

At KSAC, the transformation of the social sciences was especially dramatic. The fusionist board of regents recruited Edward Bemis, a protégé of Richard T. Ely who he had been dismissed from the University of Chicago purportedly because of his sympathies with organized labor. Bemis shared his mentor's interest in university extension as well as controversial social policies, such as public ownership of utilities. KSAC also hired Frank Parsons, a lecturer at Boston University's School of Law who was characterized by a former student as a "mild Fabian socialist." In 1895, Parsons had campaigned to become mayor of Boston as the favored candidate of a coalition of Socialists, Populists, and Prohibitionists. To fill the chair of domestic economy, the regents hired Helen Campbell, an outspoken advocate for progressive causes, a student of Ely, and an associate of Charlotte Perkins Gilman and Jane Addams.[38] Between 1892 and 1897, these professors and Thomas E. Will increased the number of social science courses from two to eight.[39] KSAC students read Ely's analysis of socialism, traveled to Topeka for independent "economic investigations," and researched the management of local utilities.[40] Yet some KSAC students were unenthusiastic about the college's new emphasis. Weekly chapel lectures on economic topics were discontinued due to low attendance. When the college revised these lectures and tested students on their content, someone protested by submitting cartoons.[41] Another student wrote "The Student's Burden," a parody of Rudyard Kipling's "The White Man's Burden."[42]

> . . . Pile on the student's burden, give him plenty and to spare;
> More studies make no difference, he's got to have his share.
> Political economy is sure salvation here,
> An extra year of "Finance" he surely need not fear . . .

Undaunted by these mixed reactions, Populist leaders remained passionate about promoting their theories of political economy from the pulpits of state colleges and universities.

Populism and Academic Freedom

When combined with the movement's skepticism toward scholarly expertise, this passion for social science encouraged Populists to discriminate against conservative professors. Although most Populist allies within the professorate were committed to emerging principles of academic freedom, the movement as a whole continued to express more traditional views about the relationship between scholars and society. Akin to the religious litmus tests administered by most colleges prior to the twentieth century, Populists sometimes demanded that scholars behave like apostles of the movement. They also encouraged partisan research and fire-breathing oratory rather than the appeals to objectivity and neutrality that were becoming standard among mainstream professors.[43] While the new school of social scientists employed moderate rhetoric, they also questioned the ideal of disinterested scholarship because they believed that personal values provided crucial sparks for academic inquiry.[44]

Occupying positions somewhere between the extremists of their own movement and the more temperate approach of these progressive social scientists, academic Populists struggled to reconcile their politics with their support for embryonic ideals of scholarly professionalism. While some denied the existence of a conflict between Populism and academic norms, others suggested that political partisanship invariably corrupted attempts to define academic freedom as a privilege granted only to neutral scholars.

Imported from Germany, the ideal of academic freedom remained fragile and ill defined in American universities during the Gilded Age, when supporters of all political parties perpetuated nepotism, patronage, and partisanship. At KSAC, for example, a Democratic governing board hired a professor in 1883 who was the brother of one regent and another professor who had allied himself with a different regent during a campaign for public office. KU Chancellor Francis Huntington Snow felt that party boss Cy Leland expected that the university would function as "part of the Republican machine." In 1889, an applicant for the presidency of NCCAMA felt that it was necessary to confide that he was a Democrat.[45] In addition to these hiring practices, administrators also restrained scholarly independence because they feared alienating political and financial supporters. Presidents and trustees threatened or dismissed professors who espoused controversial policies, such as government ownership of utilities or public protection of labor unions. Cautioned by this wave of repression, most social scientists at the turn of the century sought to distance themselves from socialism by gravitating away from partisan causes and toward the study of apolitical technical questions.[46]

Although Populists were only one of many threats to academic autonomy during the late nineteenth century, the movement appeared to be the prime example. Some Populists were even skeptical of professors just because they hailed from distant regions. Noting that only 10 percent of NU faculty members had been educated in the state, the *Nebraska Independent* urged the employment of "western workers" rather than "eastern dudes." According to the *Lawrence Journal*, Populists pressured the University of Missouri to employ natives of the state "who cultivate hair and beards and tobacco."[47] Populists were also sometimes intolerant of dissenting religious beliefs. In 1897, University of Washington President William Edwards resigned after two Populist regents questioned his faith.[48] The Populist *Jeffersonian* attacked the chancellor of KU for lecturing about the "blasphemous hogwash" of Darwinian evolution, while William Jennings Bryan eventually persuaded Oklahoma and South Carolina to outlaw paying salaries to professors who taught that subject.[49]

Controversies within the field of political economy most frequently revealed Populists' tendency to prioritize movement orthodoxy over academic freedom. In Missouri, a coalition of pro-silver Democrats and Populists hounded a new chair of history and political economy because he opposed bimetallism. University of Missouri President Richard Jesse supported the professor in spite of pressure from Populist legislators, the state's pro-silver governor, and the board of regents.[50] In 1892, a North Dakota court thwarted the efforts of a Populist governor to remove conservative members of the board of regents of the state agricultural college.[51] Reformers also lobbied against hiring a "gold bug" as president of the Colorado State Agricultural College.[52] Between 1900 and 1904, Nebraska Populists brazenly urged the fusionist majority on the NU board of regents to hire professors whose views were in "sympathy with the toiling masses." The *Nebraska Independent* criticized the fusionist governing board for supporting Professor Roscoe Pound's appointment as dean of the College of Law because Pound was a Republican and a Hamiltonian. Aside from hiring E. Benjamin Andrews as chancellor, the *Independent* believed that the board had not fulfilled its mandate and called for the election of a new slate of regents.[53]

The takeover of KSAC was the most rancorous and most publicized episode of Populist intervention. Soon after Populists assumed control in 1892, KSAC's Manhattan campus hosted controversial Populist leaders such as Mary Elizabeth Lease (who famously exhorted Kansas farmers to raise less corn and more hell). Populists also transferred responsibility for the college's two social science courses from conservative President George Fairchild to Thomas E. Will. Will revamped Fairchild's syllabi and offered new courses as well. In 1893 and 1894, KSAC sponsored weekly chapel lectures on economic subjects such as "Hard Times: Their Cause and Cure." Although it resolved that these lectures would be "fairly stated and candidly examined," the board forbade faculty speakers from ignoring or "unfairly treat[ing] the position taken by what is commonly known as the new school of political economists." Under Will's leadership, KSAC's official newspaper became an unabashed advocate for Populist economic reforms. Whereas the *Industrialist* had focused on college news and agricultural techniques since first appearing in 1875, it began publishing articles such as "Outlines of the Financial History of the United States" and "Purposes of Government."[54]

During the spring and summer of 1897, KSAC's fusionist board accelerated the college's transformation. In April, the regents informed all twenty-three professors that their contracts would expire at the end of June (replacing the customary twelve-month contract ending in September). During their July meeting, the regents offered new contracts to eighteen professors, in effect firing five members of the faculty. When President Fairchild resigned in protest, the regents replaced him with Thomas E. Will.[55] Four other professors declined to remain, leaving KSAC with fourteen of its former faculty at the start of the fall term.[56] All of the fired professors were Republicans, and at least one had been vocal about his belief that the majority of unemployed workers were to blame for their condition.[57] In a private letter, President Will revealed that KSAC sought to hire new professors possessing "liberal views." The *Kansas Commoner* applauded the eventual recruitment of Edward Bemis not only because of his intellect, but also because his "heart" seemed to have the proper sympathy for the masses.[58]

Prior to the institutionalization of tenure in the twentieth century, it was not unheard of for new administrators to dismiss professors who they judged to be underperforming. For example, Charles Dabney retained the services of only two out of ten faculty members after taking charge of the University of Tennessee in 1888.[59]

Yet criticism of the more politicized dismissals at KSAC was swift and emphatic. Comparing Populism to barbarism, *The Washington Post* reported that the movement descended on KSAC "with a ruthless proscription never before witnessed, and to an extent that either of the old parties would have found incompatible with its sense of decency."[60] Professor J. T. Willard observed that Thomas E. Will became the target of "the greatest load of contempt of anyone that ever lived in [Manhattan, Kansas]."[61] The *Manhattan Nationalist* announced, "Of all the idiotic things done under the name of Populism, the wholesale deposition of professors at the State Agricultural College at Manhattan takes the cake." The *Topeka Capital* concluded that the Populist takeover of KSAC was a "freak of partisan imbecility."[62] Inspired by these accounts, one modern author even compared the KSAC takeover with the atrocities of Hitler and Stalin.[63]

Altogether, these episodes appear to confirm the conventional wisdom about Populist disrespect for intellectualism and academic freedom. However, the attitudes of academic Populists were more complex. Academic Populists attempted to balance their ideological fervor with a degree of respect for emerging methodological and professional norms.

Populist governing boards exhibited some appreciation for academic qualifications by hiring faculty whose credentials were superior to the professors they supplanted. In Virginia, a critic of the protopopulist readjusters acknowledged that the movement replaced faculty at the state A&M college with highly qualified professors.[64] In Washington State, Populist Governor John R. Rogers removed three regents from the board of the state university because they had promoted a registrar to be the chair of American history even though he lacked a degree in the field.[65]

Kansas Populists were similarly upset when KU hired a Latin professor who had no college teaching experience. The Lawrence *Jeffersonian* complained that "scarcely a new man of note" had been hired at KU during the 1890s and urged Chancellor Snow to fire several "mediocre" professors and recruit scholars with higher profiles.[66] During their takeover of KSAC, Kansas Populists also accused the college's previous administration of having a "tendency in the past to swamp the faculty with half-educated men." A local Democratic newspaper agreed that the college employed "too many drones and inexperienced people."[67] Even Professor Julius T. Willard, a political foe of the Populists, conceded that most of the Populists' victims were either ineffective or disliked by students. Willard confided that the dismissed professor of agriculture lacked tact as well as practical experience in the field. Willard accused another former colleague of suffering from a "super-abundant egotism" and reported that the ex-professor of physiology had been especially unpopular among female students because of his "inconsiderate manners" in the classroom.[68] The recollections of two KSAC alums corroborate Willard's claim that students considered the dismissed professors to have been poorly qualified for their positions.[69]

Although political rivals claimed that the Populists valued "whiskers and loud-smelling feet" more than intellect, KSAC's regents hired professors with outstanding credentials.[70] President Will and the board of regents resisted some pressure for patronage appointments and sought candidates with degrees from "the best universities of America and Europe."[71] Whereas KSAC had previously employed only one professor with a PhD, the fusionist board added four faculty members with this degree between 1897 and 1898, including Mary Winston in math (Göttingen), Edward Bemis in sociology (Johns Hopkins), and D. J. H. Ward in English (Leipzig).[72] President Will celebrated that many of KSAC's new hires possessed "national reputation." The Riley County Populist convention also praised the new professors for raising the college to a "higher place among the educational institutions of the world." KSAC's student publication scolded "hare-brained partisan editors" of local newspapers for predicting that the fusionist board would ruin the college's reputation.[73] Even a graduate who initially opposed firing any of his former professors recognized the superior credentials of their replacements.[74] As the hiring process proceeded, Professor Willard also acknowledged that the Populists intended to hire "energetic, growing and generally young" scholars.[75]

Ironically, former President Fairchild criticized these staffing decisions by arguing that the fusionist governing board had been too easily impressed with "high-sounding degrees from eastern universities." Yet when Republicans retook control of the board of regents in 1899, they did not reinstate President Fairchild or any of the five professors who had been fired. Carl Vrooman, the one Populist regent remaining in 1899, even introduced a motion to rehire Fairchild because he was so confident that his Republicans would bury the motion in a committee and thereby prove that they no longer believed in his leadership.[76]

In addition to displaying a measure of respect for academic qualifications, academic Populists tolerated some professors who held conservative economic views. This tolerance may have reflected the movement's self-flattering perception that it was a "nonpartisan" reaction against the corruption of Democrats and Republicans alike.[77] While Populist politicians ultimately behaved much as their counterparts in other parties, the movement did develop a surprisingly strong track record of retaining conservative faculty members. Although he was a Populist sympathizer, University of South Dakota President Garrett Droppers (1899–1906) did not oversee any dramatic change in the school's faculty.[78] Contrary to the charges of their political opponents, the fusionists who ran NCCAMA between 1897 and 1899 also made few personnel moves. The board of trustees fired professor of agriculture Benjamin Irby because he lacked technical training, and they fired a professor of mathematics who was then promptly rehired. When Democrats regained control of NCCAMA after the election of 1898, their new trustees conducted a comprehensive investigation and found that no serious violations of academic freedom had occurred.[79]

In Kansas, opposition newspapers exaggerated reports of Populist intolerance at KSAC. Twelve of the fourteen professors who were offered contract renewals in 1897 were Republicans, and none were asked to describe their political beliefs. Even C. B. Daughters, one of two remaining Republican regents and a vocal opponent of Populism, acknowledged that no professor had been compelled to swear allegiance to the movement. Professor Willard confirmed that none of the rehired professors "demeaned himself in the slightest degree before the board." Willard reported that the regents only asked whether the faculty would cooperate with the new administration and "took pains to say that they didn't care anything what our political views were." According to Willard, four professors (himself included) were rehired even after they criticized the promotion of Thomas E. Will to the presidency.[80] In addition to these retained faculty members, many of the new additions to KSAC were also Republicans. The regents also hired Professor Bemis, even though he stated pointedly during his interview that he did not support silver coinage. Bemis later confided to his mentor Richard T. Ely that he had originally doubted the regents' commitment to academic freedom, but later concluded that they were sincere.[81]

According to most accounts, faculty and students felt free to express dissenting opinions at KSAC during its fusionist era. Even deposed President George Fairchild recognized that the fusionist board did not meddle with faculty instruction.[82] In response to charges of censorship leveled by Republican newspapers, KSAC students came to the defense of their professors. Several members of the junior class wrote a letter praising Frank Parsons for allowing "unfettered expression of individual opinion in class," modeling "unbiased and impartial method," and employing progressive pedagogy that encouraged student investigation rather than passive absorption. Professor Willard agreed that Parsons had been "nonpartisan," though he believed that part of Parsons's popularity resulted from lenient grading and off-color jokes.[83]

After Republicans won the election of 1898 and retook control of the board of regents, KSAC's student body called a mass meeting and passed a resolution in support of the Will administration by a margin of 396 to 24. The students asked the new regents to refrain from making "sweeping changes" in the college's faculty or course of study.[84] The junior class passed a separate resolution endorsing Professor Parsons, in particular, and requesting that the regents retain his services. Parsons believed that students rallied to the side of their professors because they had come to "love their liberty" after having experienced "free discussion and breadth of thought which deals with all sides of every question."[85] While one student complained that his sociology lectures were "regular anarchist speeches," Edward Bemis also believed that he had been an open-minded and even-handed instructor. Bemis reported that the Republican regents who terminated his contract "almost went out of their way in my praise" and admitted that they did not have "a particle of evidence that I had been guilty of partisanship." Bemis claimed that the regents confided that they felt compelled to fire both himself and Parsons because of external political pressure.[86]

To critics who noted that Bemis, Parsons, and other scholars favored by the movement all endorsed increased government intervention in the economy, Populists self-servingly responded that these doctrines were validated by rigorous research. Along with socialist intellectuals, academic Populists believed that civilized societies evolved toward increasingly complex and interrelated (regulated) organisms.[87] For example, a "Populist educator" confidently told a Kansas newspaper that these principles were found to be "scientifically correct" whenever they were subjected to fair examination.[88] After their victory in the election of 1896, Nebraska Populists pledged to continue funding the state university on the condition that "the sciences shall be taught there as expounded by the standard authorities." The party was certain that instruction in "long established and well settled principles of political economy" would counteract "the modern worship of money and mammon."[89] Similarly, the *Lincoln Independent* declared that Populists were "willing to pay generous salaries to the men who will teach science" instead of "sophistries and theories exploded and discarded by all scientists fifty years ago."[90] Thomas E. Will described the dismissals of new economists as attacks on "science" rather than on ideology.[91] Frank Parsons illustrated this perspective while responding to criticism of a speech he gave at a farmers' institute. Parsons claimed that he impartially analyzed the "the facts of history," and concluded that if these facts "seem to lend aid to some Populist ideas, I cannot help that."[92]

Yet because academic Populists rarely publicized opposing points of view, this endorsement of neutral investigation does not ring true. Indeed, Populists occasionally hinted at another definition of academic freedom, one that emphasized the right to express partisan ideas rather than the duty to remain politically neutral.

Populists had good reason to doubt the sincerity of the conventional logic of academic freedom, which held that the privilege depended on a scholar's political neutrality. Although university presidents and governing boards increasingly frowned on overt censorship, they still defended their power to oversee the manner in which ideas were expressed. University presidents argued that intemperate presentations of scholarly theories constituted evidence of poor judgment or even immoral character—neither of which were protected by the norms of academic freedom. The inevitable overlap between content and expression provided ample opportunity for the suppression of controversial ideas. Moreover, during this era when the value of dissent and the free exchange of ideas had yet to become enshrined within American higher education, administrators had few incentives to protect controversial professors.

For example, although University of Chicago President William Rainey Harper endorsed the principle of academic freedom, he maintained that firing a "partisan" professor would not violate this ideal. Even the landmark "General Report of the Committee on Academic Freedom and Academic Tenure" (1915) produced by the American Association of University Professors (AAUP) still agreed that it was appropriate to dismiss professors who expressed ideas in an intemperate fashion. Harper and other university leaders tended to define academic freedom as *freedom from* partisan loyalties rather than *freedom to* follow research wherever it might lead. Academic freedom hinged on professors' abilities to appear autonomous of controversial political movements, rather than on administrators' abilities to tolerate controversial views.[93]

Pleas for nonpartisanship or neutrality seemed hollow to Populists when most courses in political economy had boldly promoted orthodox theories of laissez-faire, even in states such as Nebraska and Kansas. Prior to the Populist electoral victories, Republican stewardship of NU had become so entrenched that the party floated the idea of assessing a 2 percent tax on all professors for "campaign purposes." Populist and fusionist reporters also believed that Republican Party operatives extorted campaign contributions from professors who were concerned about their job security and paid the train fare of Republican students traveling home to their polling places.[94] In 1897, Populist suspicions of Republican bias at NU appeared to be confirmed by the dismissal of

Henry K. Wolfe, a professor of psychology and the son of the chair of the Nebraska People's Independent Party.[95] After Populists won a majority on the NU board of regents, these memories prompted one supporter to make the dubious argument that a wholesale purge of NU faculty might not be "wholly ethical," but would still be justified by the treatment of radical professors during the previous decades of Republican administration.[96]

In Kansas, a few legislators proposed banning the allocation of state funds to pay John Hulme Canfield's salary when he was a KU professor because he expressed sympathy for the Farmers' Alliance. After Canfield emerged as a possible candidate for chancellor of KU in 1889, Republican newspapers suggested that his stance on tariff policies should disqualify him. One Populist accused the railroads of influencing the appointment of KU regents who, in return, invited a company lawyer to lecture students in the law department.[97]

According to a KSAC regent, the college's lone Populist professor had endured "sneers and jeers" from the other faculty members before the fusionist takeover of 1893. Another regent agreed that Populists and children from Populist families had been "hooted at and subjected to ridicule."[98] Thomas E. Will claimed that conservative KSAC faculty members criticized his speeches and speeches by several Populist regents for being too "political," even as they applauded a Republican regent for attacking William Jennings Bryan at the McKinley Club of Manhattan. Across the nation, university presidents campaigned for McKinley in 1896, while hypocritically questioning whether it was appropriate for a professor to publicly support Bryan.[99] As in Nebraska, rumors circulated that the former KSAC president and Republican Party operatives had paid rail fare for Republican students to ride home and vote.[100]

Populists had been particularly alarmed by the University of Chicago's dismissal of Edward Bemis. Although President Harper claimed that he fired Bemis in 1895 because of his poor teaching and lack of scholarly achievement, Populists believed that chief donor John D. Rockefeller forced Harper's hand because he opposed Bemis's sympathy for organized labor. The *Wealth Makers of the World* asserted that the Bemis case proved that privately endowed universities "are not and cannot be free."[101] The *Caucasian*, published by the Populist Marion Butler, reported that Bemis's scalp "dangle[d] at the belt of monopoly," while the *Plowboy* accused conservative economists of being "hired prostitutes."[102] Five years later, Nebraska Populists objected to Rockefeller's offer to donate a large portion of the construction cost for a student commons and religious center at NU. One newspaper derided Rockefeller's interest in laying "his foul hands upon Nebraska State University." William Jennings Bryan agreed that

"Rockefeller's money smells too much of oil to allow him to put a building on our campus."[103]

Similarly, the passions of North Carolina Populists were aroused by a large gift from the Duke family (owners of the American Tobacco Trust) to Trinity College (precursor to Duke University). Trustee and Populist sympathizer Judge Walter Clark denounced the contribution as akin to "the attempts of Northern multi-millionaires to capture by gifts and endowments the control of the education of the children of the people." When the Trinity board asked for Clark's resignation, the Populist press seized on the conflict as evidence of corporate corruption. The *Caucasian* predicted that Trinity would join the University of Chicago in the ranks of schools that forbid teaching "any system of economics that declares the positive popular injustice of the legislation whereby the donor has gathered his millions." While acknowledging that no North Carolina professors had been fired for their economic views, the paper editorialized that the Clark incident revealed a disconcerting "spirit" of censorship.[104]

Prompted by their marginalization within colleges and universities, Populists sometimes defined academic freedom as a right to advocate for controversial causes. The scholars most admired by Populists defined "objectivity" not as nonpartisanship, but as willingness to reject preexisting theories in response to new evidence. In this sense, many of the Populists who discussed academic freedom conformed to Antonio Gramsci's characterization of "organic" intellectuals—those who identified openly with a social group and rejected the possibility of neutral scholarship.[105] Some academic Populists gravitated toward this stance because they suspected that they might always seem controversial. One KSAC regent was emboldened by his belief that the new Populist administration would be accused of partisanship regardless of its actions. While recruiting Edward Bemis, President Will cautioned him against worrying about the appearance of political bias because many Republicans would automatically consider him to be a "pop" if he expressed any ideas that challenged business leaders.[106]

Whereas he had originally claimed to be politically unaffiliated, Will eventually asserted that KSAC's brief war against the trusts had been "conducted absolutely in the open, and with our flag flying." In retrospect, Will felt that it was appropriate for institutions of higher education to use "propaganda, literary and oral" in order to discourage students from becoming "servants and serfs for the multiplication of the wealth of the wealthy."[107] Written almost fifteen years after Will was fired from KSAC, these words characterize his feelings about the nature of academic freedom more forthrightly than his earlier declarations of nonpartisanship.

Academic Populists also argued that public institutions of higher education had a special duty to protect controversial scholarship. KSAC's Populist regents stated that the college should insulate scholars from being pressured by wealthy donors into "prostituting their science to the service of their masters."[108] Concerned that many colleges had been "muzzled," President Will was eager to offer Bemis a job after his dismissal from Chicago.[109] In a similar spirit, Nebraska Populists exalted that an independent state university could become "the grandest institution for original research, freedom of thought, and energizing power to lift mankind on the face of the earth."[110] Possessing little faith in conventional standards of academic freedom, some Populists argued that professors in a nonpartisan public institution should still be permitted to express controversial ideas that were associated with political parties.[111]

Conclusion

In 1899, as a new Republican governing board decided their fates, Thomas E. Will, Edward Bemis, and Frank Parsons attended a "National Social and Political Conference" in Buffalo, New York. The conference exposed the extent of disagreement about the nature of academic freedom, even among a self-selected community of radical scholars. While Bemis and John Commons emphasized the need to insulate researchers from political pressure, Will was more interested in publicizing partisan economic theories. Conference participants agreed to divide their efforts into a social science research bureau and a propagandistic correspondence school.[112] When the correspondence school failed to materialize, Will joined the faculty of Ruskin College, a short-lived institution in Missouri. Over time, Will grew increasingly comfortable with the idea of a college controlled by "the people's friends" and explicitly devoted to radical politics.[113]

Will and other academic Populist were so passionate about the potential of social science and so confident about their relationship with the so-called masses that they often ignored the likelihood that free expression of conservative as well as radical theories could serve the greater good. These Populists occasionally sought to reconcile partisan loyalty and academic freedom by stating that conservative professors did not deserve protection because they had been corrupted by the power of entrenched wealth. This convenient rationalization led some Populists to dismiss the ideal of scholarly neutrality at the very moment that it was securing modern institutional protection for the first time.

Indeed, although it did not mention Populism by name, the AAUP's watershed report on academic freedom appeared to single out the movement. Most of the report's authors had lived through the era of peak Populist strength, and Professor Roscoe Pound had personally faced attacks at NU during its period of Populist control. After discussing the threats posed by conservative business interests, the report noted the special vulnerability of professors at state universities. "Where there is a definite government policy or a strong public feeling on economic, social, or political questions," the committee stated, "the menace to academic freedom may consist in the repression of opinions that in the particular political situation are deemed ultra-conservative rather than ultra-radical." The report urged university administrators to "check the more hasty and unconsidered impulses of popular feeling."[114]

The AAUP sensibly concluded that neither Populists nor conservatives monopolized academic intolerance during the Gilded Age. While the Populists highlighted the fragile nature of academic freedom in ideologically charged environments, the flip side of this analysis also warrants attention—the behavior of academic Populists did not differ dramatically from the actions of more conventional university leaders. Academic Populists were neither as tolerant as they claimed to be nor as wildly out of step with Gilded Age norms as their critics charged. This similarity may reflect the fact that many academic Populists had attended mainstream institutions (as well as the fact that the conventional standards for academic freedom were so flimsy). Still, the episodes of Populist rule were more complex than stereotypical equations of Populism and intolerance would suggest.

Despite the movement's distrust of professorial autonomy, Populist interventions amount to more than cautionary tales about the impact of popular pressure on higher education. Some academic Populists mounted a precocious defense of the right of professors to advocate for controversial ideas. In contrast, even the AAUP initially argued that professors would be protected only if they somehow managed to discuss controversial issues without causing scandal. In this respect, the position of many academic Populists foreshadowed subsequent revisions to the AAUP's statement, which eventually concluded that neutrality or political "balance" should not be required as long as faculty met professional expectations regarding evidence, logic, and presentation.[115]

Conceptualizing Populist interventions in higher education as part of an ongoing debate over scholarly neutrality also reveals the remarkable degree to which elements of this anti-elitist movement still believed in the power of advanced scholarship. In addition to asserting that higher education could improve the status of laborers and farmers, academic Populists also hoped that experts could devise social policies that might end financial depressions and expand economic opportunity. As discussed in the next and final chapter, the willingness of Populist legislatures to allocate public resources to colleges and universities indicates the sincerity of these aspirations.

7

Watchdogs of the Treasury

Populism and Public Funding
for Higher Education

In 1887, President Samuel S. Laws of the University of Missouri learned
of the demise of "Emperor," the second largest elephant in captivity.
Convinced that the circus elephant could become the centerpiece for a university museum, Laws paid to have Emperor's skeleton prepared and shipped
to the university. The Missouri legislature, however, was less enthusiastic
about taxidermy and rejected Laws's request for reimbursement. After the
university's board of trustees nevertheless purchased the elephant for $1,100, a
joint committee of the state legislature concluded: "However good the bargain
in this elephant trade, it was made in direct contravention of the expressed will
of the last general assembly. If the people of Missouri don't want elephants
they have a right to say so, and [university administrators] have no right to
force elephants on them at any price."[1] The elephant attracted public ridicule
and served as the focal point of a legislative investigation into university
management that culminated in the resignation of President Laws.

Albeit an extreme example, this incident illustrates widespread suspicions
about the management of state university funds. Having campaigned on
platforms of fiscal responsibility, Populist politicians scrutinized public expenditures for higher education with special intensity. The supporters of a Populist
regent of the University of Nebraska even expressed concern about whether
the director of the school of music should be paid to play the piano at chapel
services because it was a job "which any one of one hundred girls could and
would do well and gladly and freely."[2] In Washington State, Populist Governor

John R. Rogers investigated if the state agricultural college was paying too much for coal.[3]

These episodes support the conventional wisdom that Populists epitomized agrarian prejudice against funding public institutions of higher education.[4] Traditionally, farmers were skeptical about government officials, who they suspected of funding unnecessary projects and bloating their salaries with tax revenues squeezed from the nation's producing classes. Indeed, some Populists opposed funding state colleges and universities altogether. Other Populists demanded that professors accept salary cuts in order to balance budgets during hard times or to align their pay more closely with the average income of state residents. This stance toward faculty compensation may have disproportionately colored scholarly perspectives on the Populists, casting a shadow over the movement's support for public higher education as a whole. And to be sure, it is easy to find examples of Populist criticism of university budgets—especially during years when the movement remained outside the halls of government.

However, when the movement won elections and gained power over state universities, many Populist politicians acted as if they could please their constituents by aligning themselves with the classic mission of public higher education. Movement leaders often agreed with the common assertion that westerners and southerners deserved state universities that were equal to the quality of elite eastern private institutions. Other Populists understood that increasing college access required corresponding increases in university budgets. Populist legislators were most likely to look kindly on appropriations that included funds for the physical plant, especially new buildings for the sciences or vocational studies. Historians of universities that came under the movement's control have routinely noted that Populists ultimately adopted a surprisingly "friendly view" of state funding.[5]

Perhaps because Populist support for higher education can seem counterintuitive, historians have not yet appreciated this overall pattern. Some skeptical scholars have attributed these appropriations to the willingness of politicians to ignore the wishes of their constituents. Indeed, American Populism drifted away from its radical grassroots as the movement engaged in electoral politics over the course of the 1890s.[6] Other historians have associated Populists with supporters of private denominational colleges, who invoked similar anti-elitist arguments while attacking appropriations to public institutions of higher education. As the preceding chapters have discussed, however, academic Populists believed that state universities could address their concerns by increasing access, providing vocationally oriented training, and offering courses in progressive political economy. Wherever the movement gained the opportunity to implement these policies, Populists supported public funding for higher education.

Populist Challenges to Public Funding

Public funding for higher education had been contested throughout the nineteenth century. Americans did not even universally support allocating tax revenues to support public high schools. In Kalamazoo, Michigan, public officials were compelled to defend the legality of secondary school appropriations in 1874. The Knights of Labor opposed public funding for high schools, for example, because they believed that these institutions did not benefit workers. The Supreme Court of North Carolina ruled in 1886 that education was not "a necessary expense" that could justify exceeding constitutional limits on taxation. On the basis of this ruling, North Carolina courts overturned several efforts to establish state funding for education, leaving support of common schools entirely in local hands until 1908.[7] Because they served relatively few students, state colleges faced greater opposition to their public funding than common schools or high schools. Citizens had challenged public spending on state colleges since the era of the early republic. As late as 1874, a U.S. representative proposed revising the Morrill Act in order to transfer the proceeds of its federal land grants away from colleges toward common schools and normal schools.[8]

Yet state university presidents in the late nineteenth century hoped that opposition to public funding for higher education had finally subsided. In 1898, University of Wisconsin President Charles Kendall Adams announced that American voters believed that "the welfare of the commonwealth demands the higher education of the few quite as much as the elementary education of the many." That same year, University of Illinois President Andrew S. Draper told the National Education Association that he was confident that any state legislator proposing to abolish funding for state universities "would start as much fun as a motion to annul the constitution and go back to a nomadic life."[9]

However, these proclamations of victory were premature. Most state legislatures did not commit to steady and substantial funding for universities until the 1910s. In North Carolina, where six separate constitutional conventions had affirmed the appropriateness of public funding for higher education, the University of North Carolina (UNC) still faced challenges to the legitimacy of its appropriations.[10] An 1887 proposal to end the university's funding was hotly debated by the legislature, where it was defeated by a disconcertingly close vote of sixty-two to thirty-eight. Ten years later, high school debate teams in North

Carolina still reenacted disputes over whether the appropriation to the state university should be preserved or abolished.[11]

In private, state university presidents were more candid about the vulnerability of their funding. When Edwin Alderman left the presidency of UNC to become president of Tulane, he confessed that he had become "very sick of the legislature." Years later, when mulling whether to become president of the University of Virginia, Alderman worried that he would once again be forced "to make bricks without straw."[12] University of Nebraska (NU) Chancellor James Hulme Canfield confided that each lobbying trip to the state capitol building consisted of "a sickening round of explanation and argument and concession."[13] In the Nebraska legislature, Populist representative William "Crookneck" Taylor built a political career on his opposition to NU funding. While representing Custer County, Taylor served as a self-appointed "watchdog of the treasury" and attacked proposals to give NU a permanent tax levy.[14]

Public colleges and universities in other states, such as Kentucky, Missouri, and New Jersey, also faced challenges to their use of tax revenue.[15] Leaders of denominational colleges were at the forefront of many of these campaigns, and they often framed their arguments in populistic as well as religious terms. Because of the longstanding association between secularism and elitism in American culture, egalitarian and spiritual critiques of state universities overlapped. Though influential donors would eventually quiet this impulse, leaders of denominational colleges often criticized the spirit of industrial "mammonism." Kentucky church leaders, for example, claimed that the state college only benefited the corrupt "aristocracy of Lexington." The issue of state support of universities became so delicate that an 1887 National Education Association panel tiptoed around the question. An audience member finally commented that she was "ashamed" of the experts because they "ought not to dodge such a question."[16]

Although many Populist legislators would ultimately support appropriations for public universities, the movement tended to scrutinize state expenditures. The second plank of the 1890 platform of the National Farmers' Alliance and Industrial Union opposed the use of tax revenues to "build up one class at the expense of another." More succinctly, the Kansas People's Party platform stated that government should serve all citizens "equally and alike."[17] Populists also tapped into longstanding popular perceptions that political elites were inclined to endorse expensive pet projects.[18] During the financial depression of the 1890s, Populist spokespeople argued that states faced a moral imperative to cut taxes and curtail spending on nonessential projects, just like ordinary households in hard times.[19] The North Carolina Farmers' Alliance agreed that money should be keep "in the hands of the people" whenever possible.[20] One Georgia Populist elected to the state legislature regarded all appropriations bills like a "hawk eye[ing] a chicken."[21]

Despite this orientation toward state budgets, Populists did not need to be cajoled into spending tax revenues on common schools, whose service to the masses was self-evident. Farmers' Alliances and state People's Parties routinely endorsed school board candidates who pledged to strengthen primary-level education. In 1891, a state legislature dominated by members of the North Carolina Farmers' Alliance approved a 25 percent increase in school taxes (the state supreme court invalidated the bill). In 1892, the Populist Party of North Carolina became the first party in the state to demand that all common schools stay open for four months, as required by the state constitution. A Populist-controlled legislature of 1895 also tried to raise school taxes and lengthen the school year but was once again overruled by the state judiciary. In 1899, a Populist state superintendent of public education proposed new inheritance taxes and taxes on corporate earnings for the purpose of funding North Carolina's common schools.[22] The Populist Party of Washington State supported a "barefoot schoolboy law," which instituted a state tax for public schooling in order to equalize funding between wealthy urban districts and poor rural districts. Populists also advocated for the distribution of free textbooks at state expense, as well as for cutting-edge policies such as free lunches, playgrounds, school-based health care, and regional high schools.[23]

At first glance, state colleges and universities did not seem to fare as well at the hands of Populist politicians. Many Populists were so committed to improving common schools that they opposed diverting any funds to higher education. In South Carolina, where nearly 40 percent of the white population was illiterate, many greenbackers and agrarian leaders regarded expenditures on state colleges as unjustifiable extravagances.[24] Similarly, a Kansas Populist in the state legislature was unwilling to vote for a university appropriation bill until every child had access to a thorough common school education.[25] After vetoing appropriations to two state normal schools, Washington's Populist Governor John R. Rogers proclaimed that the state's education system was "top heavy" because most common schools were open for only a few months a year.[26]

In Mississippi, "wool hat" Frank Burkitt waged a long campaign to persuade the legislature to redirect college appropriations toward common schools. Born in 1843, Burkitt had attended one year of an upper-level academy before the Civil War and "finished his college course in the saddle." Active in the Mississippi Farmers' Alliance and editor of the *People's Messenger*, Burkitt served in the state legislature, where he also earned the nickname "watchdog of the treasury." In

1886, Burkitt, who had been one of the first trustees of Mississippi A&M, argued that the school was an incredible expense for the sake of twenty-seven graduates. He expressed outrage that Mississippi A&M's yearly per-pupil expenditure was $100, "when the poor boy who helps his father make a crop cannot from all sources find more than three dollars to pay his tuition in the common schools during the winter months." Burkitt also charged that it was "exceedingly unjust" to pay college professors ten times the salary of common school teachers. He concluded that the college contributed to the "building up of a privileged class at the expense of the working people of the country." As chair of the legislature's appropriations committee, Burkitt attempted to cut the college's state appropriation. As the Populist nominee for governor of Mississippi in 1894, Burkitt proposed ending all tuition subsidies for public higher education unless the state could find another means of increasing funding for common schools.[27]

In Georgia, the Farmers' Alliance was riled by similar comparisons of yearly per-pupil spending at the state university ($170) and at Georgia common schools ($1.95). The alliance recommended focusing all state education appropriations on the common schools.[28] Threatened by the growth of the University of Georgia, President Warren Candler of Emory College also built his opposition to public higher education on these Populist arguments. The movement appeared to be a natural ally to the Methodist college because many Populists infused their political rhetoric with biblical allusions, millennial fervor, and the spiritual equality of humankind. James K. Hines, chair of Emory's board of trustees during the 1890s, even converted to Populism while holding that office.[29] Though not a Populist himself, Candler courted the support of the Farmers' Alliance. He argued that the University of Georgia should charge tuition instead of providing free higher education to wealthy students. Candler predicted that state universities would "create a ruling class" and a "yawning chasm" between elites and laborers.[30]

While a majority of Populist legislators in North Carolina would eventually vote in favor of funding for public higher education, the movement also expressed some reluctance and, as in Georgia, denominational colleges sought to amplify these doubts. Referring to the campaign for public funding for a new state A&M college as a "fraud," a member of the Scotland Neck Farmers' Club asked his neighbors to oppose any tax increase earmarked for that purpose. After a period of intense debate, the club approved this antitax resolution by a vote of eleven to four.[31] The Farmers' Alliance of Randolph County agreed that common school funding should take priority, editorializing that "this blow and bluster we hear about 'higher education' is a snare and a cheat. We need a brawnier manliness everywhere, and in order to have this we must see to it that the foundation work is solid."[32]

Many Populists campaigned against state aid for UNC during the elections of 1894. A reader of the Populist Wadesboro *Plowboy* warned politicians that the people had "made up their minds to stop the appropriation to the University and other state institutions of learning for the rich and their pets."[33] Advocates of private denominational colleges marshaled these Populist arguments while challenging public higher education. North Carolina evangelicals and Populists shared a commitment to preserving mechanisms of "democratic localism" in the face of pressure toward centralized, expert leadership. Methodist and Baptist clergy were prominent among the leadership of North Carolina Populist organizations, which often convened their meetings at churches. For North Carolina evangelicals affiliated with private colleges, no organization was more representative of the rising power of secular bureaucracy than UNC.[34]

This overlap between Populists and evangelicals has clouded assessments of Populist support for higher education.[35] The ambivalence of North Carolina Populists may have resulted from their interest in wooing Baptist voters rather than from their own genuine concerns. Some leaders of the North Carolina fusion movement hoped to skirt the issue of UNC's appropriation in order to avoid alienating Baptists.[36] In South Carolina, Methodist attacks on the state university preceded the more infamous criticism lobbed by "Pitchfork" Ben Tillman. The state university's president believed that South Carolina's denominational leaders were the college's most potent enemy. South Carolina Methodists accused the state university of being a "luxury of the rich, provided by the taxation of the poor." By the end of 1885, South Carolina College replaced its tuition-free policy with a charge of forty dollars (with a limited number of scholarships available for poor students).[37]

While religious leaders had opposed state funding for UNC since the 1870s, the denominational campaign against public universities intensified during the mid-1890s when North Carolina Populism approached its peak period of influence. Targeting Populist anxieties, Wake Forest President Charles E. Taylor warned that UNC could establish an elitist "state monopoly in higher education" for a "fortunate minority" at taxpayer expense.[38] Trinity College president and Methodist Reverend John C. Kilgo also raised doubts about the democratic *bone fides* of the state university by claiming that UNC supporters never "stop and shake hands with a ragged country boy peddling eggs or kindling pine along the streets."[39] By the end of the year, North Carolina Methodists sought to end scholarships to UNC, while the state's Baptist leadership lobbied to eliminate state funding for higher education altogether. Furnifold

Simmons, boss of North Carolina's Democratic Party, recruited supporters of denominational colleges during the election of 1898 by promising that a Democratic legislature would not increase UNC's funding. After the Democratic victory, Simmons made good on his promise.[40] At UNC, President George Winston exclaimed that the state's religious denominations "roared and surged and threatened us."[41]

In Kansas and Nebraska, the Populist arguments against state appropriations were similar, though the involvement of church leaders was less intense.[42] In 1887, the *Cloud County Kansan* accused the University of Kansas (KU) of catering to "nabobs" who "learn a smattering of law and Latin, part their hair in the middle, wear tight pants and gain other emblems of greatness." The newspaper argued that university funding was unacceptable because poor rural farmers had to "crawl out of their dugouts and haul corn 40 miles and sell it for 15 cents a bushel to help foot the bill."[43] During legislative debate of 1897, KU students lamented that some Populist legislators continued to regard their school as "a hot bed of aristocracy," while others simply seemed to be "constitutionally ag'in book larnin', especially of an advanced sort." A Populist politician confided to Kansas State Agricultural College (KSAC) President George Fairchild that it was difficult to justify funding the school because it was already one of the wealthiest institutions in the state.[44]

A state representative explained his opposition to the construction of a library at the University of Nebraska by stating that he would rather give money to "the poor boy on the prairie" instead of to "the Latin and Greek professor in his warm room." Another Nebraska Populist complained that the general appropriation bill of 1893, which included funds for the completion of the university library, was "a robbery in every particular . . . calculated to deceive the great mass of the people." Populist legislators helped to defeat the library amendment by a vote of fifty-one to thirty-seven.[45]

Professors' salaries, as opposed to tuition subsidies or facilities, caused the greatest consternation among Populist politicians mulling how much funding to direct toward public higher education. During an era of volatile and declining farm incomes, Populists argued that all state employees should have to sacrifice a portion of their wages. Populist Governor John R. Rogers of Washington State called on the president and the faculty of the state agricultural college to accept salary reductions in 1897 in order to reduce the school's deficit. Arkansas Populists also compelled the president of the state university to accept a lower salary.[46] Salary cuts attracted Populists because they lowered taxes and harmonized with the movement's belief in the equal status of all forms of labor. A reader of the *Kansas Commoner*, for example, demanded a 25 percent cut in salaries for all public officials and private-sector professionals.[47] "Wool hat" Frank Burkitt of Mississippi asserted that the salaries of state officials "should correspond, to some extent at least, to the ordinary incomes of the people whose interests they are designed to subserve [*sic*]."[48]

While Populist salary cut legislation applied to all state officials, professors became especially attractive symbols of pampered public employment. Professors reasoned that their special training and accomplishments justified their relatively high salaries. When the Nebraska state legislature set a $2,000 ceiling on faculty salaries during the grasshopper plague of the 1870s, sociologist Edward A. Ross was "galled" because "the average merchant in a county-seat had a better living than scholars of national reputation."[49] In contrast, Populists were often skeptical about the special talents of scholars and tended to view teaching, rather than research, as the primary duty of college faculty. Downplaying the demands of research, Populists mocked the small number of hours that faculty spent in the classroom. Burkitt believed that many professors opposed Populist ideology because it would "force them to earn a living like honest educators."[50]

The Lawrence *Jeffersonian* conducted a similar campaign against the salaries of KU faculty members, especially Chancellor Francis H. Snow, the state's highest-paid official ($5,000 a year, plus housing and fuel). The newspaper asked if professors really deserved to earn five times the amount of the average farmer and noted incredulously that it would take 12,000 bushels of corn to pay the $2,000 annual salary of a KU professor.[51] Making matters more unjust in the eyes of Populists, professors clamored for even higher salaries, costly research trips, and additional assistants for their departments. Claiming that the professors were angling for frivolous "pin money," the *Jeffersonian* was offended that professors requested additional salary for teaching summer sessions. The newspaper also argued that funds spent hiring replacements for faculty sabbaticals amounted to "robbery of the taxpayers." "Such schemes as these are what disgust the farmers of Kansas," the newspaper editorialized, "they do not desire to be niggardly with their educational institutions, but they want value received." The *Jeffersonian* expressed satisfaction when the KU board of regents ended paid sabbaticals in 1896.[52]

Accusing Chancellor Snow of disrespecting "common people" and making "a great distinction between the man who earns his living by his muscle and the man who makes it by scheming," the newspaper also criticized the large gap between the salaries of faculty and other university laborers. While the KU maintenance workers were "underpaid and overworked," the university's "brain workers" were given light schedules, high pay, and long vacations. The Republican *Nationalist* newspaper objected to this Populist tendency of considering professors to be "on a par with the unskilled hedger or ditcher."[53] The Populists declared that manual labor was just as productive as scholarly labor, if not more so.

After statewide Populist victories in the election of 1896, university advocates scrambled to articulate a rationale for faculty salaries. The Republican *Lawrence Journal* argued that KU's standard salary of $2,000 was already much lower than the $3,000 rate at state universities in Iowa, Michigan, Illinois, and California. The newspaper claimed that several professors had already forsaken Kansas in order to earn more elsewhere. Chancellor Snow's salary of $5,000, similarly, seemed more than reasonable when compared to the $8,000 and $7,500 paid to the presidents of the University of California and the University of Illinois, respectively. Concerned that KU would lose its national reputation, the *Journal* warned that salary cuts would be "the death warrant of that institution." The Populist *Topeka Advocate* broke ranks with its Lawrence counterpart in order to express ambivalence about the salary controversy.[54]

Undaunted, the Populist-controlled legislature of 1897 ordered the reduction of all salaries at KU and KSAC. The bill cut a total of $8,000 from KU salaries, including a $1,000 reduction in Chancellor Snow's pay and cuts of $250 for each senior faculty member. Salaries at KSAC were reduced by roughly 10 percent across the board.[55] President Will sympathized with the reasoning behind the salary cuts. When informing Frank Parsons that KSAC could only pay him $1,450 to be the professor of history and political science, Will explained that the legislature had capped salaries "in wholesome fashion" because of "the general hard times and the callousness of many of the salaried classes toward the suffering of the people."[56] Ultimately, the salary bill of 1897 had little tangible effect because professors were unable to find more favorable jobs.[57] That same year, the Nebraska legislature also cut the salaries of most state officials, including university faculty. As in Kansas, Populists constituted the driving force behind this action, although party sentiment was not unanimous.[58]

The Populist Party did not monopolize these concerns about state funding for higher education. The Republican-controlled Iowa legislatures of the late 1880s and early 1890s routinely disappointed university advocates, perhaps because the school was located in a Catholic, Democratic county. An Iowa Republican, for example, attacked a university appropriation bill as "a grab at the state treasury for the education of doctors and lawyers."[59] Nevertheless, Populists voiced these criticisms most frequently and intensely across the nation. As a result, state university presidents and faculty braced for devastating funding cuts when Populist parties won majorities in state legislatures.

In January 1895, with Populist-Republican fusion gaining momentum, Professor Edwin Alderman was deeply concerned about the fate of UNC. Alderman believed that the university faced a situation of "grave danger," in which "a false step, an ill-considered word, an impolitic act" could cripple the institution. An ally responded to the specter of Populist rule by praying, "God save the state and the university."[60] When Populists won control of the Kansas legislature in 1897, the Republican *Lawrence Journal* also predicted that the Populists would sacrifice the state university "to the Moloch of reform." After witnessing the start of this legislative session, Chancellor Snow reported that he was staggered by the criticisms of higher education expressed in the hallways of the state capitol.[61]

Populist Support for Public Funding

More often than not, however, university advocates were pleasantly surprised by Populist stances toward public funding. With the exception of their scrutiny of faculty salaries, most state Farmers' Alliances endorsed university appropriations. Even in Mississippi, where "wool hat" Frank Burkitt had campaigned against public higher education, the alliance ultimately came to the defense of the state agricultural college. The alliance held its statewide convention on the college's campus during the early 1890s and complained that it received much less funding than the University of Mississippi.[62] The Farmers' Alliances of North Carolina, Kansas, Texas, Tennessee, and Georgia also eventually rallied behind their respective state institutions of higher education, especially land grant colleges.[63]

Although they did not control the state purse strings, fusionist governors in the Dakotas and Nebraska generally favored funding public colleges and universities.[64] Other reform governors also supported public university appropriations during the 1890s. Democratic Governor John P. Altgeld from Illinois was elected by a farmer-labor coalition and endorsed a tax increase earmarked for public higher education.[65] Donning a floppy hat and attacking wealthy urbanites, Missouri's quasi-populist Governor William "Gumshoe Bill" Stone advocated for a permanent stream of tax revenue for the University of Missouri.[66] In Texas, Governor James S. Hogg co-opted most of the state Farmers' Alliance platform and endorsed public funding for higher education.[67] Most dramatically, South Carolina Governor "Pitchfork" Ben Tillman, who had campaigned against the state university and eliminated twelve faculty positions, eventually defended the school's public funding, while also promoting the establishment of Clemson Agricultural College and a state college for white women.[68]

Kansas's two fusionist governors also advocated for public higher educa-tion. Orphaned as a young man, Lorenzo Lewelling worked his way through Whittier College and eventually served as president of the Iowa State Normal School. As governor (1893–95), he supported public higher education and planned to send his daughter to KU.[69] Governor John Leedy (1897–99), who moved his family to Lawrence instead of Topeka so that his daughter could live at home while attending KU, was a vocal spokesperson for the state university, agricultural college, and normal school. Proclaiming, "Only intelligent citizens of Kansas can maintain a republic," Leedy endorsed each institution's request for additional facilities and boasted that Kansas's children need not go east for higher education. Leedy's political opponents expressed relief.[70]

As Populists gained power in North Carolina, advocates for the state university attracted the movement's support by highlighting the democratic aspects of public higher education. UNC President George Winston, for ex-ample, noted that the university was independent of corporate donors, whereas private colleges accepted donations from Standard Oil and the American Tobacco Trust.[71] Winston also assured skeptics that many UNC students taught in the common schools of the state.[72] To the pleasant surprise of UNC's board of trustees, North Carolina's fusion Governor Daniel Russell endorsed public funding for higher education. In 1897, Russell announced that UNC had become "popular in the highest sense of the word" because it remained "open to all." "I would not have the men who rode to victory on this popular move-ment in North Carolina antagonize the university," Russell proclaimed, "we are not its enemies but its friends."[73]

While the support of the alliance or a governor could be influential, legisla-tures ultimately determined the budgets of state colleges and universities. Even though many Populist politicians attacked their rivals for wasteful spending and appropriation bills rarely attracted unanimous Populist support, legisla-tures controlled by movement supporters tended to match or exceed previous support for state universities. While legislative actions might not reflect the views of the movement's grassroots, the intimate size of many state political districts, the amount of time representatives spent outside of the capital, and the frequency of letters and petitions suggest that legislators could understand the will of their constituencies.[74] Tentative generalizations about the Populist perspective on higher education, therefore, can be based on analysis of the actions of state-level elected officials.

When faced with the burden of governance and the opportunity to leave their mark on public higher education, the majority of Populist politicians embraced stewardship of the state universities under their authority. Dominated by politicians loyal to the Farmers' Alliance, the Arkansas legislature of 1887 passed an appropriation bill that surpassed the level of the subsequent four sessions.[75] The Colorado legislature of 1893, which had a plurality of Populists, increased the size of the state university's tax levy and funded the state agricultural college more generously than the previous Republican-controlled session.[76] After a fire destroyed the University of Missouri in 1892, a legislature controlled by the Farmers' Alliance passed a substantial appropriation to rebuild the campus. In 1895, when an alliance of Populists and Republicans ruled the Missouri House, the legislature approved most of the state university's funding requests.[77] In North Dakota, a fusionist legislature passed the largest-ever appropriation to the state university in 1893.[78] When a coalition of Populists, Democrats, and Silver-Republicans won a majority of the South Dakota legislature in 1896, they doubled the state university's appropriations, completed construction of the main hall, repaired the heating plant, and allocated additional funds for science equipment.[79]

Populists in Washington State, who constituted a majority of the legislature during the 1897 session, threatened the appropriation for the state university and agricultural college. However, favorable reports from visiting committees helped persuade the assembly to pass appropriation bills. The legislature eventually allocated $80,000 to the university, $10,000 less than its previous biannual grant, but still a substantial sum during an economic depression. The state agricultural college received $30,000, only slightly less than prior funding levels. Despite this budget cut, President Enoch Bryan later acknowledged that Populists had been among "the most sympathetic helpers of the institution."[80]

In North Carolina, Kansas, and Nebraska, where Populists controlled legislatures for multiple sessions, state colleges and universities also emerged either relatively unscathed or even stronger than before. As late as 1887, North Carolina's funding for state higher education had ranked among the lowest in the nation. Beginning with their campaign to found an agricultural college, Populists contributed to a revival of support for public colleges statewide. Although many representatives were concerned about tax increases, the "farmers' legislature" of 1891 ultimately founded two new institutions—the North Carolina A&M College for the Colored Race and the North Carolina Normal and Industrial School for white women (NCNIS). When the North Carolina Populist Party fused with the Republican Party and formed a majority

bloc during the state legislative session of 1895, most of the new fusionist representatives pledged their support for funding UNC, even though many had
criticized the school during their campaigns.

In March 1895, for example, a joint legislative committee voted in favor of
continuing appropriations to UNC by an overwhelming margin of thirty-eight
to two. Ultimately, the legislature of 1895 passed a standard UNC appropriation bill while also providing additional funding for equipment and renovation.
UNC President George Winston was relieved to learn that the university had
been saved from the attack of "revolutionists."[81] By 1897, North Carolina Populists had become more divided on the issue of state aid. At one point, ten out of
twenty-four Populist state senators and eighteen out of twenty-nine Populist
state representatives opposed funding the university. Eventually, enough Populists voted to keep UNC's appropriation alive. During a session dominated by
the Populist-Republican alliance, the legislature granted UNC $50,000—
$10,000 more than any previous appropriation.

To equalize funding for white men's and white women's state higher education, the legislature doubled funding for NCNIS. Reflecting the influence of
African American Republicans, the legislature gave equal appropriations of
$25,000 to the black and white state agricultural and mechanical colleges,
exceeding the previous funding level of both institutions. Altogether, the fusion
regime increased the proportion of higher education funding directed to black
institutions from 10 percent to 25 percent during the 1890s (when roughly 33
percent of North Carolina's population was African American). Populists even
came under fire from their political enemies for being "extravagant" and
"lavish." Contrary to most predictions, North Carolina Populists eventually
took pride in their support for public higher education.[82]

The political opponents of the North Carolina Populists did not believe
that this support was heartfelt at the grassroots. Instead, Edwin Alderman,
Charles McIver, and other reformers aligned with the Democratic Party have
been credited with converting the North Carolina Farmers' Alliance to the
cause of public higher education. As president of NCNIS, McIver claimed that
it had become "fashionable" to endorse public schools at all levels.[83] The *Biblical
Recorder*, a foe of state funding of higher education, attributed Populist support
to their political inexperience. "A crowd of new men, some of them ignorant,
many of them without real convictions," the newspaper editorialized, "are
liable to be pressed or led to do many things which as individuals they would
not do." The *Recorder* claimed that lobbyists rather than voters controlled Populist leaders.[84]

Skeptics of Populist support for public higher education also highlighted the influence of Senator Marion Butler. A Populist Party leader and editor of the *Caucasian* newspaper, Butler was a graduate of UNC who pleaded the university's case during the legislative sessions of 1895 and 1897. With language that might have alienated some of his allies, Butler criticized "the 'I-didn't-have-no-eddication' fossil," "revelers in ignorance," and "demagogues" who complained about being burdened by school taxes.[85] University supporters hoped that Butler would determine the Populists' position. William A. Guthrie, also a Populist UNC graduate, joined the effort to attract support for the university appropriation in order to prevent the party from "making a fool of itself."[86] Historians have tended to agree that Populist votes for UNC appropriations can be attributed to the influence of Butler, Guthrie, and other UNC alums among the party elite, rather than genuine Populist enthusiasm.[87]

In Nebraska and Kansas, where Populist stance toward higher education has received less attention from scholars, no such explanations have been offered. While they did not always support these institutions to the same extent as their Republican rivals, Populists did not interrupt a steadily increasing flow of funds to NU during their intermittent hold on the legislature during the 1890s. In 1891, when fifty-four out of one hundred Nebraska representatives and eighteen out of thirty-three Nebraska senators were Populists, the legislature allocated an additional $37,000 to the state university for the construction of a library. As the passage of this bill was announced, NU students in the statehouse gallery burst into celebratory yells. The faculty was also grateful for the nearly unanimous general appropriation, the highest amount that the university had ever received. To mark the occasion, NU held a "grand jubilee," during which the university band led a line of students, faculty, and Lincoln residents on a march through the city. On campus, students dressed in their class colors, played music, waved flags, fired cannon, built a bonfire, and set off fireworks.[88]

Nebraska Populists endorsed the policies of Chancellor James Hulme Canfield and supported his requests for state funding. Canfield's commitment to increasing attendance at NU harmonized with Populist interest in expanding college access. Canfield believed that the fusionist legislature of 1893, which was also dominated by Populists, would be "very friendly" toward the university, though he worried that the Republican leader Church Howe might interfere with the appropriation bill. An hour-long discussion with Republican Governor Lorenzo Crounse provided little reassurance, leading Canfield to exclaim that the meeting had been "no good!" While Crounse opposed increasing university funding, a Republican legislator warned Canfield that the party's strategy was to bait the Populist legislative majority into throttling "every institution in the state" so that the Republicans could campaign against these cuts during the following election.[89]

The fusionist legislature of 1893 rewarded the Canfield administration with a virtually unanimous general appropriation of $231,000 (while rejecting a request for more library funds), causing even the Republican-controlled board of regents to remark that it was "a marked advance over previous legislation." The student newspaper cheered "Rah for the U. of N."[90] When the Republicans retook the state legislature in 1894, however, Populist enthusiasm for university appropriations sagged. Although a generous salary bill passed the house by a vote of 73 to 15, Populists cast thirteen out of the fifteen "no" votes (eight Populists supported the bill). When the senate passed a bill establishing a permanent university tax, Populists were the most vocal opponents. Populist senators stated that they could not support extra funding for the university when tight state finances had forced a reduction in the amount of drought relief provided to struggling farmers. Many Republican representatives agreed, and the house rejected the senate bill by a vote of forty-eight to forty-seven.[91]

Despite their ambivalence about higher education, Nebraska Populists bristled at Republican accusations that they were stingy with the university. Populist newspapers rejected the notion that Populism was antithetical to public higher education. After purporting to have had conversations with party leaders, a reader of the *Wealth Makers of the World* promised that "the cause of the people has nothing to fear from higher education." The letter writer endorsed the newspaper's pro-NU stance, explaining that the school needed to accommodate increasing enrollment.[92]

After fusing with Democrats and reclaiming control of the state legislature in 1896, Populist politicians acted on these assertions. Even though Nebraska farmers were still facing hard times and Chancellor Canfield had been succeeded by a conservative supporter of the gold standard, the fusionist legislature of 1897 gave the university $232,500. This sum was one of the largest-ever university appropriations and included $30,000 for a mechanic arts building. The student editors of the *Hesperian* were satisfied with the legislature's "especially favorable" attitude toward the university. Populists also supported the state normal school in Peru at a slightly higher level than the previous session of the legislature.[93] Judging from the party's reversal between the sessions of 1895 and 1897, Populist legislators may have been more likely to vote for university funding when they enjoyed majorities and could take credit for the appropriations.

Populist propaganda celebrated these votes and rebutted Republican predictions that Populists would short-change the university. After lauding the "truly wise" university bill of 1897, the *People's Champion* reminded readers that political foes had forecast that Nebraska institutions of higher education would "suffer at the hands of the fusionists." In response, some Republicans merely changed their tune and argued that the Populist appropriations had been excessive.[94] Undaunted, the 1898 Nebraska Populist platform pledged to deliver a large appropriation to the state university while endorsing NU's focus on teaching students how to earn "an honest living."[95] In 1902, after Republican Governor Charles Henry Dietrich vetoed a $90,000 university funding bill, Populists reiterated their support for "liberal appropriations" to the university, and accused Dietrich of opposing the university because he had "nothing in common" with the school or its students.[96]

In Kansas, Populist legislatures established a similar pattern of consistent, though not unanimous, support for the agricultural college and the state university. Despite the desperate condition of Kansas's farmers, many Populists voted to fund public institutions of higher education at levels similar to or greater than Republican precedents. After the election of 1892, when Kansas Populists occupied a majority of the seats in the state senate as well as nearly half of the house, KU Chancellor Francis H. Snow fretted about the "unsettled condition" of the university's funding. A month later, however, Snow realized that most Populists felt "very favorable" toward KU even though he had not embraced their curricular priorities. Despite the bitter partisanship that characterized the session of 1893, Snow rejoiced over a $50,000 grant for the construction of an electrical engineering and physics building as well as a general appropriation that exceeded the university's previous level of funding. Although he griped that many other state agencies were being "crippled by the false economy of the Populist Party," Snow had no reason to complain about the treatment of KU. He confided to Cornell Professor Benjamin Ide Wheeler that "the Populist Movement has not affected us unfavorably."[97] In light of Populist curricular preferences, it is not surprising that the proportional increase in the funding of KSAC was even higher than that of KU. The legislature of 1893 gave KSAC over $75,000 for construction of a library, museum, classrooms, laboratories, and a power plant—nearly six times higher than the appropriation of 1891.[98]

Populist support for higher education appropriations in Kansas remained steady in 1895 and 1897. Stipulating that KU should remain tuition-free, the Populist majority in the Kansas Senate endorsed a $100,000 appropriation to the university in 1895.[99] The senate also approved appropriations to KSAC for construction and equipment, to which the house added $2,000 for a steam heating system and $1,500 for student uniforms.[100] After the Democratic-Populist alliance won the governorship and both branches of the state legislature in 1897, party leaders reassured Chancellor Snow that they intended to preserve KU's appropriation. As a candidate, Governor John Leedy had responded to Republican attacks by positioning Populism as a "sensible, practical, and successful" movement rather than a radical fringe that would make hasty changes to state policy. A Republican regent confessed to Snow that he believed the university would come out of the legislative session of 1897 "in better shape then if the Republicans had won." The regent's apprehensions about Republican rule stemmed from party boss Cy Leland's threat to take revenge after Chancellor Snow refused his requests for patronage appointments.[101]

In contrast, the Populist press was uniformly supportive. A reader of the Populist *Topeka Advocate* warned politicians who might be stingy with public institutions of higher education that they should expect to be condemned by all citizens. The letter asserted that Kansas youth deserved the same access to knowledge "as can be learned in the schools and universities of the foremost army-ridden countries of Europe." In Lawrence, the *Jeffersonian* reminded anxious onlookers that Populists had already endorsed KU during the legislative session of 1893. The state Populist Party strenuously objected to any accusation that its supporters were "wreckers of educational institutions."[102]

While Snow trusted that the Populists would not cause "serious harm," he predicted that it would be necessary "to use great caution and make great exertions in order to secure the desired advance in [the university's] equipment." Throughout the session of 1897, Populist State Senator and KU Regent William Barton Rogers rallied support while Snow rushed from Lawrence to Topeka whenever the outcome seemed in doubt. Snow reported to University of Michigan President James B. Angell that he waged a "hard fight for existence with our Populist legislature." Although legislators rejected the university's requests for three additional buildings, they approved a $100,000 general appropriation, only $8,000 less than the sum approved by the house and only "somewhat" less than the level that Snow had desired. While not overjoyed by the appropriation, the student editors of the *Kansas University Weekly* also understood that the institution had been relatively fortunate.[103]

The fusionist legislature of 1897 also supported KSAC, which had been recently reorganized by a Populist board and its newly promoted president, Thomas E. Will. Worried that KSAC could suffer a significant budget cut, Will requested the aid of Carl Vrooman, a member of the Populist State Central Committee (and eventual KSAC regent). Vrooman used his influence to defend most of KSAC's funding requests, although he was unable to undo cuts to faculty salaries. At the end of the session, the legislature earmarked roughly

$50,000 for KSAC's general expenses, a sum nearly twice as large as the college's appropriation of 1895. In addition, legislators approved Will's request for $16,000 to construct a building for the school's domestic science program. The legislature also agreed to bail the college out of a $7,000 deficit that had accumulated during the previous biennium. In light of a strained state budget and a weak farm economy, Will felt that he could not complain.[104]

After losing their legislative majority in the election of 1898, Populist advocates for public higher education still remained influential. During the session of 1899, Populist editors continued to endorse institutional appropriations, especially for the KSAC experiment station, farmers' institutes, and other measures designed to promote agricultural science. The *Advocate and News* even supported creating a permanent funding stream for KSAC in the form of a dedicated mill tax.[105] Populist political operative William H. Sears intensified his lobbying on behalf of KU. Although Sears had been critical of the insularity of the university's administration, he remained a steadfast booster. Convinced that public higher education was consistent with Populist ideals, Sears asked the influential Populist Senator H. G. Jumper to support the university. "The Populist party must go on record as being in favor of higher education," Sears wrote the senator, "if it would keep in touch with the people and the progress of the age." Sears personally visited over fifty legislators, secured free passes from the Santa Fe Railroad for their travel from Topeka to Lawrence, and arranged a series of receptions with the KU faculty. With Jumper's support, KU received its largest ever appropriation in 1899, including $120,000 in general appropriations for each of the next two years, $90,000 for a new chemistry building, and $30,000 for repairing fire damage on campus.[106] Despite most predictions, the Populist era in Kansas did not spell doom for the state university. The annual appropriation to KU gradually increased from $75,000 in 1889 to over $100,000 in 1896.[107]

Conclusion

The political scientist John W. Burgess once remarked that university appropriations were the most attractive targets for the "universal demagoguism of American politics." According to Burgess, most voters did not understand the purposes of these institutions and allowed shortsighted legislatures to prevent public institutions of higher education from becoming truly great. In 1889, a KU regent agreed that the university was vulnerable to "the political cry of the pauper and the demagogue."[108] Motivated by a combination of genuine concern for common school funding, jealousy of faculty salaries, and opportunistic demagoguery, Populist politicians have appeared to epitomize the periodic miserliness of state legislatures.

However, the history of the Populist movement indicates that self-styled representatives of the masses still lobbied for state institutions of higher education. Despite loud criticisms from segments of the movement, Populists never united behind a campaign to destroy a state institution of higher learning. Although some Populists regularly attacked funding for state universities, this opposition was motivated in large part by concerns that these institutions lay outside of popular control and did not enroll enough ordinary residents. Wherever academic Populists won the authority to influence university policies, the movement's legislators tended to support public funding at levels similar to or in excess of previous appropriations. In Kansas, Thomas E. Will even claimed that the Populists deserved credit for "habituating the legislature to the idea of appropriating liberally" to public higher education.[109] Of course, Populists prioritized particular items on universities' wish lists; they were more sympathetic to requests for tuition subsidies and new buildings, as opposed to support for faculty salaries or research. Despite these problematic omissions, the extent to which Populist legislators funded state universities indicates that they believed that the movement's values could be compatible with public higher education.

The movement's track record suggests that academic Populists persuaded enough supporters that state universities were (or could become) accessible and practical enough to provide direct benefits to farmers and workers. As political scientist Elizabeth Sanders has demonstrated, agrarian social movements may have opposed government bureaucracy, but they still often lobbied to increase the scope of the American state through statutory funding for particular programs that benefitted their constituencies.[110] While Populists sometimes argued that state budgets should be slashed across the board in order to provide tax relief to struggling farmers, the movement still accepted public spending if it seemed to serve the interests of its supporters. An Alabama Farmers' Alliance editor, for example, argued that categorical opposition to government spending was "bosh" because tax revenue funded many public goods, such as schools, militias, and state departments of agriculture.[111] Some Populists even believed that the state should use tax revenue to compensate for unequal economic opportunity. The Populist chief justice of the Kansas Supreme Court argued that a government that neglected to "provide for the leveling and equalizing of the conditions . . . has failed in the purpose of its creation."[112] To the extent that state colleges and universities aspired to provide this "leveling and equalizing," their funding could be consistent with Populist principles.

Conclusion

It may be settled that the university man will offer the people
only what the people are persistent in demanding.

Elbridge Gale,

Professor of Horticulture, Kansas State Agricultural College,

1898

Kansas State Agricultural College (KSAC) never named a building in honor
of Thomas E. Will—he is the only former KSAC president who has
not been thus memorialized.[1] In Kansas, Nebraska, North Carolina, and elsewhere, new governing boards worked quickly to erase remnants of academic
Populism after the movement fell from power.

Kansas Republicans wasted little time before pursuing a counterrevolution
at KSAC following the election of Governor William Stanley in the fall of
1898. Railroad executives were eager to replace Populist regents who had
advocated for rate regulation. Executives of the First National Bank looked
forward to resuming their administration of the college's accounts. H. A.
Perkins, editor of the *Nationalist*, hoped to regain the business of printing
KSAC's publications, which the fusionist board had produced on the college's
own press. Perkins precipitated the end of fusionist control by accusing regents
Christian Balzac Hoffman and J. N. Limbocker of donating seasoned firewood
to the college in exchange for green wood; the charges triggered their temporary
suspension from the board and created a Republican majority.[2] After a partisan
vote of five to two, the reconstituted board fired five professors, including Will,
Edward Bemis, and Frank Parsons. The regents also reduced the college's social
science offerings by combining the professorships of history and economics.
Last, the Republican board rescinded a commencement invitation to William

Jennings Bryan. "Too bad is it not," Hoffman would later write to Parsons, "that a lot of wily politicians should ruthlessly wreck the people's institution."[3]

In North Carolina, the Democratic Party engaged in a violent white supremacist campaign in order to defeat the Populist-Republican alliance during the election of 1898. During the next legislative session, Democrats overturned most of the reform legislation passed by the fusionists and created literacy tests that disenfranchised many of the African American and rural white voters who had formed the base of that alliance.[4] A special committee appointed by Democratic officials recommended dismissing every Populist and Republican appointee at the North Carolina College of Agriculture and Mechanic Arts, from faculty to security guards. Afterward, the new Democratic majority on the college's board fired three professors, prompting protests from students in the college's agricultural society and a leader of the North Carolina Farmers' Alliance.[5] In Nebraska, fusionists maintained a majority on the board of the state university until 1904. While their appointee to the chancellorship, E. Benjamin Andrews, continued to serve until 1909, he became politically moderate and academically conventional.[6] As early as 1900, a member of the National Education Association (NEA) was confident that "the demagogic period" of these land grant colleges had passed.[7]

The students, faculty, and administrators who had been inspired by Populism disputed this association with demagoguery. They characterized their interventions at state universities as principled efforts to empower the children of ordinary Americans. To this end, academic Populists advocated for three overlapping propositions: public institutions should be accessible to poor students from rural areas; public institutions should emphasize vocational curricula and regional service; and public institutions should train students to become civic leaders by exposing them to the field of political economy. While other proponents of state universities articulated similar purposes, Populists pursued a radical version of this agenda, which they hoped would temper the elitism of higher education. Often falling short of this goal, the Populist campaign demonstrated how the institutional culture of higher education could absorb and redirect the ambitions of egalitarian movements. Nevertheless, Populist demands revealed important fault lines that lay beneath conventional tributes to the accessibility, relevance, and democratic governance of public universities. As historian Daniel Rodgers has stated about American protest movements generally, academic Populists pushed conventional ideals to the point where "commonplaces turn[ed] suddenly subversive."[8]

After the Populist movement faded, political opponents rejected or diluted many of these subversive ideas, some of which were ill-conceived or contrary to student ambitions. Yet small "p" academic populism did not vanish after the demise of the Farmers' Alliance and the Populist Party.[9] While the "dema-gogic" pressures facing state universities may have subsided, another speaker at the aforementioned NEA meeting indicated the extent to which populistic ideas had infused the conventional rationale for state universities. In an address titled "The State University," Indiana University President Joseph Swain empha-sized that public institutions of higher education were duty bound to offer admission to "the whole people." Swain noted the importance of financial accessibility, reminding his audience that only wealthy residents could send their children to private institutions. He sounded a populistic refrain about status and curriculum, declaring that a "people's university" should not promote any "aristocracy of trade, profession, or wealth." Swain also repeated a popu-listic contrast between the protection of academic freedom at public univer-sities and the powerful interests that could limit expression at private institu-tions.[10] When state universities pursued these ideals during the Progressive era, they used vocabulary honed (though not invented) by academic Populists. And while radical egalitarians would rarely, if ever, exercise as much influence on public higher education, the movement's priorities continued to pose impor-tant challenges for American higher education.

The political might of populistic ideals waned during the early twentieth century after the divergence of the movement's economic and cultural strands. Evangelical Christians embraced the movement's cultural critique, whereas unions and socialists championed populistic economic grievances.[11] While organized labor shared a similar vision of higher education as the Farmers' Alliance and the Populist Party, unions tended to create their own small colleges in the 1920s and 1930s rather than lobbying for greater control over existing state universities.[12] Relatively free from popular oversight, the boards of state universities adopted corporate models of governance and defined themselves in opposition to the sort of contentious public control that the Populists had championed.[13] Progressive reformers inside and outside of academia tended to have fewer qualms about prioritizing efficient administration over democratic processes.[14] Professors' efforts to protect academic freedom also limited popular influence over public higher education.

These developments meant that state universities faced less vigorous dissent when they gravitated toward elite models of higher education during the first few decades of the twentieth century. Land grant institutions expanded their liberal arts programs and gradually morphed into closer approximations of prestigious universities.[15] Fewer state college presidents or professors mentioned an obligation to serve particular classes or, more radically, to level distinctions between classes. By 1936, the socialist muckraker (and City College graduate) Upton Sinclair mourned the extent to which higher education was becoming an "instrument of special privilege" rather than a force for collective uplift.[16]

Sinclair was too cynical—most leaders of public higher education remained committed to the trinity of access, practicality, and public service that Populists had helped to enshrine as central themes of university policy and rhetoric. For example, Populist demands preceded the crystallization of extension efforts at "Progressive" institutions, such as the University of Wisconsin (UW). These programs helped to quell rural dissatisfaction by encouraging broader dissemination of agricultural science.[17] However, whereas Populists had demanded access to both regular admissions and extension services, state universities increasingly emphasized their research expertise and extension programs rather than enrollment in the university proper.[18]

Significantly, Charles McCarthy's canonical portrait of the "Wisconsin Idea" detailed UW's contributions to state and municipal government but did not discuss admissions policies or financial aid.[19] This approach to public higher education appeared across the nation, including within the former heartlands of Populism. University of Kansas (KU) regents soon felt comfortable warning that "low standards of education and a cheap degree" would result from any attempt to align entrance standards to the level of poor farm children.[20] The annual reports of KSAC no longer publicized the enrollment of ordinary rural youth. Instead, the college added a lengthy section on the "Public Work of the KSAC," which described applied research, open lectures, and bulletins.[21] Making matters worse (at least from the Populist perspective), the research and extension programs of land grant colleges tended to conform to the interests of large commercial farmers and resisted input from dissident agricultural organizations.[22]

Faced with expanding enrollment and increased expectations for facilities and research, state universities also sometimes compromised their commitment to affordability. In 1902, with Populism fading as an organized political movement, Kansas legislators authorized KU to raise its fees.[23] KU's chancellor sounded a defensive note when claiming that the majority of students remained partially or wholly self-supported. In response to the perception that many students wore expensive clothing, the chancellor asserted, "Democracy is not a question of dress—it is a state of mind."[24] State university leaders could also point out that public institutions of higher education remained less costly than private institutions. In 1933, for example, tuition and fees at public colleges and universities averaged $61 compared to $265 at private institutions.[25]

By the 1920s, nevertheless, land grant colleges and state universities served relatively few of the poorest college students, who were more likely to enroll at less expensive normal schools and small private colleges. Revealingly, the parents of students at public universities had higher incomes, on average, than parents of students at private institutions. While cultural and academic factors contributed to this dynamic, most public universities had increased expenses and decreased the relative amount of scholarship aid, even in states once governed by Populists.[26] As state appropriations failed to keep pace with expenses, KU fees rose by 25 percent during the 1920s. In 1923, the Nebraska legislature authorized fees and legalized the first tuition charges in the history of the state university.[27]

Public universities also began to adopt more substantial admission requirements despite the persistent inferiority of many rural school systems. While broad enrollment remained a central goal of public higher education, few trustees ever matched the Populists' willingness to accommodate poor students from farming districts. To a certain extent, secondary school administrators continued to criticize admission standards at state universities. These officials sought to strip universities of the authority to set entrance requirements because they believed that professors lacked sufficient respect for vocational course credits. Some state superintendents convinced legislators to obligate universities to relinquish control over admissions. The legislatures of Kansas and Ohio ordered their state universities to accept all graduates of accredited high schools. Going even further, the Wisconsin legislature forced UW to offer probationary admission to students from nonaccredited high schools. Across the country, school administrators compelled most public universities to count some nontraditional subjects as valid credits toward admission.[28]

However, in contrast to the academic Populists of the 1890s, these principals and superintendents hoped to bolster the status of their own institutions and did not question whether requiring four years of high school disqualified an unacceptable proportion of rural students. Elite organizations such as the NEA's Committee of Ten and the College Entrance Examination Board had promoted this standard during the peak period of Populist activism. Endorsed by regional accreditation associations and the National Association of State Universities, the four-year standard spread rapidly across the nation after the turn of the century. In 1905, the Carnegie Foundation for the Advancement of Teaching (CFAT) required universities participating in its influential faculty pension program to require four years of high school preparation.

Most public institutions adopted toward this standard, even though many public high schools were still unable to provide four years of preparatory courses.[29] Universities that resisted increasing their entrance requirements jeopardized their accreditation and lowered their status in the eyes of the foundation. The CFAT classified any land grant college that did not require four years of high school as a mongrel secondary/tertiary institution.[30] Led by William Jennings Bryan, the Nebraska legislature objected to Carnegie's influence and ordered the state university to reject its pension program. The foundation's priorities also encountered resistance in California, Illinois, and Ohio.[31] Yet these were exceptional cases; most land grant colleges required four years of high school by 1910.[32]

Dissatisfied with the quality of students who were admitted automatically after graduating from accredited high schools, administrators of state universities pushed for further increases to entrance standards during the 1920s.[33] As high schools multiplied, state universities could add requirements without reducing their enrollments or drawing attention to enduring urban-rural inequalities.[34] Most dramatically, UW considered shifting responsibility for the first two years of college to high schools and focusing exclusively on advanced students, graduate education, and professional training.[35] More typically, the University of North Carolina (UNC) moderately increased its admission requirements, even though graduates of public schools constituted a minority of qualified applicants.[36] Kansas State College (formerly KSAC) and the University of Nebraska began to require freshman to enter with four years of high school credits, despite the fact that many rural districts still provided only three years of courses.[37] By 1930, twenty land grant colleges and universities no longer accepted all graduates of accredited public high schools, and twenty-eight no longer offered conditional admissions to students lacking one or two subjects.[38] A professor at the flagship University of Virginia called for even higher entrance standards by arguing that "the best brains in the state should have the best training available, but mediocre and stupid persons should be positively discouraged from entering college."[39]

Ironically, while Populists denounced the sort of attitude expressed by this professor, their advocacy for lax admissions policies and extension programs at land grant colleges promoted the institutional differentiation that justified increasing standards at flagship universities. The movement's tendency to support separate schools or programs for the masses is emblematic of a central trend of American higher education—the development of new and less prestigious institutions to accommodate the growing demand for enrollment.

Populist support for accessible agricultural colleges diverted their attention away from flagship state universities and, arguably, tempered the egalitarian character of public higher education. For example, after Populists helped strip UNC of its land grant status, President Kemp Plummer Battle felt liberated to emulate "Harvard, Yale, Columbia, Princeton" without the strain of serving a "diverse" student-body.[40] Similarly, Populist enthusiasm for short courses and farmers' institutes encouraged the creation of separate extension divisions, rather than the integration of adult education within the regular academic core.[41] Academic Populists tended to agree with liberal university reformers who viewed institutional differentiation as a beneficial and perhaps inevitable characteristic of mass higher education. Progressive academic leaders, most notably in California, would eventually create a tiered system of higher education designed to maximize access without sacrificing the entrance standards or research mission of flagship universities.[42] Scattered evidence suggests that Populists might have endorsed this strategy—movement newspapers sometimes argued that states should establish small regional colleges.[43]

Indeed, regional four-year and two-year colleges embodied much of the original Populist emphasis on accessible and practical higher education; they offered professional training or general education to students who were unable or disinclined to enroll at flagship universities. According to sociologists Christopher Jencks and David Riesman, it was "populist hostility" toward elite higher education that fueled the expansion of public community colleges, the fastest growing sector of higher education during the interwar period.[44] The history of academic Populism, therefore, suggests that institutional stratification was not exclusively a top-down strategy for diverting "the masses" away from flagship universities.[45]

Yet prior to the explosion of enrollment in two-year and regional state colleges, Populists could not have anticipated the extent of institutional differentiation in terms of resources, retention, and prestige. Ultimately, the stratification of state colleges and universities would confirm some of the original Populist anxiety about the elitism of higher education. Indeed, lingering populistic sensibilities have tempered the degree of institutional stratification within some midwestern states.[46] Stances taken by some of the movement's heirs appear to corroborate the notion that Populists would have been uncomfortable with these hierarchies. In North Dakota and Washington State, farmers and other populistic activists resisted attempts to reduce the course offerings and increase the subordination of the agricultural college in relation to the state university. They argued that providing farmers with broad higher education was well worth the inefficiency of duplicating courses in both institutions.[47]

This reaction exposes an essential dilemma of academic Populism. Expanding access to prestigious institutions might increase the probability that poor rural youth would either feel unwelcome or become alienated from the producing classes. However, establishing special institutions for these students might generate narrow or second-class forms of higher education. Perhaps because their movement dissented more often than it governed, academic Populists never developed a coherent resolution to this tension.

Nevertheless, the populistic tradition continued to influence public institutions of higher education. While the radical Populism of the 1890s never resurfaced in the same form, universities still faced decisions about how to embrace, accommodate, or deflect a similar set of public expectations.

In particular, academic Populism represented one facet of a long campaign to enshrine vocational training as a primary purpose of American postsecondary education. The belief that university training should be compatible with the farm or workshop encouraged land grant institutions to continue investing in their agricultural programs despite early years of lean enrollment. When the farm economy thrived during the early twentieth century, these programs were poised to accommodate major increases in demand.[48] This utilitarian emphasis spread across the entirety of American higher education—albeit without the anti-elitist or "leveling" objectives of the Populists. In the 1930s, advocates for unapplied curricula, such as University of Chicago President Robert Maynard Hutchins, rued the incessant demand for practical courses at public and private institutions alike. Hutchins regretted the development of the "service-station" approach to higher education, in which universities courted consumers by presenting an array of vocational and extension programs.[49]

Although this model of higher education satisfied part of the Populists' demands, little trace has remained of the movement's attempt to infuse vocational training with either an antihierarchical spirit or a commitment to working-class political engagement. These dimensions of Populism proved to be unpopular. The movement's emphasis on social leveling and producerism conflicted with the ambitions of most students, parents, business leaders, professors, and administrators. Instead, the increasing focus on vocational education stratified students according to occupational status and shifted the primary rationale for higher education away from civics and toward economic efficiency and social mobility.[50]

Throughout the twentieth century, new advocates also periodically championed populistic perspectives on access to state universities and won significant, yet incomplete, victories. These advocates demanded that the most selective public institutions account for unequal educational opportunity. In contrast to their ideas about vocational training, the Populists' commitment to access harmonized with the interests of many parents and students, as well as with the ideals of a number of twentieth-century administrators and activists. In 1912, University of South Carolina President Samuel Mitchell bucked national trends by lowering admissions standards and reminding departments of their obligation to support struggling students. Mitchell noted that less than 10 percent of South Carolina's high schools provided students with full college preparation.[51] After World War I, the University of California set aside a number of seats for rural students, veterans, and artists who might not otherwise have qualified for admission through conventional routes.[52] Between 1916 and 1921, farm/labor political parties advocated for rural students at the University of Montana, the University of North Dakota, and Oklahoma State University.[53] When faculty at the University of Missouri attempted to increase admission requirements in the 1920s, they surrendered in the face of public protest and the threat of litigation.[54] Western and midwestern residents, in particular, continued to draw proud contrasts between their state universities and elite eastern private institutions.

During this era, University of Minnesota President Lotus Coffman became a prominent evangelist for academically marginal applicants. Coffman told colleagues who wanted to raise entrance standards that every graduating class contained "thousands of those who were supposed to be mentally incompetent." Similarly, George Zook was reluctant to raise admission standards at Akron University. Zook, who had attended KU just after its Populist period, believed that higher entrance requirements were inconsistent with the mission of a public institution.[55] At the University of Iowa, psychologist E. F. Lindquist promoted American College Testing (ACT), a populistic alternative to the Scholastic Aptitude Test (SAT). Lindquist developed examinations that focused on identifying applicants who could benefit from higher education, rather than identifying the finer distinctions between students sought by selective institutions.[56]

These populistic attitudes reintensified during the Great Depression. In 1933, the Nebraska legislature revived old charges against the "aristocratic" state university, while the Kansas legislature ordered the state flagship to reduce student fees by 25 percent. That same year, a newly elected Democratic governor compelled the University of Washington to reduce entrance requirements, causing enrollment to increase by 1,000 students. In Wisconsin, farmer organizations monitored the number of students who failed out of UW and accused the university of snobbery when the rate increased. Parents across the nation continued to expect that state universities remain accessible to most students. According to one journalist, voters whose taxes supported public higher education insisted that their children receive "the benefit of whatever doubt there may be as to their ability to profit by it."[57] During World War II, a new generation of southern populists lobbied to prevent the GI Bill from being limited to high-achieving veterans (they also insisted on local control in order to impede benefits for African American veterans).[58]

A few years later, the president's Commission on Higher Education appointed by Harry Truman and chaired by George Zook published a landmark report that called for a 50 percent increase in college enrollment. The report lent federal support to a standard Populist prescription—generous subsidies for low-income students. Proclaiming that college students should not constitute "an intellectual elite, much less a small elite drawn largely from families in the higher income brackets," the commission struck an unmistakably egalitarian tone.[59] By the end of the 1950s, relatively few critics raised traditional concerns about whether needs-based scholarships promoted dependency or socialist attitudes. Governors and legislators from both major parties began to discuss states' responsibility for financial aid. Especially in the Midwest and West, legislatures provided larger and more reliable appropriations in order to maintain relatively low tuition charges.[60]

During the 1960s and 1970s, populistic values helped fuel campaigns for college access for African American and Latino students. Whereas these students had rarely concerned the white majority of the movement during the 1890s, modern civil rights activists marshaled arguments that resonated with classic Populist critiques of selectivity. In particular, the campaign for open admissions to the City University of New York (CUNY) echoed earlier concerns about the extent to which university standards discriminated against students who had received inferior secondary education.[61] Advocates demanded that CUNY revise minimum grade point average (GPA) requirements in order to increase access for students of color, who constituted roughly half of the city's high school population but occupied a small fraction of CUNY's student body. By attracting support from representatives of New York's white working class, these protests generated a broad-based populist campaign. Indeed, the switch to open admissions benefited large numbers of white students, especially Italian Americans—whose enrollment doubled between 1969 and 1971. While open admissions presented difficult challenges to CUNY campuses, the policy minimized racial competition for limited resources.[62]

Although CUNY soon began a steady retreat from open admissions, populistic attitudes toward college access remained strong in other (less racially diverse) circumstances, even with regard to flagship institutions.[63] Populist logic helps to account for the extent to which many of these universities have prioritized access rather than selectivity or retention.[64] For example, University of Colorado

President J. Quigg Newton sparked indignant protests in 1963 after pledging to transform the institution into the "Harvard of the West." During the 1980s, public dissent also halted the University of Minnesota's attempt to cap enrollment, increase standards, and focus more intensively on research.[65]

While important controversies persist over race, legacies, and athletics within the admissions offices of a number of highly selective "public ivies," such as the University of California and the University of Michigan, acceptance rates remain relatively high at the majority of state colleges and universities. Most community colleges accept nearly all applicants and most regional state universities verge on open enrollment. Many flagship universities admit over half of their applicants and some operated with virtually open admissions as recently as the last two decades.[66] Ohio State University only implemented semi-selective standards in 1987 and maintained a modern-day "conditional admission" policy for years afterward.[67] Louisiana State University adopted a list of course requirements along with modest GPA and standardized test score minimums in 1988 as part of an effort to increase graduation rates.[68] In Kansas, concerns about access for rural students motivated state legislators to reject proposals by the governor and the KU board of regents for course requirements, GPA standards, and ACT/SAT expectations up until 1996. The legislature narrowly approved these changes to KU's entrance policy and has since rejected calls from some KU students and administrators to relinquish authority over the university's modest standards. As of 2008, KU admitted all students who scored a 21 or better on the ACT, 980 or better on the SAT, or who had a 2.0 cumulative GPA and ranked in the top one-third of their high school class.[69]

Equally significant as these permissive entrance requirements, 80 percent of public universities continue to offer some form of remediation. Many flagship institutions have attempted to reduce remedial courses, which have had debatable effects on student retention and performance. Nevertheless, 30 percent to 40 percent of students nationwide take at least one remedial course.[70] Stubborn inequalities between local K-12 school districts still elicit populist reservations about higher standards, frustrating efforts to reduce attrition and complicating attempts to form consensus about the nature of college-level work.[71]

The populist spirit also lingers behind recent calls to moderate status distinctions within public systems of higher education by increasing enrollment in top-tier institutions or reducing funding gaps between selective and non-selective institutions.[72]

While Populist warnings about oligarchic college graduates can seem quaint, recent trends in college access provide reason enough for serious consideration of the movement's concerns. In particular, socioeconomic status continues to be the most significant and most persistent determinant of a student's odds of attending college. In the twenty-first century, one out of every two students whose parents earn more than $90,000 a year graduate from college—compared to one out of seventeen students whose parents earn less than $35,000.[73] Populist concerns about the elitism of higher education remain all too relevant in light of the wide disparities between the income, status, and political engagement of individuals with and without college degrees.[74] Furthermore, when students from low-income families enter college, they are more likely to enroll in two-year institutions, where educational outcomes tend to compare unfavorably with the outcomes of similar students who begin at four-year programs.[75] Poor students also continue to suffer from misalignment between their high school curriculum and university entrance standards—a problem that academic Populists publicized a century ago.[76]

While unequal academic preparation contributes to these disparities, rising expenses have also been a factor. As costs have spiraled upward and legislative appropriations have failed to keep pace, even public campuses dedicated to broad access have increasingly relied on tuition to generate revenue. During the last decade, for example, KU has raised tuition and fees by a factor of five. These increases, along with shifts in federal policies, compel working-class students to take out substantial loans that can discourage degree obtainment.[77] In addition to the external forces that have contributed to tuition increases and reductions of need-based assistance, flagship universities have sometimes redistributed financial aid away from low-income students in order to recruit students whose test scores and graduation rates boost national rankings.[78] While these public universities remain far more affordable than most private institutions, they appear out of reach to some qualified students. Meanwhile, flagship institutions attract applicants from wealthy families seeking bargains and prestige. As was the case during the 1920s, the average family income at some state universities is actually higher than at private universities.[79] The history of academic Populism provides few clear answers to these dynamics. Yet the movement's focus on social class, at least, remains integral to the pursuit of equal educational opportunity. Recently, state universities in Arizona, Florida, Michigan, and North Carolina have begun to increase aid for low-income students in order to reduce or eliminate the need for loans.[80]

Populist values also offer some hope for reframing the contentious disputes that surround selective admissions and racial representation. Recent critics have challenged racially conscious admissions policies through the ballot initiative, a mechanism that evolved out of the Populist movement's efforts to promote government by the masses. These activists embrace *procedural* Populism by favoring majoritarian rule rather than policies set by academic elites. Yet advocates of affirmative action support *substantive* Populism insofar as they champion applicants from underperforming high schools and emphasize the political and economic ramifications for communities that are underrepresented at prestigious universities.[81]

The history of academic Populism reveals that policies designed to increase the representativeness of student bodies are not radical forms of minority privilege; they follow classic precedents for broadening access to American higher education in the context of unequal secondary schooling. This history highlights disturbing inconsistencies between latter-day support for geographic- or class-based accommodations and modern-day objections to race-based considerations.[82] Equally important, the substance of the populist ethic redirects debates away from disagreements over the relative merits of individual applicants. Instead, at KSAC during the 1890s and CUNY during the 1970s, protesters conceived of access to higher education as a public good that should be distributed broadly despite uneven academic preparation.[83] During an era when race-based access policies have become legally and politically fragile, perhaps reemphasizing the original categories of class and geography (along with race) offers a path toward expanding the coalition of voters who would support consideration of a variety of applicant attributes. These approaches, in other words, might reunite the majoritarianism and the egalitarianism of the original Populist movement.[84]

The history of academic Populism may also reassure professors who engage with controversial political topics as teachers, scholars, or activists. Having witnessed the hypocrisy of administrators who only provided academic freedom to "neutral" scholars, some Populist sympathizers believed that professors should be able to support partisan causes. More than a century later, professors continue to debate whether it is appropriate for them to advocate for specific policies or candidates, or whether it is even possible to achieve political objectivity.[85] According to some scholars, attempts to legislate "balanced" approaches to teaching represent one of the greatest menaces to academic freedom in the twenty-first century.[86] This discord has had a chilling effect on the willingness of professors to discuss controversial issues. While attempts to indoctrinate students certainly violate the spirit of higher education, excessive caution threatens to inhibit debate, constrain intellectual exchange, and reinforce conventional wisdom.[87] The history of academic Populism suggests that the risks associated with professors' political engagement may be the lesser of two evils.

Finally, episodes of Populist intervention can inspire professors who seek meaningful engagement with higher education policy. Even to scholars who strongly disagree with the movement's stances, academic Populism exemplifies how deliberations over financial aid, remediation, and entrance standards can engage intellectuals in practical questions about civic ideals. Reviving the memory of academic Populism can counteract the constriction of campus political concerns to debates over rhetoric and curriculum, which are important yet incomplete conversations about the meaning of democratic higher education.[88]

The spirit of academic Populism animated some of the most powerful public demands facing American institutions of higher education. Confirming academia's greatest anxieties about external influences, Populism prioritized social equality over individual achievement, vocational training over liberal arts, and public opinion over expert research. The movement also tended to ignore or endorse racial discrimination (though this tendency did not trouble most mainstream university leaders at the time, exposure of this racist dimension has rendered Populism even more troubling to scholars in recent decades). Populism has also become more problematic for many professors as religious fundamentalists and skeptics of multiculturalism have effectively employed its rhetoric to attack university curricula, research, and admissions.[89]

Indeed, without tolerance of opposing points of view, Populism can degrade into unsavory majoritarianism, bigotry, and anti-intellectualism. Absent the utopian mass movement that energized academic Populism, public demands can stress narrow vocationalism and shortsighted metrics of accountability. These iterations of populistic pressure underscore the importance of faculty governance and help justify the privileged status of institutions that stand apart, to a certain extent, from politics and popular opinion. Without a healthy degree of autonomy, universities could degrade into mere merchants of credentials and services. Any institution of higher education that caters excessively to external demands, whether populist or elitist in nature, invites the deterioration of its core mission.[90]

Yet the history (and historiography) of academic Populism suggests that academic insiders can exaggerate the threat and obscure the contributions of public pressure. Of course, populistic ideology animates only a fraction of the external demands facing American colleges.[91] Still, the movement's track record should encourage administrators and professors to listen carefully to lay critics who may communicate important messages within disconcerting, even crude, complaints. Despite its brashness, demagoguery, and occasional incoherence, the Populist campaign was fundamentally optimistic about higher learning.

Finally, the history of academic Populism highlights the manner in which egalitarian values have competed with equally problematic rival visions of higher education.[92] When public universities are tempted by elitism, vintage Populist ideals offer important, if imperfect, counterarguments.

Notes

Reference Abbreviations

Butler Papers	Marion Butler Papers, Southern Historical Collection, University of North Carolina
Canfield Journal	James Canfield's Chancellor's Journal, James Hulme Canfield Papers, Office of the Chancellor, RG 05, Archives and Special Collections, University of Nebraska–Lincoln Libraries
Hoffman Papers	Christian Balzac Hoffman Papers, Kansas Collection, RH MS 92, Kenneth Spencer Research Library, University of Kansas
Kelley Papers	Harrison Kelley Papers, Kansas State Historical Society
KSAC Catalog	Catalogue of the Kansas State Agricultural College
KSAC Report	Biennial Report of the Kansas State Agricultural College
KS Bios	Kansas State Historical Society Biographical Scrapbooks
KSC Letters	Kansas State College History in Letters, 1897–1899, Collected and Arranged by J. T. Willard, Morse Department of Special Collections, Hale Library, Kansas State University
KSU Clippings	J. T. Willard, "History of Kansas State College: A Collection of Newspaper Clippings," vol. 1 to vol. 4, Morse Department of Special Collections, Hale Library, Kansas State University
KU Report	University of Kansas, Biennial Report
NCCAMA Catalog	Catalog of the North Carolina College of Agriculture and Mechanic Arts
NCCAMA Report	Annual Report of the North Carolina College of Agriculture and Mechanic Arts
NC Fac Mins	Faculty Meeting Minutes of the North Carolina College of Agriculture and Mechanic Arts, North Carolina State University Office of the Chancellor Records, UA 002, Special Collections Research Center, North Carolina State University Libraries, Raleigh, North Carolina

NC Super	Biennial Report of the Superintendent of Public Instruction of North Carolina
NC Trustees Mins	North Carolina State University Board of Trustees, Meeting Minutes, UA 001.001, Special Collections Research Center, North Carolina State University Libraries, Raleigh, North Carolina
NE Super	Biannual Report of the Nebraska State Superintendent of Public Instruction
NU Regents Mins	Record of the Proceedings of the Board of Regents of the University of Nebraska, RG 01, Archives and Special Collections, University of Nebraska–Lincoln Libraries
NU Regents Papers	Papers of the Board of Regents, University of Nebraska, 1869–1910, RG 01, Archives and Special Collections, University of Nebraska–Lincoln Libraries
NU Report	University of Nebraska, Biennial Report of the Board of Regents
Parsons Papers	Frank Parsons Papers, Manuscripts and Archives, Yale University Library
Peele Papers	William J. Peele Papers, MC 12, Special Collections Research Center, North Carolina State University Libraries, Raleigh, North Carolina
Polk Papers	Leonidas L. Polk Papers, #3708, Southern Historical Collection, Wilson Library, University of North Carolina at Chapel Hill
Sears Papers	William Henry Sears Papers, Kansas State Historical Society, Topeka, Kansas
SGC	Chancellor's Office, Francis Huntington Snow, General Correspondence, University Archives, Series 2/6/1, Kenneth Spencer Research Library, University of Kansas
SRC	Chancellor's Office, Francis H. Snow, Correspondence, Regents et al., June 1892–April 1899, University Archives, Series 2/6/3, Kenneth Spencer Research Library, University of Kansas
UNC	University of North Carolina Papers, #40005, University Archives, Wilson Library, University of North Carolina at Chapel Hill
UNC Report	Annual Report of the University of North Carolina
UNC Trustees	Board of Trustees of the University of North Carolina Records, #40001, University Archives, Wilson Library, University of North Carolina at Chapel Hill
Will Letterbook	Thomas Elmer Will presidential letterbook, RG 2, box 4, Morse Department of Special Collections, Hale Library, Kansas State University

Will Papers   Thomas Elmer Will Papers, Morse Department of Special
                     Collections, Hale Library, Kansas State University

Introduction

1. *Harper's Weekly*, November 9, 1895, 1057. Technically, Bemis was pressured to resign. Mary O. Furner, *Advocacy and Objectivity: A Crisis in the Professionalization of American Social Science, 1865–1905* (Lexington: University of Kentucky, 1975), 163–204.

2. Charles Postel, *The Populist Vision* (New York: Oxford University Press, 2007), 139.

3. The Populist *Kansas Commoner* applauded the hire because it believed that Bemis's "heart and head are right." *Kansas Commoner*, June 17, 1897, 4. The Populist press had expressed outrage over Bemis's dismissal from Chicago, which the movement attributed to the influence of John D. Rockefeller. *Jeffersonian*, December 5, 1895, 2; *Progressive Farmer*, August 23, 1898, 2; *Lincoln Independent*, November 8, 1895, 1.

4. Steven Hahn, *The Roots of Rural Populism: Yeoman Farmers and the Transformation of the Georgia Upcountry, 1850–1890* (New York: Oxford University Press, 1983).

5. On Populist support for common schools and informal education, see Theodore Mitchell, *Political Education in the Southern Farmers' Alliance, 1887–1900* (Madison: University of Wisconsin Press, 1987).

6. Thomas D. Snyder, ed., *120 Years of American Education: A Statistical Portrait* (Washington, DC: National Center for Education Statistics, 1993), 64.

7. For a classic treatment, see Merle Curti and Vernon Carstensen, *University of Wisconsin: A History, 1848–1925* (Madison: University of Wisconsin Press, 1949).

8. Laurence R. Veysey, *The Emergence of the American University* (Chicago: University of Chicago Press, 1965), 70–72.

9. James T. Kloppenberg, *Uncertain Victory: Social Democracy and Progressivism in European and American Thought, 1870–1920* (New York: Oxford University Press, 1988); Leon Fink, *Progressive Intellectuals and the Dilemmas of Democratic Commitment* (Cambridge, MA: Harvard University Press, 1997).

10. Postel, *The Populist Vision*, 73.

11. Robert W. Cherny, *Populism, Progressivism, and the Transformation of Nebraska Politics, 1885–1915* (Lincoln: University of Nebraska Press, 1981), 32; Scott McNall, *The Road to Rebellion: Class Formation and Kansas Populism, 1865–1900* (Chicago: University of Chicago Press, 1988), 83.

12. Veysey, *The Emergence of the American University*, 15–16. Also see Alan Nevins, *The State Universities and Democracy* (Urbana: University of Illinois Press, 1962); Edward D. Eddy Jr., *Colleges for Our Land and Time: The Land-Grant Idea in American Education* (New York: Harper and Brothers, 1956); Earle Dudley Ross, *Democracy's College: The Land-Grant Movement in the Formative Stage* (Ames: Iowa State College Press, 1942). For the impact of fascism and McCarthyism on interpretations of Populism, see C. Vann Woodward, "The Populist Heritage and the Intellectual," in *The Burden of Southern History* (Baton Rouge: Louisiana State University Press, 1960); Theodore Saloutos, "The Professors and the Populists," *Agricultural History* 40 (Oct. 1966), 235–54.

13. Richard Hofstadter, *The Age of Reform: From Bryan to F.D.R.* (New York: Vintage, 1955). Also see Richard Hofstadter, *Anti-Intellectualism in American Life* (New York: Vintage, 1963).

14. Classic revisions include Lawrence Goodwyn, *Democratic Promise: The Populist Moment in America* (New York: Oxford University Press, 1976), and Robert C. McMath Jr., *Populist Vanguard: A History of the Southern Farmers' Alliance* (Chapel Hill: University of North Carolina Press, 1975). For a more recent reaffirmation of Hofstadter's perspective on Populists and higher education, see Daniel P. Carpenter, *The Forging of Bureaucratic Autonomy: Reputations, Networks, and Policy Innovation in Executive Agencies, 1862–1928* (Princeton: Princeton University Press, 2001), 210. For the latest sympathetic interpretation of Populism, including a perceptive discussion of education, see Postel, *The Populist Vision*, 45–68. For other brief, yet important, corrections to the conventional account of Populism and higher education, see John R. Thelin, *A History of American Higher Education* (Baltimore, MD: Johns Hopkins University Press, 2004), 140; Edward L. Ayers, *The Promise of the New South: Life After Reconstruction* (New York: Oxford University Press, 1992), 225–27.

15. *Progressive Farmer*, March 2, 1887, 1. For evidence of similar sentiments in mainstream periodicals, see Daniel A. Clark, *Creating the College Man: American Mass Magazines and Middle-Class Manhood, 1890–1915* (Madison: University of Wisconsin Press, 2010).

16. *Country Life*, September 1890, 1.

17. *Appeal to Reason*, August 14, 1897, 4.

18. *Manhattan Republic*, August 28, 1896, 4.

19. People's Party (KS), *People's Party Campaign Handbook* (Hiawatha, KS: Harrington Printing Company, 1898).

20. *Atlanta Constitution*, October 31, 1897, 19 & July 16, 1893, 17.

21. Veysey, *The Emergence of the American University*, 16, 63–65.

22. On the value of college credentials, see Burton J. Bledstein, *The Culture of Professionalism: The Middle Class and the Development of Higher Education in America* (New York: Norton, 1976).

23. Harris quoted in Merle Curti, *The Social Ideas of American Educators* (Totowa, NJ: Littlefield, [1935], 1971), 331–32. Also see William James, "The Social Value of the College-Bred," in Frederick H. Burkhardt, ed., *Essays, Comments, and Reviews* (Cambridge, MA: Harvard University Press, 1987), 109–10; E. L. Godkin, "The Duty of Educated Men in a Democracy," *Forum* 17 (March 1894), 39–45.

24. *Student's Journal*, November 9, 1894, 6; *Rocky Mountain Collegian*, November 1894, 23. Also see *Nebraskan*, October 25, 1895, 2 & November 2, 1894, 2; *Kansas University Weekly*, March 13, 1896, 1. State universities did indeed produce many political leaders. As of 1900, UNC graduates constituted 44 percent of North Carolina's U.S. senators, 40 percent of its U.S. representatives, and 58 percent of its governors. Kemp P. Battle, *History of the University of North Carolina*, vol. 2 (Raleigh, NC: Edwards and Broughton, 1912), 587. Also see The University of Nebraska, *Semi-Centennial Anniversary Book* (Lincoln: University of Nebraska Press, 1919), 65–66.

25. See, for example, *Topeka Advocate*, August 25, 1897, 11.

26. G. Lynn to L. Kellie, March 10, 1893. Nebraska Farmers' Alliance Papers, Nebraska State Historical Society, microfilm reel 1.

27. Bryan quoted in Hofstadter, *Anti-Intellectualism in American Life*, 128.

28. *Appeal to Reason*, August 14, 1897, 4.

29. Kloppenberg, *Uncertain Victory*, 267–77, 289, 379.

30. Bruce Palmer, *Man over Money: The Southern Populist Critique of American Capitalism* (Chapel Hill: University of North Carolina Press, 1980), 40–41. In contrast, many Progressives were ambivalent about majoritarian democracy. William A. Link, *The Paradox of Southern Progressivism, 1880–1930* (Chapel Hill: University of North Carolina Press, 1992), 59, 85.

31. Mitchell, *Political Education in the Southern Farmers' Alliance*, 3–5, 97–98, 108–15, 130–40; Postel, *The Populist Vision*, 49–50, 62–66.

32. Postel, *The Populist Vision*, 53–56.

33. *The Biblical Recorder*, March 21, 1894, 1. Also see Steve Kantrowitz, *Ben Tillman and the Reconstruction of White Supremacy* (Chapel Hill: University of North Carolina Press, 2000), 4–5, 212–13 n1. For definitions of Populism, see Michael Kazin, *The Populist Persuasion: An American History* (Ithaca: Cornell University Press, 1998); Francisco Panizza, "Populism and the Mirror of Democracy," in Francisco Panizza, ed., *Populism and the Mirror of Democracy* (New York: Verso, 2005).

34. David B. Danbom, *The Resisted Revolution: Urban America and the Industrialization of Agriculture, 1900–1930* (Ames: Iowa State University Press, 1979), 22. On the relationship between Populism and Protestantism, see Joseph W. Creech Jr., "Righteous Indignation: Religion and Populism in North Carolina, 1886–1906" (PhD dissertation, University of Notre Dame, 2000); Peter Argersinger, "Pentecostal Politics in Kansas: Religion, the Farmers' Alliance, and the Gospel of Populism," in *The Limits of Agrarian Radicalism: Western Populism and American Politics* (Lawrence: University Press of Kansas, 1995).

35. Farmers began to depart the Grange after its cash-based cooperative ventures failed. Farmers' Alliances were also more militant, charged lower membership fees, and eschewed the Grangers' elaborate hierarchical rankings. McMath Jr., *Populist Vanguard*, 3–5, 20, 96–99, 116–17.

36. Postel, *The Populist Vision*, 12–13, 206.

37. McMath Jr., *Populist Vanguard*, 141–42; Goodwyn, *Democratic Promise*, 160–61, 209, 245, 259–62, 322, 415, 422; Jeffrey Ostler, *Prairie Populism: The Fate of Agrarian Radicalism in Kansas, Nebraska, and Iowa, 1880–1892* (Lawrence: University of Kansas Press, 1993); Donna A. Barnes, *Farmers in Rebellion: The Rise and Fall of the Southern Farmers Alliance and People's Party in Texas* (Austin: University of Texas Press, 1984); Barton C. Shaw, *The Wool-Hat Boys: Georgia's Populist Party* (Baton Rouge: Louisiana State University Press, 1984); James M. Beeby, *Revolt of the Tar Heels: The North Carolina Populist Movement, 1890–1901* (Jackson: University Press of Mississippi, 2008).

38. Goodwyn, *Democratic Promise*, 539, 551–52.

39. Christopher Lasch, *The True and Only Heaven: Progress and Its Critics* (New York:

Norton, 1991); Catherine McNicol Stock, *Rural Radicals: Righteous Rage in the American Grain* (Ithaca, NY: Cornell University Press, 1996), 15–86.

40. D. McKay to L. L. Polk, July 14, 1880, Polk Papers, box 4, folder 46. Also see Postel, *The Populist Vision*, 224; McMath Jr., *Populist Vanguard*, 6, 36–38, 43, 58–59, 156; Hahn, *The Roots of Rural Populism*, 9, 273–78. Populist membership may have correlated more strongly with regional levels of debt than with property value or income. J. Rogers Hollingsworth, "Populism: The Problem of Rhetoric and Reality," *Agricultural History* 39 (April 1965), 83–84; Stanley B. Parsons, "Who Were the Nebraska Populists?" *Nebraska History* 44 (June 1963), 83–99; John Dibbern, "Who Were the Populists? A Study of Grass-Roots Alliancemen in Dakota," *Agricultural History* 56 (October 1982), 677–91. However, Cherny found that the Populist Party in Nebraska was strongest in the poorest rural areas. Cherny, *Populism, Progressivism, and the Transformation of Nebraska Politics*, 55.

41. *Lincoln Independent*, October 11, 1895, 4.

42. Michael L. Goldberg, *An Army of Women: Gender and Politics in Gilded Age Kansas* (Baltimore, MD: Johns Hopkins University Press, 1997); Postel, *The Populist Vision*, 69–101; Maryjo Wagner, "Farms, Families, and Reform: Women in the Farmers' Alliance and Populist Party" (PhD dissertation, University of Oregon, 1986), 35–44.

43. Joseph Gerteis, *Class and the Color Line: Interracial Class Coalition in the Knights of Labor and the Populist Movement* (Durham, NC: Duke University Press, 2007). Foster quoted in William Chafe, "The Negro and Populism: A Kansas Case Study," *Journal of Southern History* 34 (August 1968), 408–9.

44. Gerald Gaither, *Blacks and the Populist Revolt: Ballots and Bigotry in the "New South"* (Tuscaloosa: University of Alabama Press, [1977], 2005), 36, 76, 112–13, 123–27; Omar Hamid Ali, "Black Populism in the New South, 1886–1898" (PhD dissertation, Columbia University, 2003).

45. Goodwyn, *Democratic Promise*.

46. For a discussion of these pitfalls, see James L. Hunt, *Marion Butler and American Populism* (Chapel Hill: University of North Carolina, 2003), 2–7.

47. This broad definition includes most fusionists, silverites, members of the Farmers' Alliance, and socialists who were sympathetic to the Populist cause. This approach has been informed by Michael Kazin's contention that Populism is "too elastic and promiscuous" to be defined solely by organization membership. Kazin, *The Populist Persuasion*, 1–3, 286.

48. Veysey, *The Emergence of the American University*, 60–61.

49. John J. Fry, *The Farm Press, Reform, and Rural Change, 1895–1920* (New York: Routledge, 2005).

50. Robert Sinclair, "Agricultural Education and Extension in Vermont" and Seymour Bassett, "President Matthew Buckham and the University of Vermont," in Robert Daniels, ed., *The University of Vermont: The First Two Hundred Years* (Hanover, NH: University Press of New England, 1991); Roy V. Scott, *The Reluctant Farmer: The Rise of Agricultural Extension to 1914* (Urbana: University of Illinois Press, 1970), 52–54. This book uses upper-case "Populist" and "Populism" when describing the late-nineteenth-century

movement and proponents thereof. Lower-case "populist," "populism," and the term "populistic" are used to refer to similar ideologies expressed by unaffiliated individuals or in other time periods. This distinction is important because many individuals supported particular aspects of the movement's ideals without endorsing all of its core values and because the meaning of populism shifted over time.

51. *Report of the Commissioner of Education for the Year 1890–91*, vol. 1 (Washington, DC: Government Printing Office, 1894), 43–44; *Report of the Commissioner of Education for the Year 1900–01*, vol. 1 (Washington, DC: Government Printing Office, 1902), xiii. On distinctions between wholesome western "freshwater colleges" and elite eastern colleges in the mainstream press, see Clark, *Creating the College Man*, 56.

52. Steve Kantrowitz, *Ben Tillman and the Reconstruction of White Supremacy* (Chapel Hill: University of North Carolina Press, 2000).

53. Hofstadter, *The Age of Reform*, 18–19; Hofstadter, *Anti-Intellectualism in American Life*, 23.

Chapter 1. Preludes to Populism

1. Frank C. Abbott, *Government Policy and Higher Education: A Study of the Regents of the University of the State of New York, 1784–1949* (Ithaca, NY: Cornell University Press, 1958), 50.

2. John S. Whitehead, *The Separation of College and State: Columbia, Dartmouth, Harvard, and Yale, 1776–1876* (New Haven, CT: Yale University Press, 1973).

3. Richard Hofstadter, *Anti-Intellectualism in American Life* (New York: Vintage, 1963), 151–55.

4. Abbott, *Government Policy and Higher Education*, 18–19.

5. Ronald P. Formisano, *For the People: American Populist Movements from the Revolution to the 1850s* (Chapel Hill: University of North Carolina Press, 2008), 65–159; Walter Hugins, *Jacksonian Democracy and the Working Class: A Study of the New York Workingmen's Movement, 1829–1837* (Stanford: Stanford University Press, 1960), 110, 146, 220.

6. Hofstadter, *Anti-Intellectualism in American Life*, 155–59.

7. Legislator quoted in Frederick Rudolph, *The American College and University* (New York: Knopf, 1962), 219.

8. Evans quoted in Hugins, *Jacksonian Democracy and the Working Class*, 142. On vernacular speech, see Kenneth Cmiel, *Democratic Eloquence: The Fight over Popular Speech in Nineteenth-Century America* (New York: William Morrow, 1990), 64.

9. Hofstadter, *Anti-Intellectualism in American Life*, 162–64.

10. Joseph F. Kett, "A Class Act: Collegiate Competition and American Society," in Michael C. Johanek, ed., *A Faithful Mirror: Reflections on the College Board and Education in America* (New York: College Entrance Examination Board, 2001), 105–42.

11. Rudolph, *The American College and University*, 217–18; Robert Samuel Fletcher, *A History of Oberlin College: From Its Foundation through the Civil War*, vol. 2 (Oberlin, OH: Oberlin College, 1943), 634–39, 659–63.

12. S. Willis Rudy, *The College of the City of New York: A History, 1847–1947* (New York: City College Press, 1949), 5–29, 59–60, 120–27.

13. Hawthorne quoted in David F. Allmendinger Jr., *Paupers and Scholars: The Transformation of Student Life in Nineteenth-Century New England* (New York: St. Martin's Press, 1975), 2.

14. Colin B. Burke, *American Collegiate Populations: A Test of the Traditional View* (New York: New York University Press, 1982), 97, 107, 138, 149–50; Joseph F. Kett, *The Pursuit of Knowledge under Difficulties: From Self-Improvement to Adult Education in America, 1750–1990* (Stanford: Stanford University Press, 1994), 131–32; Maxwell H. Bloomfield, "Law: The Development of a Profession," in Nathan O. Hatch, ed., *The Professions in History* (Notre Dame, IN: University of Notre Dame Press, 1988), 35–36.

15. Rudolph, *The American College and University*, 187.

16. E. Merton Coulter, *College Life in the Old South* (Athens: University of Georgia Press, [1928], 1951), 170–72.

17. Hugins, *Jacksonian Democracy and the Working Class*, 142; "The Report of the Working Men's Committee," in John R. Commons, et al., eds. *A Documentary History of American Industrial Society*, vol. 5 (New York: Russell and Russell, 1958), 98–99.

18. Bruce Sinclair, *Philadelphia's Philosopher Mechanics: A History of the Franklin Institute, 1824–1865* (Baltimore, MD: Johns Hopkins University Press, 1974), 2–15, 119; Kett, *The Pursuit of Knowledge under Difficulties*, 39–45, 102, 110–11, 120, 130–32.

19. Kett, *The Pursuit of Knowledge under Difficulties*, 40, 133; Sinclair, *Philadelphia's Philosopher Mechanics*, 4–5, 67, 124.

20. Roger L. Geiger, "The Rise and Fall of Useful Knowledge: Higher Education for Science, Agriculture and the Mechanic Arts, 1850–1875," *History of Higher Education Annual* 18 (1998), 53; R. Freeman Butts, *The College Charts Its Course* (New York: McGraw-Hill, 1939), 131–50; Rudolph, *The American College and University*, 113–14.

21. Julianna Chaszar, "Leading and Losing in the Agricultural Education Movement: Freeman G. Cary and Farmers' College, 1846–1884," *History of Higher Education Annual* 18 (1998), 25–46; Gary T. Lord, "Alden Partridge's Proposal for a National System of Education: A Model for the Morrill Land Grant Act," *History of Higher Education Annual* 18 (1998), 11–24; Daniel Lang, "People's College: The Mechanics Mutual Protection and the Agricultural Act," *History of Education Quarterly* 18 (1978), 295–321.

22. Superintendent quoted in J. Gregory Behle and William E. Maxwell, "The Social Origins of Students at the Illinois Industrial University, 1868–1894," *History of Higher Education Annual* 18 (1998), 93.

23. Eldon L. Johnson, "Misconceptions about the Early Land Grant Colleges," *Journal of Higher Education* 52 (July/August 1981), 333–51.

24. The Morrill Act of 1862, 12 *United States Statutes at Large*, 503–5; Coy F. Cross II, *Justin Smith Morrill: Father of the Land grant Colleges* (East Lansing: Michigan State University Press, 1999); Roger L. Williams, *The Origins of Federal Support for Higher Education: George Atherton and the Land Grant Movement* (University Park: Pennsylvania State University Press, 1991).

25. Margaret Rossiter, *The Emergence of Agricultural Science: Justus Liebig and the Americans, 1840–1880* (New Haven, CT: Yale University Press, 1975); Earle D. Ross, *Democracy's College: The Land Grant Movement in the Formative Stage* (Ames: Iowa State College Press, 1942), 87, 119; Alan Marcus, *Agricultural Science and the Quest for Legitimacy: Farmers, Agricultural Colleges, and Experiment Stations, 1870–1890* (Ames: Iowa State University Press, 1985), 220–21.

26. Harry Kersey Jr., *John Milton Gregory and the University of Illinois* (Urbana: University of Illinois Press, 1968), 70–71; James E. Pollard, *History of the Ohio State University: The Story of Its First Seventy-Five Years, 1873–1948* (Columbus: Ohio State University Press, 1952), 16, 40; Williams, *The Origins of Federal Support for Higher Education*, 2, 7, 55, 59–61, 72, 83.

27. Kersey Jr., *John Milton Gregory and the University of Illinois*, 107–8; Richard Gordon Moores, *Fields of Rich Toil: The Development of the University of Illinois College of Agriculture* (Urbana: University of Illinois Press, 1970), 48, 56–57, 73; Ross, *Democracy's College*, 87.

28. Ross, *Democracy's College*, 120.

29. *Southern Cultivator*, August 1876, 329–31.

30. Thomas A. Woods, *Knights of the Plow: Oliver H. Kelley and the Origins of the Grange in Republican Ideology* (Ames: Iowa State University Press, 1992), xx, 147, 178; Solon Justus Buck, *The Granger Movement: A Study of Agricultural Organization and Its Political, Economic, and Social Manifestations* (Cambridge, MA: Harvard University Press, 1913), 64–69, 102, 182.

31. William Henry Denton, "The Impact of Populism upon the Southern Educational Awakening" (PhD dissertation, University of North Carolina, 1965), 76.

32. *Proceedings of the Annual Session of the Kansas State Grange, 1877*, Kansas Collection, Kenneth Spencer Research Library, Kansas University.

33. Marcus, *Agricultural Science and the Quest for Legitimacy*, 38.

34. Mabel Hardy Pollitt, *A Biography of James Kennedy Patterson* (Louisville, KY: Westerfield-Bonte, 1925), 143.

35. Scott, *The Reluctant Farmer*, 57; D. Sven Nordin, *Rich Harvest: A History of the Grange, 1867–1900* (Jackson: University Press of Mississippi, 1974), 63.

36. Ezra S. Carr, *The Patrons of Husbandry on the Pacific Coast* (San Francisco: Bancroft, 1875), 187–88, 371, 377–83. Also see John Aubrey Douglass, *The California Idea and American Higher Education: 1850 to the 1960 Master Plan* (Stanford: Stanford University Press, 2000), 37–69. On Jeanne Carr, see Donald Marti, *Women of the Grange: Mutuality and Sisterhood in Rural America, 1866–1920* (New York: Greenwood Press, 1991), 41.

37. Kersey Jr., *John Milton Gregory and the University of Illinois*, 128–30, 135, 160; Jonathan Periam, *The Groundswell: A History of the Origin, Aims, and Progress of the Farmers' Movement* (Cincinnati, OH: Hannaford, 1874), 508.

38. *Transactions of the Kansas State Board of Agriculture, 1872*, 72, 25–41. Also see James Carey, *Kansas State University: The Quest for Identity* (Lawrence: The Regents Press of Kansas, 1977), 39–40, 41–43.

39. O. Gene Clanton, *Kansas Populism: Ideas and Men* (Lawrence: University Press of Kansas, 1969), 26–27; Peter H. Argersinger, *Populism and Politics: William Alfred Peffer and the People's Party* (Lexington: University of Kentucky Press, 1974), 2; Scott McNall, *The*

Road to Rebellion: Class Formation and Kansas Populism, 1865–1900 (Chicago: University of Chicago Press, 1988), 220–21, 269.

40. Jeffrey Ostler, *Prairie Populism: The Fate of Agrarian Radicalism in Kansas, Nebraska, and Iowa, 1880–1892* (Lawrence: University of Kansas Press, 1993), 72–73; Bertha Evelyn Wentworth, "The Influence of the Grange Movement upon the Educational and Social Development of the Agricultural Class of Kansas from 1872–1876" (master's thesis, Kansas State Agricultural College, 1929), 30–31.

41. *Transactions of the Kansas State Board of Agriculture, 1872*, 40.

42. *Junction City Union*, April 26, 1873, 1.

43. *Transactions of the Kansas State Board of Agriculture, 1872*, 13.

44. Carey, *Kansas State University*, 43–44; George Washington Martin, *John A. Anderson — A Character Sketch* (n.p., 1902), 1–6; *Manhattan Republic*, April 23, 1897, 4.

45. Anderson quoted in Carey, *Kansas State University*, 45.

46. KSAC Catalog, 1875–77, 3–5.

47. Handbook of the Kansas State Agricultural College (Manhattan, 1874), 16.

48. Anderson quoted in Carr, *The Patrons of Husbandry on the Pacific Coast*, 383–84.

49. KSAC Catalog, 1875–77, 17.

50. *Industrialist*, November 9, 1878.

51. *Chickasaw Messenger*, May 12, 1881, 2; James Ferguson, "The Grange and Farmer Education in Mississippi," *Journal of Southern History* 8 (November 1942), 497, 502–4; Herman Hattaway, *General Stephen D. Lee* (Jackson: University Press of Mississippi, 1976), 3–4, 157–62, 173–74.

52. John K. Bettersworth, *People's University: The Centennial History of Mississippi State* (Jackson: University Press of Mississippi, 1980), 28, 59.

53. *Progressive Farmer*, February 26, 1889, 4; *Proceedings of the Annual Convention of American Agricultural Colleges and Experiment Stations, 1892*, 27–28; *Chickasaw Messenger*, December 23, 1880, 1.

54. Gould P. Colman, *Education and Agriculture: A History of the New York State College of Agriculture at Cornell University* (Ithaca, NY: Cornell University Press, 1963), 67–69; George H. Callcott, *A History of the University of Maryland* (Baltimore: Maryland Historical Society, 1966), 146–47, 176–77, 181–82, 190–92.

55. Periam, *The Groundswell*, 541, 552–53.

56. KSAC Catalogue, 1875–77, 17; *Industrialist*, June 1, 1878; KSAC Handbook, 5, 9, 31–32, 52–53; Carey, *Kansas State University*, 48–50, 55.

57. William H. Sikes, *Bill Sikes, The Preacher's Boy: An Autobiography of a Ninety-Year-Old Rebel* (n.p., 1948), 16–18, 22.

58. The Mississippi State Grange, "The State Grange and A&M College," 1–3; Ferguson, "The Grange and Farmer Education in Mississippi," 502–4; Lilibel Hurshel Henry Broadway, "Frank Burkitt: The Man in the Wool Hat" (master's thesis, Mississippi State University, 1948), 13–14.

59. *Progressive Farmer*, March 12, 1889, 1.

60. *Progressive Farmer*, March 5, 1889, 1 and April 2, 1889, 1; *Proceedings of the Annual Convention of American Agricultural Colleges and Experiment Stations, 1892*, 27–28.

61. Mari Jo Buhle, *Women and American Socialism, 1870–1920* (Urbana: University of Illinois Press, 1981), 82–84; Michael L. Goldberg, *An Army of Women: Gender and Politics in Gilded Age Kansas* (Baltimore, MD: Johns Hopkins University Press, 1997).

62. Marti, *Women of the Grange*, 67–84.

63. KSAC Handbook, 54; KSAC Catalogue, 1875–77, 6–7.

64. Bridget Smith Pieschel and Stephen Robert Pieschel, *Loyal Daughters: One Hundred Years at the Mississippi University for Women, 1884–1984* (Jackson: University Press of Mississippi, 1984), 6, 12.

65. Germaine M. Reed, *David French Boyd: Founder of Louisiana State University* (Baton Rouge: Louisiana State University, 1977), 162–71, 181–83, 259.

66. W. W. Folwell to A. D. White, October 24, 1874 and W. W. Folwell to T. R. Lounsbury, March 3, 1875, in Solon J. Buck, ed., *William Watts Folwell: The Autobiography and Letters of a Pioneer of Culture* (Minneapolis: University of Minnesota Press, 1933), 214–15.

67. William D. Barns, "The Influence of the West Virginia Grange upon Public Agricultural Education of College Grade, 1873–1914," *West Virginia History* 9 (January 1948), 126, 131, 137–39, 145.

68. University of New Hampshire, *History of the University of New Hampshire, 1866–1941* (Durham: University of New Hampshire, 1941), 74–78, 95, 107.

69. Scott, *The Reluctant Farmer*, 52–54; Joseph B. Edmond, *Magnificent Charter: The Origin and Role of the Morrill Land Grant Colleges and Universities* (Hicksville, NY: Exposition Press, 1978), 23.

70. Merle Curti and Vernon Carstensen, *University of Wisconsin: A History, 1848–1925*, vol. 1 (Madison: University of Wisconsin Press, 1949); Scott, *The Reluctant Farmer*, 56–57; James E. Hansen II, *Democracy's College in the Centennial State: A History of Colorado State University* (Fort Collins: Colorado State University Press, 1977), 1, 24–25; Henry Dethloff, *A Centennial History of Texas A&M University, 1876–1976*, vol. 1 (College Station: Texas A&M Press, 1975), 47, 72–73, 96, 124, 143, 219, 383; Colman, *Education and Agriculture*, 92, 179; Andrew Dickson White, *Autobiography* (New York: Century Company, 1906), 370.

71. Wentworth, "The Influence of the Grange Movement," 59; Harold J. Smith, "History of the Grange in Kansas, 1883–1897" (master's thesis, University of Kansas, 1940), 171.

72. The Mississippi State Grange, "The State Grange and A&M College," 2–3; Bettersworth, *People's University*, 12; Ferguson, "The Grange and Farmer Education in Mississippi," 502–4, 508.

73. James B. Angell, "The State Universities of the West," in *State Aid to Higher Education: A Series of Addresses Delivered at the Johns Hopkins University* (Baltimore, MD: Johns Hopkins Press, 1898), 35.

74. Konrad H. Jarausch, "Higher Education and Social Change: Some Comparative Perspectives," in Konrad H. Jarausch, ed., *The Transformation of Higher Learning, 1860–1930: Expansion, Diversification, Social Opening, and Professionalization in England, Germany, Russia, and the United States* (Stuttgart, Germany: Klett-Cotta, 1982), 23.

75. KU Report, 1877–1878, 8–9.

Chapter 2. Scaling the Gilded Halls of the University

1. *Nebraska Independent*, December 15, 1898, 4.

2. *Proceedings of the Annual Meeting of the National Educational Association, 1895*, 982–83.

3. Kemp Plummer Battle, *History of the University of North Carolina*, vol. 2 (Raleigh, NC: Edwards and Broughton, 1912), 70; D. McKay to L. L. Polk, June 12, 1880, Polk Papers, box 4, folder 45, and D. McKay to L. L. Polk, March 13, 1886, Polk Papers, box 6, folder 81.

4. J. Daniels to K. P. Battle, January 30, 1886, UNC, box 16, folder 524; J. Daniels to K. P. Battle, February 5, 1886, UNC, box 16, folder 525; James L. Leloudis, *Schooling the New South: Pedagogy, Self, and Society in North Carolina, 1880–1920* (Chapel Hill: University of North Carolina Press, 1996), 52–59.

5. "An Industrial School," February 5, 1885, Walter Hines Page Papers, Letters from Various Correspondents, American Period, bMS Am 1090 (1101), Houghton Library, Harvard University; "The Need of an Industrial School in North Carolina," MC 229, box 2, "Publications, 1884–1927" folder, the Watauga Club Records, Special Collections Research Center, North Carolina State University Libraries, Raleigh, North Carolina; Charles Dabney, *Universal Education in the South* (New York: Arno Press, 1936, 1969), 182–87; Dwight B. Billings Jr., *Planters and the Making of a "New South": Class, Politics, and Development in North Carolina, 1865–1900* (Chapel Hill: University of North Carolina Press, 1979), 206–7.

6. Polk's Handwritten Account of the Farmers' Mass Convention and Galley Proofs of "Farmers' Mass Convention," January 26, 1887, Polk Papers, box 6, folder 88; M. Slaughter to L. L. Polk, January 20, 1887, Polk Papers, box 6, folder 88; D. McKay to L. L. Polk, March 13, 1886, Polk Papers, box 6, folder 81; *Progressive Farmer*, February 2, 1887, 4 and February 9, 1887, 5; David A. Lockmiller, *History of the North Carolina State College of Agriculture and Engineering of the University of North Carolina, 1889–1939* (Raleigh: North Carolina State College of Agriculture and Engineering, 1939), 32. While they clashed over control of the industrial school, Populists and New South reformers shared many interests. Philip Roy Muller, "New South Populism: North Carolina, 1884–1900" (PhD dissertation, University of North Carolina, 1972), 47–48.

7. William J. Peele, "A History of the Agricultural and Mechanical College" (n.d., n.p.), 8.

8. *Journal of the House of Representatives of the General Assembly of the State of North Carolina* (Raleigh: North Carolina State Printer, 1887), 624–31.

9. Minutes of the Board of Trustees of the University of North Carolina, February 16, 1888 and June 6, 1888, UNC Trustees, vol. S-8; Battle, *History of the University of North Carolina*, 220, 376–78; Kemp Plummer Battle, *Memories of an Old-Time Tar Heel* (Chapel Hill, University of North Carolina Press, 1945), 253–54.

10. Notes from November 10, 1897 and December 5, 1898, untitled notebook, Watauga Club Collection, box 1; NCCAMA Catalog, 1890, 2–3; Alice Reagan, *North Carolina State University: A Narrative History* (Ann Arbor, MI: Edwards Brothers, 1987), 18; William L. Carpenter, *Knowledge Is Power: A History of the School of Agriculture and Life Sciences at North Carolina State University, 1877–1984* (Raleigh: North Carolina State University, 1987), 71–73.

11. NCCAMA Catalog, 1890, 2–3, 52–53; NCCAMA Report, 1896, 10.

12. Paul Escott, *Many Excellent People: Power and Privilege in North Carolina, 1850–1900* (Chapel Hill: University of North Carolina Press, 1985), 243–49; Edward P. Bailey Jr. to Mother, September 5, 1900, MSS 67, Special Collections Research Center, North Carolina State University Libraries, Raleigh, NC.

13. Jeffrey J. Crow and Robert F. Durden, *Maverick Republican in the Old North State: A Political Biography of Daniel L. Russell* (Baton Rouge: Louisiana State University Press, 1977), 46.

14. Governor Russell also gave trustee seats to three NCCAMA professors. *News and Observer*, June 12, 1897, 1, 5 and September 8, 1897, 5. On Harris, see James M. Beeby, *Revolt of the Tar Heels: The North Carolina Populist Movement, 1890–1901* (Jackson: University Press of Mississippi, 2008), 64.

15. *News and Observer*, March 6, 1895, 1, 5.

16. *Journal of Proceedings and Addresses of the National Educational Association, 1897*, 184–86.

17. Scott McNall, *The Road to Rebellion: Class Formation and Kansas Populism, 1865–1900* (Chicago: University of Chicago Press, 1988), 5, 66–69, 245–46; Peter H. Argersinger, *Populism and Politics: William Alfred Peffer and the People's Party* (Lexington: University of Kentucky Press, 1974), 11, 23; O. Gene Clanton, *Kansas Populism: Ideas and Men* (Lawrence: University Press of Kansas, 1969), 29, 207; Lawrence Goodwyn, *Democratic Promise: The Populist Movement in America* (New York: Oxford University Press, 1976), 95–97, 182; Robert C. McMath Jr., *American Populism: A Social History, 1877–1898* (New York: Hill and Wang, 1993), 136, 193–94.

18. Clyde Kenneth Hyder, *Snow of Kansas: The Life of Francis Huntington Snow, with Extracts from His Journals and Letters* (Lawrence: University of Kansas Press, 1953), 210.

19. Untitled typescript, Sears Papers, box 1, letterbook, 239–42. On Sears, see Sara Mullin Baldwin and Robert M, Baldwin, eds., *Illustriana Kansas* (Hebron, NE: Illustriana, 1933), 1032.

20. Newspaper quoted in Clifford S. Griffin, *The University of Kansas* (Lawrence: University of Kansas Press, 1974), 186.

21. *Jeffersonian*, March 2, 1893, 1; Griffin, *The University of Kansas*, 185–86; F. H. Snow to G. L. Raymond, November 9, 1896, SRC. Snow remained concerned about the potential for "partisan action" should the Populists ever gain one more seat and achieve a majority. F.H. Snow to C. R. Mitchell, May 29, 1894, SRC.

22. In contrast, Professor Frank Blackmar claimed that the regent, Charles Robinson, resigned because he had felt that KU was not serving the commoners of Kansas. Frank W. Blackmar, *The Life of Charles Robinson: The First State Governor of Kansas* (Topeka, KS: Crane, 1902), 34–36, 294, 298–300, 349. The Populist regents of KU during Snow's tenure also included A. S. Olin (a KU alum and high school principal), J. P. Sams (a farmer), and William Rogers (a farmer and former state senator). Alfred Thayer Andreas, *The History of the State of Kansas* (Chicago: A. T. Andreas, 1883), 342, 890, 963; KS Bios, vol. 142, 241. On Snow's cordial relations, see F. H. Snow to A. Olin, March 6, 1893; F. H. Snow to W. Rogers, May 25, 1895; and F. H. Snow to C. R. Mitchell, May 29, 1894, SRC. Lewelling replaced Robinson with a carpenter and former sheriff named H. S. Clarke, who was more apt to challenge university policies. KS Bios, vol. 34, 134.

23. W. H. Sears to L. S. Stebbins, December 4, 1896, Sears Papers, box 2, letterbook; *Jeffersonian*, April 22, 1897, 2 and July 29, 1897, 2. When Leedy was elected, five Republican and two fusionist regents governed KU. In 1897, Populists almost maneuvered to create a majority by revising appointment procedures. Fifteen Populist representatives broke party ranks to oppose the measure. F. H. Snow to C. F. Scott, February 24, 1897, F.H. Snow to Carter, March 20, 1897, and F.H. Snow to F.B. McKinnon, March 22, 1897, SRC; *Lawrence Journal*, March 13, 1897, 1 and June 12, 1897, 9; *Manhattan Nationalist*, April 22, 1897, 4.

24. F. H. Snow to G. T. Fairchild, May 27, 1897, KSC Letters.

25. The Emporia State Normal School never attracted much Populist attention, although at least two of its trustees were Populists during the mid-1890s. *State Normal Monthly*, November 1896, 24 and April 1897, 106; *Biennial Report of the Board of Regents and Faculty of the State Normal School, Emporia, Kansas, 1897-98.*

26. James Carey, *Kansas State University: The Quest for Identity* (Lawrence: Regents Press of Kansas, 1977), 69. Lewelling's appointments included E. D. Stratford (a lawyer and former probate judge) and W. D. Street (a former farmer, newspaper editor, and legislator, who speculated in real estate, the drug and grocery business, and cattle raising). KS Bios, vol. 155, 164, 181, 332; Andreas, *The History of the State of Kansas*, 1439, 1615; Kansas State Historical Society, *Transactions*, vol. 9, 33.

27. Frank W. Blackmar, *Higher Education in Kansas* (Washington, DC: Government Printing Office, 1900), 84; Carey, *Kansas State University*, 60–61.

28. On Kelley, see Andreas, *The History of the State of Kansas*, 660; Kansas State Historical Society, *Transactions* vol. 6, 219–20; *Nonconformist*, August 13, 1891, 4; *Manhattan Republic*, July 30, 1897, 4; George T. Fairchild, "Populism in a State Educational Institution," *American Journal of Sociology* 3 (November 1897), 394. On Secrest, see *Industrialist*, January 28, 1893, 91 and April 1899, 253–55; E. Secrest to H. Kelley, May 14, 1893, Kelley Papers, box 1, folder "Correspondence 1893."

29. *Industrialist*, November 4, 1893, 35; E. Secrest to L. Lewelling, June 1, 1894, box 1, folder 6, Records of the Governor's Office, Governor Lorenzo D. Lewelling, RG 27-5-4-5, Kansas State Historical Society, Topeka, Kansas.

30. Autobiography of C. B. Hoffman, Hoffman Papers, box 2, folder 16; untitled typescript dated April 1898, Will Papers, folder 1; Edward Gene Nelson, *The Company and*

the Community (Lawrence: University of Kansas, 1956); Patricia Michaelis, "C. B. Hoffman, Kansas Socialist," *Kansas Historical Quarterly* 41 (Summer 1975), 166–82; *Enterprise Antimonopolist*, April 24, 1884 and June 19, 1884; Walter T. K. Nugent, *The Tolerant Populists: Kansas Populism and Nativism* (Chicago: University of Chicago Press, 1963), 50, 79.

31. Fairchild, "Populism in a State Educational Institution," 394–95; J. D. Walters, *History of Kansas State Agricultural College* (Manhattan: Kansas State Agricultural College, 1909), 125–27.

32. Thomas E. Will, "How I Became a Socialist" (1904), Pamphlets in American History, Microfilm Series S440.

33. Joseph Dorfman, *The Economic Mind in American Civilization*, vol. 3 (New York: Viking Press, 1949), 299–303; *Manhattan Republic*, June 23, 1899, 4. On the lack of Will's formal identification with the Populist Party, see G. T. Fairchild to W. A. Kellerman, April 21, 1897, KSC Letters.

34. J. T. Willard to F. Parsons, December 25, 1899, Parsons Papers (MS 11), box 2, folder 104.

35. The Populist regents initially adhered to "rather conservative counsel" according to Julius T. Willard, KSAC's Republican chemistry professor. Julius T. Willard, *History of Kansas State College of Agriculture and Applied Science* (Manhattan: Kansas State College Press, 1940), 95.

36. Leedy's appointments to the KSAC Board included George Munger (a farmer who owned a large laundry business) and W. H. Phipps (a recent KSAC graduate who managed a creamery and had been principal of Abilene High School). On Munger, see *Kansas Commoner*, September 9, 1897, 4; *Kansas Farmer*, August 12, 1897, 508; KS Bios, vol. 107, 184, vol. 111, 197, vol. 115, 73. On Phipps, see *Industrialist*, June 1898, 428 and Ralph Sparks, "To Serve the People: The Populist Era at Kansas State," unpublished manuscript dated 1993, Morse Department of Special Collections, Hale Library, Kansas State University.

37. Limbocker worked as a bookkeeper, schoolteacher, farmer, banker, and insurance agent. He held a variety of political offices while affiliated with the Grange, the Greenbacker movement, and the Populists. *Manhattan Republic*, May 28, 1897, 4 and September 10, 1891, 1; *American Nonconformist and Kansas Industrial Liberator*, June 11, 1891, 7; KS Bios, vol. 104, 189.

38. Virginia Noah Gibson, "The Effect of the Populist Movement on Kansas State Agricultural College" (master's thesis, Kansas State College of Agriculture and Applied Science, 1932), 36.

39. *Industrialist*, August 16, 1897, 170.

40. C. B. Hoffman to H. Kelley, December 29, 1896, Kelley Papers, box 1, folder "Correspondence 1894–1898."

41. *Manhattan Nationalist*, September 16, 1897, 2.

42. Carey, *Kansas State University*, 71; Charles Correll, "Revolution and Counterrevolution," *Kansas Quarterly* 1 (4) (Fall 1969), 91–93, 99; Walters, *History of Kansas State Agricultural College*, 111.

43. *Manhattan Republic*, September 24, 1897, 1. Regent Carl Schurz Vrooman, appointed by Governor Leedy in 1899, was another reformer on the KSAC board. Part of a family of gentile radicals, Vrooman earned a BA in economics from Harvard before joining the Populist State Central Committee in Kansas. Republican editors accused Vrooman of being a violent anarchist. Ross E. Paulson, *Radicalism and Reform: The Vrooman Family and American Social Thought, 1837–1937* (Lexington: University of Kentucky Press, 1968), 96, 113, 138; Helen M. Cavanaugh, *Carl Schurz Vrooman: A Self-Styled "Constructive Conservative"* (Chicago: Lakeside, 1977), 14–16, 20, 29, 44–45; "Denouncements of Appointment of Vrooman," 1899, Kansas State University History Index, Morse Department of Special Collections, Hale Library, Kansas State University.

44. Robert W. Cherny, *Populism, Progressivism, and the Transformation of Nebraska Politics, 1885–1915* (Lincoln: University of Nebraska Press, 1981), 37, 68–76; Annabel L. Beal, "The Populist Party in Custer County, Nebraska: Its Role in Local, State, and National Politics" (PhD dissertation, University of Nebraska, 1965).

45. Albert L. Biehn, "The Development of the University of Nebraska, 1871–1900" (master's thesis, University of Nebraska, 1934), 34; The University of Nebraska, *Semi-Centennial Anniversary Book* (Lincoln: University of Nebraska Press, 1919), 15, 75–76, 83.

46. LaVon M. Gappa, *Chancellor James Hulme Canfield: His Impact on the University of Nebraska, 1891–1895* (PhD dissertation, University of Nebraska, 1985), 16, 151.

47. *Nebraska State Journal*, July 12, 1891, 7.

48. Calvin Thomas, *James Hulme Canfield* (New York: Columbia University Press, 1909), 299–302.

49. James H. Canfield, "The Farmers' Alliance in Kansas," *Christian Union*, June 25, 1891, 841–42; Dorfman, *The Economic Mind in American Civilization*, 77; *Nebraska State Journal*, June 12, 1891, 4; *Alliance Independent*, February 22, 1894, 4; *Farmers' Alliance*, July 9, 1891, 4.

50. Biehn, "The Development of the University of Nebraska, 1871–1900," 130–31; Robert Knoll, *Prairie University: A History of the University of Nebraska* (Lincoln: University of Nebraska Press, 1995), 38; *Nebraskan*, September 27, 1895, 1.

51. In the fall of 1894, Populists and Silver Democrats elected Silas Holcomb to the governorship, but lost control of the legislature. Republicans remained in control of NU's governing board. The fusion coalition retook the legislature in 1896 before losing again in 1898. Cherny, *Populism, Progressivism, and the Transformation of Nebraska Politics*, 44–47, 80.

52. *Nebraska Independent*, August 5, 1897, 4, October 14, 1897, 4, October 21, 1897, 4, November 25, 1897, 8, February 10, 1898, 4 and July 2, 1903, 4.

53. Cherny, *Populism, Progressivism, and the Transformation of Nebraska Politics*, 72–74; *Nebraska Independent*, November 9, 1899, 4 and December 28, 1899, 2; *People's Banner*, November 2, 1899, 4.

54. *Nebraska State Journal*, October 7, 1899, 4, October 14, 1899, 4, and November 7, 1899, 4; Robert Manley, *Centennial History of the University of Nebraska*, vol. 1 (Lincoln: University of Nebraska Press, 1969), 119.

55. *Nebraska State Journal*, February 16, 1900, 1; NU Regents Mins, vol. 5, February 15, 1904.

56. An opposition newspaper declared that Populists encouraged North Carolina's agricultural college to sponsor "frills," such as baseball, football, and dances. *News and Observer*, March 27, 1897, 5.

57. *Jeffersonian*, November 21, 1895, 2 and November 7, 1895, 2.

58. *Jeffersonian*, July 8, 1897, 2 and December 2, 1897, 2; *Kansas Commoner*, January 21, 1897, 4.

59. Barton C. Shaw, *The Wool-Hat Boys: Georgia's Populist Party* (Baton Rouge: Louisiana State University Press, 1984), 37; Hunt, *Marion Butler and American Populism*, 15; George R. Poage, "College Career of William Jennings Bryan," *The Mississippi Valley Historical Review* 15 (September 1928), 172. Several Populist leaders had attended UNC. D. C. Mangum, *Biographical Sketches of the Members of the Legislature of North Carolina, Session 1897* (Raleigh, NC: Edwards and Broughton, 1897), 25–26.

60. *Harper's Weekly*, November 29, 1890, 923; Norman Pollack, *The Just Polity: Populism, Law, and Human Welfare* (Chicago: University of Illinois Press, 1987), 145.

61. Maryjo Wagner, "Farms, Families, and Reform: Women in the Farmers' Alliance and Populist Party" (PhD dissertation, University of Oregon, 1986), 15; Charles Postel, *The Populist Vision* (New York: Oxford University Press, 2007), 72.

62. Omar Hamid Ali, "Black Populism in the New South, 1886–1898" (PhD dissertation, Columbia University, 2003); Gerald Gaither, *Blacks and the Populist Revolt: Ballots and Bigotry in the "New South"* (Tuscaloosa: University of Alabama Press, [1977], 2005).

63. Robert C. McMath Jr., *Populist Vanguard: A History of the Southern Farmers' Alliance* (Chapel Hill: University of North Carolina Press, 1975), 162.

64. Shaw, *The Wool-Hat Boys*, 130–31, 173–74, 64; Edward Ayers, *The Promise of the New South: Life After Reconstruction* (New York: Oxford University Press, 1992), 246.

65. Billings Jr., *Planters and the Making of a "New South,"* 168–71, 196.

66. Clanton, *Kansas Populism*, 63–65.

67. Cherny, *Populism, Progressivism, and the Transformation of Nebraska Politics*, 68–69, 104.

68. Joseph W. Creech Jr., "Righteous Indignation: Religion and Populism in North Carolina, 1886–1906" (PhD dissertation, University of Notre Dame, 2000), 294.

69. Clipping from *Wilmington Messenger*, August 21, 1892, North Carolina Biographical Files, North Carolina Collection, Wilson Library, University of North Carolina; *Country Life*, September 1890, 5.

70. Homer Clevenger, "The Teaching Techniques of the Farmers' Alliance," *Journal of Southern History* 20 (August 1945), 505.

71. Between 1881 and 1900, the proportion of land grant trustees affiliated with a rural advocacy group peaked at 29 percent, well below their proportion of the population. Clyde W. Barrow, *Universities and the Capitalist State: Corporate Liberalism and the Reconstruction of American Higher Education, 1894–1928* (Madison: University of Wisconsin Press, 1990), 37, 51–58.

72. These trustees were W. J. Peele (a Raleigh attorney); William A. Guthrie (an attorney and the Populists' nominee for governor in 1896); and Marion Butler (an editor and Populist U.S. senator). Minutes of the Board of Trustees, March 14, 1895, April 5, 1895, June 5, 1895, August 1, 1896, June 1, 1897, and January 27, 1898, UNC Trustees, vol. 9; *News and Observer*, March 27, 1897, 5.

73. The college-educated regents were C. B. Hoffman (Central Wesleyan College), E. D. Stratford (Howard College and Emporia State Normal School), Carl Vrooman (Washburn College and Harvard University), W. H. Phipps (KSAC), A. S. Olin (University of Kansas), and Charles Robinson (Amherst College). Autobiography of C. B. Hoffman, Hoffman Papers, box 2, folder 16; KS Bios, vol. 34, 104, 134, 142, 155, 164, 181, 189, 241 and 332; Cavanaugh, *Carl Schurz Vrooman*, 14, 20, 44; *Industrialist*, June 1898, 428 and April 1899, 253–55; Andreas, *The History of the State of Kansas*, 342, 963, 1439; Kansas State Historical Society, *Transactions*, vol. 6, 219–20 and vol. 9, 33; *Kansas Farmer*, August 12, 1897, 508.

74. In 1897, fusionists elected George F. Kenower (a former teacher and regent of the University of Illinois who edited the Populist *Wisner Chronicle*) and E. Von Forell (a Populist minister who had served as chaplain of the state industrial school). The victorious fusion ticket of 1899 consisted of John L. Teeters (a jeweler who graduated from the University of Iowa), and Edson Rich (a NU alum who practiced law and served in the state legislature). *Nebraska Independent*, October 7, 1897, 4, September 14, 1899, 4 and October 12, 1899, 4; *Wisner Chronicle*, September 4, 1897, 4 and September 30, 1899, 4; Manley, *Centennial History of the University of Nebraska*, 142; *Nebraskan-Hesperian*, November 14, 1899, 5; Biographical Note, John L. Teeters Papers, Nebraska State Historical Society; *Nebraskans: 1854–1904* (Omaha, NE: Bee, 1904), 44; *Nebraska State Journal*, November 16, 1899, 4.

75. *Weekly Commoner*, March 19, 1897, 4. Rogers also sent all three of his children to college. Thomas W. Riddle, *The Old Radicalism: John R. Rogers and the Populist Movement in Washington* (New York: Garland, 1991), 52; Enoch Albert Bryan, *Historical Sketch of the State College of Washington, 1890–1925* (Pullman, WA: Alumni and the Associates Students of Washington State College, 1928), 188.

76. *Jeffersonian*, May 31, 1894, 1; *Advocate and News*, May 18, 1898, 9.

77. *Alliance Independent*, September 7, 1893, 1; *People's Poniard*, October 25, 1895, 1; *Nebraska Independent*, September 14, 1899, 4 and October 12, 1899, 4. On Peattie, see Susanne George Bloomfield, ed., *Impertinences: Selected Writings of Elia W. Peattie, a Journalist in the Gilded Age* (Lincoln: University of Nebraska Press, 2005), 11–12.

78. *Jeffersonian* March 3, 1893, 1 and December 5, 1895, 2; *Advocate and News*, October 12, 1898, 8; *Hickory Mercury*, August 18, 1897, 2.

79. For example, see *Hickory Mercury*, September 1, 1897, 6.

80. James H. Baker, *Educational Aims and Civic Needs* (New York: Longmans, Green, 1913), 130.

81. *Rocky Mountain Collegian*, September 1892, 8, October 1892, 13, and November 1892, 21.

82. *Progressive Farmer,* June 14, 1898, 3.

83. *College Symposium of the Kansas Agricultural College* (Topeka, KS: Hall and O'Donald, 1891), 116.

84. Mamie Alexander Boyd, *Rode a Heifer Calf through College* (Brooklyn, NY: Pageant-Poseidon, 1972), v–vi, 14–16, 77, 94.

85. *Student Herald,* September 23, 1896, 2, September 30, 1896, 2, and October 28, 1896, 1.

86. W. H. Sears to M. Howard, September 18, 1896, Sears Papers, box 1, letter-book; *Kansas University Weekly,* April 23, 1898, 2; *Nebraskan,* October 12, 1894, 2 and October 19, 1894, 2; *Wealth Makers of the World,* May 3, 1894, 4; *Nebraska Independent,* October 5, 1899, 5.

87. *Lawrence Journal,* January 30, 1897, 8; *Nebraskan,* April 26, 1895, 2; March 13, 1896, 1 and May 1, 1899, 7.

88. Frank O'Connell, *Farewell to the Farm* (Caldwell, ID: Caxton Printers, 1962), 47, 50, 89, 153.

89. Jonathan Rose, *The Intellectual Life of the British Working Classes* (New Haven, CT: Yale University Press, 2001); Lawrence W. Levine, *Highbrow / Lowbrow: The Emergence of Cultural Hierarchy in America* (Cambridge, MA: Harvard University Press, 1988).

90. Alvin Johnson, *Pioneer's Progress* (New York: Viking, 1952), 21, 46, 53, 63–64, 80, 87; Louis Finkelstein, *American Spiritual Autobiographies: Fifteen Self-Portraits* (New York: Harpers, 1948), 41.

91. *Who's Who in Nebraska* (Lincoln: Nebraska Press Association, 1940), 684.

92. *Nebraska Independent,* March 20, 1902, 4, September 8, 1898, 4, 6, February 10, 1898, 4, January 26, 1899, 3, and December 29, 1898, 4.

93. *Nebraska Independent,* January 4, 1900, 3.

94. *Topeka Advocate,* February 3, 1897, 2. Also see *Nebraska Independent,* December 29, 1898, 4 and January 26, 1899, 3.

95. Donald M. McKale, *Tradition: A History of The Presidency of Clemson University* (Macon, GA: Mercer University Press, 1988), 47–49.

96. *Caucasian,* September 12, 1895, 3. On Butler, see Hunt, *Marion Butler and American Populism.* The *Caucasian* still occasionally attacked higher education. *Caucasian,* January 15, 1891, 2.

97. *Progressive Farmer,* September 17, 1895, 2.

98. *Chicago Daily Tribune,* November 13, 1890, 1.

99. Theodore Saloutos, *Farmers Movements in the South, 1865–1933* (Berkeley: University of California Press, 1960), 85–86, 209.

100. Rose, *The Intellectual Life of the British Working Classes,* 260–71.

101. Richard J. Altenbaugh, *Education for Struggle: The American Labor Colleges of the 1920s and 1930s* (Philadelphia, PA: Temple University Press, 1990).

102. *Proceedings of the North Carolina Farmers' Alliance, 1891,* 4–7; D. McKay to L. L. Polk, July 14, 1880, Polk Papers, box 4, folder 46; Postel, *The Populist Vision,* 11. American colleges had emphasized their development of leadership skills, such as oratory and

judgment, since the eighteenth century. Joseph F. Kett, "A Class Act: Collegiate Competition and American Society" in Michael C. Johanek, ed., *A Faithful Mirror: Reflections on the College Board and Education in America* (New York: College Entrance Examination Board, 2001), 118. On the place of the classics in American culture, see Caroline Winterer, *The Culture of Classicism: Ancient Greece and Rome in American Intellectual Life, 1780–1910* (Baltimore, MD: Johns Hopkins University Press, 2002).

103. *Progressive Farmer*, June 9, 1886, 1.

104. Hamlin Garland, *A Spoil of Office* (Boston: Arena, 1892), 30. Regarding Garland's political sympathies, see Postel, *The Populist Vision*, 231. On Bryan, see Poage, "College Career of William Jennings Bryan," 177–80.

105. Stuart Noblin, *Leonidas Lafayette Polk: Agrarian Crusader* (Chapel Hill: University of North Carolina Press, 1949), 22–41, 77–78, 144–46; Battle, *History of the University of North Carolina*, 374; John D. Hicks, "The Farmers' Alliance in North Carolina," *North Carolina Historical Review* 2 (April 1925), 162–87.

106. *Progressive Farmer*, July 21, 1887, 4 and September 15, 1887, 4.

107. Noblin, *Leonidas Lafayette Polk*, 7–8, 171, 184–89.

108. Noblin, *Leonidas LaFayette Polk*, 92; Goodwyn, *Democratic Promise*, 658 n26.

109. Frenise Logan, "The Movement in North Carolina to Establish a State Supported College for Negroes," *North Carolina Historical Review* 35 (April 1958), 167–70; Warmouth T. Gibbs, *History of the North Carolina Agricultural and Technical College, Greensboro, North Carolina* (Dubuque, IA: Wm. C. Brown, 1966).

110. "To the People of North Carolina," June 7, 1896, Butler Papers, Sub-Series 1.2, folder 20.

111. Report of the President, February 11, 1896, UNC Trustees, vol. 9; John K. Chapman, "Black Freedom and the University of North Carolina, 1793–1960" (PhD dissertation, University of North Carolina, 2006).

112. Theodore Mitchell, *Political Education in the Southern Farmers' Alliance, 1887–1900* (Madison: University of Wisconsin Press, 1987), 147.

113. No Populists appear in Kim Cary Warren's history of African American and Native American education in Kansas. Kim Cary Warren, *The Quest for Citizenship: African American and Native American Education in Kansas, 1880–1935* (Chapel Hill: University of North Carolina Press, 2010).

114. Griffin, *The University of Kansas*, 209–10; KSAC Report, 1885–86, 166; Carey, *Kansas State University*, 61–62.

115. *Industrialist*, March 1899, 153–54.

116. Thaddeus T. Smith, "Western University: A Ghost College in Kansas" (master's thesis, Kansas State College of Pittsburg, 1966), 2–10, 13–23, 27–37, 41–42; Erik Paul Conard, *A History of Kansas' Closed Colleges* (PhD dissertation, University of Oklahoma, 1970), 158–60; *Report of the Board of Trustees of the State Industrial Department at Western University, Quindaro, Kansas, 1904*.

117. Brenda J. Child, *Boarding School Seasons: American Indian Families, 1900–1940* (Lincoln: University of Nebraska Press, 1998), 7. Nor were North Carolina Populists

particularly supportive of Native American higher education. Populists apparently ignored the Lumbee (Croatan) normal school. Adolph L. Dial and David K. Eliades, *The Only Land I Know: A History of the Lumbee Indians* (San Francisco: Indian Historian Press, 1975), 91–93.

118. Louis R. Harlan, *Separate and Unequal: Public School Campaigns and Racism in The Southern Seaboard States, 1901–1915* (New York: Athenaeum, 1958, 1968); Postel, *The Populist Vision*, 61.

119. South Carolina's black land grant college charged no tuition for children whose parents earned less than $1,000 a year. North Carolina's admitted all literate students. John F. Potts, *A History of South Carolina State College, 1896–1978* (Orangeburg: South Carolina State College, 1978), 31; Gibbs, *History of the North Carolina Agricultural and Technical College*, 12.

120. Fred Humphries, "Land-Grant Institutions: Their Struggle for Survival," in Ralph Christy and Lionel Williamson, eds., *A Century of Service: Land Grant Colleges and Universities, 1890–1990* (New Brunswick, NJ: Transaction, 1992); Fred Williams, "The Second Morrill Act and Jim Crow Politics: Land-Grant Education at Arkansas A&M College, 1890–1927," *History of Higher Education Annual* 18 (1998), 81–92; Leedell W. Neyland, *Historically Black Land-Grant Institutions and the Development of Agriculture and Home Economics, 1890–1990* (Tallahassee: Florida A&M University Foundation, 1990), 19; Henry Drewry and Humphrey Doermann, *Stand and Prosper: Private Black Colleges and Their Students* (Princeton: Princeton University Press, 2001).

121. Barbara Solomon, *In the Company of Educated Women: A History of Women and Higher Education in America* (New Haven, CT: Yale University Press, 1985), 53; Rudolph, *The American College and University*, 314–15; Snyder, *120 Years of American Education*, 75–76. Also see Andrea G. Radke-Moss, *Bright Epoch: Women and Coeducation in the American West* (Lincoln: University of Nebraska Press, 2008).

122. Lynn D. Gordon, *Gender and Higher Education in the Progressive Era* (New Haven, CT: Yale University Press, 1990); Ruth Bordin, *Women at Michigan: The "Dangerous Experiment," 1870s to the Present* (Ann Arbor: University of Michigan Press, 1999).

123. *Omaha World Herald*, February 12, 1896, 8.

124. *Industrialist*, April 1899, 212; *Jeffersonian*, October 28, 1897, 2; James E. Hansen II, *Democracy's College in the Centennial State: A History of Colorado State University* (Fort Collins: Colorado State University Press, 1977), 111.

125. Postel, *The Populist Vision*, 91.

126. Daniel Walker Hollis, *University of South Carolina*, vol. 2 (Columbia: University of South Carolina Press, 1956), 170–71; William Henry Denton, "The Impact of Populism upon the Southern Educational Awakening" (PhD dissertation, University of North Carolina, 1965), 110; Steve Kantrowitz, *Ben Tillman and the Reconstruction of White Supremacy* (Chapel Hill: University of North Carolina Press, 2000), 117–19, 169, 182.

127. North Carolina Farmers' Alliance, *Proceedings of the North Carolina Farmers' State Alliance, 1890*, 35; *Prospectus of the Normal and Industrial School of North Carolina, 1892–93*, 6. NCFA leader Leonidas L. Polk sent his daughters to the Baptist Female Seminary of

Raleigh and supported the creation of a Baptist "Female University" (Meredith College). Noblin, *Leonidas Lafayette Polk*, 184–89, 251.

128. *Progressive Farmer*, February 2, 1897, 8.

129. Minutes of the Board of Trustees, February 18, 1897, UNC Trustees, vol. 9; Minutes of the Executive Committee, September 6, 1898 and Minutes of the Board of Trustees, February 14, 1899, UNC Trustees, vol. 10.

130. Few women enrolled before the 1920s. NC Trustees Mins, July 5, 1899 and August 2, 1899; Reagan, *North Carolina State University*, 50, 80.

131. *Nebraska Independent*, February 10, 1898, 4 and March 10, 1898, 4.

132. *Jeffersonian*, October 28, 1897, 2; Judy Green and Jeane Laduke, "Contributors to American Mathematics," in G. Kass-Simon and Patricia Farnes, eds., *Women of Science: Righting the Record* (Bloomington: Indiana University Press, 1990), 127–29.

133. Fairchild, "Populism in a State Educational Institution," 399.

134. *People's Poniard*, October 25, 1895, 1; *Lincoln Independent*, October 4, 1895, 4 and October 11, 1895, 4.

135. Richard Hofstadter, *Anti-Intellectualism in American Life* (New York: Vintage, 1963), 21.

Chapter 3. The Greatest Good
for the Greatest Number

1. W. Coleman to T. E. Will, November 20, 1897, box 3, folder 45, Kansas State Agricultural College Records, 1868–1902, Morse Department of Special Collections, Hale Library, Kansas State University.

2. Hugh Hawkins, "University Identity: The Teaching and Research Functions," in Alexandra Oleson and John Voss, eds., *The Organization of Knowledge in Modern America, 1860–1920* (Baltimore, MD: Johns Hopkins University Press, 1979), 289, 301. Regarding special students, see Merle Curti and Vernon Carstensen, *University of Wisconsin: A History, 1848–1925*, vol. 1 (Madison: University of Wisconsin Press, 1949), 620.

3. Alexis de Tocqueville, *Democracy in America*, vol. 1 (New York: Vintage Books, 1990), 202; Richard Hofstadter, *Anti-Intellectualism in American Life* (New York: Vintage, 1963), 25, 46–47, 51.

4. "The greatest good for the greatest number" was a common Populist slogan. For example, it graced the mastheads of *The People's Champion* (Hebron, Nebraska) and the *Hickory Mercury* (Hickory, North Carolina).

5. John R. Thelin, *A History of American Higher Education* (Baltimore, MD: Johns Hopkins University Press, 2004), 171–74; Roger L. Geiger, *To Advance Knowledge: The Growth of American Research Universities, 1900–1940* (New York: Oxford University Press, 1986), 13; Laurence R. Veysey, *The Emergence of the American University* (Chicago: University of Chicago Press, 1965), 357.

6. Josephus Daniels, *Tar Heel Editor* (Chapel Hill: University of North Carolina Press, 1939), 233–34; Marc A. VanOverbeke, *The Standardization of American Schooling:*

Linking Secondary and Higher Education, 1870–1910 (New York: Palgrave Macmillan, 2008), 102–3; Harold Wechsler, *The Qualified Student: A History of Selective College Admissions in America* (New York: Wiley, 1977), 46; Edwin C. Broome, *A Historical and Critical Discussion of College Admission Requirements* (Princeton: College Entrance Examination Board, 1963), 82.

7. W. J. Chase and C. H. Thurber, "Tabular Statement of Entrance Requirements to Representative Colleges and Universities of the United States," *The School Review* 4 (6) (June 1896), 341–412; Edward D. Eddy, *Colleges for Our Land and Time: The Land Grant Idea in American Education* (New York: Harper and Brothers, 1957), 66–67.

8. Wechsler, *The Qualified Student*, 24, 121–22.

9. See for example, E. Alderman to R. Wainwright, June 20, 1899 and E. Alderman to Uzzell, July 5, 1899, UNC Papers, box 50, vol. 1. Regarding conditioned students, see University of North Carolina, *The Record: Containing the Report of the President* (Chapel Hill: University of North Carolina Press, 1902), 19–21.

10. *The Journal of Proceedings and Addresses of the National Educational Association, 1889*, 374–75; Michael McGiffert, *The Higher Learning in Colorado: A Historical Study, 1860–1940* (Denver, CO: Sage Books, 1964), 34; VanOverbeke, *The Standardization of American Schooling*, 12.

11. George Edwin MacLean, "Present Standards of Higher Education in the United States," *United States Bureau of Education Bulletin*, no. 4 (Washington, DC: Government Printing Office, 1913), 40–41.

12. VanOverbeke, *The Standardization of American Schooling*, 120–21.

13. Charles W. Eliot, "The Gap Between Common Schools and Colleges," in *Education Reform, Essays and Addresses* (New York: Arno, 1969), 197–98; Canfield Journal, November 17, 1893.

14. *Proceedings and Addresses of the National Educational Association, 1891*, 213; Kansas Department of Public Instruction, *Biennial Report, 1897–98*, 24; NE Super, 1897–98, 5; NC Super, 1891–92, xxi, xlv; NC Super, 1898–1900, 69.

15. William A. Link, *A Hard Country and a Lonely Place: Schooling, Society, and Reform in Rural Virginia, 1870–1920* (Chapel Hill: University of North Carolina Press, 1986), 6, 53–54; Paul Theobald, *Call School: Rural Education in the Midwest to 1918* (Carbondale: Southern Illinois University Press, 1995), 119; James L. Leloudis, *Schooling the New South: Pedagogy, Self, and Society in North Carolina, 1880–1920* (Chapel Hill: University of North Carolina Press, 1996), 10–13. Pamela Riney-Kehrberg, *Childhood on the Farm: Work, Play, and Coming of Age in the Midwest* (Lawrence: University Press of Kansas, 2005), 68–71.

16. Broome, *A Historical and Critical Discussion of College Admission Requirements*, 105–6.

17. National Educational Association, *Report of Committee on College Entrance Requirements* (Chicago: University of Chicago Press, 1899), 75.

18. Jana Nidiffer and Jeffrey P. Bouman, "The Chasm Between Rhetoric and Reality: The Fate of the 'Democratic Ideal' When a Public University Becomes Elite," *Educational Policy* 15 (July 2001), 441.

19. LaVon M. Gappa, "Chancellor James Hulme Canfield: His Impact on the University of Nebraska, 1891–1895" (PhD dissertation, University of Nebraska, 1985),

105; Marjean Snyder Mallard, "The Development of the University of Texas during the 1890s" (master's thesis, University of Texas, 1970), 14; NC Fac Mins, January 6, 1890 through December 4, 1893; NCCAMA Report, 1896, 41.

20. Willa Cather, *The Professor's House* (New York: Vintage, [1925], 1990), 95–97; Willa Cather, *My Ántonia* (Lincoln: University of Nebraska Press, [1918], 1994), 220, 224, 249–50, 463.

21. President's Report, February 27, 1889, UNC Trustees, vol. S-8; G. T. Winston to W. L. Sanders, August 14, 1887, UNC, box 17, folder 554.

22. VanOverbeke, *The Standardization of American Schooling*, 123.

23. Veysey, *The Emergence of the American University*, 64.

24. Mabel Hardy Pollitt, *A Biography of James Kennedy Patterson* (Louisville, KY: Westerfield-Bonte, 1925), 266.

25. Earle Dudley Ross, *Democracy's College: The Land-Grant Movement in the Formative Stage* (Ames: Iowa State College Press, 1942), 113–14.

26. *Journal of Proceedings and Addresses of the National Educational Association, 1888*, 167.

27. On colleges' initial emphasis on social class, see Joseph F. Kett, "A Class Act: Collegiate Competition and American Society" in Michael C. Johanek, ed., *A Faithful Mirror: Reflections on the College Board and Education in America* (New York: College Entrance Examination Board, 2001), 106–10.

28. James H. Baker, *Educational Aims and Civic Needs* (New York: Longmans and Green, 1913), 145.

29. Frederick Jackson Turner, "Pioneer Ideals and the State University," in *The Frontier in American History* (New York: Henry Holt, 1920), 283.

30. Pollitt, *A Biography of James Kennedy Patterson*, 266; University of Kansas, *Biennial Report, 1883–84*, 17; University of the State of Missouri, *Biennial Report of the Board of Curators to the General Assembly, 1892*, 22–24.

31. James E. Pollard, *History of the Ohio State University: The Story of its First Seventy-Five Years, 1873–1948* (Columbus: Ohio State University Press, 1952), 37–39; Winton U. Solberg, *The University of Illinois, 1867–1894: An Intellectual and Cultural History* (Urbana: University of Illinois Press, 1968), 232, 269; Gould P. Colman, *Education and Agriculture: A History of the New York State College of Agriculture at Cornell University* (Ithaca, NY: Cornell University Press, 1963), 91–92; Michael Dennis, *Lessons in Progress: State Universities and Progressivism in the New South, 1880–1920* (Urbana: University of Illinois Press, 2001), 4, 92–93; United States Department of Agriculture, *Proceedings of the Annual Convention of American Agricultural Colleges and Experiment Stations* (Washington, DC: Government Printing Office, 1897), 61; University of New Hampshire, *History of the University of New Hampshire, 1866–1941* (Durham, NH: University of New Hampshire, 1941), 117–20.

32. Russel Nye, *Midwestern Progressive Politics: A Historical Study of Its Origins and Development, 1870–1950* (East Lansing: Michigan State College Press, 1951), 136. On populist skepticism of meritocracy, see Christopher Lasch, *The Revolt of the Elites and the Betrayal of Democracy* (New York: Norton, 1995).

33. *Alliance Independent*, May 18, 1893, 4.

34. Alvin Johnson, *Pioneer's Progress* (New York: Viking, 1952), 79.

35. Theodore Mitchell, *Political Education in the Southern Farmers' Alliance, 1887–1900* (Madison: University of Wisconsin Press, 1987), 124–27.

36. John R. Morris, *Davis H. Waite: The Ideology of a Western Populist* (Washington, DC: University Press of America, 1982), 20, 114.

37. Kansas Department of Public Instruction, *Biennial Report, 1893–94*, 61, 64; Kansas Department of Public Instruction, *Biennial Report, 1897–98*, 25–27; *Topeka Advocate*, January 6, 1897.

38. NE Super, 1895, 107, 133; *Nebraska Independent*, May 13, 1897, 4, May 20, 1897, 4, June 10, 1897, 4, June 17, 1897, 3, September 2, 1897, 4, September 23, 1897, 4, September 30, 1897, 4, and May 26, 1898, 4; NE Super, 1897–98, 14, 31.

39. *Industrialist*, July 1898, 443–49.

40. *Journal of Proceedings and Addresses of the National Educational Association, 1886*, 290; Joseph L. Henderson, *Admission to College by Certificate* (New York: Teachers College, 1912), 73, 83; *Journal of Proceedings and Addresses of the National Educational Association, 1877*, 71.

41. Pollard, *History of the Ohio State University*, 43; James Gray, *The University of Minnesota, 1851–1951* (Minneapolis: University of Minnesota Press, 1951), 49.

42. However, universities typically continued to offer remedial courses in some form or another for years after the official closure of preparatory departments. Henderson, *Admission to College by Certificate*, 82; Wechsler, *The Qualified Student*, 6, 11, 21.

43. Dennis, *Lessons in Progress*, 76, 92, 112–13.

44. Edward Krug, *The Shaping of the American High School*, vol. 1 (Madison: University of Wisconsin Press, 1969), 129.

45. United States Department of Agriculture, *Proceedings of the Annual Convention of American Agricultural Colleges and Experiment Stations* (Washington, DC: Government Printing Office, 1897), 59.

46. President's Report, February 27, 1889, UNC Trustees, vol. S-8; President's Report, February 11, 1891, UNC Trustees, vol. S-8.

47. "To Teachers Preparing Students for the University," October 1, 1889, UNC, box 18, folder 601.

48. Battle did believe that UNC had a constitutional obligation to remain accessible to teacher trainees. President's Report, February 27, 1889, UNC Trustees Papers, vol. S-8.

49. UNC Report, 1902, 19–21; UNC Report, 1903, 9–10; Louis R. Wilson, *The University of North Carolina, 1900–1930: The Making of a Modern University* (Chapel Hill: University of North Carolina Press, 1957), 22.

50. NC Trustees Mins, August 2, 1899; G. Winston to C. Alston, August 24, 1899, George T. Winston (series 2), flat box 7, North Carolina State University, Office of the Chancellor, Early Chancellors Records, UA 002.001.001, Special Collections Research Center, North Carolina State University Libraries, Raleigh, NC.

51. For a conventional statement about the closure of preparatory departments, see Johnson, "Misconceptions about the Early Land-Grant Colleges," 347.

52. Frederick Rudolph, *The American College and University* (New York: Knopf, 1962), 284.

53. *Alliance Independent*, September 8, 1892, 3.

54. Populists were not unanimous. Some complained that preparatory departments served wealthy local youth. John K. Bettersworth, *People's University: The Centennial History of Mississippi State* (Jackson: University Press of Mississippi, 1980), 132–34.

55. Attendance in the KSAC preparatory department increased from 67 in 1896–97 to 110 in 1898–99. KSAC Report, 1899–1900, 47; Minutes of the KSAC Board of Regents, vol. B, March 25, 1898, Morse Department of Special Collections, Hale Library, Kansas State University; *Industrialist*, October 1898, 580. The preparatory department continued to grow after the end of the Populist regime, especially after the college raised its entrance requirements in 1903. KSAC Report, 1903–4; KSAC Report, 1905–6.

56. Clifford S. Griffin, *The University of Kansas* (Lawrence: University of Kansas Press, 1974), 299–300.

57. NU Report, 1889–90, 32–34.

58. NU Regents Mins, vol. 3, June 11, 1890 and June 12, 1890; *Nebraska State Journal*, February 27, 1891, 4; *Farmers' Alliance*, March 7, 1891, 4; Report of the Committee Appointed by the General Faculty on Extensions of Courses of Study, June 6, 1893, NU Regents Papers, box 11, folder 86; Robert Manley, *Centennial History of the University of Nebraska*, vol. 1 (Lincoln: University of Nebraska Press, 1969), 126.

59. *Hesperian*, February 15, 1894, 2–4; Canfield, "The Opportunities of the Rural Population for Higher Education," 384; Gappa, "Chancellor James Hulme Canfield," 182.

60. Untitled clipping, February 10, 189(5?), in University of Nebraska Newspaper Clippings Scrapbook, 1895–97, Archives and Special Collections, University of Nebraska–Lincoln Libraries. Canfield was still sympathetic to school officials who were concerned that eighth graders dropped out in order to attend NU's preparatory Latin School. He agreed to phase out the Latin School when most towns had adequate secondary schools. Canfield Journal, August 29, 1891; Manley, *Centennial History of the University of Nebraska*, 126; NU Report, 1893–94, 14–19.

61. Johnson, *Pioneer's Progress*, 82; *Nebraskan*, September 27, 1895, 1; Manley, *Centennial History of the University of Nebraska*, 127; George E. MacLean, "Inaugural Address," February 14, 1896, George E. MacLean Papers, Office of the Chancellor, RG 05, box 1, "Speeches" Folder, Archives and Special Collections, University of Nebraska–Lincoln Libraries.

62. *Nebraska Independent*, May 13, 1897, 4, May 20, 1897, 4, June 10, 1897, 4, June 17, 1897, 3, September 2, 1897, 4, September 23, 1897, 4, and September 30, 1897, 4.

63. NU Report, 1896–98, 8; J. Dickinson to G. MacLean, February 7, 1898, file 101, box 13, NU Regents Papers; NU Regents Mins, vol. 4, August 3, 1897.

64. On the early struggles of the land grant colleges, see Eldon L. Johnson, "Misconceptions about the Early Land-Grant Colleges," *Journal of Higher Education* 52 (July–August, 1981): 336–42.

65. United States Department of Agriculture, *Proceedings of the Annual Convention of American Agricultural Colleges and Experiment Stations* (Washington, DC: Government Printing Office, 1896), 19.

66. Christopher Allen, "The Land Grant Act of 1862 and the Founding of NCCAMA" (master's thesis, North Carolina State University, 1984), 32.

67. *Progressive Farmer*, November 24, 1886, 3.

68. NCCAMA Catalog, 1890, 39–40. NCCAMA trustees had originally agreed on slightly higher standards but eventually decided to eliminate a history examination and ease the requirements in English and math. NC Trustees Mins, May 22, 1889 and July 11, 1889.

69. No land grant colleges required Latin or Greek, but 17 percent required French or German. U.S. Department of Agriculture, *Proceedings of the Annual Convention of American Agricultural Colleges and Experiment Stations* (Washington, DC: Government Printing Office, 1896), 19.

70. NC Fac Mins, December 30, 1889, January 27, 1890, February 10, 1890, and October 27, 1891; NCCAMA Report, 1890, 4; NC Trustees Mins, June 17, 1891 and December 3, 1891.

71. NCCAMA Report, 1890, 4, 24.

72. NC Fac Mins, February 1, 1892, February 8, 1892; David A. Lockmiller, *History of the North Carolina State College of Agriculture and Engineering of the University of North Carolina, 1889–1939* (Raleigh: North Carolina State College of Agriculture and Engineering, 1939), 50; NCCAMA Catalog, 1893–94, 4–8, 16.

73. NCCAMA Report, 1896, 12–13.

74. NCCAMA also raised the minimum age limit to 16 and launched an admission by certificate policy. NCCAMA Catalog, 1901, 14; NC Trustees Mins, August 2, 1899; NC Fac Mins, March 5, 1900; NCCAMA Report, 1899–1900, 6; *Progressive Farmer*, September 12, 1899, 2. North Carolina would not have a statewide network of high schools until 1907. Wilson, *The University of North Carolina*, 22.

75. Fifty graded county schools were approved by 1892. KSAC Report, 1891–92, 7.

76. *Proceedings of the Annual Convention of American Agricultural Colleges and Experiment Stations, 1896*, 19 n64.

77. KSAC Catalog, 1891–92; KSAC Catalog, 1897–98.

78. *Industrialist*, June 23, 1894, 163 and October 1898, 558–62; *Manhattan Republic*, September 10, 1897, 75–76.

79. *Nationalist*, October 7, 1897, 2, October 21, 1898, 2, and November 18, 1898, 2.

80. J. T. Willard to G. Fairchild, May 4, 1899 and May 15, 1899, KSC Letters.

81. Meeting of the Board of Regents, vol. B, June 6, 1899, Kansas State Agricultural College Papers, Morse Department of Special Collections, Hale Library, Kansas State University; *Industrialist*, July 1899, 468. Clipping from the *Manhattan Republic*, June 2, 1899, in KSU Clippings, vol. 4; *Student Herald*, June 1, 1899, 2.

82. *Manhattan Republic*, June 2, 1899, 1.

83. KSAC Report, 1899–1900, 41; *Industrialist*, July 1899b, 1, 12 (the Will and Nichols administrations each published issues of the *Industrialist* in July of 1899).

84. *Student Herald*, September 28, 1899, 31. In 1903, KSAC raised its entrance requirements to the level of ninth grade in the "best high schools" despite concerns

about access for rural students. KSAC Report, 1903–4, 5; Kansas State Agricultural College Faculty Record, vol. D, March 24, 1903, Morse Department of Special Collections, Hale Library, Kansas State University.

85. *The University of Nebraska, The Industrial College: A Brief Historical Sketch* (Lincoln: 1892), 12–13. The industrial college required the same number of high school credits, though it required fewer English and foreign language credits and more science credits. NU Regents Mins, vol., 4, April 11, 1900.

86. NU Report, 1887–88, 10–11.

87. Gappa, "Chancellor James Hulme Canfield," 43, 45; *Nebraska State Journal,* July 12, 1891; Manley, *Centennial History of the University of Nebraska*, 114–16.

88. Johnson, *Pioneer's Progress*, 47, 77.

89. Alvin Johnson to Don Mauricio Hochschild, April 4, 1946, box 2, folder 41a, Alvin Johnson Papers, Manuscripts and Archives, Yale University Library.

90. Canfield to Examiners, September 8, 1892, James H. Canfield General Correspondence, 1891–1895, James Hulme Canfield Papers, Office of the Chancellor, RG 05, Archives and Special Collections, University of Nebraska–Lincoln Libraries.

91. Canfield Journal, January 2, 1892 and January 4, 1892; Gappa, "Chancellor James Hulme Canfield," 105.

92. Canfield Journal, July 10, 1891; Recommendations of the General Faculty for Curricular and Calendar Changes, April 9, 1895, NU Regents Papers, box 12, folder 92.

93. *Journal of Proceedings and Addresses of the National Educational Association, 1894*, 623–24.

94. *Nebraska Independent*, May 20, 1897, 4, June 10, 1897, 4, June 17, 1897, 3, September 2, 1897, 4, September 23, 1897, 4, September 30, 1897, 4, December 29, 1898, 4, and January 26, 1899, 3.

95. On Andrews, see James E. Hansen, "Gallant, Stalwart Bennie: Elisha Benjamin Andrews (1844–1917), An Educator's Odyssey" (PhD dissertation, University of Denver, 1969).

96. Manley, *Centennial History of the University of Nebraska*, 91, 171; NU Regents Mins, vol., 4, April 11, 1900; NU Report, 1899–1900, 8, 19. Compared to the industrial college, the college of literature, science, and the arts, required a year of history and third year of language (two years had to be Latin). The board tempered this increase in requirements by accepting more elective credits. On the fourteen-unit requirement, see Ellen Condliffe Lagemann, *Private Power for the Public Good: A History of the Carnegie Foundation for the Advancement of Teaching* (Middletown, CT: Wesleyan University Press, 1983), 95.

97. NU Regents Mins, vol. 4, April 9, 1901.

98. Roy V. Scott, *The Reluctant Farmer: The Rise of Agricultural Extension to 1914* (Urbana: University of Illinois Press, 1970), 54–56; *Journal of Proceedings and Addresses of the National Educational Association, 1890*, 213–18.

99. Canfield suggested that the school only charge five dollars and require only basic common-school subjects. Canfield Journal, September 28, 1891 and October 2, 1891; NU Report, 1893–94, 14–19.

100. NU Report, 1895–96, 15–16; NU Report, 1897–98, 7, 22; Manley, *Centennial History of the University of Nebraska*, 126, 142. Report of the School of Agriculture, April 9, 1898, NU Regents Papers, box 13, folder 102.

101. NU Report, 1899–1900, 23.

102. NU Regents Mins, vol. 4, February 15, 1898 and April 13, 1898; Report of the Committee on Reorganization of the School of Agriculture, April 13, 1898, NU Regents Papers, box 13, folder 102; *The Populist*, February 22, 1998, 6.

103. *Prairie Home*, December 7, 1899, 2; *Wisner Chronicle*, November 15, 1902, 2; *Nebraska Independent*, September 8, 1898, 4, 6.

104. Manley, *Centennial History of the University of Nebraska*, 175–77; Elvin F. Frolik and Ralston J. Graham, *The University of Nebraska–Lincoln College of Agriculture: The First Century* (Lincoln: University of Nebraska, 1987), 359.

105. Alfred Charles True, *A History of Agricultural Education in the United States, 1785–1925* (Washington, DC: Government Printing Office, 1929), 274, 336.

106. George M. Woytanowitz, *University Extension: The Early Years in the United States, 1885–1915* (Iowa City: American College Testing Program, 1974), 19–26, 106–7; Joseph F. Kett, *The Pursuit of Knowledge Under Difficulties: From Self-Improvement to Adult Education in America, 1750–1990* (Stanford: Stanford University Press, 1994), 185–90, 201.

107. Woytanowitz, *University Extension*, 25–26.

108. Roger L. Geiger, "The Era of Multipurpose Colleges in American Higher Education," *The American College in the Nineteenth Century* (Nashville, TN: Vanderbilt University Press, 2000), 150.

109. Scott, *The Reluctant Farmer*, 71, 153–55.

110. Curti and Carstensen, *University of Wisconsin*, vol. 1, 470–75. Also see Scott, *The Reluctant Farmer*, 81–83. For a different interpretation, see Daniel P. Carpenter, *The Forging of Bureaucratic Autonomy: Reputations, Networks, and Policy Innovation in Executive Agencies, 1862–1928* (Princeton: Princeton University Press, 2001), 229.

111. *Weekly Commoner*, February 12, 1897, 3.

112. *Farmers' Alliance*, December 24, 1891, 5; Gappa, "Chancellor James Hulme Canfield," 159; Report of the Short Course in Agriculture, February 24, 1894, NU Regents Papers, box 11, folder 90.

113. President George Fairchild had ended the program in 1896. *Industrialist*, August 22, 1891, 1; KSAC Report, 1895–96, 11, 35; KSAC Report, 1899–1900, 35; *Advocate and News*, February 23, 1898, 12.

114. *Industrialist*, November 1898, 598.

115. Woytanowitz, *University Extension*, 69–71.

116. Scott, *The Reluctant Farmer*, 64–72.

117. Alan Marcus, *Agricultural Science and the Quest for Legitimacy: Farmers, Agricultural Colleges, and Experiment Stations, 1870–1890* (Ames: Iowa State University Press, 1985), 39; Madison Kuhn, *Michigan State: The First Hundred Years* (East Lansing: Michigan State University Press, 1955), 137–41; James Ferguson, "The Grange and Farmer Education in Mississippi," *Journal of Southern History* 8 (November 1942), 502–4; *Atlanta Constitution*,

December 14, 1891, 1. Populists were not unanimous. Some called the institutes "humbugs" run by impractical professors and wealthy landlords. Scott, *The Reluctant Farmer*, 101.

118. Frolik and Graham, *The University of Nebraska–Lincoln College of Agriculture*, 8.

119. *Farmers' Alliance*, October 4, 1890, 3 and February 14, 1891, 8.

120. *Hesperian*, February 15, 1894, 2–4.

121. Report of the Farmers Institutes, April 10, 1893, NU Regents Papers, box 11, folder 84.

122. NU Regents Mins, vol. 4, December 13, 1899.

123. Thomas E. Will, "How to Organize the Union for Practical Progress in the Villages," *Arena* 12 (64) (March 1895), 59–72; Ross E. Paulson, *Radicalism and Reform: The Vrooman Family and American Social Thought, 1837–1937* (Lexington: University of Kentucky Press, 1968), 96.

124. *Manhattan Republic*, July 14, 1899, 4; Howard V. Davis, *Frank Parsons: Prophet, Innovator, Counselor* (Carbondale: Southern Illinois University Press, 1969), 35–36, 87–88.

125. *The People's College News*, May 1916, 30, Hoffman Papers, box 2, folder 19; C. B. Hoffman to Comrade, February 8, 1915, Hoffman Papers, box 2, folder 11; E. V. Debs to C. B. Hoffman, August 15, 1914, Hoffman Papers, box 1, folder 7.

126. KSAC Report, 1899–1900, 31–32; J. D. Walters, *History of Kansas State Agricultural College* (Manhattan: Kansas State Agricultural College, 1909), 180–83; *Industrialist*, June 1898, 417 and May 1899, 301–18; Julius T. Willard, *History of Kansas State College of Agriculture and Applied Science* (Manhattan: Kansas State College Press, 1940), 66.

127. *Advocate and News*, December 22, 1897, 4 and August 24, 1898, 8.

128. KSAC's student body had grown by a yearly average of 6 percent since 1880, whereas enrollment rose by 9 percent in 1897–98 and 8 percent in 1898–99, the peak years of Populist intervention. The increase in special students was particularly substantial, rising from between one and six students a year during the previous two decades to fifteen students in 1897–98 and forty students in 1898–99. KSAC Report, 1899–1900, 47; KSAC Report, 1905–6, 30. For enrollment growth during NU's Populist era, see NE Super, 1886–88, 8; NE Super, 1902–4, 62.

129. Eddy, *Colleges for Our Land and Time*, 67.

130. NCCAMA Report, 1893, 39–40; NCCAMA Faculty Mins, June 3, 1895.

131. KSAC Reports, 1883–84 through 1903–4.

132. The proportion of freshmen leaving the college of literature had been 30 percent during the late 1880s and remained at 32 percent among students entering in 1900. NE Super, 1886–88, 8; NE Super, 1900–1902, 44–45.

Chapter 4. Looking Forward

1. Edward Bellamy, *Looking Backward 2000–1887* (Cambridge, MA: Harvard University Press, [1888], 1967), 138.

2. Edward Bellamy, *Equality* (New York: Appleton, 1897), 246–48.

3. Populist newspapers endorsed *Looking Backward* and some Farmers' Alliances gave away free copies. *The American Nonconformist and Kansas Industrial Liberator*, June 27, 1889, 1, August 29, 1889, 7, and July 4, 1889, 1; *Farmers' Alliance*, February 8, 1890, 2. Also see John L. Thomas, *Alternative America: Henry George, Edward Bellamy, Henry Demarest Lloyd, and the Adversary Tradition* (Cambridge, MA: Harvard University Press, 1983), 275.

4. *Industrialist*, January 1898, 56–61, October 1898, 563–69, March 1899, 155, and April 1899, 210–18.

5. *Lincoln Independent*, December 6, 1895, 4.

6. On the lack of scholarship about college access for poor students in the late nineteenth century, see Jana Nidiffer, "Poor Historiography: The 'Poorest' in American Higher Education," *History of Education Quarterly* 39 (Fall 1999), 321–37. An exception is Rupert Wilkinson, *Aiding Students, Buying Students: Financial Aid in America* (Nashville, TN: Vanderbilt University Press, 2005).

7. Colin B. Burke, *American Collegiate Populations: A Test of the Traditional View* (New York: New York University Press, 1982), 215.

8. Richard Henry Jesse, "The Function of the State University," *Journal of Proceedings and Addresses of the National Educational Association, 1891*, 606–7; Frederick Jackson Turner, "Pioneer Ideals and the State University," *The Frontier in American History* (Huntington, NY: Krieger, 1976), 282; Jana Nidiffer and Jeffrey P. Bouman, "The Chasm Between Rhetoric and Reality: The Fate of the 'Democratic Ideal' When a Public University Becomes Elite," *Educational Policy* 15 (July 2001), 437. G. F. Mellen, *Popular Errors Concerning Higher Education in the United States and the Remedy* (Leipsic: Gressner and Schramm, 1890), 46–47; Merle Curti and Vernon Carstensen, *University of Wisconsin: A History, 1848–1925*, vol. 1 (Madison: University of Wisconsin Press, 1949), 492; Christopher Allen, "The Land Grant Act of 1862 and the Founding of NCCAMA" (master's thesis, North Carolina State University, 1984), 19.

9. Hal Bridges, "D. H. Hill and Higher Education in the New South," *Arkansas Historical Quarterly* 15 (Summer 1956), 117–18. Also see John Thelin, "Higher Education's Student Financial Aid Enterprise in Historical Perspective," in Frederick M. Hess, ed., *Footing the Tuition Bill: The New Student Loan Sector* (Washington, DC: American Enterprise Institute, 2007), 21; Eldon L. Johnson, "Misconceptions about the Early Land-Grant Colleges," *Journal of Higher Education* 52 (July–August, 1981), 338.

10. John Aubrey Douglass, *The Conditions for Admission: Access, Equity, and the Social Contract of Public Universities* (Stanford: Stanford University Press, 2007), 18–19.

11. James R Montgomery, *The Volunteer State Forges Its University: The University of Tennessee, 1887–1919* (Knoxville: University of Tennessee Record, 1966), 4, 28; Thomas J. Giddens, "Origins of State Scholarship Programs: 1647–1913," *College and University* 46 (Fall 1970), 37–45; Daniel Walker Hollis, *University of South Carolina*, vol. 2 (Columbia: University of South Carolina Press, 1956), 188.

12. Bridges, "D. H. Hill and Higher Education in the New South," 115; David W. Levy, *The University of Oklahoma: A History*, vol. 1 (Norman: University of Oklahoma Press, 2005), 102.

13. Ray Stannard Baker, *Native American: The Book of My Youth* (New York: Scribner's, 1941), 199.

14. The University of Nebraska, *Semi-Centennial Anniversary Book* (Lincoln: University of Nebraska Press, 1919), 43; *Hesperian*, February 15, 1894, 16.

15. KSAC Report, 1885–86, 62.

16. NC Fac Mins, December 2, 1889 and January 12, 1892.

17. President's Report, February 27, 1889, UNC Trustees, vol. S-8; J. Manning to W. L. Sanders, February 8, 1888, UNC, box 17, folder 561.

18. See for example, KSAC Catalog, 1893–94, 66.

19. J. Gregory Behle and William E. Maxwell, "The Social Origins of Students at the Illinois Industrial University, 1868–1894," *History of Higher Education Annual* 18 (1998), 100–101; Nidiffer and Bouman, "The Chasm Between Rhetoric and Reality," 432–42.

20. Winton U. Solberg, *The University of Illinois, 1867–1894: An Intellectual and Cultural History* (Urbana: University of Illinois Press, 1968), 170, 380.

21. Theodore Dreiser, *Dawn: An Autobiography of Early Youth* (Santa Rosa, CA: Black Sparrow Press, 1998), 368–75, 380, 389, 442.

22. Alvin Johnson, *Pioneer's Progress* (New York: Viking, 1952), 170.

23. Daniel A. Clark, *Creating the College Man: American Mass Magazines and Middle-Class Manhood, 1890–1915* (Madison: University of Wisconsin Press, 2010), 37, 56.

24. Charles W. Eliot, "Inaugural Address as President of Harvard College," *Education Reform, Essays and Addresses* (New York: Arno, 1969), 19–20; Hugh Hawkins, *Between Harvard and America: The Educational Leadership of Charles W. Eliot* (New York: Oxford University Press, 1972), 147–48, 165–67, 170–71; David Starr Jordan, "An Apology for the American University," *The Trend of the American University* (Stanford: Stanford University Press, 1929), 69; W. Bruce Leslie, *Gentlemen and Scholars: College and Community in the "Age of the University," 1865–1917* (University Park: Pennsylvania State University Press, 1992), 113, 119, 240.

25. Mabel Hardy Pollitt, *A Biography of James Kennedy Patterson* (Louisville, KY: Westerfield-Bonte, 1925), 99, 296.

26. Nidiffer and Bouman, "The Chasm Between Rhetoric and Reality," 439–40; Oscar Handlin and Mary F. Handlin, *The American College and American Culture: Socialization as a Function of Higher Education* (New York: McGraw-Hill, 1970), 52; James B. Angell, "The State Universities of the West," *State Aid to Higher Education: A Series of Addresses Delivered at the Johns Hopkins University* (Baltimore, MD: Johns Hopkins University Press, 1898); Frederick Rudolph, *The American College and University* (New York: Knopf, 1962), 279.

27. Charles R. Van Hise, "Inaugural Address," in Hugh Hawkins ed., *The Emerging University and Industrial America* (Malabar, FL: Krieger, 1985), 27.

28. Thomas D. Clark, *Indiana University: Midwestern Pioneer*, vol. 4 (Bloomington: Indiana University Press, 1970), 269.

29. John R. Thelin, *A History of American Higher Education* (Baltimore, MD: Johns Hopkins University Press, 2004), 171. Also see Clark, *Creating the College Man*, 122.

30. Lewis Perry, *Intellectual Life in America: A History* (New York: F. Watts, 1984), 284.

31. *Biblical Recorder*, August 15, 1894, 1. On the culture of self-help, see Irvin G. Wyllie, *The Self-Made Man in America: The Myth of Rags to Riches* (New York: Free Press, 1954).

32. *Nebraskan-Hesperian*, October 31, 1899, 8. Also see J. L. Pickard, "Scholarships," *Journal of Proceedings and Addresses of the National Educational Association, 1880*, 159.

33. Willa Cather, *My Ántonia* (Lincoln: University of Nebraska Press, [1918], 1994), 250; Willa Cather, *The Professor's House* (New York: Vintage, [1925], 1990), 95.

34. Henry Seidel Canby, "College Life in the Nineties," *Harpers Monthly Magazine* (February 1936), 354.

35. *Chickasaw Messenger*, September 29, 1887, 3 and June 14, 1888, 1; John K. Bettersworth, *People's University: The Centennial History of Mississippi State* (Jackson: University Press of Mississippi, 1980), 92–97.

36. *Atlanta Constitution*, November 17, 1894, 7.

37. *Nebraska Independent*, March 13, 1902, 4.

38. Helen Horowitz, *Campus Life: Undergraduate Cultures from the end of the Eighteenth Century to the Present* (New York: Knopf, 1987), 38–39, 47.

39. *Journal of Proceedings and Addresses of the National Educational Association, 1890*, 707–11.

40. Report of the President, February 11, 1896, UNC Trustees, vol. 9; Rose H. Holder, *McIver of North Carolina* (Chapel Hill: University of North Carolina Press, 1957), 165; Allen W. Trelease, *Making North Carolina Literate: The University of North Carolina at Greensboro, from Normal School to Metropolitan University* (Durham, NC: Carolina Academic Press, 2004), 42.

41. Robert W. Topping, *A Century and Beyond: The History of Purdue University* (West Lafayette, IN: Purdue University Press, 1988), 109.

42. *Nebraskan*, February 26, 1897, 1–2.

43. *Jeffersonian*, June 24, 1897, 2; Clifford S. Griffin, *The University of Kansas* (Lawrence: University of Kansas Press, 1974), 210.

44. *Nebraska Independent*, March 13, 1902, 4, October 14, 1897, 4, and October 21, 1897, 4.

45. Johnson, *Pioneer's Progress*, 81–87. Also see "Canfield to All Students," October 2, 1894, James H. Canfield General Correspondence, 1891–1895, James Hulme Canfield Papers, Office of the Chancellor, RG 05, Archives and Special Collections, University of Nebraska–Lincoln Libraries.

46. *Wealth Makers of the World*, May 10, 1894, 3.

47. KU Report, 1889–90, 7–8; KU Report, 1893–94, 14; KU Report, 1895–96, 12–13.

48. *Lawrence Journal*, January 30, 1897, 9; *Student's Journal*, February 8, 1895, 2.

49. KSAC Report, 1885–86, 62; KSAC Report, 1887–88, 75–76; KSAC Report, 1889–90, 67; KSAC Report, 1891–92, 36; KSAC Report, 1893–94, 39; KSAC Report, 1895–96, 40; KSAC Report, 1897–98, 39.

50. NU Report, 1897–98, 8; NU Report, 1889–90, 31; NU Report, 1891–92, 11; NU Report, 1893–94, 26; NU Report, 1895–96, 22; NU Report, 1899–1900, 39.

51. UNC Report, 1887, 12–18.

52. George T. Winston, "The Influence of Universities and Public Schools on National Life and Character" (Austin, TX: 1896), 6; President's Report, February 18, 1892 and February 11, 1896, UNC Trustees, vol. 9 and vol. 10.

53. "The University of North Carolina: Necessity for Its Existence and Support," December 20, 1894, UNC, box 19, folder 649; "Facts about the University: A Statement by the Executive Committee of the Board of Trustees," 1893, UNC, box 19, folder 646; Winston, "The Influence of Universities and Public Schools on National Life and Character," 10; Report of the Visiting Committee, June 17, 1896 and June 1, 1897, UNC Trustees, vol. 9.

54. Paul M. Gaston, *The New South Creed: A Study in Southern Mythmaking* (New York: Knopf, 1970), 107–9.

55. Dumas Malone, *Edwin A. Alderman: A Biography* (New York: Doubleday, 1940), 17; *The Inauguration of Edwin A. Alderman, President of the University of North Carolina* (Chapel Hill: University of North Carolina, 1897), 23–27; Report of the President, February 18, 1897, UNC Trustees, vol. 9; Luther L. Gobbel, *Church-State Relationships in Education in North Carolina since 1776* (Durham, NC: Duke University Press, 1938), 166; *Caucasian*, June 10, 1897, 1.

56. J. Carr to E. Alderman, June 18, 1897, UNC, box 20, folder 666.

57. Between 1892 and 1900, two-thirds of NCNIS students reported that they would not have been able to afford a private college. NC Super, 1893–94, 20–23; NC Super, 1898–1900, 471–72; Pamela Dean, "Covert Curriculum: Class, Gender, and Student Culture at a New South Woman's College, 1892–1910" (PhD dissertation, University of North Carolina, 1995), 114–17.

58. Thomas Dyer, *The University of Georgia: A Bicentennial History, 1785–1985* (Athens: University of Georgia Press, 1985), 124–5; Elisha Benjamin Andrews, "Eastern Universities and Western," *The Independent* 57 (July–December 1904), 676. Also see Nidiffer and Bouman, "The Chasm Between Rhetoric and Reality," 439.

59. Hawkins, *Between Harvard and America*, 152–56.

60. Mellen, *Popular Errors Concerning Higher Education in the United States and the Remedy*, 41, 56, 61.

61. *Biblical Recorder*, July 15, 1896, 4 and August 5, 1896, 2.

62. Judges upheld the scholarships in Indiana and New York, but not in Missouri. Alexander Brody, *The American State and Higher Education: The Legal, Political, and Constitutional Relationship* (Washington, DC: American Council on Education, 1935), 58–59; Edward Elliot and M. M. Chambers, *The Colleges and the Courts: Judicial Decisions Regarding Institutions of Higher Education in the United States* (New York: Carnegie Foundation for the Advancement of Teaching, 1936), 55–58.

63. *Biblical Recorder*, July 15, 1896, 4; *News and Observer*, March 6, 1895, 1, 5. Also see James R. Montgomery, *The Volunteer State Forges Its University: The University of Tennessee, 1887–1919* (Knoxville: University of Tennessee Record, 1966), 4, 28.

64. Loans were the only form of need-based aid at the University of Michigan as

late as 1910. Nidiffer and Bouman, "The Chasm Between Rhetoric and Reality," 442. By 1930, the majority of land grant colleges offered some form of loans. Arthur J. Klein, "Survey of Land-Grant Colleges and Universities," *United States Office of Education Bulletin*, no. 9 (Washington, DC: Government Printing Office, 1930), 509.

65. Populists, however, were not unanimous. See letter to the editor in the *Caucasian*, January 15, 1891, 2.

66. Harrison Hale, *University of Arkansas, 1871–1948* (Fayetteville: University of Arkansas Press, 1948), 57–60.

67. *Progressive Farmer*, February 10, 1886, 4–5 and March 3, 1887, 4; Document dated March 2, 1887, "Legislation" box, University Archives Reference Collection, UA50.1.14, Special Collections Research Center, North Carolina State University Libraries, Raleigh, North Carolina; NC Trustees Mins, May 22, 1889 and December 5, 1889; NCCAMA Catalog, 1890, 38, 41–42; *North Carolina General Assembly, Public Laws, Regular Session, March 7, 1887*, 469; NC Super, 1887–88, 116.

68. *Biennial Report of the Board of Curators of the University of the State of Missouri, 1895–1896, 16; Biennial Report of the Board of Curators of the University of the State of Missouri, 1897–1898*, 10, 22.

69. *Farmers' Alliance*, March 7, 1891, 4. For the founding legislation of NU, see State of Nebraska, *Compiled Statutes of the State of Nebraska, 1922* (Columbia, MO: E. W. Stephens, 1922), Section 6727.

70. *Chickasaw Messenger*, March 29, 1888, 2, April 5, 1888, 1, and April 12, 1888, 1.

71. *Industrialist*, March 1899, 155–56 and May 1899, 301–18; *Advocate and News*, February 23, 1898, 12.

72. *Industrialist*, July 1898, 443–49 and October 1898, 563–69.

73. Mellen, *Popular Errors Concerning Higher Education in the United States and the Remedy*, 46–47; Nidiffer and Bouman, "The Chasm Between Rhetoric and Reality," 442.

74. F. S. Snow to C. S. Gleed, September 30, 1893, SRC; *Student's Journal*, May 4, 1894, 2; F. H. Snow to C. F. Scott, November 3, 1894, SGC, box 16; *Jeffersonian*, November 8, 1894, 4 and November 29, 1894, 2; University of Kansas Board of Regents minutes, April 8, 1892 and September 13, 1894, University Archives, Series 1/2, Kenneth Spencer Research Library, University of Kansas.

75. Untitled Typescript, 189(5?), Sears Papers, box 1, Letterbook, 239–42; *Jeffersonian*, January 28, 1897, 2; *Lawrence Journal*, January 30, 1897, 9.

76. *Compiled statutes of the state of Nebraska, 1922, comprising all the statutory law of a general character in force July 1, 1922* (Columbia, MO: E. W. Stephens, 1922). For expenses during the 1890s, see Lawrence R. Veysey, *The Emergence of the American University* (Chicago: University of Chicago Press, 1965), 292; Robert Manley, *Centennial History of the University of Nebraska*, vol. 1 (Lincoln: University of Nebraska Press, 1969), 114.

77. NU Regents Mins, vol. 4, April 9, 1901; NU Report, 1900–1902, 9; *Nebraska Independent*, September 12, 1901, 4, October 3, 1901, 1, and October 31, 1901, 1.

78. *Nebraska Independent*, October 24, 1901, 1.

79. R. Pound to J. S. Dales, December 3, 1903, NU Regents Papers, box 16, folder 132; I. D. Evans to E. C. Calkins, August 6, 1903, NU Regents Papers, box 16, folder 131; Report of Committee on Fees, May 12, 1903, NU Regents Papers, box 16, folder 129.

80. KSAC Report, 1899–1900, 34–35.

81. Joseph F. Kett, *The Pursuit of Knowledge under Difficulties: From Self-Improvement to Adult Education in America, 1750–1990* (Stanford: Stanford University Press, 1994), 196; W. Fitzhugh Brundage, *A Socialist Utopia in the New South: Ruskin Colonies in Tennessee and Georgia, 1894–1901* (Urbana: University of Illinois Press, 1996), 51–54. Regarding the "cooperative commonwealth," see Dorothy Ross, *The Origins of American Social Science* (New York: Cambridge University Press, 1991), 108–9. On Populist belief in cooperation, see Steven Hahn, *The Roots of Rural Populism: Yeoman Farmers and the Transformation of the Georgia Upcountry, 1850–1890* (New York: Oxford University Press, 1983).

82. "Robert B. Hunter on Topolobampo," Hoffman Papers, box 2, folder 1; *The American Nonconformist and Kansas Industrial Liberator,* January 1, 1891, 7 and August 6, 1891, 7; Patricia Michaelis, "C. B. Hoffman, Kansas Socialist," *Kansas Historical Quarterly* 41 (Summer 1975), 169.

83. T. E. Will to C. B. Hoffman, October 4, 1896, Will Papers, folder 1.

84. Ross E. Paulson, *Radicalism and Reform: The Vrooman Family and American Social Thought, 1837–1937* (Lexington: University of Kentucky Press, 1968), 147–51, 162–67; Thomas Elmer Will, "College for the People," *Arena* 26 (July 1901), 16–18; Howard V. Davis, *Frank Parsons: Prophet, Innovator, Counselor* (Carbondale: Southern Illinois University Press, 1969), 30–31; J. D. Walters, *History of Kansas State Agricultural College* (Manhattan: Kansas State Agricultural College, 1909), 131–32; Earl A. Collins, "The Multitude Incorporated," *Missouri Historical Review* 27 (July 1933), 303–6; Helen Owen, "Ruskin College, 1900–1903" (master's thesis, Northeast Missouri State College, 1971).

85. T. E. Will to C. B. Hoffman, July 29, 1913 and September 10, 1913, Hoffman Papers, box 1, folder 6; T. E. Will to C. B. Hoffman, September 25, 1911, Hoffman Papers, box 1, folder 3.

86. T. E. Will to J. T. Willard, October 25, 1913, Hoffman Papers, box 1, folder 6; *Manhattan Republic,* June 25, 1897, 1; *Kansas Commoner,* August 18, 1898, 4.

87. T. E. Will to W. S. Stanley, March 31, 1899, Will Papers, folder 2; KSAC Report, 1897–98, 46–47; *Industrialist,* July 1898, 512.

88. *Manhattan Republic,* June 6, 1899, in KSU Clippings, vol. 4; KSAC Report, 1897–98, 46–47. On the lack of investment in dormitories, see Julie A. Reuben, *The Making of the Modern University: Intellectual Transformation and the Marginalization of Morality* (Chicago: University of Chicago Press, 1996), 260.

89. *Nationalist,* April 15, 1898, 2; James Carey, *Kansas State University: The Quest for Identity* (Lawrence: Regents Press of Kansas, 1977), 79, 83; Charles Correll, "Revolution and Counterrevolution," *Kansas Quarterly* 1 (Fall 1969), 98.

90. Minutes of the Board of Regents, Kansas State Agricultural College, vol. B, June 6, 1899, 272; *Industrialist,* July 1899, 468; Virginia Noah Gibson, "The Effect of the

Populist Movement on Kansas State Agricultural College" (master's thesis, Kansas State College of Agriculture and Applied Science, 1932), 82.

91. J. T. Willard to Friends, May 14, 1899, KSC Letters; *Industrialist,* June 1899, 390; *Manhattan Republic,* June 23, 1899; *Student Herald,* October 6, 1899, 39.

92. W. H. Oury to Regents, April 11, 1898, NU Regents Papers, box 13, folder 102.

93. John R. Commons, *Myself* (New York: MacMillan, 1934), 55–56.

94. John H. Reynolds and David Y. Thomas, *History of the University of Arkansas* (Fayetteville: University of Arkansas, 1910), 146; Wright Bryan, *Clemson: An Informal History of the University, 1889–1979* (Columbia: R. L. Bryan, 1979), 39; Dyer, *The University of Georgia,* 158; NU Regents Mins, vol. 5, September 14, 1903.

95. Pamela Riney-Kehrberg, "Foundations of the People's College; The Early Years of Iowa State," *A Sesquicentennial History of Iowa State University* (Ames: Iowa State Press, 2007), 13.

96. Klein, "Survey of Land-Grant Colleges and Universities," 362.

97. *Progressive Farmer,* August 11, 1887, 4; NCCAMA Report, 1890, 4; David A. Lockmiller, *History of the North Carolina State College of Agriculture and Engineering of the University of North Carolina, 1889–1939* (Raleigh: North Carolina State College of Agriculture and Engineering, 1939), 51–52.

98. Hale, *University of Arkansas,* 57–60; Reynolds and Thomas, *History of the University of Arkansas,* 140.

99. Bryan, *Clemson,* 39.

100. *Jeffersonian,* January 27, 1898.

101. KSAC Report, 1897–98, 46–47.

102. Kansas State Agricultural College Faculty Record, vol. D, March 22, 1898, 82–84, Morse Department of Special Collections, Hale Library, Kansas State University; *Industrialist,* October 1898, 541–42; T. E. Will to G. E. Beckes, July 12, 1897, box 4, vol. 1, President Letterbooks, RG 2, Morse Department of Special Collections, Hale Library, Kansas State University; *Kansas Farmer,* October 28, 1897, 698; *Student Herald,* September 28, 1898, 2.

103. *Manhattan Republic,* June 6, 1899; KSAC Report, 1899–1900, 34–35.

104. *Industrialist,* November 1899, 115–16.

105. *Industrialist,* July 1899b, 14.

106. Thelin, *A History of American Higher Education,* 171.

107. Report of the Bursar, January 26, 1886, UNC Trustees, vol. S-8; Minutes of the Board of Trustees, February 16, 1888 and February 27, 1889, UNC Trustees, vol. S-8; Report of the Bursar, February 11, 1896, January 1, 1897, and December 31, 1897, UNC Trustees, vol. 9; Report of the President, February 18, 1897, UNC Trustees, vol. 9; Report of the Bursar, February 16, 1900, UNC Trustees, vol. 10; Report of the Bursar, UNC, box 50, vol. 1, and box 20, folder 677; Office of the Registrar, University Affairs, Student Records and Faculty Reports, Subgroup 2: Miscellaneous Student Records, folder 33, University Archives, Wilson Library, University of North Carolina at Chapel

Hill; James L. Leloudis, *Schooling the New South: Pedagogy, Self, and Society in North Carolina, 1880–1920* (Chapel Hill: University of North Carolina Press, 1996), 60.

108. NCCAMA Report, 1893, 39; NCCAMA Report, 1899–1900, 9.

109. KU Report, 1889–90, 7–8; KU Report, 1893–94, 14; KU Report, 1895–96, 12–13; KU Report, 1897–98, 10–11.

110. NC Trustees Mins, June 15, 1892; G. Winston to H. Clarkson, August 25, 1899, G. Winston to E. J. Jenkins, August 26, 1899, G. Winston to J. J. Broadhurst, August 24, 1899, G. Winston to H. W. Barrow, September 1, 1899, G. Winston to J. Ferrell, September 1, 1899, and G. Winston to E. Ricks, September 1, 1899, George T. Winston Letterbook, Chancellor's Office—Correspondence, Box UA 2.1.1, North Carolina State University Libraries Special Collections.

111. These questions continue to divide policymakers and the public. James J. Duderstadt and Farris W. Womack, *The Future of the Public University in America: Beyond the Crossroads* (Baltimore, MD: Johns Hopkins University Press, 2003), 42; Roger L. Geiger, *Money and Knowledge: Research Universities and the Paradox of the Marketplace* (Stanford, CA: Stanford University Press, 2004), 36–48, 80–85.

Chapter 5. Producers and Parasites

1. Thorstein Veblen, *The Theory of the Leisure Class* (New Brunswick, NJ: Transaction, [1899], 1992), 247–49, 255–56. On Veblen, see David Riesman, *Thorstein Veblen* (New Brunswick, NJ: Transaction, [1953], 1995).

2. *Journal of Proceedings and Addresses of the National Educational Association, 1888*, 170–78.

3. Bruce A. Kimball, *Orators and Philosophers: A History of the Idea of Liberal Education* (New York: Teachers College Press, 1986).

4. John Henry Newman, *The Idea of a University.* (New Haven, CT: Yale University Press, 1999); Walter Hines Page, *The Southerner: A Novel Being the Autobiography of Nicholas Worth* (New York: Doubleday, 1909), 41.

5. Roger L. Geiger, "The Era of Multipurpose Colleges in American Higher Education," *The American College in the Nineteenth Century* (Nashville, TN: Vanderbilt University Press, 2000), 141; Joseph L. Henderson, *Admission to College by Certificate* (New York: Teachers College, 1912), 85–87.

6. Roger L. Williams, *The Origins of Federal Support for Higher Education: George Atherton and the Land-Grant Movement* (University Park: Pennsylvania State University Press, 1991).

7. Julie A. Reuben, *The Making of the Modern University: Intellectual Transformation and the Marginalization of Morality* (Chicago: University of Chicago Press, 1996), 62; Laurence R. Veysey, *The Emergence of the American University* (Chicago: University of Chicago Press, 1965), 90; A. J. Angulo, *William Barton Rogers and the Idea of MIT* (Baltimore, MD: Johns Hopkins University Press, 2009).

8. Laurence R. Veysey, "Higher Education as a Profession: Changes and Continuities," in Nathan O. Hatch, ed., *The Professions in History* (Notre Dame, IN: University of Notre Dame Press, 1988), 22; R. Freeman Butts, *The College Charts Its Course* (New

York: McGraw-Hill, 1939), 216–21; Richard Hofstadter, *Anti-Intellectualism in American Life* (New York: Vintage, 1963), 237, 260–61.

9. Michael Dennis, *Lessons in Progress: State Universities and Progressivism in the New South, 1880–1920* (Urbana: University of Illinois Press, 2001).

10. Roy V. Scott, *The Reluctant Farmer: The Rise of Agricultural Extension to 1914* (Urbana: University of Illinois Press, 1970), 29.

11. Isaac P. Roberts, *Autobiography of a Farm Boy* (Ithaca, NY: Cornell University Press, 1946), 96. On farmers' attitude toward agricultural science, see Alan Marcus, *Agricultural Science and the Quest for Legitimacy: Farmers, Agricultural Colleges, and Experiment Stations, 1870–1890* (Ames: Iowa State University Press, 1985), 5–6, 15–17, 27, 220–21; Mary Neth, *Preserving the Family Farm: Women, Community, and the Foundations of Agribusiness in the Midwest, 1900–1940* (Baltimore, MD: Johns Hopkins University Press, 1995), 144; David B. Danbom, *The Resisted Revolution: Urban America and the Industrialization of Agriculture, 1900–1930* (Ames: Iowa State University Press, 1979), 22, 77; Charles E. Rosenberg, *No Other Gods: On Science and American Social Thought* (Baltimore, MD: Johns Hopkins University Press, [1961], 1976), 160–70; Margaret Rossiter, *The Emergence of Agricultural Science: Justus Liebig and the Americans, 1840–1880* (New Haven, CT: Yale University Press, 1975).

12. Inspired by German agricultural research, experiment stations were established in the 1870s and enhanced by the federal Hatch Act of 1887. Agricultural extension work improved dramatically after the development of farm demonstration during the early twentieth century. Danbom, *The Resisted Revolution*, 70–71; Marcus, *Agricultural Science and the Quest for Legitimacy*, 127; Scott, *The Reluctant Farmer*, 58; Rosenberg, *No Other Gods*, 154–58.

13. *Progressive Farmer*, September 28, 1897, 3 and November 2, 1897, 2.

14. Charles Postel, *The Populist Vision* (New York: Oxford University Press, 2007), 32, 48, 53–56. Also see Theodore Mitchell, *Political Education in the Southern Farmers' Alliance, 1887–1900* (Madison: University of Wisconsin Press, 1987), 134. For an alternative view, see Daniel P. Carpenter, *The Forging of Bureaucratic Autonomy: Reputations, Networks, and Policy Innovation in Executive Agencies, 1862–1928* (Princeton: Princeton University Press, 2001), 210.

15. Philip Roy Muller, "New South Populism: North Carolina, 1884–1900" (PhD dissertation, University of North Carolina, 1972), 25. Also see Kemp Plummer Battle, *History of the University of North Carolina*, vol. 2 (Raleigh, NC: Edwards and Broughton, 1912), 72, 92–93, 122–23, 136–37, 381–82; William L. Carpenter, *Knowledge Is Power: A History of the School of Agriculture and Life Sciences at North Carolina State University, 1877–1984* (Raleigh, NC: North Carolina State University, 1987), 12.

16. D. McKay to L. L. Polk, June 12, 1880, Polk Papers, box 4, folder 45.

17. *Progressive Farmer*, February 10, 1886, 4–5, May 19, 1886, 4, and January 19, 1887, 3.

18. *Progressive Farmer*, July 2, 1889, 1.

19. NCCAMA Report, 1890, 10; North Carolina General Assembly, Public Laws, Regular Session, March 7, 1887, Chap 410, Section 9, 718–22; NCCAMA Catalog, 1890, 2–3.

20. "Wilbur Fisk Massey: North Carolina Botanist, Horticulturalist, and Agriculturalist," *Journal of the Elisha Mitchell Scientific Society* 116 (2000), 101–12; Ira O. Schaub, *North Carolina Agricultural Experiment Station: The First 60 Years, 1877–1937* (Raleigh, NC: Agricultural Experimental Station Bulletin, January 1955), 55; "Administration of Dr. W. A. Withers, Acting Director 1897–99" (undated) and "Report and Recommendations of the Director of the Experiment Station and Professor of Chemistry," April 21, 1899, Peele Papers.

21. G. McCarthy to W. J. Peele, March 30, 1899, Peele Papers; G. McCarthy to W. J. Peele, May 1, 1899 and May 29, 1899, William J. Peele Papers, #1881, box 1, folder 7, Southern Historical Collection, Wilson Library, University of North Carolina at Chapel Hill.

22. William J. Peele, "A History of the Agricultural and Mechanical College" (n.d., n.p.), 12.

23. KSAC Report, 1891–92, 40; KSAC Catalog, 1881–82, 13–14; *College Symposium of the Kansas Agricultural College* (Topeka, KS: Hall and O'Donald, 1891), 32; *Industrialist*, January 4, 1897, 69.

24. E. B. Cowgill to G. T. Fairchild, March 25, 1897, KSC Letters; *Jeffersonian*, June 24, 1897, 2. Also see *Manhattan Republic*, April 30, 1897, 4; Ralph Sparks, "To Serve the People: The Populist Era at Kansas State," undated manuscript, Kansas State University Special Collections.

25. *Industrialist*, January 1898, 56–61 and May 1899, 301–18; KSAC Report, 1897–98, 37.

26. "The Reorganization of the Kansas State Agricultural College," Will Papers, folder 9; KSAC Report, 1897–98, 1, 4, 37–38, 43; KSAC Report, 1899–1900, 26–27; *Industrialist*, July 15, 1897, 161, August 16, 1897, 171, and May 1899, 301–18; *Kansas Commoner*, September 29, 1898, 4, October 6, 1898, 4, and November 10, 1898, 4.

27. Virginia Railsback Gunn, "Industrialists Not Butterflies: Women's Higher Education at Kansas State Agricultural College, 1873–1882," *Kansas History* 18 (Spring 1995), 2–17. On Campbell, see Glenna Matthews, *"Just a Housewife": The Rise and Fall of Domesticity in America* (New York: Oxford University Press, 1987), 155–57. Annie Diggs quoted in *Industrialist*, February 1899, 123. On home economics, see Sarah Stage, "Ellen Richards and the Social Significance of the Home Economics Movement," in Sarah Stage and Virginina B. Vincenti, eds., *Rethinking Home Economics: Women and the History of a Profession* (Ithaca, NY: Cornell University Press, 1997), 19–25.

28. The university fended off attempts to revoke its land grant status in 1885 and 1889. The University of Nebraska, *Semi-Centennial Anniversary Book* (Lincoln: University of Nebraska Press, 1919), 31; Robert P. Crawford, *These Fifty Years: A History of the College of Agriculture of the University of Nebraska* (Lincoln: University of Nebraska Press, 1925), 56–57; Howard W. Caldwell, "Education in Nebraska," *United States Bureau of Education Circular* 3 (1902), 45–46; Thomas R. Walsh, "Charles E. Bessey and the Transformation of the Industrial College," *Nebraska History* 52 (1971), 395–96, 404–5; NU Report, 1889–90, 8; The University of Nebraska, *The Industrial College: A Brief Historical Sketch* (Lincoln: University of Nebraska, 1892), 16.

29. Canfield Journal, September 8, 1891, December 9, 1891 and December 10, 1891; LaVon M. Gappa, "Chancellor James Hulme Canfield: His Impact on the University of Nebraska, 1891–1895" (PhD dissertation, University of Nebraska, Lincoln, 1985), 126–27, 186.

30. *Nebraska State Journal*, April 1, 1893, 3; *Nebraska Independent*, October 14, 1897, 4, October 21, 1897, 4, and September 8, 1898, 4, 6; Robert Manley, *Centennial History of the University of Nebraska*, vol. 1 (Lincoln: University of Nebraska Press, 1969), 117–19.

31. *Nebraska Independent*, October 7, 1897, 4 and September 8, 1898, 4, 6; *Wisner Chronicle*, November 18, 1899, 4; NU Regents Mins, vol. 4, April 13, 1898.

32. "Preliminary Report of the Committee on Agricultural Education in the University," April 11, 1900, NU Regents Papers, box 14, folder 115; NU Report, 1901–2, 8, 13–14.

33. C. MacMillan to C. E. Bessey, December 7, 1899, Charles Edwin Bessey Papers, microfilmed by the University of Nebraska Archives, reel 9; *Nebraska Independent*, July 29, 1897, 4; NU Regents Mins, April 11, 1900, vol. 4. On Andrews, see *Nebraska Independent*, January 15, 1903, 1; James E. Hansen, "Gallant, Stalwart Bennie: Elisha Benjamin Andrews (1844–1917), An Educator's Odyssey" (PhD dissertation, University of Denver, 1969).

34. *Nebraska Independent*, September 27, 1900, 9–10 and November 14, 1901, 4; Elisha Benjamin Andrews, *The Call of the Land: Popular Chapters on Topics of Interest to Farmers* (New York: Orange Judd, 1913), 174–211, 216–17.

35. Elizabeth Sanders, *Roots of Reform: Farmers, Workers, and the American State, 1877–1917* (Chicago: University of Chicago Press, 1999), 314–16.

36. Mary Summers, "Conflicting Visions: Farmers' Movements and the Making of the United States Department of Agriculture" (PhD dissertation in progress, Yale University), Chapter 4; Robert A. Leflar, *The First 100 Years: Centennial History of the University of Arkansas* (Fayetteville: University of Arkansas Foundation, 1972), 25, 47–50; Harrison Hale, *University of Arkansas, 1871–1948* (Fayetteville: University of Arkansas Press, 1948), 57–61; John H. Reynolds and David Y. Thomas, *History of the University of Arkansas* (Fayetteville: University of Arkansas, 1910), 137–40.

37. Steve Kantrowitz, *Ben Tillman and the Reconstruction of White Supremacy* (Chapel Hill: University of North Carolina Press, 2000), 117–19, 128, 214; Wright Bryan, *Clemson: An Informal History of the University, 1889–1979* (Columbia, SC: R. L. Bryan, 1979), 37–38; Francis Butler Simkins, *Pitchfork Ben Tillman: South Carolinian* (Baton Rouge: Louisiana State University Press, 1944), 117; Daniel Walker Hollis, *University of South Carolina*, vol. 2 (Columbia: University of South Carolina Press, 1956), 138.

38. Gerald Gaither, *Blacks and the Populist Revolt: Ballots and Bigotry in the "New South"* (Tuscaloosa: University of Alabama Press, [1977], 2005), 210; Omar Hamid Ali, "Black Populism in the New South, 1886–1898" (PhD dissertation, Columbia University, 2003), 15–16; James D. Anderson, *The Education of Blacks in the South: 1860–1935* (Chapel Hill: University of North Carolina Press, 1988), 54.

39. Gaither, *Blacks and the Populist Revolt*, 12. For Murray's views, see G. W. Murray to B. T. Washington, July 7, 1894, in Louis R. Harlan, ed., *The Booker T. Washington Papers*,

vol. 3 (Urbana: University of Illinois Press, 1974), 451–52; Gregg Cantrell, *Kenneth and John B. Rayner and the Limits of Southern Dissent* (Urbana: University of Illinois Press, 1993), 251–59; Jack Abramowitz, "John B. Rayner—A Grassroots Leader," *Journal of Negro History* 36 (April 1951), 168–70; George R. Woolfolk, *Prairie View: A Study in Public Conscience, 1878–1946* (New York: Pageant Press, 1962), 132–33.

40. Robert J. Norrell, *Up From History: The Life of Booker T. Washington* (Cambridge, MA: Harvard University Press, 2009), 146. For the absence of correspondence with the CFA, see Harlan, ed., *The Booker T. Washington Papers*, vols. 2 and 3.

41. Anderson, *The Education of Blacks in the South*, 245.

42. Maryjo Wagner, "Farms, Families, and Reform: Women in the Farmers' Alliance and Populist Party" (PhD dissertation, University of Oregon, 1986), 37.

43. *Annual Catalog of the North Carolina Agricultural and Mechanical College for the Colored Race, 1902–03*, 57. Also see Robert L. Jenkins, "The Black Land Grant Colleges in their Formative Years, 1890–1920," *Agricultural History* 65 (Spring 1991), 63–72.

44. *Wealth Makers of the World*, November 8, 1894, 8. Also see Caroline Winterer, *The Culture of Classicism: Ancient Greece and Rome in American Intellectual Life, 1780–1910* (Baltimore, MD: Johns Hopkins University Press, 2002).

45. *Industrialist*, August 16, 1897, 175 and October 1898, 563–69; Thomas E. Will, "The End of Education," *The Open Court* 9 (October 1895), 425–31; *Advocate and News*, February 23, 1898, 12.

46. Helen M. Cavanaugh, *Carl Schurz Vrooman: A Self-Styled "Constructive Conservative"* (Chicago: Lakeside, 1977), 19.

47. Herbert Kliebard, *Schooled to Work: Vocationalism and the American Curriculum, 1876–1946* (New York: Teachers College Press, 1999); Robert C. McMath Jr., et al, *Engineering the New South: Georgia Tech, 1885–1985* (Athens: University of Georgia Press, 1985), 18.

48. John Dewey, *Democracy and Education: An Introduction to the Philosophy of Education* (New York: Macmillan, 1916), 140.

49. Theodore Mitchell, *Political Education in the Southern Farmers' Alliance, 1887–1900* (Madison: University of Wisconsin Press, 1987), 135–38; *Nebraska Independent*, June 15, 1899, 4.

50. *Weekly Commoner*, March 26, 1897, 4 and May 12, 1899, 4; George A. Frykman, *Creating the People's University: Washington State University, 1890–1990* (Pullman: Washington State University Press, 1990), 32.

51. *Industrialist*, May 1899, 301–18; KSAC Report, 1893–94, 10; *Manhattan Republic*, April 8, 1898, 4; *Kansas Commoner*, October 21, 1897, 4. Also see T. E. Will to J. Walters, April 10, 1909, Will Papers, Folder 5; KSAC Catalog, 1896–97, 31.

52. D. Sven Nordin, *Rich Harvest: A History of the Grange, 1867–1900* (Jackson: University Press of Mississippi, 1974), 73; *Journal of Proceedings and Addresses of the National Educational Association, 1890*, 222; *Progressive Farmer*, June 23, 1886, 4.

53. *Progressive Farmer*, February 10, 1886, 4–5, February 17, 1886, 4, April 21, 1886, 4, July 28, 1886, 4, July 7, 1886, 3, and October 13, 1886, 4.

54. *Industrialist*, April 1899, 213; *Manhattan Republic*, February 19, 1897, 4. Populists were not unanimous on this issue. See *Manhattan Republic*, September 10, 1897, 1.

55. Postel, *The Populist Vision*, 54.

56. Radicals and conservatives both endorsed the idea that physical labor provided the backbone of morality. Daniel T. Rodgers, *The Work Ethic in Industrial America, 1820–1920* (Chicago: University of Chicago Press, 1978), xi, 211–13; Kliebard, *Schooled to Work*, 1–25. Also see Daniel A. Clark, *Creating the College Man: American Mass Magazines and Middle-Class Manhood, 1890–1915* (Madison: University of Wisconsin Press, 2010), 100.

57. Joseph F. Kett, *The Pursuit of Knowledge under Difficulties: From Self-Improvement to Adult Education in America, 1750–1990* (Stanford: Stanford University Press, 1994), 230–31; Richard J. Altenbaugh, *Education for Struggle: The American Labor Colleges of the 1920s and 1930s* (Philadelphia: Temple University Press, 1990), 22.

58. *Manhattan Republic*, June 25, 1897, 4; *Chickasaw Messenger*, June 28, 1888, 1; *Progressive Farmer*, October 15, 1889, 1.

59. David B. Danbom, *Born in the County: A History of Rural America* (Baltimore, MD: Johns Hopkins University Press, 1995), 127–28, 148, 161–84.

60. *Nebraska Independent*, November 14, 1901, 4; Pamela Riney-Kehrberg, *Childhood on the Farm: Work, Play, and Coming of Age in the Midwest* (Lawrence: University Press of Kansas, 2005), 15–18.

61. *Progressive Farmer*, May 12, 1886, 4.

62. *Caucasian*, December 18, 1890, 2.

63. Simkins, *Pitchfork Ben Tillman*, 92–93, Hollis, *University of South Carolina*, 152; Edward Ayers, *The Promise of the New South: Life After Reconstruction* (New York: Oxford University Press, 1992), 225–26; Kantrowitz, *Ben Tillman*, 135–36.

64. Kantrowitz, *Ben Tillman*, 117–19; Donald M. McKale, *Tradition: A History of The Presidency of Clemson University*, 36–39. According to the *Oxford English Dictionary*, "dude" originated in the early 1880s as a term to denigrate men who "exaggerated fastidiousness in dress, speech, and deportment." See http://dictionary.oed.com (accessed on June 18, 2007).

65. Clark, *Creating the College Man*, 35. For discussion of the evolution of concerns over manliness in this era, see Gail Bederman, *Manliness and Civilization: A Cultural History of Gender and Race in the United States, 1880–1917* (Chicago: University of Chicago Press, 1995).

66. *Country Life*, December 1890, 4; *Caucasian*, June 26, 1890, 1.

67. Opposition to this cultural authority can be mislabeled as anti-intellectualism rather than anti-authoritarianism. Lawrence W. Levine, *Highbrow / Lowbrow: The Emergence of Cultural Hierarchy in America* (Cambridge, MA: Harvard University Press, 1988), 7, 239–40.

68. *Nebraskan*, October 25, 1895, 2.

69. *Progressive Farmer*, February 9, 1897, 3.

70. Hermione Lee, *Willa Cather: Double Lives* (New York: Pantheon, 1989), 43–44.

71. Willa Cather, *One of Ours* (New York: Knopf, 1922), 24–26.

72. Willa Cather, *O Pioneers!* (New York: Fine Creative Media, [1913], 2003), 64, 33, 97, 130, 165. Similar to Lou and Oscar, the Populist *Manhattan Republic* speculated that a University of Kansas student accused of murdering his father had been corrupted by "a giddy whirl—wine suppers, balls, etc." *Manhattan Republic*, July 1, 1898, 1.

73. Ellen Glasgow, *Voice of the People* (New York: A. L. Burt, [1900], 1902).

74. Glasgow, *Voice of the People*, 135. Similarly, a young rural Nebraskan from a Populist family who was considering college in this era recalled hearing a neighbor predict that too much education would "spoil all the young'uns in the country." Frank O'Connell, *Farewell to the Farm* (Caldwell, ID: Caxton Printers, 1962), 94–95.

75. Glasgow, *Voice of the People*, 135, 126.

76. Leon Fink, *Progressive Intellectuals and the Dilemmas of Democratic Commitment* (Cambridge, MA: Harvard University Press, 1997), 5–7, 14.

77. John Dos Passos, *The Big Money* (Boston: Houghton Mifflin, [1933], 2000), 74–83; Dorfman, *Thorstein Veblen and His America*, 16–17, 29–30; Riesman, *Thorstein Veblen*, 4. Theodore Dreiser's siblings also worried that he would have a "swelled head" when he returned home from the University of Indiana. Theodore Dreiser, *Dawn: An Autobiography of Early Youth* (Santa Rosa, CA: Black Sparrow Press, [1931], 1998), 372–75.

78. Hamlin Garland, "Up the Coulee: A Story of Wisconsin," *Main-Traveled Roads* (New York: Penguin, [1891], 1962), 66, 96.

79. John Williams, *Stoner* (New York: New York Review Book, 1965), 22, 108–9, 218.

80. Clark, *Creating the College Man*, 12.

81. *Rocky Mountain Collegian*, November 1895, 15.

82. *Nebraskan*, May 12, 1894, 2; *Nebraska Independent*, July 9, 1903, 11; Alvin Johnson, *Pioneer's Progress* (New York: Viking, 1952), 85.

83. *Lincoln Independent*, October 11, 1895, 4.

84. Kliebard, *Schooled to Work*, 229–30.

85. Danbom, *Born in the County*, 150–51; Marcus, *Agricultural Science and the Quest for Legitimacy*, 8–13.

86. *Progressive Farmer*, October 15, 1889, 1.

87. *Progressive Farmer*, December 22, 1886, 1. Also see *Farmers' Alliance*, January 11, 1890, 2.

88. *Progressive Farmer*, February 10, 1886, 4–5 and July 26, 1898, 1.

89. Edward Bellamy, *Looking Backward 2000–1887* (Cambridge, MA: Harvard University Press, [1888], 1967), 133–36; Lloyd cited in James B. Gilbert, *Work Without Salvation: America's Intellectuals and Industrial Alienation, 1880–1910* (Baltimore, MD: Johns Hopkins University Press, 1977), 104. Also see Christopher Lasch, *The Revolt of the Elites and the Betrayal of Democracy* (New York: Norton, 1995), 64; John L. Thomas, *Alternative America: Henry George, Edward Bellamy, Henry Demarest Lloyd, and the Adversary Tradition* (Cambridge, MA: Harvard University Press, 1983).

90. *Progressive Farmer*, July 21, 1887, 4; NCCAMA Catalog, 1890, 10.

91. Canfield Journal, May 4, 1893.

92. *Nebraska Independent*, June 15, 1899, 4.

93. "Farewell: Address on Behalf of the Alumni Association of the KSAC," Will Papers, folder 9; *Industrialist*, October 1898, 558–62; KSAC Catalog, 1900–1901, 24.

94. Jane Addams, *Twenty Years at Hull-House* (Urbana: University of Illinois, [1910], 1990), 249; Jane Addams, *Democracy and Social Ethics* (Urbana: University of Illinois Press,

[1902], 2002), 86–87; Rodgers, *The Work Ethic in Industrial America*, 81–83; Fink, *Progressive Intellectuals and the Dilemmas of Democratic Commitment*, 22–23.

95. Robert B. Westbrook, "Pullman and the Professor," in *Democratic Hope: Pragmatism and the Politics of Truth* (Ithaca, NY: Cornell University Press, 2005), 87–96.

96. Dewey, *Democracy and Education*, 275, 316–20.

97. Helen Owen, "Ruskin College, 1900–1903" (master's thesis, Northeast Missouri State College, 1971), 13; Jonathan Rose, *The Intellectual Life of the British Working Classes* (New Haven, CT: Yale University Press, 2001), 286; Altenbaugh, *Education for Struggle*, 69, 80.

98. Winton U. Solberg, *The University of Illinois, 1867–1894: An Intellectual and Cultural History* (Urbana: University of Illinois Press, 1968), 101.

99. Upton Sinclair, *The Goose-Step: A Story of American Education* (New York: Albert and Charles Boni, 1936), 142.

100. Earle Dudley Ross, *Democracy's College: The Land-Grant Movement in the Formative Stage* (Ames: Iowa State College Press, 1942), 159.

101. Burton J. Bledstein, *The Culture of Professionalism: The Middle Class and the Development of Higher Education in America* (New York: Norton, 1976); David K. Brown, *Degrees of Control: A Sociology of Educational Expansion and Occupational Credentialism* (New York: Teachers College Press, 1995), 138–39; David F. Labaree, *The Making of an American High School: The Credentials Market and the Central High School of Philadelphia, 1838–1939* (New Haven, CT: Yale University Press, 1988).

102. Kett, *The Pursuit of Knowledge under Difficulties*, 230–31, 511 n22.

103. Especially after 1890, the growth in higher education occurred primarily in the fields of teacher training, law, and medicine. Colin B. Burke, *American Collegiate Populations: A Test of the Traditional View* (New York: New York University Press, 1982), 221–22; Geraldine Jonçich Clifford, "'Marry, Stitch, Die, or Do Worse': Educating Women for Work," in David B. Tyack and Harvey Kantor, eds., *Work, Youth, and Schooling: Historical Perspectives on Vocationalism in American Education* (Stanford: Stanford University Press, 1982), 253–56.

104. *Student Herald*, January 29, 1896, 4.

105. Riney-Kehrberg, *Childhood on the Farm*, 79–81, 203–6; Liahna Babener, "Bitter Nostalgia: Recollections of Childhood on the Midwestern Frontier," in Elliott West and Paula Petrik, eds., *Small Worlds: Children and Adolescents in America: 1850–1950* (Lawrence: University Press of Kansas, 1992).

106. Alice Reagan, *North Carolina State University: A Narrative History* (Ann Arbor, MI: Edwards Brothers, 1987), 1; Michael McGiffert, *The Higher Learning in Colorado: A Historical Study, 1860–1940* (Denver: Sage Books, 1964), 101–2; *The Weekly Toiler*, February 5, 1890, 1 and March 5, 1890, 4.

107. Reynolds and Thomas, *History of the University of Arkansas*, 148; O. P. Hood to G. T. Fairchild, February 20, 1898 and J. T. Willard to G. T. Fairchild, May 4, 1899, KSC Letters; Carpenter, *Knowledge Is Power*, 67, 99; Christopher Allen, "The Land Grant Act of 1862 and the Founding of NCCAMA" (master's thesis, North Carolina State University,

1984), 87–97; Eldon L. Johnson, "Misconceptions about the Early Land-Grant Colleges," *Journal of Higher Education* 52 (July–August, 1981), 339–40.

108. Manley, *Centennial History of The University of Nebraska*, 138; David A. Lockmiller, *History of the North Carolina State College of Agriculture and Engineering of the University of North Carolina, 1889–1939* (Raleigh: North Carolina State College of Agriculture and Engineering, 1939), 48; Madison Kuhn, *Michigan State: The First Hundred Years* (East Lansing: Michigan State University Press, 1955), 226; Kett, *The Pursuit of Knowledge Under Difficulties*, 227.

109. Bruce Sinclair, "Episodes in the History of the American Engineering Profession," in Nathan O. Hatch, ed., *The Professions in History* (Notre Dame, IN: University of Notre Dame Press, 1988), 138; Monte A. Calvert, *The Mechanical Engineer in America, 1890–1910* (Baltimore, MD: Johns Hopkins Press, 1967), 139–45.

110. Paul H. Mattingly, *The Classless Profession: American Schoolmen in the Nineteenth Century* (New York: New York University Press, 1975).

111. Burke, *American Collegiate Populations*, 220; Arthur J. Klein, "Survey of Land-Grant Colleges and Universities," *United States Office of Education Bulletin*, no. 9 (Washington, DC: Government Printing Office, 1930), 369, 382.

112. *Rocky Mountain Collegian*, January 1892, 9. Originally printed in the *Lafayette Sunday Times*.

113. *The Agricultural and Mechanical College Record, 1902*, 110–13.

114. NU Report, 1891–92, 60; NU Report, 1895–96, 15–16; University of Nebraska, *Semi-Centennial Anniversary Book*, 47; Caldwell, "Education in Nebraska," 63; Report of the Committee Appointed by the General Faculty on Extensions of Courses of Study, June 6, 1893, NU Regents Papers, box 11, folder 86.

115. KSAC Report, 1885–86, 65; KSAC Report, 1893–94, 39, 66; KSAC Catalog, 1900–1901, 134.

116. Dwight B. Billings Jr., *Planters and the Making of a "New South": Class, Politics, and Development in North Carolina, 1865–1900* (Chapel Hill: University of North Carolina Press, 1979), 72–73.

117. Andrea G. Radke-Moss, *Bright Epoch: Women and Coeducation in the American West* (Lincoln: University of Nebraska Press, 2008), 152–59.

118. Neth, *Preserving the Family Farm*, 100–106; Frederick Rudolph, *The American College and University* (New York: Knopf, 1962), 251, 264–65.

119. NCCAMA Catalog, 1890, 14; G. T. Winston to W. H. Page, December 15, 1902, Houghton Library, Harvard University, Walter Hines Page Papers, Letters from Various Correspondents, American Period, bMS Am 1090 (45).

120. *Annual Catalog of the North Carolina Agricultural and Mechanical College for the Colored Race, 1901–02*, 7.

121. *Industrialist*, September 23, 1893, 9.

122. *Progressive Farmer*, June 25, 1895, 4.

123. Klein, "Survey of Land-Grant Colleges and Universities," 357.

124. *Watchman*, July 30, 1891, 4; *Nebraska Independent*, November 14, 1901, 4.

125. *The Agricultural and Mechanical College Record, 1902*, 109–10; KSAC Report, 1895–96, 5.

126. MaryJo Wagner, "'Helping Papa and Mamma Sing the People's Songs': Children in the Populist Party," in Wava G. Haney and Jane B. Knowles, eds., *Women and Farming: Changing Roles, Changing Structures* (Boulder. CO: Westview Press, 1988), 322–23.

127. Garland, *A Son of the Middle Border*, 197, 205.

128. Johnson, *Pioneer's Progress*.

129. O'Connell, *Farewell to the Farm*, 117, 135, 190, 195.

130. F. J. Smith to J. T. Willard, March 30, 1937, vertical file, presidents, Thomas Elmer Will, 1897–1899, Morse Department of Special Collections, Hale Library, Kansas State University; Mamie Alexander Boyd, *Rode a Heifer Calf through College* (Brooklyn: Pageant-Poseidon, 1972), 94; *Lawrence Journal*, August 31, 1895, 5.

131. Hal Bridges, "D. H. Hill and Higher Education in the New South," *Arkansas Historical Quarterly* 15 (Summer 1956), 114.

132. President's Report, February 27, 1889, UNC Trustees, vol. S-8; D. McKay to L. L. Polk, July 14, 1880, Polk Papers, box 4, folder 46.

133. Garland, *A Son of the Middle Border*, 210.

134. Johnson, *Pioneer's Progress*, 23–27.

135. O'Connell, *Farewell to the Farm*, 44, 94, 102, 147, 166.

136. Ray Stannard Baker, *Native American: The Book of My Youth* (New York: Scribner's, 1941), 201; Richard H. Harms, "Farmers vs. Scientists," *Michigan History* 67 (1983), 26–31. Also see Morris Bishop, *A History of Cornell* (Ithaca, NY: Cornell University Press, 1962), 127–28.

137. Louis R. Harlan, *Booker T. Washington: The Making of a Black Leader, 1856–1901* (New York: Oxford University Press, 1972), 275–80.

138. Marcus, *Agricultural Science and the Quest for Legitimacy*, 33; *Proceedings of the Annual Convention of American Agricultural Colleges and Experiment Stations, 1898*, 74.

139. Reagan, *North Carolina State University*, 23, 36; Lockmiller, *History of the North Carolina State College*, 65.

140. Canfield Journal, May 4, 1893, May 13, 1893, November 4, 1893 and November 6, 1893; "Report of the Committee Appointed by the General Faculty on Extensions of Courses of Study," June 6, 1893, NU Regents Papers, box 11, folder 86; NU Regents Mins, vol. 3, April 17, 1896.

141. All students still had to perform a few hours of labor as freshman, when they all took the same set of basic courses. *Industrialist*, February 2, 1895, 87; *Student Herald*, March 24, 1897, 2 and May 26, 1897, 2; Julius T. Willard Diary, June 20, 1897, Morse Department of Special Collections, Hale Library, Kansas State University; Kansas State Agricultural College Faculty Record, vol. D, November 30, 1897, 31, Morse Department of Special Collections, Hale Library, Kansas State University.

142. Carnegie Foundation for Advancement of Teaching, *Fourth Annual Report, 1909*, 103–5.

143. Rodgers, *The Work Ethic in Industrial America*, 86–87; Kliebard, *Schooled to Work*, 124–29, 231–36.

144. *Industrialist*, August 16, 1897, 170.

145. Thorstein Veblen, *The Higher Learning in America: A Memorandum on the Conduct of Universities by Business Men* (Stanford: Academic Reprints, [1918], 1954), 191–99, 203, 212.

Chapter 6. The Tastes of the Multitude

1. *Kansas University Weekly*, April 17, 1897, 2. Also see N. M. Butler to G. Fairchild, April 12, 1897, KSC Letters.

2. Hugh Hawkins, *Between Harvard and America: The Educational Leadership of Charles W. Eliot* (New York: Oxford University Press, 1972), 164–66.

3. Laurence R. Veysey, *The Emergence of the American University* (Chicago: University of Chicago Press, 1965), 64–65; Adam R. Nelson, *Education and Democracy: The Meaning of Alexander Meikeljohn, 1872–1964* (Madison: University of Wisconsin Press, 2001), 196.

4. *Industrialist*, August 16, 1897, 174–75 and November 1898, 644–45.

5. Richard Hofstadter and Walter P. Metzger, *The Development of Academic Freedom in the United States*, vol. 2 (New York: Columbia University Press, 1955), 247, 399, 419–51. The sources were deposed president George Fairchild and conservative professor Julius Willard.

6. Theodore Mitchell, *Political Education in the Southern Farmers' Alliance, 1887–1900* (Madison: University of Wisconsin Press, 1987); Charles Postel, *The Populist Vision* (New York: Oxford University Press, 2007), 62–66; Solon Justus Buck, *The Granger Movement: A Study of Agricultural Organization and Its Political, Economic, and Social Manifestations* (Cambridge, MA: Harvard University Press, 1913), 285–89.

7. Mary O. Furner, *Advocacy and Objectivity: A Crisis in the Professionalization of American Social Science, 1865–1905* (Lexington: University Press of Kentucky, 1975); Thomas Haskell, *The Emergence of Professional Social Science: The American Social Science Association and the Nineteenth-Century Crisis of Authority* (Chicago: University of Illinois Press, 1977); Dorothy Ross, *The Origins of American Social Science* (New York: Cambridge University Press, 1991).

8. *Alliance Weekly*, January 7, 1896, 2.

9. *Alliance*, June 26, 1889, 1.

10. Mitchell, *Political Education in the Southern Farmers' Alliance*, 3–5, 97–98, 108–15, 130–32.

11. William Allen White, *The Autobiography of William Allen White* (New York: Macmillan, 1946), 282.

12. Michael Kazin, *A Godly Hero: The Life of William Jennings Bryan* (New York: Knopf, 2006), 296; Helen M. Cavanaugh, *Carl Schurz Vrooman: A Self-Styled "Constructive Conservative"* (Chicago: Lakeside, 1977), 31.

13. *Nebraska Independent*, January 30, 1896, 4. In particular, Populists resented the manner in which Professor J. Laurence Laughlin dismissed Harvey's arguments. Laughlin,

political economist at the University of Chicago, debated Harvey in 1895. Theodore Saloutos, "The Professors and the Populists," *Agricultural History* 40 (October 1966), 239.

14. *Jeffersonian*, April 2, 1896, 2.

15. Alvin Johnson, *Pioneer's Progress* (New York: Viking, 1952), 95.

16. *Industrialist*, July 15, 1897, 161.

17. See for example, *Hickory Mercury*, October 20, 1897, 4.

18. Vernon L. Parrington, *Main Currents in American Thought: An Interpretation of American Literature from the Beginnings to 1920* (New York: Harcourt, Brace, 1930), 125; W. Bruce Leslie, *Gentlemen and Scholars: College and Community in the "Age of the University," 1865–1917* (University Park: Pennsylvania State University Press, 1992), 75.

19. William H. Harvey, *A Tale of Two Nations* (Chicago: Coin, 1894), 106.

20. John L. Thomas, *Alternative America: Henry George, Edward Bellamy, Henry Demarest Lloyd, and the Adversary Tradition* (Cambridge, MA: Harvard University Press, 1983), 70.

21. *The New York Times*, November 14, 1897, 12.

22. Robert B. Westbrook, "Pullman and the Professor," in *Democratic Hope: Pragmatism and the Politics of Truth* (Ithaca, NY: Cornell University Press, 2005), 78–80; Mark Pittenger, *American Socialists and Evolutionary Thought, 1870–1920* (Madison: University of Wisconsin Press, 1993), 60.

23. Julie A. Reuben, *The Making of the Modern University: Intellectual Transformation and the Marginalization of Morality* (Chicago: University of Chicago Press, 1996), 157–60.

24. Johnson, *Pioneer's Progress*, 95, 112–14; Peter M. Rutkoff and William B. Scott, *New School: A History of the New School for Social Research* (New York: Free Press, 1986), 28–31.

25. Russel Nye, *Midwestern Progressive Politics: A Historical Study of Its Origins and Development, 1870–1950* (East Lansing: Michigan State College Press, 1951), 138; Mitchell, *Political Education in the Southern Farmers' Alliance*, 75–76.

26. *Nebraska Independent*, April 23, 1896, 4.

27. Ellen Fitzpatrick, *Endless Crusade: Women Social Scientists and Progressive Reform* (New York: Oxford University Press, 1990).

28. Daniel T. Rodgers, *Atlantic Crossings: Social Politics in a Progressive Age* (Cambridge, MA: Harvard University Press, 1998), 99; Leon Fink, *Progressive Intellectuals and the Dilemmas of Democratic Commitment* (Cambridge, MA: Harvard University Press, 1997), 59.

29. Richard T. Ely, *Ground Under Our Feet: An Autobiography* (New York: Macmillan, 1937), 79–81; Furner, *Advocacy and Objectivity*, 122; Ross, *The Origins of American Social Science*, 117.

30. Ely, *Ground Under Our Feet*, 184; Benjamin G. Rader, *The Academic Mind and Reform: The Influence of Richard T. Ely in American Life* (Lexington: University of Kentucky Press, 1966), 113–14, 126; E. Bemis to R. T. Ely, May 10, 1899, Richard T. Ely Papers, Wisconsin Historical Society (microfilm), reel 14; Bemis to Ely, April 23, 1897, Ely Papers, reel 12; David Riesman, *Thorstein Veblen* (New Brunswick: Transaction, [1953], 1995), 3, 12–13, 107.

31. James H. Canfield, *Taxation: A Plain Talk for Plain People* (New York: G. P. Putnam's, 1883).

32. Manley, *Centennial History of the University of Nebraska*, 204.

33. Thomas, *Alternative America*, 70. Also see *Nebraska Independent*, February 24, 1898, 4.

34. *Lincoln Independent*, November 22, 1895, 4.

35. NCCAMA Catalog, 1897–98, 16; Alice Reagan, *North Carolina State University: A Narrative History* (Ann Arbor, MI: Edwards Brothers, 1987), 43–44; William L. Carpenter, *Knowledge Is Power: A History of the School of Agriculture and Life Sciences at North Carolina State University, 1877–1984* (Raleigh: North Carolina State University Press, 1987), 124.

36. *Nebraska State Journal*, April 1, 1893, 3; Canfield Journal, April 4, 1893; *Lincoln Independent*, November 22, 1895, 4 and December 13, 1895, 4; W. J. Bryan to G. MacLean, September 13, 1897, NU Regents Papers, box 12, folder 99; *Nebraska Independent*, August 4, 1898, 1 and March 26, 1903, 1. Clyde W. Barrow, *Universities and the Capitalist State: Corporate Liberalism and the Reconstruction of American Higher Education, 1894–1928* (Madison: University of Wisconsin Press, 1990), 92.

37. Roy V. Scott, *The Reluctant Farmer: The Rise of Agricultural Extension to 1914* (Urbana: University of Illinois Press, 1970), 61.

38. Charles Correll, "Revolution and Counterrevolution," *Kansas Quarterly* 1 (Fall 1969), 94–97; William J. Barber, "Political Economy in an Atmosphere of Academic Entrepreneurship: The University of Chicago," in Barber, ed., *Economists and Higher Learning in the Nineteenth Century*, 241–65; Howard V. Davis, *Frank Parsons: Prophet, Innovator, Counselor* (Carbondale: Southern Illinois University Press, 1969), 11–13; James Carey, *Kansas State University: The Quest for Identity* (Lawrence: Regents Press of Kansas, 1977), 73–75.

39. Correll, "Revolution and Counterrevolution," 91; "The Reorganization of the Kansas State Agricultural College," July 1, 1897, Will Papers, folder 9; Kansas State Agricultural College Faculty Record, vol. D, November 12, 1897, 20, Morse Department of Special Collections, Hale Library, Kansas State University; KSAC Report, 1895–96, 81; KSAC Report, 1897–98, 38; *Industrialist,* July 15, 1897, 161, August 16, 1897, 171, January 1898, 56–61 and May 1899, 301–18.

40. *Manhattan Republic*, April 28, 1899, 4; T. E. Will to Whom It May Concern, December 23, 1897, Will Letterbook; KSAC Report, 1897–98, 70; *The Students' Herald*, October 5, 1898, 1.

41. Julius T. Willard, *History of Kansas State College of Agriculture and Applied Science* (Manhattan: Kansas State College Press, 1940), 95; Kansas State Agricultural College Faculty Record, vol. D, January 18, 1897, 51, Morse Department of Special Collections, Hale Library, Kansas State University.

42. "The Student's Burden," Vertical File, Presidents, Thomas E. Will, Morse Department of Special Collections, Hale Library, Kansas State University.

43. Rodgers, *Atlantic Crossings*, 323; Furner, *Advocacy and Objectivity*, 5–8, 228; Ross, *The Origins of American Social Science*, 108–9; Haskell, *The Emergence of Professional Social Science*; Christopher Lasch, *The New Radicalism in America, 1889–1963: The Intellectual as a Social Type* (New York: Knopf, 1965), xiv.

44. Reuben, *The Making of the Modern University*, 192.

45. Willard, *History of Kansas State College of Agriculture and Applied Science*, 73; Clyde Kenneth Hyder, *Snow of Kansas: The Life of Francis Huntington Snow, with Extracts from His Journals and Letters* (Lawrence: University of Kansas Press, 1953), 207–10; F. W. Simonds to K. P. Battle, July 1, 1889, UNC, box 18, folder 589.

46. Ross, *The Origins of American Social Science*, 177; Thomas Bender, "E.R.A. Seligman and the Vocation of Social Science," in *Intellect and Public Life: Essays on the Social History of Academic Intellectuals in the United States* (Baltimore, MD: Johns Hopkins University Press, 1993), 63.

47. *Nebraska Independent*, February 10, 1898, 4; *Lawrence Journal*, May 29, 1897, 9.

48. Thomas C. McClintock, "J. Allen Smith and the Progressive Movement: A Study in Intellectual History" (PhD dissertation, University of Washington, 1959), 125–31.

49. *Jeffersonian*, January 16, 1896, 2; Upton Sinclair, *The Goose-Step: A Story of American Education* (New York: Albert and Charles Boni, 1936), 352. Populists also sometimes supported religious freedom. *Jeffersonian*, April 5, 1894, 2; *Advocate and News*, February 23, 1898, 12.

50. Eric Goldman, "J. Allen Smith: The Reformer and his Dilemma," *Pacific Northwest Quarterly* 35 (July 1944), 198–99.

51. Bill G. Reid, *Five for the Land and Its People* (Fargo: North Dakota Institute for Regional Studies, 1989), 24, 144.

52. I. D. Chamberlain to C. S. Thomas, May 31, 1899, in "Thomas Elmer Will: Letters on Educational Work, 1899," unprocessed addition to Will Papers.

53. *Nebraska Independent*, April 12, 1900, 6, June 18, 1903, 9, June 25, 1903, 9, July 2, 1903, 10, and July 9, 1903, 10.

54. "Comments of J. T. Willard Re: Statement Issued by Board of Regents to the Reorganization of KSAC Faculty, April 1897," KSC Letters; KSAC Report, 1893–94, 33–34; KSAC Report, 1897–98, 47; *Industrialist*, April 14, 1894, 123; Ralph Sparks, "To Serve the People: The Populist Era at Kansas State," unpublished manuscript dated 1993, Morse Department of Special Collections, Hale Library, Kansas State University; George Thompson Fairchild, "Populism in a State Educational Institution," *American Journal of Sociology* 3 (November 1897), 394–98; Correll, "Revolution and Counterrevolution," 91; E. Secrest to L. Lewelling, June 1, 1894, box 1, folder 6, Correspondence file, Gov. Lorenzo D. Lewelling, Records of the Governor's Office, Kansas State Historical Society.

55. Virginia Noah Gibson, "The Effect of the Populist Movement on Kansas State Agricultural College" (master's thesis, Kansas State College of Agriculture and Applied Science, 1932), 37–38, 68; Correll, "Revolution and Counterrevolution," 91–95; Julius T. Willard Diary, July 4, 1897, Morse Department of Special Collections, Hale Library, Kansas State University; C. B. Hoffman to H. Kelley, July 7, 1897, Kelley Papers, box 1, folder "Correspondence 1894–1898"; *Manhattan Nationalist*, July 8, 1897, 2.

56. Carey, *Kansas State University*, 71–73. The *Topeka Capital*, however, spread misinformation with the headline "Deposed Nearly Entire Faculty." The *Capital's* source was a professor who had left Manhattan and did not realize that many of his colleagues

had been rehired. *Topeka Capital*, April 10, 1897. Some historians were misled into repeating the claim that the Populists fired almost all KSAC professors. Hofstadter and Metzger, *The Development of Academic Freedom in the United States*, 429; Furner, *Advocacy and Objectivity*, 221.

57. *The American Nonconformist and Kansas Industrial Liberator*, June 27, 1889, 1; J. T. Willard to F. Parsons, June 27, 1899, Parsons Papers, box 2, folder 104.

58. T. E. Will to J. Wiley, May 13, 1897, Will Letterbook, vol. 1, 118–19; *Kansas Commoner*, June 17, 1897, 4. For Republican outrage, see KSU Clippings.

59. James R. Montgomery, *The Volunteer State Forges Its University: The University of Tennessee, 1887–1919* (Knoxville: University of Tennessee Record, 1966), 20.

60. *The Washington Post*, June 19, 1899, 6.

61. J. T. Willard to F. Parsons, June 27, 1899 and December 25, 1899, Parsons Papers, box 2, folder 104.

62. *Manhattan Nationalist*, April 22, 1897, 1–2, 4; KSU Clippings, vol. 1, 6.

63. Hyder, *Snow of Kansas*, 211.

64. Duncan L. Kinnear, *The First 100 Years: A History of Virginia Polytechnic Institute and State University* (Blacksburg: Virginia Polytechnic Institute, 1972), 99–119.

65. *Seattle Post-Intelligencer*, October 17, 1897, 1, 4; E. S. Meany to A. A. Lindsey, February 25, 1898 and E. S. Meany to W. B. Judson, Edmund S. Meany Papers, University of Washington Archives (microfilm), Edmund S. Meany letterpress copybook, vol. 4, 678–81, 816; Charles Gates, *The First Century at the University of Washington, 1861–1961* (Seattle: University of Washington Press, 1961), 67–71; McClintock, "J. Allen Smith and the Progressive Movement," 125–31; Thomas W. Riddle, *The Old Radicalism: John R. Rogers and the Populist Movement in Washington* (New York: Garland, 1991), 93.

66. *Jeffersonian*, June 17, 1897, 2, July 8, 1897, 2 and July 15, 1897, 2.

67. "The Reorganization of the Kansas State Agricultural College," July 1, 1897, Will Papers, folder 9; *Industrialist*, July 15, 1897, 161; *Manhattan Mercury*, June 17, 1896, 4.

68. J. T. Willard to father, April 18, 1897, KSC Letters; J. T. Willard Re: "Statement Issued by Board of Regents to the Reorganization of KSAC Faculty," April, 1897, KSC Letters; J. T. Willard to G. T. Fairchild, May 4, 1899, KSC Letters. Edward Bemis agreed that president Fairchild had not hired a high-quality faculty, though he questioned the dismissal of a conservative professor of history. E. Bemis to R. T. Ely, October 4, 1897, Ely Papers, reel 12.

69. Correll, "Revolution and Counterrevolution," 94; *Industrialist*, August 16, 1897, 171; *Manhattan Republic*, May 14, 1897, 4.

70. *Manhattan Republic*, April 30, 1897, 4; *Industrialist*, August 16, 1897, 171.

71. T. E. Will to C. B. Hoffman, May 18, 1897, KSC Letters; T. E. Will to H. Kelley, May 31, 1897, KSC Letters; T. E. Will to J. Wiley, May 31, 1897, KSC Letters; T. E. Will to C. B. Hoffman, May 31, 1897, Will Letterbook, vol. 1, 243; Correll, "Revolution and Counterrevolution," 96.

72. C. B. Hoffman to H. Kelley, July 7, 1897, Kelley Papers, box 1, folder "Correspondence 1894–1898"; Carey, *Kansas State University*, 73–76; *Industrialist*, October 1898, 583.

73. *The Students' Herald,* April 14, 1897, 2, May 12, 1897, 2, and May 19, 1897, 2.

74. *Industrialist,* July 1898, 511; *Manhattan Mercury,* June 9, 1897 and September 1, 1897; *Manhattan Republic,* July 2, 1897, 4; T. E. Will to J. Walters, January 6, 1909, Will Papers, folder 5.

75. T. E. Will to H. Kelley, May 4, 1897, Will Letterbook, vol. 1, 20; "The Reorganization of the Kansas State Agricultural College," July 1, 1897, Will Papers, folder 9; *Industrialist,* July 15, 1897, 161; J. T. Willard to father, April 18, 1897, KSC Letters.

76. Fairchild, "Populism in a State Educational Institution," 403; F. White to G. T. Fairchild, July 11, 1897, KSC Letters; *Manhattan Republic,* June 23, 1899, 1.

77. Postel, *The Populist Vision,* 139–41.

78. *The University of South Dakota, 1862–1966* (Vermillion: University of South Dakota Press, 1975), 65–66, 70–75.

79. Irby was later rehired by a Democratic board of trustees and then fired again. The fusionists also dismissed the director of the agricultural experiment station. David A. Lockmiller, *History of the North Carolina State College of Agriculture and Engineering of the University of North Carolina, 1889–1939* (Raleigh: North Carolina State College of Agriculture and Engineering, 1939), 60; Carpenter, *Knowledge Is Power,* 77, 89 n9.

80. *Industrialist,* August 16, 1897, 171; *Nationalist,* April 22, 1897, 1; *Manhattan Republic,* May 5, 1899, 8; J. T. Willard to father, April 18, 1897, KSC Letters; Correll, "Revolution and Counterrevolution," 94; Carey, *Kansas State University,* 71–73. Fairchild claimed that he eventually would have been fired. He also claimed that none of the rehired professors had the temperament to challenge Populist policies. G. T. Fairchild to E. M. Fairchild, April 25, 1897, KSC Letters.

81. T. E. Will to E. Bemis, June 1, 1897, KSC Letters; T. E. Will to E. Bemis, July 8, 1897, Will Letterbook, vol. 1, 378; F. Parsons to C. Thomas, May 29, 1899, "Thomas Elmer Will: Letters on Educational Work, 1899," unprocessed addition to Will Papers; T. E. Will to J. T. Willard, October 25, 1913, Hoffman Papers, box 1, folder 6; T. E. Will to J. T. Willard, December 17, 1943, Vertical File, Presidents, Thomas E. Will, Morse Department of Special Collections, Hale Library, Kansas State University; untitled, undated typescript, Will Papers, folder 8; "The Reorganization of the Kansas State Agricultural College," July 1, 1897, Will Papers, folder 9; *Industrialist,* July 1899, 472; *Manhattan Republic,* April 16, 1897, 1 and April 28, 1899, 1; E. Bemis to R. T. Ely, October 4, 1897, Ely Papers, reel 12.

82. Fairchild, "Populism in a State Educational Institution," 397–98.

83. L. B. Jolly and H. B. Kempton to F. Parsons and Whom It May Concern, March 25, 1899, Parsons Papers, box 1, folder 8; J. T. Willard to F. Parsons, June 27, 1899 and December 25, 1899, Parsons Papers, box 2, folder 104.

84. Minutes of the Board of Trustees, Kansas State Agricultural College, vol. B, June 6, 1899, 272; *Industrialist,* July 1899, 468; *Manhattan Republic,* June 2, 1899; *Student Herald,* June 1, 1899, 2; E. Bemis to R. T. Ely, June 3, 1899, Ely Papers, reel 14.

85. Junior Class Meeting Resolutions, May 20, 1899, Parsons Papers, box 1, folder 8; F. Parsons to C. Thomas, May 29, 1899, Thomas Elmer Will: Letters on Educational

Work, 1899, unprocessed addition to the Will Papers; F. A. Metcalf to Whom It May Concern, June 21, 1899, Parsons Papers, box 2, folder 80. The KSAC alumni association condemned the Populists, though some students claimed that Fairchild appointed its member before his resignation. "Facts about Alumni Association," Will Papers, folder 9.

86. C. C. Georgeson to G. T. Fairchild, October 6, 1897, KSC Letters; E. Bemis to R. T. Ely, June 12, 1899, Ely Papers, reel 14; E. Bemis to Whom It May Concern, June 17, 1899, Parsons Papers, box 1, folder 18; E. Bemis to R. T. Ely, January 19, 1899, Ely Papers, reel 14.

87. Pittenger, *American Socialists and Evolutionary Thought*, 7; Postel, *The Populist Vision*, 139.

88. *Wealth Makers of the World*, November 8, 1894, 8.

89. Tibbles, *Nebraska Redeemed*, 93.

90. *Lincoln Independent*, December 6, 1895, 4.

91. T. E. Will to R. T. Ely, June 24, 1897, Ely Papers, reel 12.

92. *Industrialist*, July 1898, 505.

93. Reuben, *The Making of the Modern University*, 194–200; Veysey, *The Emergence of the American University*, 386; Ellen W. Schrecker, *No Ivory Tower: McCarthyism and the Universities* (New York: Oxford University Press, 1986), 14; "General Report of the Committee on Academic Freedom and Academic Tenure," *Bulletin of the American Association of University Professors* 1 (December 1915), 17–43.

94. Louis Finkelstein, *American Spiritual Autobiographies: Fifteen Self-Portraits* (New York: Harper, 1948), 41; Canfield Journal, November 25, 1891; *Wisner Chronicle*, April 21, 1900, 4; *Nebraska Independent*, November 15, 1900, 4.

95. Ludy T. Benjamin Jr., *Harry Kirke Wolfe: Pioneer in Psychology* (Lincoln: University of Nebraska Press, 1991), 90; Robert Manley, *Centennial History of the University of Nebraska*, vol. 1 (Lincoln: University of Nebraska Press, 1969), 119–20; Canfield Journal, August 25, 1891 and April 18, 1893; H. K. Wolfe to Board of Regents, June 10, 1897, NU Regents Papers, box 12, folder 97; Robert Knoll, *Prairie University: A History of the University of Nebraska* (Lincoln: University of Nebraska Press, 1995), 39.

96. Ross E. Paulson, *Radicalism and Reform: The Vrooman Family and American Social Thought, 1837–1937* (Lexington: University of Kentucky Press, 1968), 145.

97. Hyder, *Snow of Kansas*, 207; Manley, *Centennial History of the University of Nebraska*, 113; "Mounted Clippings, James Canfield," Charles Sumner Gleed Papers, Kansas State Historical Society, box 51; *Kansas Commoner*, April 15, 1897, 4; *Jeffersonian*, May 27, 1897, 2; *The Advocate*, June 24, 1891.

98. E. Secrest to H. Kelley, May 14, 1893, Kelley Papers, box 1, folder "Correspondence 1893"; *Manhattan Republic*, June 23, 1899, 8; *Jeffersonian*, June 24, 1897, 2.

99. T. E. Will to C. B. Hoffman, October 4, 1896, Will Papers, folder 1.

100. Fairchild denied the story. *Manhattan Republic*, May 7, 1897, 4; *Kansas Commoner*, April 15, 1897, 4; *Topeka Advocate*, April 28, 1897, 11; G. T. Fairchild to W. A. Peffer, April 30, 1897, KSC Letters.

101. *Wealth Makers of the World*, July 4, 1895, 4 and August 15, 1895, 4; *Jeffersonian*, December 5, 1895, 2; *Lincoln Independent*, November 8, 1895, 1.

102. *Caucasian*, September 5, 1895, 1 and October 24, 1895, 1; *Plowboy*, January 8, 1896, 1.

103. Manley, *Centennial History of the University of Nebraska*, 152–54, 209–10; NU Regents Mins, vol. 5, May 14, 1903; J. D. Whitmore to J. S. Dales, February 7, 1904, NU Regents Papers, box 16, folder 133; F. W. Russell to J. S. Dales, February 4, 1904, NU Regents Papers, box 16, folder 133.

104. J. W. Grainger to W. Clark, April 21, 1896, W. Clark to J. H. Southgate, June 25, 1898, and W. Clark to J. H. Southgate, June 30, 1898, in Aubrey Lee Brooks and Hugh T. Lefler, eds., *The Papers of Walter Clark*, vol. 1 (Chapel Hill: University of North Carolina Press, 1948), 283–84, 369–72, 377–80; *Caucasian*, June 30, 1898, 1–2 and July 7, 1898, 3; *Progressive Farmer*, August 23, 1898, 2, 6; Aubrey Lee Brooks, *Walter Clark: Fighting Judge* (Chapel Hill: University of North Carolina Press, 1944), 104–5.

105. Fink, *Progressive Intellectuals*, 212–13; Reuben, *The Making of the Modern University*, 192.

106. E. D. Stratford to H. Kelley, June 6, 1893, Kelley Papers, box 1, folder "Correspondence 1893"; T. E. Will to E. Bemis, July 8, 1897, Will Letterbook, vol. 1, 378.

107. T. E. Will to J. T. Willard, October 25, 1913, Hoffman Papers, box 1, folder 6.

108. "The Reorganization of the Kansas State Agricultural College," July 1, 1897, Will Papers, folder 9.

109. KSAC Report, 1899–1900, 25–26; *Industrialist*, October 1898, 563–69 and November 1898, 600–3; Thomas E. Will, "A Menace to Freedom: The College Trust," *Arena* 26 (September 1901), 248–55; Thomas E. Will, "College for the People," *Arena* 26 (July 1901), 15–16.

110. *Nebraska Independent*, November 9, 1899, 4.

111. *Jeffersonian*, June 24, 1897, 2; *Alliance Independent*, February 22, 1894, 4.

112. Paulson, *Radicalism and Reform*, 140–43; Cavanaugh, *Carl Schurz Vrooman*, 47–49.

113. Will, "A Menace to Freedom," 248, 257.

114. "General Report of the Committee on Academic Freedom and Academic Tenure," 31–32.

115. Matthew W. Finkin and Robert C. Post, *For the Common Good: Principles of American Academic Freedom* (New Haven, CT: Yale University Press, 2009), 100–101.

Chapter 7. Watchdogs of the Treasury

1. Jonas Viles, *The University of Missouri: A Centennial History* (Columbia: University of Missouri Press, 1939), 197–201.

2. "Many Tax Payers" to J. L. Teeters, February 12, 1900, NU Regents Papers, box 14, folder 114.

3. *Weekly Commoner*, September 10, 1897, 5.

4. David B. Danbom, *The Resisted Revolution: Urban America and the Industrialization of Agriculture, 1900–1930* (Ames: Iowa State University Press, 1979), 17.

5. For example, see Charles Gates, *The First Century at the University of Washington, 1861–1961* (Seattle: University of Washington Press, 1961), 57–64.

6. Steven Hahn, *The Roots of Rural Populism: Yeoman Farmers and the Transformation of the Georgia Upcountry, 1850–1890* (New York: Oxford University Press, 1983), 286; Robert C. McMath Jr., *Populist Vanguard: A History of the Southern Farmers' Alliance* (Chapel Hill: University of North Carolina Press, 1975), 143.

7. David Tyack, Thomas James, and Aaron Benavot, *Law and the Shaping of Public Education, 1785–1954* (Madison: University of Wisconsin Press, 1987), 74–108; Alexander Brody, *The American State and Higher Education: The Legal, Political, and Constitutional Relationship* (Washington, DC: American Council on Education, 1935), 49–50; Merle Curti, *The Social Ideas of American Educators* (Totowa, NJ: Littlefield, [1935], 1971), 239; Louis R. Harlan, *Separate and Unequal: Public School Campaigns and Racism in the Southern Seaboard States, 1901–1915* (New York: Atheneum, [1958], 1968), 46–54.

8. Edward A. Ross, *Seventy Years of It: An Autobiography* (New York: Appleton, 1936), 175. Also see Eldon L. Johnson, "Misconceptions about the Early Land-Grant Colleges," *Journal of Higher Education* 52 (July–August 1981), 342–44.

9. Charles K. Adams, "State Aid to Higher Education," in *State Aid to Higher Education: A Series of Addresses Delivered at the Johns Hopkins University* (Baltimore, MD: Johns Hopkins Press, 1898), 13; *Journal of Proceedings and Addresses of the National Educational Association, 1898*, 109.

10. William Snider, *Light on the Hill: A History of the University of North Carolina at Chapel Hill* (Chapel Hill: University of North Carolina Press, 1992), 101–2, 115–17.

11. North Carolina General Assembly, *Journal of the House of Representatives of the General Assembly of the State of North Carolina, 1887*, 623–24; J. Daniel to E. Alderman, April 12, 1897, UNC, box 20, folder 664; B. Craven to E. Alderman, February 3, 1898, UNC, box 20, folder 669. On the acceleration of public funding after 1910, see Roger L. Geiger, *To Advance Knowledge: The Growth of American Research Universities, 1900–1940* (New York: Oxford University Press, 1986), 42.

12. Frederick A. Bode, *Protestantism in the New South: North Carolina Baptists and Methodists in Political Crisis, 1894–1903* (Charlottesville: University Press of Virginia, 1975), 134–36; E. A. Alderman to W. H. Page, April 4, 1904, Walter Hines Page Letters from Various Correspondents, American Period, bMS Am 1090 (10), Houghton Library, Harvard University.

13. Canfield Journal, February 1, 1893.

14. Robert Manley, *Centennial History of the University of Nebraska*, vol. 1 (Lincoln: University of Nebraska Press, 1969), 119, 123–25, 196. For Taylor's biography, see Sara M. Baldwin and Robert M. Baldwin, eds., *Nebraskana* (Hebron, NE: Baldwin, 1932), 1180.

15. Brody, *The American State and Higher Education*, 51–57.

16. Henry Dethloff, *A Centennial History of Texas A&M University, 1876–1976*, vol. 1 (College Station: Texas A&M Press, 1975), 47, 72–73; Louis G. Geiger, *University of the Northern Plains: A History of the University of North Dakota, 1883–1958* (Grand Forks: University of North Dakota Press, 1958), 102; C. Vann Woodward, *Origins of the New South, 1877–1913* (Baton Rouge: Louisiana State University Press, [1951], 1971), 172–73; George M. Marsden, *The Soul of the American University: From Protestant Establishment to Established*

Nonbelief (New York: Oxford University Press, 1994), 276; Mabel Hardy Pollitt, *A Biography of James Kennedy Patterson* (Louisville, KY: Westerfield-Bonte, 1925), 4, 125, 261–63; *Proceedings and Addresses of the National Educational Association, 1887*, 175.

17. *The American Nonconformist and Kansas Industrial Liberator*, July 10, 1890, 6; *Jeffersonian*, July 21, 1892, 5.

18. Daniel T. Rodgers, *Contested Truths: Keywords in American Politics since Independence* (New York: Basic Books, 1987), 89; Bruce Palmer, *"Man over Money:" The Southern Populist Critique of American Capitalism* (Chapel Hill: University of North Carolina Press, 1980), 41–42.

19. People's Party of Kansas, Central State Committee, *People's Party Campaign Handbook* (Hiawatha, KS: Harrington Printing, 1898).

20. Joseph W. Creech Jr., "Righteous Indignation: Religion and Populism in North Carolina, 1886–1906" (PhD dissertation, University of Notre Dame, 2000), 236.

21. Barton C. Shaw, *The Wool-Hat Boys: Georgia's Populist Party* (Baton Rouge: Louisiana State University Press, 1984), 132–33.

22. H. Leon Prather Sr., *Resurgent Politics and Educational Progressivism in the New South, 1890–1913* (Rutherford, NJ: Fairleigh Dickinson University Press, 1979), 123–24; William H. Denton, "The Impact of Populism upon the Southern Educational Awakening" (PhD dissertation, University of North Carolina, 1965), 156; *Progressive Farmer*, May 30, 1899, 2.

23. Thomas W. Riddle, *The Old Radicalism: John R. Rogers and the Populist Movement in Washington* (New York: Garland, 1991), 176–77. Also see William J. Reese, *Power and Promise of School Reform: Grassroots Movements during the Progressive Era* (New York: Teachers College Press, 2002), 64–69, 97.

24. Daniel Walker Hollis, *University of South Carolina*, vol. 2 (Columbia: University of South Carolina Press, 1956), 100–101; Steve Kantrowitz, *Ben Tillman and the Reconstruction of White Supremacy* (Chapel Hill: University of North Carolina Press, 2000), 99.

25. *Lawrence Journal*, January 30, 1897, 9.

26. *Seattle Post-Intelligencer*, March 14, 1897, 1; *Weekly Commoner*, March 19, 1897, 5.

27. *Chickasaw Messenger*, January 6, 1887, 1, August 25, 1887, 6, March 15, 1888, 1, and April 12, 1888, 1; *Progressive Farmer*, August 4, 1887, 4. Also see John K. Bettersworth, *People's University: The Centennial History of Mississippi State* (Jackson: University Press of Mississippi, 1980), 92–103, 132–34.

28. *Atlanta Constitution*, September 13, 1889, 3, and December 1, 1892, 4.

29. Thomas Dyer, *The University of Georgia: A Bicentennial History, 1785–1985* (Athens: University of Georgia Press, 1985), 144–50, 193; Shaw, *The Wool-Hat Boys*, 106–7. On the relationship between populism and evangelicalism, see Bode, *Protestantism in the New South*, 6, 42; 172–73; Peter Argersinger, "Pentecostal Politics in Kansas: Religion, the Farmers' Alliance, and the Gospel of Populism" in *The Limits of Agrarian Radicalism: Western Populism and American Politics* (Lawrence: University Press of Kansas, 1995).

30. *Atlanta Constitution*, June and July, 1893, November 25, 1894, 14, November 18, 1897, 5, and November 19, 1897, 4; *Biblical Recorder*, May 9, 1894, 1, 4.

31. S. C. Randolph to L. L. Polk, February 21, 1887, Polk Papers, box 6, folder 89.

32. *Country Life*, September 1890, 1.

33. *Plowboy*, February 6, 1895, 3 and January 9, 1895, 2; *News and Observer*, March 6, 1895, 1, 5. Also see Philip Roy Muller, "New South Populism: North Carolina, 1884–1900" (PhD dissertation, University of North Carolina, 1972), 215.

34. James L. Leloudis, *Schooling the New South: Pedagogy, Self, and Society in North Carolina, 1880–1920* (Chapel Hill: University of North Carolina Press, 1996), 109–16; Luther L. Gobbel, *Church-State Relationships in Education in North Carolina since 1776* (Durham, NC: Duke University Press, 1938), 67, 92, 106, 122, 131; Bode, *Protestantism in the New South*, 24; President's Report, February 8, 1893, UNC Trustees Papers, vol. 9.

35. For example, one historian concluded that the North Carolina Farmers' Alliance was divided about supporting public higher education, but cited a source printed by a suballiance affiliated with the Methodist Trinity College. James L. Hunt, *Marion Butler and American Populism* (Chapel Hill: University of North Carolina, 2003), 36. The source was an issue of *Country Life*, the organ of the Randolph County Farmers' Alliance, which included a Trinity professor and convened on campus. *Country Life*, September 1890, 5.

36. Josephus Daniels, *Editor in Politics* (Chapel Hill: University of North Carolina Press, 1941), 102; Bode, *Protestantism in the New South*, 30–35.

37. Hollis, *University of South Carolina*, 128–33, 138–41; Hal Bridges, "D. H. Hill and Higher Education in the New South," *Arkansas Historical Quarterly* 15 (Summer 1956), 117.

38. *Biblical Recorder*, April 4, 1894, 1, January 10, 1894, 1, May 9, 1894, 1, 4, February 24, 1897, 1 and August 5, 1896, 2; *Western Carolina Advocate*, February 9, 1893, 1.

39. *Biblical Recorder*, July 15, 1896, 4.

40. E. Alderman to M. Butler, December 17, 1896, Butler Papers, Collection 114, folder 44; Rose H. Holder, *McIver of North Carolina* (Chapel Hill: University of North Carolina Press, 1957), 159; Gobbel, *Church-State Relationships in Education in North Carolina since 1776*, 149, 155–56.

41. Gobbel, *Church-State Relationships in Education in North Carolina since 1776*, 140 n40.

42. F. H. Snow to S. D. Jewell, November 21, 1894 and F. H. Snow to S. F. Jewell, November 26, 1894, SGC, box 16; Clifford S. Griffin, *The University of Kansas* (Lawrence: University of Kansas Press, 1974), 88–92; Manley, *Centennial History of the University of Nebraska*, 135.

43. Griffin, *The University of Kansas*, 88.

44. *Kansas University Weekly*, March 20, 1897, 126; G. T. Fairchild to J. T. Willard, May 5, 1899, KSC Letters.

45. Newspaper clippings of February 8, 189(5?), University of Nebraska Newspaper Clippings Scrapbook, 1895–97, RG 0/4, Archives and Special Collections, University of Nebraska–Lincoln Libraries; *Nebraska State Journal*, April 1, 1893, 3.

46. *Seattle Post-Intelligencer*, September 17, 1897, 3; George A. Frykman, *Creating the People's University: Washington State University, 1890–1990* (Pullman: Washington State University Press, 1990), 27–28; Bryan, *Historical Sketch of the State College of Washington*,

172–78; Harrison Hale, *University of Arkansas, 1871–1948* (Fayetteville: University of Arkansas Press, 1948), 57–60; John H. Reynolds and David Y. Thomas, *History of the University of Arkansas* (Fayetteville: University of Arkansas, 1910), 144.

47. *Kansas Commoner,* January 14, 1897, 4.

48. Lilibel Hurshel Henry Broadway, "Frank Burkitt: The Man in the Wool Hat" (master's thesis, Mississippi State University, 1948), 25–26. Also see *Wealth Makers of the World,* August 29, 1895, 1; *Prairie Home,* June 1897, 1; *Kansas Commoner,* January 14, 1897, 4.

49. Ross, *Seventy Years of It,* 90.

50. *Chickasaw Messenger,* March 22, 1888, 1 and April 12, 1888, 8; Bettersworth, *People's University,* 96–97.

51. *Jeffersonian,* November 5, 1896, 2, November 22, 1894, 2 and April 2, 1896, 2.

52. *Jeffersonian,* December 31, 1896, 3, April 9, 1896, 2, and April 2, 1896, 2. Also see Untitled and undated typescript, Sears Papers, box 1, letterbook, 239–42.

53. *Jeffersonian,* January 31, 1895, 2; *Nationalist,* May 13, 1897, 2.

54. *Lawrence Journal,* February 6, 1897 1 and February 27, 1897, 8; *Topeka Advocate,* February 24, 1897, 4.

55. F. H. Snow to F. B. McKinnon, March 22, 1897 and F. H. Snow to J. B. Angell, March 29, 1897, SRC; *Kansas University Weekly,* February 27, 1897 81; *Lawrence Journal,* February 20, 1897, 1 and March 13, 1897, 1; *Topeka Advocate,* March 24, 1897, 12; *Jeffersonian,* March 18, 1897, 1–2.

56. *Jeffersonian,* June 3, 1897, 2; T. E. Will to F. Parsons, May 8, 1897, KSC Letters.

57. F. H. Snow to F. B. McKinnon, March 22, 1897, SRC; *Jeffersonian,* June 17, 1897, 2 and January 6, 1898, 2.

58. *Nebraska Independent,* March 18, 1897, 1; NU Regents Mins, April 13, 1898, vol. 4.

59. Ballard C. Campbell, *Representative Democracy: Public Policy and Midwestern Legislatures in the Late Nineteenth Century* (Cambridge, MA: Harvard University Press, 1980), 71, 169.

60. Alderman cited in Bode, *Protestantism in the New South,* 30–32, 81; H. Clarkson to E. Alderman, October 23, 1896, UNC, box 20, folder 659.

61. *Lawrence Journal,* January 30, 1897, 9; F. H. Snow to Kellogg, November 4, 1896, SRC; F. H. Snow to Carter, January 28, 1897, SGC, box 21.

62. Some Populists, however, wanted to cut Ole Miss's budget instead. Bettersworth, *People's University,* 99–103; *Progressive Farmer,* April 2, 1889, 1.

63. *Proceedings of the North Carolina Farmers' State Alliance, 1889,* 22; *Proceedings of the North Carolina Farmers' State Alliance, 1891,* 20, 30; *The News and Observer,* July 22, 1890; T. B. Parker to E. Alderman, July 16, 1898, UNC, box 20, folder 671; KU Report, 1889–90, 29; David Brooks Cofer, *First Five Administrators of Texas A. and M College, 1876–1890* (College Station, TX: 1952), 40–41; Theodore Saloutos, *Farmers Movements in the South, 1865–1933* (Berkeley: University of California Press, 1960), 86; Denton, "The Impact of Populism upon the Southern Educational Awakening," 122–26. On the initial opposition of the Tennessee Farmers' Alliance, see Connie L. Lester, *Up From the Mudsills of Hell: The Farmers' Alliance, Populism, and Progressive Agriculture in Tennessee, 1870–1915* (Athens: University of Georgia Press, 2006), 142–48.

64. Cedric Cummins, *The University of South Dakota, 1862–1966* (Vermillion: University of South Dakota Press, 1975), 63; Geiger, *University of the Northern Plains*, 101–3; Manley, *Centennial History of the University of Nebraska*, 121–23; *Nebraskan*, March 12, 1897, 1; *Nebraska Independent*, January 12, 1897, 5.

65. Winton U. Solberg, *The University of Illinois, 1867–1894: An Intellectual and Cultural History* (Urbana: University of Illinois Press, 1968), 338–40.

66. David Thelen, *Paths of Resistance: Tradition and Dignity in Industrializing Missouri* (New York: Oxford University Press, 1986), 212; Homer Clevenger, "Agrarian Politics in Missouri, 1880–1896" (PhD dissertation, University of Missouri, 1940), 200; Ruth Warner Towne, "The Public Career of William Joel Stone" (PhD dissertation, University of Missouri, 1953); *Missouri Statesman*, January 15, 1897, 4; University of the State of Missouri, *Biennial Report of the Board of Curators to the General Assembly for the Two Years Ending December 31, 1896*, 26.

67. Denton, "The Impact of Populism upon the Southern Educational Awakening," 128–29.

68. Hollis, *University of South Carolina*, 168–69; Francis Butler Simkins, *Pitchfork Ben Tillman: South Carolinian* (Baton Rouge: Louisiana State University Press, 1944), 153, 171–79, 306.

69. *Jeffersonian*, December 17, 1896, 2. On Lewelling, also see Peter H. Curtis, "Lorenzo D. Lewelling: A Quaker Populist," *Quaker History* 61 (1972), 113–15; F. H. Snow to L. Lewelling, May 31, 1894, box 1, folder 25, Correspondence file, Gov. Lorenzo D. Lewelling, Records of the Governor's Office, Collection 27-5-4-5, Kansas State Historical Society, Topeka, Kansas.

70. *Manhattan Republic*, January 15, 1897, 6; *Kansas Commoner*, January 14, 1897, 7; *Lawrence Journal*, November 14, 1896; F. H. Snow to E. C. Little, November 9, 1896, SRC; *Lawrence Journal*, January 16, 1897, 9.

71. Leloudis, *Schooling the New South*, 119; Gobbel, *Church-State Relationships in Education in North Carolina since 1776*, 167.

72. "The University of North Carolina: Necessity for Its Existence and Support," December 20, 1894, UNC, box 19, folder 649; Kemp Plummer Battle, *History of the University of North Carolina*, vol. 2 (Raleigh, NC: Edwards and Broughton, 1912), 482–93.

73. *Progressive Farmer*, January 19, 1897, 3; *News and Observer*, March 6, 1895, 1, 5. Also see Trustee Minutes and President's Report, February 18, 1897, UNC Trustees, Subgroup 1, vol. 9.

74. Campbell, *Representative Democracy*, 53.

75. Reynolds and Thomas, *History of the University of Arkansas*, 145.

76. *Colorado State Board of Agriculture and State Agricultural College, Eighteenth Annual Report, 1896*, 31; James Edward Wright, *The Politics of Populism: Dissent in Colorado* (New Haven, CT: Yale University Press, 1974), 153, 163; Frederick Allen, Ernest Andrade Jr., Mark Foster, Phillip Mitterling, and H. Lee Scamehorn, *The University of Colorado, 1876–1976* (New York: Harcourt Brace Jovanovich, 1976), 68–69; *Senate Journal of the General Assembly of Colorado, 1893*, 939–40, 1179, 1290; *House Journal of the General Assembly of the State of Colorado, 1893*, 1313, 1778–79.

77. Viles, *The University of Missouri*, 236–39.

78. State of North Dakota, *Journal of the House of the Third Legislative Assembly, 1893*, 518–22; Geiger, *University of the Northern Plains*, 101–8, 134.

79. Cummins, *The University of South Dakota*, 68.

80. *Seattle Post-Intelligencer*, March 2, 1897, 2, March 3, 1897, 4, March 7, 1897, 2, March 9, 1897, 1, March 11, 1897, 1–2, March 12, 1897, 1–2, and March 13, 1897, 2; *Weekly Commoner*, March 19, 1897, 6; Bryan, *Historical Sketch of the State College of Washington*, 172–78.

81. Winston cited in Bode, *Protestantism in the New South*, 30–35.

82. 1897 North Carolina General Assembly, Public Laws, Regular Session, Chapter 165, Chapter 171, Chapter 486, and Chapter 535; State Executive Committee of the People's Party of North Carolina, *People's Party Hand-Book of Facts: Campaign of 1898* (Raleigh, NC: Capital Printing, 1898), 58–59; *Journal of the House of Representatives of the General Assembly of the State of North Carolina, 1897*, 562, 612, 770–71; *Progressive Farmer*, October 17, 1899, 6; Wade H. Boggs III, *State Supported Higher Education for Blacks in North Carolina, 1877–1945* (PhD dissertation, Duke University, 1972), 147–48, 171–79; *News and Observer*, March 17, 1897, 5.

83. McIver cited in Pamela Dean, "Covert Curriculum: Class, Gender, and Student Culture at a New South Woman's College, 1892–1910" (PhD dissertation, University of North Carolina, 1995), 71.

84. *Biblical Recorder*, February 24, 1897, 1 and July 14, 1897, 1.

85. *Caucasian*, June 10, 1897, 2. Also see M. Butler to E. Alderman, October 14, 1897, UNC, box 20, folder 668; E. Alderman to M. Butler, December 17, 1896, Butler Papers, Subseries 1.2, folder 44.

86. T. H. Battle to E. Alderman, October 17, 1896, UNC, box 20, folder 659; W. A. Graham to E. Alderman, October 29, 1896, UNC Papers, box 20, folder 659; Guthrie cited in Bode, *Protestantism in the New South*, 30–35.

87. James M. Beeby, *Revolt of the Tar Heels: The North Carolina Populist Movement, 1890–1901* (Jackson: University Press of Mississippi, 2008), 108; Muller, "New South Populism," 169–72; Gobbel, *Church-State Relationships in Education in North Carolina since 1776*, 144 n38. James Leloudis has suggested that no populist attack on UNC materialized because the movement fractured after the Bryan campaign of 1896. Leloudis, *Schooling the New South*, 125.

88. Thomas Henry Tibbles, *Nebraska Redeemed* (Lincoln, NE: Independent Publishing, 1897), 93; *Nebraska State Journal*, March 29, 1891, 3, April 5, 1891, 6, April 7, 1891, 8 and April 12, 1891, 13.

89. Canfield Journal, January 3, 1893, January 24, 1893, January 25, 1893, and January 26, 1893; *Wealth Makers of the World*, October 25, 1894, 5, November 1, 1894, 4, and January 17, 1895, 4. Regarding Populist influence over the fusion alliance, see Robert W. Cherny, *Populism, Progressivism, and the Transformation of Nebraska Politics, 1885–1915* (Lincoln: University of Nebraska Press, 1981), 76, 87–88.

90. Report of the Regents Committee on Legislation, April 11, 1893, NU Regents Papers, box 11, folder 84; *Nebraskan*, May 1893, 1; *House Journal of the Legislature of the State of Nebraska, Twenty-Third Regular Session, 1893*, 462–63.

91. *House Journal of the Legislature of the State of Nebraska, Twenty-Fourth Regular Session, 1895,* 895; *Nebraskan,* February 14, 1895, 1; *Nebraska State Journal,* February 6, 1895, 2, and February 8, 1895, 2.

92. *Wealth Makers of the World,* November 8, 1894, 8.

93. *Hesperian,* March 19, 1897, 4; NU Report, 1897–98, 60; *Senate Journal of the Legislature of the State of Nebraska, Twenty-Fifth Regular Session, 1897,* 677; *Nebraska State Journal,* April 3, 1897, 2, *Nebraska Independent,* March 18, 1897, 1, April 8, 1897, 2, April 15, 1897, 1, and May 6, 1897, 4–5; Manley, *Centennial History of the University of Nebraska,* 121–23.

94. *People's Champion,* May 7, 1897, 3 and May 14, 1897, 3.

95. *People's Advocate,* November 4, 1898, 4; *Nebraska Independent,* August 4, 1898, 1, December 29, 1898, 4, and January 26, 1899, 3; NU Report, 1899–1900, 6; *Nebraska Independent,* December 22, 1898, 2 and October 31, 1901, 1; Elvin F. Frolik and Ralston J. Graham, *The University of Nebraska–Lincoln College of Agriculture: The First Century* (Lincoln: University of Nebraska, 1987), 9; Manley, *Centennial History of the University of Nebraska,* 123–25.

96. *Nebraska Independent,* September 12, 1901, 4, October 3, 1901, 1, October 31, 1901, 1, and June 26, 1902, 6; *Nebraskan-Hesperian,* March 26, 1901, 1, April 10, 1901, 1, and April 17, 1901, 1.

97. The general appropriation passed the House unanimously, but twenty-two Populists voted against funding for the science building. Kansas State Legislature, *Journal of the House of Representatives* (1893), iii–iv, 531, 625. For Snow's responses, see F. H. Snow to W. R. Cone, January 12, 1893, SRC; F. H. Snow to G. F. Weida, March 6, 1893, SGC, box 9; F. H. Snow to W. H. Brown, April 24, 1893, SGC, box 9. On the Kansas election of 1892, see Scott McNall, *The Road to Rebellion: Class Formation and Kansas Populism, 1865–1900* (Chicago: University of Chicago Press, 1988), 258, 282.

98. KSAC Report, 1893–94, 11; *Industrialist,* May 10, 1897, 139; Kansas State Legislature, *Journal of the House of Representatives, 1893,* 184, 548.

99. Kansas State Legislature, *Journal of the House of Representatives, 1895,* 554, 1289; *Jeffersonian,* February 21, 1895, 1 and April 4, 1895, 2.

100. Kansas State Legislature, *Journal of the Senate, 1895,* 553, 882–83, 1036; Kansas State Legislature, *Journal of the House of Representatives, 1895,* 452, 849, 1140.

101. McNall, *The Road to Rebellion,* 287; F. H. Snow to Kellogg, November 19, 1896 and F. H. Snow to C. F. Scott, February 24, 1897, SRC; *Jeffersonian,* August 22, 1895, 2; Clyde Kenneth Hyder, *Snow of Kansas: The Life of Francis Huntington Snow, With Extracts from His Journals and Letters* (Lawrence: University of Kansas Press, 1953), 206–8.

102. *Topeka Advocate,* January 6, 1897, 8 and February 3, 1897, 2; *Jeffersonian,* November 5, 1896, 2; *People's Party Campaign Handbook.*

103. F. H. Snow to G. L. Raymond, November 9, 1896, F. H. Snow to E. C. Little, November 9, 1896, F. H. Snow to A. S. Draper, November 11, 1896, F. H. Snow to W. H. Brown, December 1, 1896, F. H. Snow to C. F. Scott, February 24, 1897, F. H. Snow to Carter, March 20, 1897, F. H. Snow to W. H. Brown, March 20, 1897, and F. H. Snow to J. B. Angell, March 29, 1897, SRC; F. H. Snow to G. E. MacLean, February 6, 1897,

SGC, box 21; Kansas State Legislature, *Journal of the Senate, 1897*, 1082, 1113–16; Kansas State Legislature, *Journal of the House of Representatives, 1897*, 268, 1076–77; *Kansas University Weekly*, March 20, 1897, 126.

104. Helen M. Cavanaugh, *Carl Schurz Vrooman: A Self-Styled "Constructive Conservative"* (Chicago: Lakeside, 1977), 44; Ross E. Paulson, *Radicalism and Reform: The Vrooman Family and American Social Thought, 1837–1937* (Lexington: University of Kentucky Press, 1968), 129; *Industrialist*, March 22, 1897, 111–12, May 10, 1897, 139, and April 1899, 249–51; KSAC Report, 1899–1900, 36; "Retrospect" in KSC Letters; Kansas State Legislature, *Journal of the House of Representatives, 1895*, 303–4, 1015.

105. *Advocate and News*, January 4, 1899, 2; *Manhattan Republic*, February 24, 1899, 1.

106. Populist Regent Clarke disagreed with the request for fire repair funds. W. H. Sears to F. H. Snow, October 8, 1898, W. H. Sears to H. G. Jumper, November 14, 1898, and W. H. Sears to H. G. Jumper, April 19, 1899, Sears Papers, box 1, Letterbook; untitled, undated typescript, Sears Papers, box 3, folder "Misc. Material, letters; some dated 1931–32"; Hyder, *Snow of Kansas*, 211; F. H. Snow to W. C. Clock, March 18, 1899 and F. H. Snow to W. Rogers, April 6, 1898, SRC.

107. KU Report, 1907–8, 13.

108. Burgess cited in Merle Borrowman, "The False Dawn of the State University," *History of Education Quarterly* 1 (June 1961), 6; Joel Moody, "The University and the Student" (Topeka, KS: 1889), 9.

109. T. E. Will to J. D. Walters, January 6, 1909, Will Papers, folder 5.

110. Elizabeth Sanders, *Roots of Reform: Farmers, Workers, and the American State, 1877–1917* (Chicago: University of Chicago Press, 1999), 387–88.

111. Palmer, *Man over Money*, 41.

112. Peter H. Argersinger, *Populism and Politics: William Alfred Peffer and the People's Party* (Lexington: University of Kentucky Press, 1974), 137.

Conclusion

1. James Carey, *Kansas State University: The Quest for Identity* (Lawrence: Regents Press of Kansas, 1977), 86. In 1983, KSU graduate students arranged for a "non-dedication' of a classroom to Will. Clipping from *Kansas State Collegian*, March 10, 1983, Vertical File, Presidents, Thomas E. Will, 1897–1899, Morse Department of Special Collections, Hale Library, Kansas State University.

2. Carey, *Kansas State University*, 78–82; KSU Clippings, vol. 3 and vol. 4, 312–420; Julius T. Willard, *History of Kansas State College of Agriculture and Applied Science* (Manhattan: Kansas State College Press, 1940), 123; Charles Correll, "Revolution and Counter-revolution," *Kansas Quarterly* 1 (Fall 1969), 99–101.

3. Abstracts from Proceedings of the Board of Regents, June 6–12, 1899 and untitled typescript of Susan St. John's comments, Will Papers, folder 6; *Industrialist*, June 1899, 391 and July 1899, 465–67; *Manhattan Republic*, June 30, 1899, 8 and June 16, 1899, 1, 8; J. T. Willard to "Friends," December 10, 1899, KSC Letters; KSU Clippings, vol. 4,

457–59; C. B. Hoffman to F. Parsons, January 19, 1900, Parsons Papers, box 1, folder 48; E. Bemis to R. T. Ely, June 12, 1899, Richard T. Ely Papers, Wisconsin Historical Society, reel 14.

4. James M. Beeby, *Revolt of the Tar Heels: The North Carolina Populist Movement, 1890–1901* (Jackson: University Press of Mississippi, 2008), 163–88.

5. Untitled typescript, April 18, 1899, Peele Papers; *Progressive Farmer*, April 25, 1899, 2 and May 2, 1899, 2; T. B. Parker to W. J. Peele, July 2, 1899 and July 8, 1899, William J. Peele Papers, #1881, box 1, folder 8, Southern Historical Collection, Wilson Library, University of North Carolina at Chapel Hill.

6. Robert Knoll, *Prairie University: A History of the University of Nebraska* (Lincoln: University of Nebraska Press, 1995), 39–43.

7. *Journal of the Proceedings and Addresses of the National Educational Association, 1900*, 474.

8. Daniel T, Rodgers, *The Work Ethic in Industrial America, 1820–1920* (Chicago: University of Chicago Press, 1978), 215.

9. See note 50 in the introduction for a discussion of upper-case "Populist" and "Populism" versus lower-case "populistic."

10. *The Journal of Proceedings and Addresses of the National Educational Association, 1900*, 106–14.

11. Michael Kazin, *The Populist Persuasion: An American History* (Ithaca, NY: Cornell University Press, 1998).

12. Richard J. Altenbaugh, *Education for Struggle: The American Labor Colleges of the 1920s and 1930s* (Philadelphia: Temple University Press, 1990).

13. Clyde W. Barrow, *Universities and the Capitalist State: Corporate Liberalism and the Reconstruction of American Higher Education, 1894–1928* (Madison: University of Wisconsin Press, 1990), 115.

14. Leon Fink, *Progressive Intellectuals and the Dilemmas of Democratic Commitment* (Cambridge, MA: Harvard University Press, 1997), 42; Lawrence R. Veysey, *The Emergence of the American University* (Chicago: University of Chicago Press, 1965), 180–251.

15. Roger L. Geiger, "The Rise and Fall of Useful Knowledge: Higher Education for Science, Agriculture and the Mechanic Arts, 1850–1875," *History of Higher Education Annual* 18 (1998), 59.

16. Upton Sinclair, *The Goose-Step: A Story of American Education* (New York: Albert and Charles Boni, 1936), 18.

17. Extension services ultimately blossomed in the form of county demonstration programs rather than institutes run by land grant colleges. Daniel P. Carpenter, *The Forging of Bureaucratic Autonomy: Reputations, Networks, and Policy Innovation in Executive Agencies, 1862–1928* (Princeton: Princeton University Press, 2001).

18. Jana Nidiffer and Jeffrey P. Bouman, "The Chasm Between Rhetoric and Reality: The Fate of the 'Democratic Ideal' When a Public University Becomes Elite," *Educational Policy* 15 (3) (July 2001), 432–51.

19. Charles McCarthy, *The Wisconsin Idea* (New York: Macmillan, 1912).

20. KU Report, 1907–08, 55–59.

21. See KSAC's annual reports between 1900 and 1912. Regarding southern universities, see Michael Dennis, *Lessons in Progress: State Universities and Progressivism in the New South, 1880–1920* (Urbana: University of Illinois Press, 2001), 28–32.

22. Mary Neth, *Preserving the Family Farm: Women, Community, and the Foundations of Agribusiness in the Midwest, 1900–1940* (Baltimore, MD: Johns Hopkins University Press, 1995), 100–106.

23. KU Report, 1903–04, 2; Clifford S. Griffin, *The University of Kansas* (Lawrence: University of Kansas Press, 1974), 233.

24. KU Report, 1905–06, 34–35.

25. Claudia Goldin and Lawrence F. Katz, "The Shaping of Higher Education: The Formative Years in the United States, 1890–1940," *Journal of Economic Perspectives* 13 (Winter 1999), 50. The dollar amounts in 2007 terms would be $1,033 vs. $4,489, according to the United States Bureau of Labor Statistics (http://data.bls.gov/cgi-bin/cpicalc.pl).

26. O. Edgar Reynolds, *The Social and Economic Status of College Students* (New York: Teachers College Bureau of Publications, 1927), 16; Rupert Wilkinson, *Aiding Students, Buying Students: Financial Aid in America* (Nashville: Vanderbilt University Press, 2005), 31; David O. Levine, *The American College and the Culture of Aspiration, 1915–1940* (Ithaca, NY: Cornell University Press, 1986), 165, 212–14; Colin B. Burke "The Expansion of American Higher Education" in Konrad H. Jarausch, ed., *The Transformation of Higher Learning, 1860–1930: Expansion, Diversification, Social Opening, and Professionalization in England, Germany, Russia, and the United States* (Stuttgart, Germany: Klett-Cotta, 1982).

27. Griffin, *The University of Kansas*, 422; Henry H. Foster and George E. Price, *Laws Relating to the University of Nebraska* (n.p., 1929); Knoll, *Prairie University*, 69.

28. Merle Curti and Vernon Carstensen, *University of Wisconsin: A History, 1848–1925* (Madison: University of Wisconsin Press, 1949), 244–48; William Estus McVey, "Standards for the Accreditation of Secondary Schools" (PhD dissertation, University of Chicago, 1942), 39–41; Griffin, *The University of Kansas*, 307–9, 675–76.

29. Ellen Condliffe Lagemann, *Private Power for the Public Good: A History of the Carnegie Foundation for the Advancement of Teaching* (Middletown, CT: Wesleyan University Press, 1983), 95–98; David B. Tyack and Larry Cuban, *Tinkering Toward Utopia: A Century of Public School Reform* (Cambridge, MA: Harvard University Press, 1995), 91–93; Marc A. VanOverbeke, *The Standardization of American Schooling: Linking Secondary and Higher Education, 1870–1910* (New York: Palgrave Macmillan, 2008), 164–66.

30. Richard McCormick, *Rutgers: A Bicentennial History* (New Brunswick, NJ: Rutgers University Press, 1966), 128, 143–44; *Fourth Annual Report of the Carnegie Foundation for Advancement of Teaching, 1909*, 85, 98–101.

31. Barrow, *Universities and the Capitalist State*, 90–94.

32. Edward D. Eddy, *Colleges for Our Land and Time: The Land Grant Idea in American Education* (New York: Harper and Brothers, 1957), 85.

33. Harold Wechsler, *The Qualified Student: A History of Selective College Admissions in America* (New York: Wiley, 1977), 238–43.

34. Levine, *The American College and the Culture of Aspiration*, 162; David Riesman and Christopher Jencks, *Academic Revolution* (Garden City, NY: Doubleday, 1968), 490.

35. Curti and Carstensen, *University of Wisconsin*, vol. 2, 6.

36. UNC Report, 1905, 7–8. On public and private school enrollment at UNC see Kemp Plummer Battle, *History of the University of North Carolina*, vol. 2 (Raleigh, NC: Edwards and Broughton, 1912), 572; UNC Report, 1903, 9–10.

37. Carey, *Kansas State University*, 116–17; Robert Manley, *Centennial History of the University of Nebraska*, vol. 1 (Lincoln: University of Nebraska Press, 1969), 200.

38. Eddy, *Colleges for Our Land and Time*, 85; Arthur J. Klein, "Survey of Land-Grant Colleges and Universities," *United States Office of Education Bulletin*, no. 9 (Washington, DC: Government Printing Office, 1930), 272.

39. Virginuis Dabney, *Mr. Jefferson's University: A History* (Charlottesville: University of Virginia Press, 1981), 170.

40. Battle, *History of the University of North Carolina*, vol. 2, 376–78. Regarding stratification, see Levine, *The American College and the Culture of Aspiration*, 21, 113–14, 133.

41. Joseph F. Kett, *The Pursuit of Knowledge under Difficulties: From Self-Improvement to Adult Education in America, 1750–1990* (Stanford: Stanford University Press, 1994), 187–88, 289; George M. Woytanowitz, *University Extension: The Early Years in the United States, 1885–1915* (Iowa City: American College Testing Program, 1974), 150–51.

42. John Douglass, *The California Idea and American Higher Education: 1850 to the 1960 Master Plan* (Stanford: Stanford University Press, 2000).

43. *Progressive Farmer*, February 19, 1889, 4 and March 3, 1886, 1; *Jeffersonian*, February 4, 1897, 2; *Industrialist*, July 1898, 443–49.

44. Jencks and Riesman, *Academic Revolution*, 484.

45. A study of higher education in Minnesota has indicated that rural residents continued to demand local junior colleges and regional universities in the decades following World War II. Jodi Vandenberg-Daves, "'A Look at the Total Knowledge of the World': The University of Minnesota, the Land-Grant Ideal, and the Politics of US Public Higher Education, 1950–1990," *History of Education* 32 (1) (January 2003), 57–79. Regarding the diversion theory of community colleges, see Steven Brint and Jerome Karabel, *The Diverted Dream: Community Colleges and the Promise of Educational Opportunity in America, 1900–1985* (New York: Oxford University Press, 1989).

46. Douglass, *The California Idea and American Higher Education*, 8–9.

47. William C. Hunter, *Beacon across the Prairie: North Dakota's Land Grant College* (Fargo: North Dakota Institute for Regional Studies, 1961), 89; Barrow, *Universities and the Capitalist State*, 115–16.

48. W. Norton Grubb and Marvin Lazerson, *The Education Gospel: The Economic Power of Schooling* (Cambridge, MA: Harvard University Press, 2004). For enrollments in agricultural courses, see Klein, "Survey of Land-Grant Colleges and Universities," 776.

49. Robert Maynard Hutchins, *The Higher Learning in America* (Westport, CT: Greenwood Press, [1936], 1979), 1–14, 29–38, 70–73, 85–87, 117–18.

50. David F. Labaree, *How to Succeed in School Without Really Learning: The Credentials Race in American Education* (New Haven, CT: Yale University Press, 1997).

51. Dennis, *Lessons in Progress*, 181-82.

52. Students admitted through this informal policy constituted roughly 10 percent of UC enrollment until the implementation of the master plan of 1960, when the percentage dropped sharply. John Aubrey Douglass, *The Conditions for Admission: Access, Equity, and the Social Contract of Public Universities* (Stanford: Stanford University Press, 2007), 90, 99, 117.

53. Barrow, *Universities and the Capitalist State*, 58. On North Dakota, in particular, see Louis G. Geiger, *University of the Northern Plains: A History of the University of North Dakota, 1883-1958* (Grand Forks: University of North Dakota Press, 1958), 282-85, 308-9.

54. Edward Krug, *The Shaping of the American High School*, vol. 2 (Madison: University of Wisconsin Press, 1969), 65; Frank Stephens, *A History of the University of Missouri* (Columbia: University of Missouri Press), 503-4.

55. Lotus D. Coffman, *The State University, Its Work and Problems* (Minneapolis: University of Minnesota Press, 1934), 43; Wechsler, *The Qualified Student*, 240-43; George Knepper, *New Lamps for Old: One Hundred Years of Urban Higher Education at the University of Akron* (Akron, OH: University of Akron Press, 1970), 171-75. Zook felt pressured to raise standards, however, in order to cut costs by limiting enrollment and he expressed concern about freshman attrition. Griffin, *The University of Kansas*, 675-76.

56. Nicholas Lemann, *The Big Test: The Secret History of the American Meritocracy* (New York: Farrar, Straus, and Giroux, 1999), 25.

57. Knoll, *Prairie University*, 88-89; Griffin, *The University of Kansas*, 444; Charles Gates, *The First Century at the University of Washington, 1861-1961* (Seattle: University of Washington Press, 1961), 179-80; Sinclair, *The Goose-Step*, 236; R. L. Duffus, *Democracy Enters College: A Study of the Rise and Decline of the Academic Lockstep* (New York: Scribners, 1936), 178.

58. Kathleen J. Frydl, *The GI Bill* (New York: Cambridge University Press, 2009).

59. *Higher Education for American Democracy: A Report of the President's Commission on Higher Education*, vol. 3 (Washington, DC: Government Printing Office, 1947-1948), 6.

60. Wilkinson, *Aiding Students, Buying Students*, 99; John R. Thelin, *A History of American Higher Education* (Baltimore, MD: Johns Hopkins University Press, 2004), 254; John Thelin, "Higher Education's Student Financial Aid Enterprise in Historical Perspective," in Frederick M. Hess, ed., *Footing the Tuition Bill: The New Student Loan Sector* (Washington, DC: American Enterprise Institute, 2007), 25.

61. Daniel Bell, "Meritocracy and Equality," *The Coming of the Post-Industrial Society: A Venture in Social Forecasting* (New York: Basic Books, 1973), 410; Wechsler, *The Qualified Student*, 280-88.

62. CUNY senior colleges accepted students with high school GPAs over 80 or rankings in the top half of their classes. David E. Lavin and David Hyllegard, *Changing the Odds: Open Admissions and the Life Chances of the Disadvantaged* (New Haven, CT: Yale University Press, 1996), 13-15, 34; Joshua B. Freeman, *Working-Class New York: Life and Labor Since World War II* (New York: New Press, 2000), 229-33.

63. Lavin and Hyllegard, *Changing the Odds*, 209–12.

64. Less-selective schools have higher attrition rates, even for students with similar demographic and academic profiles. William G. Bowen, Matthew M. Chingos, and Michael S. McPherson, *Crossing the Finish Line: Completing College at America's Public Universities* (Princeton: Princeton University Press, 2009).

65. Frederick Allen, et al., *The University of Colorado, 1876–1976* (New York: Harcourt Brace Jovanovich, 1976), 53, 194; Vandenberg-Daves, "'A Look at the Total Knowledge of the World,'" 75–77.

66. Robert K. Fullinwider and Judith Lichtenberg, *Leveling the Playing Field: Justice, Politics, and College Admissions* (New York: Rowman and Littlefield, 2004), 6–7; *The College Blue Book*, 36th Edition, vol. 1 (Detroit: Macmillan Reference USA, 2009).

67. Leo Reisberg, "Faced With Enrollment Crunch, Many Colleges Shut the Back Door," *Chronicle of Higher Education*, September 8, 2000, A65.

68. Mary Crystal Cage, "Fewer Students Get Bachelor's Degrees in 4 Years," *Chronicle of Higher Education*, July 15, 1992; Scott Jaschik, "Overhaul to End Segregation Ordered in Louisiana," *Chronicle of Higher Education*, January 6, 1993.

69. Mary Crystal Cage, "Optimism Returns to Higher Education in Kansas After Nearly a Decade of Belt Tightening," *Chronicle of Higher Education*, October 4, 1989; Goldie Blumenstyk, Mary Crystal Cage, and Benjamin Schonberger, "The Outlook for Higher Education in the 50 States," *Chronicle of Higher Education*, January 9, 1991; Peter Schmidt, "Kansas Institutes Admissions Standards for State Universities," *Chronicle of Higher Education*, April 12, 1996; "U. Kansas Lacks Strict Admission Standards," *University Daily Kansan*, September 28, 2006; "U. Kansas Should Raise Standards," *University Daily Kansan*, August 29, 2006; Goldie Blumenstyk, "20 Years Later: How One Flagship Has Changed," *Chronicle of Higher Education*, December 12, 2008, A1.

70. Fullinwider and Lichtenberg, *Leveling the Playing Field*, 72; Mary Soliday, *The Politics of Remediation: Institutional Needs in Higher Education* (Pittsburgh: University of Pittsburgh Press, 2002), 101, 192 n5; Lavin and Hyllegard, *Changing the Odds*, 203 n5.

71. Ronald A. Phipps, *College Remediation: What It Is, What It Costs, What's at Stake* (Washington, DC: Institute for Higher Education Policy, 1998).

72. See for example, Theda Skocpol and Suzanne Mettler, "Back to School," *Democracy: A Journal of Ideas* (Fall 2008), 8–18; Christopher Newfield, *Unmaking the Public University: The Forty-Year Assault on the Middle Class* (Cambridge, MA: Harvard University Press, 2008), 191–93.

73. James J. Duderstadt and Farris W. Womack, *The Future of the Public University in America: Beyond the Crossroads* (Baltimore, MD: Johns Hopkins University Press, 2003), 40–41, 125; Gene R. Nichol, "Public Universities at Risk Abandoning Their Mission," *Chronicle of Higher Education*, October 31, 2008, A50.

74. Douglass, *The Conditions for Admission*, 280.

75. Kevin Dougherty, *The Contradictory College: The Conflicting Origins, Impacts, and Futures of the Community College* (Albany: State University of New York Press, 2001).

76. Andrea Venezia, Michael W. Kirst, and Anthony Antonio, *Betraying the College Dream: How Disconnected K-12 and Postsecondary Education Systems Undermine Student Aspirations* (Stanford: Stanford Institute for Higher Education Research, 2003).

77. Katharine Lyall and Kathleen R. Sell, *The True Genius of America at Risk: Are We Losing Our Public Universities to De Facto Privatization?* (Westport, CT: Praeger, 2006), 78, 141; Douglass, *The Conditions for Admission*, 246–47, 274; Blumenstyk, "20 Years Later: How One Flagship Has Changed," A1; James C. Hearn and Janet M. Holdsworth, "Federal Student Aid: The Shift from Grants to Loans," in Edward P. St. John and Michael D. Parsons, eds., *Public Funding of Higher Education: Changing Contexts and New Rationales* (Baltimore, MD: Johns Hopkins University Press, 2004).

78. Danette Gerald and Kati Haycock, *Engines of Inequality: Diminishing Equity in the Nation's Premier Public Universities* (Washington, DC: Education Trust, 2006).

79. Duderstadt and Womack, *The Future of the Public University in America*, 125.

80. For details, see the list of programs posted by the Project on Student Debt, an initiative of the Institute for College Access and Success at http://projectonstudentdebt .org/pc_institution.php (accessed July 8, 2010).

81. For analysis of the unpopularity and elitism of affirmative action, see Jeffrey D. Skrenty, *The Ironies of Affirmative Action: Politics, Culture, and Justice in America* (Chicago: University of Chicago Press, 1996).

82. White Americans seem comfortable with offering special treatment to many groups, including veterans, seniors, and relatives, but tend to see African Americans as undeserving. Skrenty, *The Ironies of Affirmative Action*.

83. For further analysis, see Julie A. Reuben, "Merit, Mission, and Minority Students: The Historical Debate over Special Admission Programs," in Michael C. Johanek, ed., *A Faithful Mirror: Reflections on the College Board and Education in America* (New York: College Entrance Examination Board, 2001), 195–243.

84. On class-based access policies, see Ronald Dworkin, "The Court and the University," *New York Review of Books*, May 15, 2003, 8–11; William G. Bowen, Martin A. Kurzweil, and Eugene M. Tobin, *Equity and Excellence in American Higher Education* (Charlottesville: University of Virginia Press, 2005), 175–83. On class and access to selective colleges, see Anthony P. Carnevale and Stephen J. Rose, "Socio-economic Status, Race/Ethnicity, and Selective College Admissions," in Richard D. Kahlenberg, ed., *America's Untapped Resource: Low-Income Students in Higher Education* (New York: Century Foundation Press, 2004). Yet if universities focus on class and ignore race altogether, minority enrollment could fall drastically because of the large pool of low-income white students. Douglass, *The Conditions for Admission*, 168.

85. Louis Menand, "The Limits of Academic Freedom," in Louis Menand, ed., *The Future of Academic Freedom* (Chicago: University of Chicago Press, 1996), 5–6; Charles M. Ambrose, "Academic Freedom in American Public Colleges and Universities," *Review of Higher Education* 14 (Fall 1990), 5–32; Stanley Fish, "Conspiracy Theories 101," *New York Times*, July 23, 2006; Sherman Dorn, "The Buttons We Bear . . . or the Crosses,

or Other Things" (October 19, 2008) and "Stanley Fish and the False Dichotomy" (October 13, 2008), www.shermandorn.com/mt/archives/cat_academic_freedom.html (accessed May 12, 2009).

86. Sixteen states have considered passing laws requiring "balanced" instruction. Robert O'Neil, *Academic Freedom in the Wired World: Political Extremism, Corporate Power, and the University* (Cambridge, MA: Harvard University Press, 2008), 237.

87. A. Lee Fritschiler and Bruce L. R. Smith, "The New Climate of Timidity on Campuses," *Chronicle of Higher Education* 55 (23) (February 13, 2009), A80.

88. For an example of one university's efforts, see Lee Benson, Ira Richard Harkavy, and John L. Puckett, *Dewey's Dream: Universities and Democracies in an Age of Education Reform* (Philadelphia: Temple University Press, 2007). On the struggle of intellectuals to ally themselves with reform movements, see Richard Rorty, "Intellectuals in Politics," *Dissent* (Fall 1991), 483–90; Thomas Bender, "Epilogue," in *Intellect and Public Life: Essays on the Social History of Academic Intellectuals in the United States* (Baltimore, MD: Johns Hopkins University Press, 1993).

89. On Populism's conservative turn, see Kazin, *The Populist Persuasion.*

90. Duderstadt and Womack, *The Future of the Public University in America*, 23–25.

91. Financial strains, in particular, exert powerful influence over institutional missions. Sheila Slaughter and Gary Rhoades, *Academic Capitalism and the New Economy: Markets, State, and Higher Education* (Baltimore, MD: Johns Hopkins University Press, 2004); Nichol, "Public Universities at Risk Abandoning Their Mission," A50; Duderstadt and Womack, *The Future of the Public University in America*, 13.

92. In particular, academic elitists have tended to believe that high-ranking students, scholarly research, and other markers of institutional prestige ultimately benefit the public at large. Thomas Bender, "Politics, Intellect, and the American University," in Thomas Bender and Carl Schorske, eds., *American Academic Culture in Transformation* (Princeton: Princeton University Press, 1998), 17; Levine, *The American College and the Culture of Aspiration*, 165–66; Douglass, *Conditions for Admission*, 112–17; Richard Freeland, *Academia's Golden Age: Universities in Massachusetts, 1945–1970* (New York: Oxford University Press, 1992), 358–60.

Index

faculty: on admissions standards, 66, 77; as advocates for social reform, 130; affiliations with Farmers' Alliance, 49; controversial political topics addressed by, 4, 141–43, 179; dismissals, 8, 126, 133, 136–37, 139, 141–42, 235n80; elected officials on, 126–27; "General Report of the Committee on Academic Freedom and Academic Tenure" (1915), 141, 145; on higher education policy, 19, 104, 179–80; hiring of, 8, 25, 33, 134–38; isolation of, 39, 127–28, 129, 144; Nebraska legislature appropriations for, 162; on open admission policies, 76–77; performance evaluations, 136–37; on preparatory programs, 69, 71; Republican Party oversight of, 141–42; resistance to required manual labor, 123; salaries of, 33, 148, 152, 154–56, 162; salary cuts at state colleges and universities, 154–56; social science, 40–41, 110, 130–36; viewed as elites, 155; on vocational education, 101–2, 104–5; women as, 49, 59, 133. *See also* academic freedom

Fairchild, George T.: on academic freedom at KSAC, 139; on enrollment of farmers' children at KSAC, 85, 89–90; on faculty dismissals, 235n80; on Populist influence at KSAC, 40, 139; relations with fusionist regents, 40, 44; replaced by Thomas Will, 40, 136, 138; social science courses, 136; support for humanities courses, 105–6

Farmers' Alliance: African Americans, 12, 56–57, 108; common school education endorsed by, 151; on egalitarian social reform promoted by universities, 35; gender norms in, 11; Hatch Act supported by, 107–8; independent political campaigns supported by, 10; Alvin Johnson's membership in, 51–52; H. L. Loucks, 131; mobile farmers' institutes supported by, 79; Morrill Act (1862) supported by, 108; in Nebraska, 44, 49, 71, 79, 80, 92; NFAIU (National Framers' Alliance and Industrial Union), 10, 150, 187n35; professors' affiliations with, 49; support for state

universities, 157, 159. *See also* the Grange; NCCAMA (North Carolina College of Agriculture and Mechanical Arts)

Farmers' Alliance (Populist newspaper), 46

Farmers' College, 23

farmers' institutes, 15, 79–81, 133, 165, 173, 211–12n117

Farmers' Mass Convention, 37

FCA (Farmers' Cooperative Association of the State of Kansas), 28

financial aid: attrition due to financial need, 85, 86; campus employment, 15, 30, 96, 97–99; denominational challenges to, 150, 152–54; economic access to higher education, 84–87; at elite institutions, 20–21; GI Bill, 176; need-based assistance, 92, 178; scholarships as, 20, 85, 91–92; at state universities, 92, 171, 178

Florida State College of Agriculture, 25

Folwell, William Watts, 32, 69

Forell, Ernest Von, 46, 78, 200n74

Foster, Benjamin F., 11–12, 49

Franklin, Benjamin, 22, 23

Franklin Institute for the Promotion of the Mechanic Arts in Philadelphia, 22, 23

fraternities, 39, 86, 88–89

Free Academy, 21

Frieze, Henry S., 63

funding: of agricultural short courses, 79; challenges to funding higher education, 20, 149, 151–55, 160; for common schools, 20, 149, 151–53; denominational campaigns against state funding for public universities, 150, 152–54; for farmers' institutes, 80–81; for land grant colleges, 4, 14, 20–21, 37, 107–8, 150, 152–54; of North Carolina higher education, 36–37, 149–50, 153, 154, 157–60; opposition to state funding for public universities, 150–54; for secondary schools, 149; tax revenues for, 94, 149, 150–51, 154–55, 165

fusionist governors: on common school education, 151–52; election of, 38, 39; on funding for public higher education, 154–55, 157–58; Silas Holcomb, 198n51;

Polk, Leonidas Lafayette: the agricultural college as the people's college, 37, 54–56; on campus job opportunities, 98; founding of NCCAMA, 37, 73–74, 104; higher education for women, 104, 203–4n127; on the importance of practical education, 37, 111, 112, 116; racism of, 56; tuition limits and financial assistance at NCCAMA, 92; UNC criticized by, 105

poor students: access to higher education, 85, 87–89, 171; campus housing for, 97; college expenses of, 85, 94, 170; Greek societies, 88–89; impact of free public higher education on, 91; negative impact of free tuition, 91; NU enrollment statistics, 90; romanticization of, 88, 90; social discrimination of, 86, 87, 88–89, 90

Populism: demise of, 168–69; educated leadership of, 6, 48–50, 200n73; egalitarianism, 3–4, 8, 9, 12–13, 35, 52, 62, 101, 116, 154–56, 166, 188n47; electoral politics, 4, 10, 75, 97, 140, 141, 148, 153–54; on faculty compensation, 135–38, 148, 155–56; informal education endorsed by, 4, 15, 22–23, 35, 79–81, 127–29, 133, 173, 211–12n117; on intellectual capabilities of lay people, 128, 129–30; membership of, 10–11; People's Parties, 9–10, 35, 39, 127, 151; producerism, 10–11, 13; racial discrimination, 11–12, 38, 56–58, 62, 67, 92–93, 160, 168; on the scholarly community, 39, 127–28, 131, 132–34, 144, 145–46; silverites, 51, 135, 198n51; use of term, 9–10, 12–13, 188n47, 188–89n50; women in, 49. *See also* academic freedom; academic Populists; black Populists; common schools; Farmers' Alliance; *Farmers' Alliance*; fusionist governors; fusionist leadership; fusionist regents at KSAC; the Grange; *specific school headings (e.g., KSAC); specific Populist parties (e.g., North Carolina Populist Party)*

Populist Party of Washington State, 151, 159

Populist press: on academic freedom, 142; on agricultural education, 78, 104, 121; challenges to faculty salaries, 154–56;

circulation of, 13; on corporate corruption at universities, 143; on elitism at universities, 39, 48, 111–13; employment of in-state educated faculty endorsed by, 135; on higher education, 6, 52–53, 61–62, 70, 154, 162, 164, 6162; on hiring practices at KU, 137; incidental fees criticized by, 93–94; KSAC affairs in, 40, 74–75, 106; on lay understanding of economics, 129, 132–33; on rural women, 11; on social science education, 110, 131; support for student employment, 98; tributes to working classes in, 35; on university leadership, 46, 48, 49–50; on value of preparatory courses, 71–72

Postel, Charles, 8

Pound, Roscoe, 136, 145

Prairie View A&M University, 108

preparatory programs, 4, 15, 31, 62–65, 67–73, 78, 177, 207n42, 208n54, 208n55

presidents of colleges and universities: admissions for special students, 61; on admission standards, 175; advocacy for academically marginal applicants at, 77; on censorship, 141; curriculum decisions of, 25; educational backgrounds of, 46; elitism of, 46; on faculty dismissals, 141, 235n80; fiscal mismanagement, 147; fraternities opposed by, 88; on freedom of expression, 141; of land grant colleges, 25, 36–38, 86, 90, 104, 122, 131, 172–73; on making colleges accessible to poor students, 87; on practical applications of scientific research, 103; on public funding of higher education, 149–50; search for faculty, 25; support of Farmers' Alliance, 46; on termination of preparatory programs, 69–70; vocational training supported by, 46

primary-level education. *See* common schools

Princeton University, 20, 86

producerism, 10–11, 13

The Professor's House (Cather), 87–88

Progress and Poverty (Lloyd), 41, 116

Progressive Farmer, 6, 54, 104, 113, 116